ENTERTAINING AMERICA

# ENTERTAINI

## Jews, Movies, and Broadcasting

# NG AMERICA

**J. HOBERMAN**

**AND**

**JEFFREY SHANDLER**

With contributions by

Maurice Berger
Michael Bronski
Mel Gordon
Amelia S. Holberg
David Marc
Deborah Dash Moore
Samuel J. Rosenthal
Ben Singer
Mark Slobin
Judith Thissen
Donald Weber

THE JEWISH MUSEUM, NEW YORK
UNDER THE AUSPICES OF THE JEWISH THEOLOGICAL SEMINARY OF AMERICA

PRINCETON UNIVERSITY PRESS
PRINCETON AND OXFORD

EXHIBITION TOUR

The Jewish Museum, New York
February 21–September 14, 2003

The Jewish Museum of Maryland, Baltimore
October 16, 2003–January 18, 2004

Front cover: Frédéric Brenner, *Marxists*,
New York, 1994.
Spine: Betty Boop.
Back cover: Gertrude Berg as Molly Goldberg,
1951.
Half title: Gertrude Berg as Molly Goldberg.
Frontispiece: Marquee of the Roxy Theater,
New York, 1928.
Images used on contents spread: Logo for
Dr. S. Lubin, 1907; Natalie Wood as Marjorie
Morningstar; Eddie Cantor in blackface; Danny
Kaye in *The Secret Life of Walter Mitty*; Judy
Holliday.
Images used on divider pages: *Nickelodeon
Nation*: Crystal Hall, New York, c. 1915;
*Moguldom*: Irving Thalberg, Louis B. Mayer,
Will Hays, and Harry Rapf; *An American at
Home, a Jew on the Air*: Gertrude Berg as
Molly Goldberg, 1951; *Star Gallery*: Frédéric
Brenner, *Marxists*, New York, 1994; *Stand-Up
Jews*: The arrival of refugees in Palestine as
portrayed in *Exodus*.

Published by The Jewish Museum, New York, in association with Princeton University Press on the
occasion of the exhibition *Entertaining America: Jews, Movies, and Broadcasting.*

The Jewish Museum
1109 Fifth Avenue
New York, New York 10128
www.thejewishmuseum.org

Princeton University Press
41 William Street
Princeton, New Jersey 08540
In the United Kingdom:
Princeton University Press
3 Market Place, Woodstock
Oxfordshire OX20 1SY
www.pupress.princeton.edu

Guest Curators: J. Hoberman and Jeffrey Shandler
Project Director: Fred Wasserman, Associate Curator
Manager of Curatorial Publications: Michael Sittenfeld
Project Assistants: Ivy Epstein and Jason Glassman
Manuscript Editor: Sarah Swartz
Copyeditor: Diana Murphy
Exhibition Design: Robin Russell Parkinson
Media Producers: Owen Electric Pictures

Publisher, Art Group, Princeton: Nancy Grubb
Art Book Production Coordinator: Sarah Henry
Fine Arts Production Editor: Devra K. Nelson
Production Manager: Ken Wong
Managing Editor: Kate Zanzucchi

Designed by Katy Homans with David Frisco
Composed by Katy Homans, David Frisco, and Matt Mayerchak
Printed by Graphicom, Inc.

Credits for all illustrations and previously published texts appear on pages 332–33.

Printed and bound in Verona, Italy
(Cloth) 10 9 8 7 6 5 4 3 2 1
(Paper) 10 9 8 7 6 5 4 3 2 1

*Library of Congress Cataloging-in-Publication Data*
Entertaining America: Jews, movies, and broadcasting /
J. Hoberman and Jeffrey Shandler, with contributions by Maurice Berger . . . [et. al].
    p.   cm.
    Includes bibliographical references and index.
    ISBN 0-691-11301-7 (alk. paper)—ISBN 0-691-11302-5 (pbk. : alk. paper)
        1. Jews in the performing arts—United States. I. Hoberman, J. II. Shandler, Jeffrey.

PN1590.J48 E58 2003
791'.089'924—dc21

2002030263

*Entertaining America: Jews, Movies, and Broadcasting* is sponsored by

HSBC
The world's local bank

Major support has also been provided by the National Endowment for the Humanities, The Blanche and Irving Laurie Foundation, special appropriations obtained by New York State Senator Roy M. Goodman and New York State Governor George E. Pataki and administered by the Office of Parks, Recreation and Historic Preservation, The Martin and Doris Payson Charitable Foundation, The Skirball Foundation, Eugene M. and Emily Grant Foundation given in honor of Evelyn G. Clyman, and public funds from the New York State Council on the Arts, A State Agency.

NATIONAL ENDOWMENT FOR THE HUMANITIES

State of the Arts
NYSCA

# CONTENTS

## STAND-UP JEWS

# FOREWORD

From the first neighborhood nickelodeons to today's mass television programming, Jews have intersected with film and broadcasting in ways that have helped to build the entertainment industry. New Americans of all backgrounds became part of an evolving mass culture, and many first- and second-generation Jews were involved in its emergence and development—as actors, producers, directors, studio heads, theater owners and distributors, musicians, composers, comedians, and inventors. National attention and widespread discussion have been generated by some of the issues implicit in this history. Among them are the history of Jewish immigration to this country, experiences of American anti-Semitism, and the creation of a cultural identity. While the focus here is on a Jewish story, the subject illuminates two broader themes: the challenge of becoming fully American while holding on to a specific ethnic or religious identity; and the dynamic and variegated fabric of American popular culture. Thus *Entertaining America* is both celebratory and complex.

One challenge in creating the exhibition and this book was selecting those people, programs, trends, and films from an immense number of possibilities that would vividly illuminate the subject. Another challenge was to create a visitor experience in the form of an exhibition that would capture the magic and dynamism of works that have been made to exist in real time. It was a difficult task, yet the museum benefited greatly from taking several years to plan and from turning to a variety of consultants for their knowledge and experience. Ultimately a curatorial and design team emerged that created an emotionally, intellectually, and visually engaging presentation, finding a thought-provoking path through a vast world of material. Their synthesis of this multifaceted subject is admirable, and the final result turned out to be both enlightening and fun.

This book sets a new standard for the research and examination of Jewish involvement in American entertainment. The authors have shed light on a remarkable range of subjects—from the mistaken identification of Charlie Chaplin as a Jew to the long-running commentary on the influence of Jewish movie moguls, from the early days of Yiddish radio to the more recent proliferation of Jewish characters on television—and have collected a fascinating array of source materials. Our hope is that this volume and the exhibition will spark much lively discussion and inspire further scholarship in the years ahead.

In the many years the project took to be realized, a large number of people were involved. I am deeply indebted to everyone for their generosity on every level—with funding, time, wisdom, talent, and patience. I include here our donors, current and past staff members, consulting scholars, designers, and technicians. Our gratitude goes especially to the two guest curators and principal authors of this book, Jim Hoberman and Jeff Shandler. Their knowledge and energy are the very heart of this project. They worked intimately with two people: the clever and resourceful designer of the exhibition, Robin Parkinson, and Associate Curator Fred Wasserman, who as project director efficiently and creatively ensured that the project came to fruition. I also want to acknowledge Robin White and her colleagues at Owen Electric Pictures for their work on the media pieces in the exhibition, and Glenn Polly for his valued technical assistance.

Championing *Entertaining America* from its inception were Trustee and donor Martin Payson, and Life Trustee and consultant Stuart Silver. Both were indomitable in their belief in the importance of this subject and the ability of the staff to address it in a fascinating way. Additionally Stuart Silver helped greatly in shaping the conceptual plans for the exhibition. Guiding the project through its many developmental iterations, Deputy Director of Program Ruth Beesch supervised all of the planning and implementation with her usual good spirits and judgment. Michael Sittenfeld, Manager of Curatorial Publications, played a crucial role in the creation of this wonderful book; Al Lazarte, Director of Operations, handled a complicated installation superbly; Gregory Fienhold, Director of Development, and Elana Yerushalmi Kamenir, former Director of Program Funding, were instrumental in securing funds for this project; Jane Rubin, Head Registrar, and Erin Tohill, Associate Registrar, supervised innumerable aspects of the exhibition; Alessandro Cavadini, Audio Visual Coordinator, managed the installation of the exhibition's media programs; and several other individuals and whole departments contributed enormously to making *Entertaining America* a reality. I thank all of them, including the museum's Development, Education, Public Programs and Media, Collections and Exhibitions, and Marketing and Public Relations Departments. Much appreciation goes to those consultants who played important roles in the formative stages of the project, helping the museum to research and shape early versions of the exhibition. Included were Maurice Berger, Lynda Kaplan, Leonard Majzlin, Andrea Most, Richard Rabinowitz, Jack Salzman, Andrea Simon, and Hal Tiné. I am grateful as well to Walter Lippincott, Nancy Grubb, and their colleagues at Princeton University Press for collaborating in the creation of this book.

The lengthy planning period and the interactive nature of the exhibition, with its many media presentations, made *Entertaining America* an undertaking of considerable magnitude. Consequently, a high level of financial support was required to realize our vision. I am tremendously grateful to all of those corporations, government agencies, individuals, and foundations that contributed to this project. I especially wish to acknowledge the leadership support of our corporate sponsor, HSBC. Major funding was also provided by the National Endowment for the Humanities. Of great importance to this project were the special appropriations obtained by New York State Senator Roy M. Goodman and New York State Governor George E. Pataki and administered by the Office of Parks, Recreation, and Historic Preservation. The Blanche and Irving Laurie Foundation and The Martin and Doris Payson Charitable Foundation helped enormously at an early stage. Much appreciated assistance came from The Skirball Foundation and from the New York State Council on the Arts. We also thank the lenders of artworks and artifacts to the exhibition for their generous cooperation.

As always, I have been privileged to receive the support and counsel of The Jewish Museum Board of Trustees. I wish to express my great appreciation to the members of the Board for their role in creating this landmark publication and exhibition.

Joan Rosenbaum
*Helen Goldsmith Menschel Director*
*The Jewish Museum, New York*

# ACKNOWLEDGMENTS

As editors of this catalogue and curators of its attendant exhibition, we are indebted to many. It is our great pleasure to acknowledge their creativity and intelligence.

We are fortunate to have collaborated with the many authors who contributed to this volume, all of whom responded enthusiastically to our invitation to participate and were especially generous in meeting deadlines, tracking down visuals, and responding to editorial queries. We are also extremely grateful to Henry Popkin and Philip Roth for allowing us to excerpt previously published work, and we wish to thank Frédéric Brenner and Art Spiegelman for graciously granting us permission to include their artworks.

Our researchers, Pamela Brown-Lavitt and Lacey Torge, discovered many invaluable texts and images. We are further indebted to Mary Corliss and Terry Geesken of the Museum of Modern Art Film Stills Archive for their generosity, thoughtfulness, and expertise. Sarah Swartz brought an attentive and thoughtful editorial eye to all the texts as we brought this complicated volume together. Katy Homans, with the assistance of David Frisco, crafted an inspired book design that is a model of clarity as well as a pleasure to view. We also thank Nancy Grubb, Ken Wong, Devra K. Nelson, Sarah Henry, and Kate Zanzucchi at Princeton University Press for the careful attention that they brought to the publication process. Above all, we are indebted to Michael Sittenfeld, Manager of Curatorial Publications at The Jewish Museum, for his tireless and cheerful dedication to every aspect of the creation of this book.

The daunting task of coordinating the exhibition's many facets was ably supervised by Fred Wasserman, Associate Curator at The Jewish Museum. He was aided by project assistants Ivy Epstein and Jason Glassman. Robin Parkinson tackled the challenge of designing the environment in which visitors would encounter the media and artifacts that made up the exhibition, and it has been an illuminating experience for us to watch the design take shape. The work of the artists Mark Bennett, Aline Kominsky-Crumb, Ben Katchor, Rhonda Lieberman, and Mark Rappaport greatly enriched the exhibition.

We are also grateful to Andy Ingall, Collections Manager of the National Jewish Archive of Broadcasting at The Jewish Museum, and Lorin Sklamberg, Sound Archivist of the YIVO Institute for Jewish Research, for their help in tracking down obscure radio and television programs. For their generous assistance with media and artifacts for the installation, we thank Janie Klain of the Museum of Television and Radio; Anne Coco of the Margaret Herrick Library at the Academy of Motion Picture Arts and Sciences; Marguerite Lavin at the Museum of the City of New York; Carolyn Davis and Diane Cooter at the Syracuse University Library; and Cherney Berg, Henry Sapoznik, Stuart Schear, Peter Schweitzer, and Bruce Hershenson. And it has been a true pleasure to collaborate with the staff of Owen Electric Pictures—Robin White, Gunjan Prakash, and especially Natacha Ruck—on creating the media pieces that are at the core of the exhibition.

Finally, we wish to express our gratitude to Joan Rosenbaum, Ruth Beesch, and Stuart Silver for inviting us to work with The Jewish Museum on this project, enabling us to explore in a new setting issues that have engaged us for years.

J. Hoberman and Jeffrey Shandler

# ENTERTAINING "ENTERTAINING AMERICA"

J. HOBERMAN AND JEFFREY SHANDLER

This volume and the exhibition that it accompanies address a topic that has provoked one of the most extensive public discussions of identity and culture in America: the relationship between American Jews and the nation's entertainment media.

It is a charged and sprawling topic; simply to raise it is to prompt further questions. Which relations between Jews and the mass media are under consideration? Are we discussing Jews as the creators of media institutions or Jews as individual artists? Do we mean Jews as producers of entertainment or as its subject? Is it possible to speak of a Jewish audience, or is it more accurate to speak of Jewish audiences? Moreover, what assumptions are being made about "Jewishness" (a religious conviction? an ethnicity? a national or racial identity? a sensibility or consciousness?) and "Americanness" (especially in a discussion whose locus is largely confined to New York and Los Angeles)?

Other questions follow: How can Jews be seen simultaneously as cultural outsiders—a minority seeking integration into the American mainstream—and as the ultimate insiders—a group with decisive, "disproportionate" influence over a nation's cultural sensibilities? Do popular films and broadcasts now provide Americans with the most widely familiar stories about Jews? If so, what are the implications of this phenomenon? Is the Jewish case unique or is it a paradigm for other communities—African-Americans, Italian-Americans, Muslims, women, gays and lesbians—and their relationships to the nation's popular culture?

Such questions testify not only to the subject's challenge, but also to its enduring appeal. Collecting the names of Jewish celebrities, especially those prominent in popular entertainment, is not a recent phenomenon. This activity even extends to the debates over the Jewish identity of fictional characters on television series. (Is Sgt. Bilko *really* Jewish? Sally Rogers? Mr. Spock? Barney Miller? George Costanza?) In recent years, this practice, once largely confined to private conversations in front of the TV set or on the way home from the movies, has grown increasingly elaborate and public, sometimes becoming the subject of media works themselves. When comedian Adam Sandler recites an inventory of Jewish entertainment celebrities in a live recording of his 1994 "Chanukah Song," the youthful audience cheers this open declaration of a communal secret.

Similarly, one of the most popular displays in New York's Museum of Jewish Heritage, which opened in 1997, is a multiscreen video installation that celebrates the Jewish contribution to contemporary culture, featuring a preponderance of performers and others who have worked in American film and broadcasting. Frequently, a rapt museum visitor can be heard to exclaim, "I didn't know so-and-so was Jewish!" (Of course, he or she can always check on www.jewhoo.com to make sure.) Nor is this simply a pastime for enthusiasts; since the early decades of the twentieth century, anti-Semites have avidly listed the names of Jewish producers, writers, and performers in the entertainment industry as a means of exposing and rooting out a Jewish presence in American culture that they consider to be as hegemonic as it is pernicious.

What inspires people—Jews and non-Jews, fans and detractors—to keep track of who's Jewish in American show business? To debate the Jewishness of characters, dialogue, and plots? To characterize an entire industry as a Jewish "empire"? What can we learn when we collect these collections, debate these debates? What can they tell us about the role of popular entertainment in modern American life, the place of Jews in American society, the ways that Americans talk about culture and identity? This is the agenda of *Entertaining America*.

Discussions of American Jews and the media can be extensive, passionate, and contentious; they are anything but trivial. Indeed, debates over the presumed Jewishness of a stand-up comedian's material or the submerged Jewish themes in a particular television series have often been an indirect, even encrypted, means of analyzing something more substantial. The central argument of this volume and the exhibition is that the discourse about American Jews and entertainment media, far from being at the periphery, is at the heart of the matter. The topic of *Entertaining America* has not been called into existence by something inherent either in Jews or in the American entertainment industry. Rather, it arises from the public observation of the connections made between this community and that component of American culture. To approach our subject, therefore, it is essential to scrutinize the nature of its discourse and to treat the discussion as a cultural phenomenon in itself—or, to think of it in museological terms, as an array of artifacts.

*Entertaining America* is not simply an inventory of people or works or institutions. Nor does it strive to offer a comprehensive history of American Jews and entertainment media. It does not collect Jews so much as it examines the ways in which the subject of Jews and the entertainment media has been presented from the beginning of the twentieth century to the start of the current millennium—in fan magazines as well as literary fiction, by religious and political leaders as well as journalists and historians, and by Jews working in the entertainment business themselves. These primary materials are complemented by reflections on this discourse by contemporary scholars of media, American culture, and Jewish history.

Like the exhibition, this volume deals with film and broadcasting, as they are the "new" mass media of the past century in which the consideration of American Jews figures most prominently. Taking a selective approach to this vast subject, *Entertaining America* focuses on a key group of widely discussed works (such as the 1960 film *Exodus*), figures (Gertrude Berg, creator and star of the long-running radio and television situation comedy *The Goldbergs*), institutions (early-twentieth-century nickelodeons on New York's Lower East Side), and events (anti-Communist blacklisting in the entertainment industry during the years immediately after World War II).

While it is organized according to a general chronology, this book makes occasional leaps across the decades to demonstrate the resilience of particular issues, some of which endure for generations. For example, important as it may be in its own right, the landmark 1927 film *The Jazz Singer* is but one realization of a particular American Jewish myth that runs throughout the twentieth century. Similarly, the Star Gallery at the center of the book samples the extensive scrutiny of Jewish performers in film and broadcasting from the silent era to the present, tracing the dynamics of the Jewish celebrity as a subject of public discourse over the decades.

At any given moment, the discourse on American Jews and the entertainment media gives prominence to certain issues while leaving others largely unaddressed. This balance, too, shifts over time. Jewish professional involvement in the film and, later, broadcasting industries has been an especially widely discussed topic. Now over three generations old, the discourse on the Jewish presence in Hollywood—which is

the subject of "Hollywood's Jewish Question," the central essay in this volume—
chronicles shifting notions of Jewish distinctiveness and visibility in America and,
more generally, of identity politics in the public sphere.

While examining the most widely known examples of this discussion, *Entertaining
America* considers some that are either less familiar or more oblique. In approaching
American Jews and the entertainment media as a discursive phenomenon, these prove
to be as telling as more obvious cases. Thus, notions of Jewish essentialism have been
complicated, as well as clarified, by the projection of a Jewish identity onto non-
Jewish performers, epitomized by the example of Charlie Chaplin. And while Jewish
religious media generally lie beyond the scope of mainstream American entertainment, *The Eternal Light*, the Jewish Theological Seminary's broadcasts of ecumenical
dramas during the 1940s and 1950s and, more recently, the annual telethons aired by
the Lubavitcher hasidim are revealing examples of how Jewish religious communities
in America employ the conventions of popular entertainment to address moral and
spiritual issues before a national audience.

The examination of American Jews and the entertainment media that took shape
over the course of the twentieth century continues to develop. The Jewish Museum's
exhibition and the debates that it, too, generates—including those that accumulate
on the exhibition's Web site (www.thejewishmuseum.org)—are yet another marker in
this remarkable process. Similarly, readers of this volume will have their own say on
the matter. We hope they will find herein ample material that will help them locate
their personal responses within this contentious and polyvalent discussion.

**FIVE YEARS** INTO THE NEW CENTURY, AMERICA DISCOVERED
A NEW FORM OF ENTERTAINMENT AND A NEW ENTERTAINMENT AUDIENCE. THE NATION'S URBAN
WORKING CLASS WAS FLOCKING TO ATTEND HALF-HOUR MOVING PICTURE SHOWS THAT COST FIVE
CENTS AND CHANGED EACH DAY. SINCE THEIR INTRODUCTION IN 1896, MOVING PICTURES HAD
BEEN SHOWN MAINLY IN THE CONTEXT OF VARIETY SHOWS OR PENNY ARCADES. In June 1905, a Pittsburgh
show business entrepreneur remodeled a storefront as a moving picture theater in
McKeesport, Pennsylvania, and offered continuous performances from eight in
the morning until midnight. The idea spread. *Variety* first reported the proliferation
of 199-seat storefront theaters in March 1906; within eighteen months, these "nickelodeons" were a bona fide sociological phenomenon.[1]

"This is the boom time in the motion picture business," Chicago journalist
Joseph Medill Patterson told the readers of the *Saturday Evening Post* in late 1907,
the peak year of the Great Immigration and not long after the *Chicago Tribune*
editorialized that the nickelodeons were "without a redeeming feature to warrant
their existence." Patterson, later an editor-owner of the *Tribune*, had a more reasoned perspective: "Everybody is making money—manufacturers, renters, jobbers,
exhibitors. . . . The nickelodeon is tapping an entirely new stratum of people, is
developing into theatergoers a section of population that formerly knew and cared
little about the drama as a fact in life."[2]

Particularly popular on New York's Lower East Side, the nickelodeons—which
largely kept their seating capacity at 299 or less to avoid compliance with strict
building regulations—supplanted the primitive Yiddish-language variety shows found
in the back rooms of Bowery saloons. (Later, the two forms would learn to coexist.)
*Variety*'s December 14, 1907, issue calculated that one typical Lower East Side
nickelodeon, the Golden Rule Hall on Rivington Street, reported weekly grosses of
$1,800 against expenses of $500. Moreover, the five-cent theaters seemed impervious
to economic downturns. In May 1908, after some months of economic depression,
the *Jewish Daily Forward* reported that although "most musical halls have shut
down, Yiddish theaters are badly hurt, and candy stores have lost customers," people
were still lining up for the nickelodeons. "There are now about a hundred movie
houses in New York, many of them in the Jewish quarter."[3]

In fact, nearly a fourth of Manhattan's 123 movie theaters were located amid
Lower East Side tenements, with another thirteen squeezed among the Bowery's
Yiddish theaters and music halls, and seven more clustered in the somewhat tonier
entertainment zone to the north at Union Square. That this Manhattan area, then
home to a half-million Jews, was not only the most densely populated but also the

Audience at the Boody
Theatre, location unknown,
c. 1910.

most nickelodeonized part of America has added to the mythology of the Lower East Side. The "old neighborhood" was the legendary locus of the great Jewish immigration out of Eastern Europe—and the cradle of the movie industry as well. The origins of Hollywood were to be found in the new, substantially immigrant mass audience, and its founding fathers among the entrepreneurs of New York's preeminent pre–World War I Jewish neighborhood, including such garment merchants turned exhibitors as Marcus Loew, Adolph Zukor, and William Fox.[4]

For the immigrant and working-class audience, nickelodeons were cheap entertainment and perhaps something more. In her study of silent movie spectatorship, *Babel and Babylon*, Miriam Hansen argues that "the neighborhood character of many nickelodeons—the egalitarian seating, continuous admission and variety format, nonfilmic activities like illustrated songs, live acts and occasional amateur nights—fostered a casual, sociable, if not boisterous atmosphere and made moviegoing an interactive rather than merely passive type of experience."[5]

For civic leaders and crusading reformers, however, these dark, unsanitary holes where unsavory men, unchaperoned women, and unsupervised children partook of unlicensed enjoyment—much of it imported from France—were a potential vice problem. Moreover, the nickelodeons were open seven days a week, often doing their best business on Sunday. New York's police commissioner at the time, Theodore Bingham, an outspoken nativist whose pronouncements on crime in the city verged on anti-Semitism, was a foe of nickelodeons, penny arcades, and cheap theater. He

Grand Opening
for LADIES And GENTLEMEN at
384 Myrtle Ave.
Near Vanderbilt Ave.        Brooklyn, N. Y.

I take pleasure in announcing to the public
that I have opened at the above address a first
class **Moving Picture** place, where Ladies
and Gentlemen with their families can have a
pleasant time for a little money. It will be my
special duty to procure the **Latest and Best Pictures** obtainable; such as
will be fit for the youngest and oldest of my patrons to look at and enjoy.
Come and be convinced yourself. **The price is small, the FUN is great**
**Admission** only **5 Cents**
Open daily at 3.30 p. m.                Our pictures do all but speak.

**Laugh and Be Merry**

ABOVE, TOP
Princess Theatre, St. Cloud,
Minnesota, 1911.

ABOVE, BOTTOM
Handbill announcing a new
nickelodeon theater in
Brooklyn, c. 1908.

ABOVE
International Theatre, Los
Angeles, 1910.

was supported by the Children's Aid Society, which, in 1907, began a campaign against the nickelodeons that resulted in the arraignment of a First Avenue theater-owner for permitting minors to attend a documentary reenactment of the Stanford White murder, featuring White's erstwhile mistress, Evelyn Nesbitt Thaw. Erratic attempts at censorship reached their climax in December 1908, following the collapse of a balcony guardrail in a Rivington Street nickelodeon, which killed one person and injured fifteen (including several children). New York's mayor, George B. McClellan, held hearings at which a number of clergymen testified on the "open exhibition of depravity" that the film theaters afforded young children.[6]

BALKED

Editorial cartoon from *Film Index*, August 14, 1909, by Ralph Ince. This cartoon was published soon after immigrant Jewish exhibitors like Carl Laemmle began to produce their own movies in defiance of the Motion Picture Patents Company. Big-eared and bug-eyed, the stoop-shouldered "junk dealer" is an anti-Semitic stereotype. Laemmle's riposte to the "film trust" appears on the opposite page.

On Christmas Eve 1908, New York police padlocked the city's five-cent theaters, by now 550 in number. As recounted by Terry Ramsaye, the morning after Mayor McClellan "clamped the lid of the law down on the city's motion picture theatres as unclean and immoral places of amusement . . . [a] wail of deep grief and pain rose from the five hundred motion picture exhibitors affected by the order. A call went out for a mass meeting, held Christmas Day at the Murray Hill Lyceum, Third Avenue and Thirty-fourth Street. Israel was smitten and there was no balm in Gilead."[7]

The embattled nickelodeon proprietors—who had already formed the Moving Picture Exhibitors Association (MPEA)—met to plan a counterattack. The *New York Tribune* characterized this conclave in ethnic terms, almost as if describing Biograph's 1907 farce *The Fights of Nations*. The paper noted that the "greater portion" of the assembled Irishmen, Hungarians, Italians, Greeks, Germans, and "Jewish Americans" were the latter group. Indeed, it was the twenty-nine-year-old garment-cutter William Fox and the thirty-eight-year-old former newsboy Marcus Loew who led the exhibitors in their successful struggle to reopen their theaters.[8]

To regain their licenses, the MPEA pledged to refrain from Sunday performances and to bar films that offended community morals. In March 1909, the exhibitors asked the People's Institute, already responsible for the voluntary censorship of the city's live theaters, to organize a board of censorship. Four years later, Fox would enter movie production—as a major opponent of the Motion Picture Patents Company, a trust formed in January 1909 to secure monopoly control over the burgeoning film industry.[9]

Almost immediately, enterprising exhibitors—notably the German-Jewish immigrant Carl Laemmle, a founder of the Independent Motion Picture Company of America (IMP)—began to produce and distribute their own movies. In 1912, Laemmle defeated the Patents Company in court and, having merged IMP with several smaller firms to create the Universal Film Manufacturing Company, led an exodus from New York to southern California.

At the same time, venues where motion pictures were exhibited began to change. Legitimate theaters, burlesque palaces, and even opera houses had been converted to show photoplays (or, more frequently, the mixture of movies and vaudeville associated with Fox's first theaters). Now the trade press began to call for better pictures and more luxurious venues, advising exhibitors to strive for a "mixed house" by avoiding

Advertisement in *Motion Picture World* for the Laemmle Film Service, c. 1910. Distributor Carl Laemmle explained his opposition to the Motion Picture Patents Company in this ad. Laemmle hired a well-known advertising man and conducted a full-scale campaign in the trade press against the Motion Picture Patents Company—often caricatured as the embodiment of rapacious capitalism.

entertainment directed at any one ethnic group. This may be seen as part of a drive toward Americanization, notably by favoring westerns and Anglo-Saxon stars, in an attempt to counter the French company Pathé, the world's largest motion picture manufacturer, which dominated the nickelodeon market at the time.[10]

Exhibitors had their own sense of expressing an American ideology. Inspired by the aspirations of his immigrant audiences, Chicago exhibitor A. J. Balaban created theaters that would allow customers to "live in a fairyland and to make them forget their troubles," forming a chain that Ramsaye would describe as "a piece of Arabian Nights magic emerging from the kaleidoscope of Chicago's West Side and the push-cart markets of Jefferson Street." In New York, the pace was set by immigrant or first-generation Jewish exhibitors Fox, Loew, and the former furrier's assistant Adolph Zukor (soon to enter film production with the formation of the Famous Players).[11]

Bidding to overcome middle-class distaste for popular amusements and recognizing that popular luxury and freedom from daily life were intrinsic to the movies' escapist appeal, the Fox and Loew's circuits offered lengthy programs at popular prices in increasingly plush surroundings. In the June 1914 issue of the *Fox Exhibitor's Bulletin*, Fox attached his name to a manifesto— "Possibilities of the Motion Picture Unlimited"—that identified these new cinemas with American democracy: "Movies breathe the spirit in which the country was founded, freedom and equality. In the motion picture theaters there are no separations of classes. Everyone enters the same way. There is no side door thrust upon those who sit in the less expensive seats. There is always something abhorrent in different entrances to theaters. . . . In the movies the rich rub elbows with the poor and that's the way it should be. The motion picture is a distinctly American institution." It hardly seems coincidental that Laemmle—who had been the first of the Jewish immigrant exhibitors to cross over into production—would call the weekly column, which began appearing in 1915 under his name in Universal's trade journal, the "Melting Pot."[12]

Broadway's first lavish movie theater, the Strand, opened on April 11, 1914,

Marquee of the Roxy
Theater, the "Cathedral of
Motion Pictures," at the
corner of Seventh Avenue
and Fiftieth Street, New
York, 1928.

under the direction of Samuel "Roxy" Rothafel. Thus, according to Ramsaye, the Nickelodeon Age ended: "The motion picture had risen from the peep show novelty to the status of a vehicle of pretentious drama, and now stepped forth to contest the supremacy of the speaking stage on 'The Great White Way.'" By 1916, New York could boast ten such "luxury" houses, where, as Roxy noted, "the man who comes to the theater on foot rubs elbows with the man who arrives in a limousine, and no favoritism is shown to either one or the other."[13]

*"Mama—does God live here?"*

Whereas Jews were a significant presence as movie exhibitors and viewers during the nickelodeon period and thereafter, they were far less prominent as screen subjects. Jewish characters are found amid the mix of ethnic and racial "types" that populate one-reel comedies and urban melodramas. Typically, they reproduce stereotypes familiar from stage melodrama, vaudeville, and humor magazines. The few Jews among the nascent film industry's first "stars" were not known to their public as Jews. Indeed, setting what would prove a long-standing precedent for the American film industry, actors such as Bronco Billy Anderson and Theda Bara obscured their Jewish backgrounds.

However, American cinema's first superstar was widely imagined as Jewish. Rather than explaining that this was not in fact the case, Charlie Chaplin coyly encouraged this misidentification, which was embraced with equal fervor by his Jewish admirers and political enemies. For those who insist on such a reading, Chaplin is the first of an array of non-Jews to have made their reputations, at least in part, by "playing Jewish."
—J.H./J.S.

# THE NICKELODEON BOOM IN MANHATTAN

BEN SINGER

At the close of 1905, movies were still a relatively marginal amusement in Manhattan, mainly filling brief slots at the end of vaudeville shows. Two years later, nickelodeons had revolutionized urban recreation and altered the commercial landscape.

Early movie exhibition in Manhattan holds special interest for film history, not because it was necessarily the most extensive or important (although it may well have been, since New York was the nation's commercial and cultural capital, as well as the center of the pre-Hollywood film industry) or because it was particularly representative of the emergence of cinema elsewhere in the country. Rather it is because Manhattan's nickelodeon boom has so often functioned as historical shorthand for the rise of movies in general. Although exhibition sites varied considerably from the very beginning, for most people today the image of cramped, dingy nickelodeons on the Lower East Side stands as a symbol for the cinema's emergence in America. The same association prevailed ninety years ago.

The holy grail for historians of early cinema in New York would be a master list of all the movie theaters in the city, with information on locations, seating capacities, names of owners and managers, and so on. It would be invaluable to historians of early cinema. Unfortunately, none has been unearthed. Without such a list, the best historians can do is to cobble together scraps of information from sources such as business directories, fire insurance maps, building permits, newspaper ads, and trade-journal references. It is fairly certain, from various municipal government memos and audits, that at any one time during the boom of 1907–10 there were roughly 325 movie theaters in Manhattan. Given the considerable rate of failures and start-ups, the total number of movie theaters that appeared during this period would have been much higher. About three-quarters of them were very small: true nickelodeons with fewer than 300 seats. The rest were converted larger theaters with all-movie policies or theaters that interspersed movies with vaudeville routines. So far, historians have been able to locate about 225 theaters.

Although nickelodeons mushroomed all over Manhattan, there is no question that the Lower East Side–Union Square area had, by far, the thickest concentration in the city and probably in the world. The cultural predispositions of the working-class, immigrant, and first-generation Jews and Italians who predominated in this area may have had something to do with the superabundance of theaters, but the primary factor was most likely the exceptional customer base provided by the extraordinarily high population density and commercial traffic in these neighborhoods.

While it remains an open question, there is little to suggest that ethnic groups differed appreciably in their moviegoing habits. It is clear, however, that there was considerable variation in ethnic patterns of cinema entrepreneurship. The mythology of early cinema emphasizing the prominence of Jews as exhibitors turns out to be accurate. A genealogical analysis of the 190 exhibitors listed by name in 1908 and 1909 Manhattan business directories reveals that 60 percent were Jewish, while Jews constituted only about one-quarter of the total Manhattan population. Italians and native-born Americans ventured into the exhibition business in numbers that roughly reflected their proportion of the local population (about 18 percent and 14 percent, respectively). Irish were underrepresented among exhibitors (7 percent, compared with 13 percent of the population). Germans were not at all inclined toward this

ABOVE
Brooklyn nickelodeon,
1913. Joseph Seiden, whose
family owned the business,
would later become a pro-
ducer of Yiddish talking
pictures.

OPPOSITE
Nickelodeon theaters
on the Lower East Side,
c. 1910. Map by Adrian
Kitzinger, based on research
by Ben Singer.

venture. While one person in ten in Manhattan was either German or of German parentage, this group accounted for only one exhibitor in fifty.

A comparison of theater addresses in listings from 1908 and 1909 indicates that despite the nickelodeon's explosive growth, this was an extremely unstable period for exhibitors. There was an almost fifty-fifty chance that a nickelodeon operating at the end of 1907 would be out of business one year later.

249 3rd Ave.

25 E. 14

People's Vaudeville
126 Univ. Pl.

The Comedy
46 E. 14

The Pastime
18 W. 11

Automatic Vaudeville
48 E. 14

The City
116 E. 14

The Fair 122 E. 14

The Union Square/Bijou Dream
56 E. 14

The Unique 134 E. 14

138 3rd Ave.

120 E. 14

112 3rd Ave.

The Dewey 128 E. 14

Automatic Vaudeville
134½ E. 14

236 1st Ave.

762 Broadway

406 E. 13

235 Ave. A

176 1st Ave.

181 Bleecker

157 Bleecker

152 Bleecker

180 Thompson

124 W. Houston

140 Sullivan

419 Lafayette

126 2nd Ave.

131 Ave. A

89 1st Ave.

128 E. 7

The Fycent 103 Ave. A

Tompkins Square Vaudeville
103 Ave. B

110 Ave. C

314 Bowery

The Florence 331 Bowery

302 Bowery

60 Ave. A

273 Bowery

257 Bowery

13 2nd Ave.

51 Ave. A

129 E. Houston

52 Stanton

Houston Hippodrome
141–143 E. Houston

People's Vaudeville
287 E. Houston

44 Ave. C

303 E. Houston

214 Bowery

197 Bowery

Essex Street Theater
133 Essex

178 Stanton

357 E. Houston

48 Ave. D

187 Bowery

118 Rivington

190 Stanton

192 Grand

196 Grand

125 Rivington

435 E. Houston

147 Mulberry

135 Eldridge

120 Delancey

114 Cannon

Automatic Vaudeville

Union Vaudeville
133 Eldridge

263 Grand

269 Broome

90 Clinton

115 Bowery

236 Broome

66 Columbia

103 Bowery

The Fycent
265 Grand

79 Orchard

126 Clinton

412 Grand

387 Grand

27 Bowery

Star Vaudeville
8 Forsyth

525 Grand

8 Bowery

21 Bowery

19 Bowery

11 Market

155 E. Broadway

64 Catherine

45 James

158 Monroe

FEET
0  200 400        1000             2000            3000            4000            5000            6000

1 MILE

# SIGMUND LUBIN

Once an eyeglass salesman by profession, Sigmund "Pop" Lubin (1851–1923), a Jewish immigrant from Breslau, Germany, entered the American filmmaking industry during its infancy in the mid-1890s, as an outgrowth of his knowledge of optics and interest in photography. Within a few years, Lubin was creating, distributing, and exhibiting hundreds of short films on a wide range of subjects: dramas, comedies, westerns, histories, scientific documentaries, as well as "smokers" (pornographic films). An innovator in film promotion, he also claimed to have erected America's first purpose-built cinema in 1899. In 1912, Lubin established his own studio, Betzwood, in the Philadelphia suburbs. During the early 1910s he produced a number of longer, more elaborate films, notably *The Battle of Gettysburg* (1912). But by 1917 Lubin's company folded, and by the time of his death his career as a pioneer of American movies had been eclipsed by the founders of Hollywood's studios.
—J.S.

LEFT
Lubin's Cineograph, 1899, believed to be the first purpose-built cinema. The admission cost of ten cents was double the customary rate.

BELOW
Logo for Dr. S. Lubin, Manufacturer of Life Motion Picture Machines, Films, Slides, and Stereopticons, Philadelphia, 1907.

RIGHT
Lubin Films recording a silent movie on a rooftop in Philadelphia.

# CHARLES STEINER AND THE HOUSTON HIPPODROME

JUDITH THISSEN

Charles Steiner, c. 1925.

During the first two decades of the twentieth century, moving pictures replaced vaudeville as America's dominant mass entertainment form. Although Jewish film exhibitors played a crucial role in this revolution, only a few became Hollywood moguls. The career of Charles Steiner (1883–1946)—a contemporary and competitor of Marcus Loew, William Fox, and Adolph Zukor in early motion pictures—offers the model of a Jewish showman who capitalized on specific local demands by investing in exhibition practices that aimed at building audiences on the basis of a shared ethnic identity.

Before the nickelodeon era, East Side Jews who wished to see moving pictures could either attend one of the large and lavish vaudeville theaters on Union Square and East Fourteenth Street or visit the much cheaper penny arcades on the nearby Bowery. In the summer, many enjoyed free moving picture shows in Coney Island saloons just as other New Yorkers did. It was also possible to see films in a specifically Jewish setting. The Lower East Side counted some dozen Yiddish *myuzik hols* (music halls), which offered Yiddish vaudeville in combination with moving pictures for an admission price that ranged from ten to thirty-five cents.

The first storefront theaters that specialized in moving pictures sprang up in the tenement district east of the Bowery during the 1906–7 season, when the "motion picture craze" hit New York. "Just like the music halls, this novelty comes from uptown, from the Christians," the *Jewish Daily Forward* explained to its readers.[1] The following season, more Jewish entrepreneurs tried their luck in the booming nickelodeon business. Most of the older Yiddish music halls were converted into movie houses during the economic recession of 1907–8, as patrons flocked to the less expensive nickel shows. Soon, the Lower East Side was dotted with small movie houses that charged five or ten cents for admission. By mid-1908, although the maximum density had not yet been reached, the area already had the thickest concentration of film exhibition outlets in Manhattan. The *Forward* of May 24, 1908, reported: "When you go through the streets of our neighborhood you will be amazed by the mass of moving picture houses. Four or more 'shows' can be found on one street. In some streets, there are even two 'shows' on one block, facing each other."[2]

This was certainly the case at the corner of Rivington and Essex Streets, in the midst of the overcrowded Tenth Ward, where many blocks counted more than three thousand inhabitants. Here three nickelodeons (as well as a fourth, which opened in 1910) competed for the Jewish immigrant audience. In February 1908, twenty-four-year-old Charlie Steiner turned his father's livery stable at 133 Essex Street (near Rivington Street) into a 250-seat nickelodeon. By the end of the year, this success allowed him to open another moving picture show in a former kosher sausage factory on Monroe Street. When the market for Yiddish vaudeville revived in late 1909, Steiner entered the Yiddish music-hall business. With Abe Minsky as a partner, he took over an old Protestant church on East Houston Street and converted it into a five-and-ten-cent variety theater, the Houston Hippodrome. While the pulpit gave way to a stage and the religious scenes on the walls were painted over with blue, white, and gold, the wooden pews continued to serve as seats. According to Minsky's brother, Morton, "the customers found that the racks that once held hymnals were marvelous storage bins for the bagels, salamis and other eatables they brought with them for nourishment during the long program."[3] A tiny dairy restaurant in the basement of the building provided inexpensive kosher refreshments, as did Yonah Shimmel's knish bakery next door.

The Houston Hippodrome offered its immigrant patrons a mixed bill of "*hay kles englishe un yidishe vodevil un muving piktshurs,*" for a nickel in the afternoon and a dime in the evening. The vaudeville routines included comic sketches, single-turns, songs and dances, as well as an occasional animal act, acrobatic number, or piece of jugglery. In late 1910, three- and even four-act melodramas were added to the bill. Most of these plays, which were written and performed by local Yiddish stock companies, dealt with Jewish themes. In fact, many productions dramatized the immigrants' experiences in the New World. In contrast with the live programs, we know little about the moving pictures shown at the Houston Hippodrome. Exhibitors seldom advertised specific moving pictures because the regular film programs in their theaters consisted primarily of one-reelers, which changed almost every day.[4]

In December 1912, Steiner and Minsky downgraded the Hippodrome to a common show without live entertainment, and moved their successful "vaud-pic" formula two blocks down Houston Street to the new National Winter Garden, a thousand-seat rooftop theater. It was here that Abe and Billy Minsky would reinvent

# MOVIES VS. YIDDISH THEATER:
## "THE GRAND SCANDAL"

The Grand Street Music Hall on the Lower East Side, c. 1900.

In December 1909, Nathan Fleissig, the manager of the Grand Street Music Hall, announced triumphantly that the moving pictures had been defeated and that his theater would again be devoted to "first-class Yiddish variety." By presenting this shift in exhibition practices in terms of a cultural war, Fleissig shrewdly linked the reopening of the Grand Street Music Hall with the "Grand scandal," which had roused the emotions of the Yiddish press, some weeks earlier, when Yiddish theater star and impresario Jacob P. Adler sold the lease of the two-thousand-seat Grand Theater.

The new owners, Marcus Loew and Adolph Zukor, turned the home of Yiddish literary drama into an English-language vaudeville house in which moving pictures featured prominently on the bill. It was the *Jewish Daily Forward's* opinion that Adler's selling the Grand Theater to a "million-dollar trust of American theater managers" dishonored the entire East Side. Editor Abraham Cahan and

his staff never mentioned that the new lessees were themselves Jews. Rather, they repeatedly emphasized, along with other Yiddish newspapers, that the Grand had been turned into a *goyish* (Gentile) moving picture theater, and as such, symbolized the loss of yiddishkeit in the New World.

In the aftermath of the Grand scandal, the *Forward's* staff began to redefine the cultural positions within Jewish immigrant entertainment. Cinema was constructed as the new "low Other" and relegated to the bottom of the hierarchy, a position previously occupied by Yiddish vaudeville. The latter was legitimized as a Yiddish theatrical tradition and elevated to a middlebrow position, while the "legitimate" Yiddish stage maintained its status as a highbrow institution.

—Judith Thissen

American burlesque by installing a runway to give the audience a closer look at the chorus girls.

Charlie Steiner went a different route. In 1913, he ended his partnership with the Minsky family and began to consolidate his activities in the film business. Backed by real estate dealer Hyman Weisner, Steiner set up a medium-sized chain of movie theaters that extended from the Lower East Side to Harlem. This development was stimulated by a new law regulating movie exhibition in New York.

After lingering on the city council's agenda for almost two years, the so-called Folk's Ordinance was finally passed by the Board of Aldermen during the summer of 1913, in the aftermath of a fire panic at the Houston Hippodrome in which two people were trampled to death and eleven seriously injured. The law set rigorous fire and construction codes for moving picture theaters, in particular for those that offered live entertainment. Although the stringent safety standards put many music hall proprietors out of business, the law offered good prospects for enterprising film exhibitors because the seating limit for new moving picture theaters was raised from three hundred to six hundred. Steiner seized the opportunity.

The week before Passover 1914, he opened his first purpose-built six-hundred-seat cinema, the American Movies Theater, on East Third Street (between Avenues B and C). The name of the theater suggests that Steiner geared his offerings to more mainstream, Americanized tastes. He relied heavily, however, on Jewish-theme films to build an audience. During the opening weeks, he promoted the following titles in the *Forward*: *Esther and Mordechai* (Gaumont, 1910), *Judith and Holophernes* (Biograph, 1914), *Samson the Hero* (Universal, 1914), *Joseph's Trials in Egypt* (Eclectic Film Co./Pathé, 1914), *Mendel Beilis, Bar Kochba—The Hero of a Nation* (Supreme, 1913), *Uriel Acosta* (Goldin, 1914), and *The Slaughter* (a film released in Warsaw in 1914 from the play by Yiddish dramatist Jacob Gordin). In fact, throughout the 1910s, Steiner continued to show moving pictures that were of special interest to East European Jews.[5]

While Marcus Loew and William Fox erected large and luxurious movie palaces in traditional entertainment and retail districts, Steiner's low-cost brick theater building at 238–240 East Third Street became the prototype of the modern, but modest, neighborhood movie theaters. Picture-palace-style film exhibition was not the only way to run a chain. The Steiner group (Greater M and S Circuit) presented its patrons with a middle ground between the luxury of a Loew's theater and the shabbiness of the old-style storefront. It offered immigrant workers surroundings where they could feel at home while participating in the American dream of abundance.

A few months after the opening of the American Movies Theater, the Essex Street Theater, where Steiner began his career as a showman, was demolished to make way for the six-hundred-seat Palace Theater. The Palace was followed in 1916 by the New 14th Street Theater and in 1917 by a $25,000 renovation of the Houston Hippodrome, thereafter known as the Sunshine Theatre. By the mid-1920s, the Greater M and S Circuit had assumed control of most movie theaters on the Lower East Side, including the Clinton, the Odeon, the Ruby, the Palestine, the New Law, and the New Delancey Street. The Great Depression and unfair competition from Hollywood-owned theaters forced this independent chain to curtail its activities. Yet, Steiner continued to cater to Jewish immigrants and other New Yorkers who could not afford much more than a dime for an evening's entertainment. Shortly after his death in 1946, the three remaining Steiner theaters closed their doors for good.

Full-page advertisement in the *Jewish Daily Forward* for the grand opening of the Sunshine Theatre, Houston Street, New York, July 1, 1917. The advertisement proclaims the Sunshine Theatre's cooling system as unique on the East Side, and boasts of a large, $25,000 Wurlitzer organ and a thirty-five-piece orchestra.

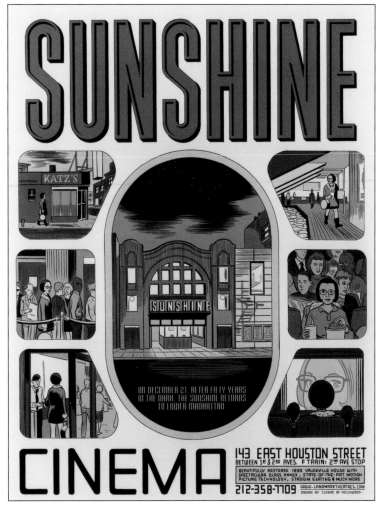

Poster announcing the 2001 reopening of the Sunshine Theatre, now called the Landmark Sunshine Cinema. Although the renovated theater features a "spectacular glass annex, state-of-the-art motion picture technology, stadium seating and much more," the advertisement places it in the context of the historic Lower East Side as embodied by the venerable Katz's Delicatessen. The illustration by cartoonist Daniel Clowes shows his character Enid Coleslaw going to watch herself in the film version of Clowes's graphic novel *Ghost World* (2001).

# DEBATING *COHEN'S FIRE SALE*

The Lower East Side milliner, who is the eponymous protagonist of *Cohen's Fire Sale*, is a Jewish stock character—portly, gesticulating, and obsequious (at least toward his customers). When a new shipment of French hats is inadvertently carted away by the trash collector, S. Cohen checks his insurance policy and decides to recoup his loss by torching his store. A prompt fire department puts out the blaze but does not preclude a successful fire sale. The movie's final shot, in which Cohen presents his wife with a diamond (and their outsized, false noses prevent them from kissing), suggests that the merchant has benefited considerably from this apparent misfortune.

Produced by the Edison company during the summer of 1907, *Cohen's Fire Sale* was a relatively elaborate comedy, running over thirteen minutes and incorporating several locations (most likely near the company's studio on Decatur Avenue in the Bronx), as well as a detailed background flat representing the neighborhood around Cohen's store. One of many series of early-twentieth-century "Cohen" shorts—drawn from routines popular on the vaudeville stage and, later, early sound recordings—the film's negative stereotypes offended some Jewish audience members. As reported in the conservative New York Yiddish daily *Yidishes Tageblat*, the protest sparked by the film's projection in one Jewish-owned nickelodeon presages late-twentieth-century debates over identity politics and political correctness. That the incident occurred more than a year after *Cohen's Fire Sale*'s release is suggestive of the movie's popularity.

—J.H.

Ephraim Koplan, "Jews Who Spit in Their Own Faces," *Yidishes Tageblat* (Jewish Daily News), September 1, 1908.

Not long ago a priest criticized Jews for their indifference toward the spread of anti-Semitism in theaters that present all manner of strange, wild Jewish "types." At first, the Irish also suffered from their portrayal in the theater, the priest declared, but then they took the situation in their own hands. Why, then, do Jews allow someone to spit in their faces? Why don't they do as much to protect their honor?

If this priest knew more about us he certainly wouldn't ask such a naive question. If our fault were only that we let someone spit in our faces it would be bad enough; the problem is that we ourselves are often the ones spitting in our faces, and we don't realize how disgusting and debasing this is.

If Jews visit Christian playhouses where they are mocked and don't protest, it's certainly a disgrace; it's indefensible, of course. The grimness of diaspora, one might say, has accustomed Jews to fear, and when they enter an unfamiliar environment they're afraid to open their mouths, even when they are treated in the most abusive manner. But what diaspora, however grim it may be, can debase people to such a degree that they begin to insult and mock their own people?

Scenes from *Cohen's Fire Sale*
(1907).

And yet, unfortunately, there are plenty of such creatures, the likes of which exist, perhaps, among no other people. In New York and Brooklyn, for example, right in the middle of the Jewish ghetto, cheap five-cent theaters are spreading like a plague. Their owners, regrettably, are Jews, as are their patrons. We might therefore expect that these temples of art would offer at least some small number of authentically Jewish pictures to satisfy the patriotic feelings of the patrons. But not only don't they do this; they grab every insulting picture that portrays Jews as devils, swindlers, and impostors. The creators of these pictures are usually staunch anti-Semites, and their inclinations are quite obvious, but the Jewish owners of the vaudeville houses care as little about this as they do about last year's snow.

It is even more of a wonder that it doesn't occur to any member of the Jewish public to protest against this disgraceful fact. Jews on the Lower East Side are as they were in the Old Country; they refrain from expressing their discontent out of fear. If they don't do this, they have only themselves to blame for spitting in their own faces. You might perhaps say that the public that frequents these "temples of art" is far from intelligent, and that they don't have the brains to understand the malice at the heart of the matter.

But that would be a false assumption on your part. The same public that attends either the Jewish or the Christian theater also frequents these vaudeville houses for cheaper and lighter entertainment.

One of the latest pictures currently being shown is called *Cohen's Fire Sale*. In a very hateful manner, this picture shows how a Jew, whose business is in trouble, burns down his millinery store; as a result of his cleverness, he makes a considerable profit and gives his wife a large, valuable diamond. A young man, a Zionist, who saw this picture in a Jewish-owned motion picture house, protested against it. He shouted that it was disgraceful to portray Jews as arsonists, but the owner of the theater answered him by shouting even louder that "Jews wouldn't be accused of setting such fires if they didn't do it. No one is so quick to set fires as we Jews are." The audience, a Jewish audience, found all this very amusing and applauded the owner.

The young Zionist walked out to the street, defeated, but his heart would not be stilled, and he demanded that the theater take down the sign depicting Cohen the Jew and his wife abandoning their store to the fire. A large crowd gathered, most of them Jews. They listened to both sides—and, can you imagine, almost all sided with the

owner! "What business is this of yours, mister? What makes you the expert about this? The one thing you can do is not go where you don't feel like going." And that sentiment was shared by the many Jews in the crowd. It was also the opinion of the policeman, who made his point with the assistance of his club.

Should one be silent about such things? Should everyone be allowed to spit in our faces? Should *Cohen's Fire Sale* be presented by Jews? We leave it to our people to be the judge!

—Translated by Jeffrey Shandler

# THE FIRST "JEWISH" SUPERSTAR: CHARLIE CHAPLIN

### J. HOBERMAN

*Sunday, after lunch, I and my friend Mike (who used to be called Mendel not so long ago) go to the moving pictures to see the great movie star, Charlie Chaplin. My brother Eli and our friend Pinney also go along with us. All the way to the picture house, we talk about Charlie Chaplin. What a great man he is, how much he must make, and the fact that he's a Jew.*
—Sholem Aleichem, "Motl in America" (1916)[1]

Has there ever been a more universal performing artist than Charles Chaplin (1889–1977)? Or a non-Jew so persistently identified—by both admirers and detractors, Jews and Gentiles—as a Jew?

That the movies' first Jewish superstar was not in fact a Jew suggests the intimate connection between immigrant East European Jews and the dynamics of modern mass culture. In the years just before World War I, the Irish-American ingenue Irene Wallace enjoyed brief celebrity playing Jewish roles, while American-born Jews like Theda Bara (born Theodesia Goodman) and Bronco Billy Anderson (born Max Aronson) achieved stardom as types—the exotic temptress and honest cowpoke, respectively. Chaplin's "Little Tramp" *was* a comic type that struck Jews and non-Jews alike as essentially "Jewish."[2]

*The Immigrant* (1917).

For audiences throughout the world, Chaplin embodied the twentieth century's movie-driven mass culture; for some, he represented its revolutionary (or desecratory) potential as well. The construction of Chaplin as a Jew suggests a popular perception of a new "Jewish" style and attitude identified with modern forms of popular entertainment and an impoverished, rootless urban or immigrant underclass. Given Chaplin's extraordinary visibility both as a movie star and arguably the most widely known personality of the twentieth century, it is remarkable that this identification persisted throughout his life and, at times, even posthumously—despite the fact that he did not play a specifically Jewish character until *The Great Dictator* (United Artists, 1940).[3]

Arriving in the United States in 1913, Chaplin made his first two-reel comedy in early 1914 and required barely more than a year to become the most sensational attraction in American movies. His emergence as the Little Tramp roughly coincides with the rise of foreign-born Jewish exhibitors William Fox, Carl Laemmle, and Adolph Zukor as leaders in the American film industry. Indeed, the first objections to Chaplin's vulgarity and the suggestion that he was in some fashion impure—"never anything dirtier was placed on the screen," *Variety* complained of the Little Tramp in 1915—presage criticisms that would be increasingly leveled against Hollywood in general after 1920.[4]

In his study of ethnicity in Hollywood movie comedy, Mark Winokur singles out Chaplin as the silent comic most concerned with "the fairy-tale transformation of immigrant into American," and from the American perspective, the London-born

Charlie Chaplin as the Little Tramp.

Chaplin was most obviously an immigrant. That the dark-eyed, frizzy-haired, sharp-featured comic did not appear stereotypically English encouraged curiosity regarding his origins. Early press profiles identified him as the child of Jewish variety performers, possibly at Chaplin's own suggestion.[5]

Over half a century later, Chaplin explained that when he broke into the movies, his first producer—presumably Adam Kessel, who proffered him several offers to join Keystone—"naturally" mistook him for a Jew named "Chapman." Chaplin did not disabuse his new employer: "Born in the poorest class in England, with no past, nor castles, nor ancestors to defend, I was not a man to encumber myself with prejudice. If they wanted me Jewish, they would have me Jewish." Not for the last time would Chaplin serve as a screen for audience projection.[6]

According to his biographer David Robinson, the star's earliest published comment on his background dates to 1915. Asked by a reporter if he was Jewish, Chaplin tactfully replied, "I have not that good fortune." Despite such denials, the association stuck. In a 1924 tribute to Charlot, as Chaplin was known in France, Florent Fels wrote that "a Jew renders comic even the most tragic circumstances." Profiling Chaplin in 1925, a *New Yorker* writer noted that "at three a.m., he was a wistful, bewildered lad of the East End. If words of the Kabala had come from his hard mouth, I should not have wondered. He seemed a Jew." Indeed, depending on the circumstances, Chaplin left certain admirers with the unmistakable impression that he was of Jewish descent. The star delighted an eight-year-old Jewish child met on a transatlantic steamer in October 1921 with the observation that "all great geniuses have Jewish blood in them." Although not himself Jewish, he felt that "there must be some somewhere in me. I hope so."[7]

Hollywood director Edward Sutherland, who assisted on *The Gold Rush* (United Artists, 1925), remembered Chaplin telling him that he thought he might have Jewish origins: "I notice my characteristics are very Semitic, my gestures are, my thinking is certainly along money lines." Samuel Rosenblatt, the son of the celebrated cantor Yossele Rosenblatt, wrote that when his father visited Chaplin at home in Hollywood in 1927, Chaplin told him, "I have all the records you have ever produced. I cherish them as among my most treasured possessions. Whenever I feel a little blue, I take them out and play them. They do something to me. They unite me—oh so closely— with my Jewish ancestors."[8]

Chaplin greeting Cantor Yossele Rosenblatt, Beverly Hills, California, 1927. That same year, Rosenblatt had a featured role—as himself— in the movie version of *The Jazz Singer*.

Jewish audiences, meanwhile, simply assumed Chaplin was Jewish. Comparing the three most notable figures in Hollywood silent comedy, a reviewer for the *Jewish Tribune* deemed Buster Keaton "the typical English comedian" and Harold Lloyd "the Yankee par excellence." Chaplin, however, was the "eternal Jewish 'schlemiel.'" The critic reported that "a typical Jewish mother" seated beside him in the theater was overcome by Chaplin's on-screen vicissitudes in *The Gold Rush*, shedding tears and histrionically crying out, "What do they want from him, the *goyim*? Why do they pick on him? What has he done to them?"[9]

The 1948 edition of *Universal Jewish Encyclopedia* discussed the possible relationship between the names Chaplin and Kaplan, and cited two 1931 newspaper articles in support of Chaplin's Jewish origins. The *New York Herald Tribune* characterized his eyes as "simultaneously, the happiest, the saddest and the most intelligent eyes ever formed in a Jewish face," while a Budapest Jewish periodical traced Chaplin's roots to a Central European Jewish family named Thonstein. Suggestively, the name "Israel Thonstein" was the alias the FBI used for Chaplin (whose file dates back to the summer of 1922, when an informant reported that the star had hosted a fund-raiser for the American Communist William Z. Foster, a leader of the 1919 steel strike).[10]

For the immigrant boys in Sholem Aleichem's 1916 story "Motl in America," Chaplin is a source of ethnic pride as well as an inspiration. His success is proof of the possibilities America offered East European Jews. In her 1944 essay, "The Jew as Pariah," the German-Jewish refugee Hannah Arendt similarly assumed that Chaplin was a Jew: "In Chaplin the most unpopular people in the world inspired what was long the most popular of contemporary figures." Searching for positive evidence of Jewish European culture in the face of the Nazi onslaught, Arendt links Chaplin with Heinrich Heine, Bernard Lazare, and Franz Kafka as a quintessential Jewish artist and imagines that Chaplin's Jewishness is the source of his universal appeal: "Standing outside the pale, suspected by all the world, the pariah—as Chaplin portrays him—could not fail to arouse the sympathy of the common people, who recognized in him the image of what society had done to them. Small wonder, then, that Chaplin became the idol of the masses."

For Arendt, Chaplin is Jewish because he suffered and prevailed. His childhood "taught him the traditional Jewish fear of the 'cop'—that seeming incarnation of a hostile world." He embodied the "effrontery of the poor 'little Yid' who does not recognize the class order of the world because he sees in it neither order nor justice for himself."[11]

Similarly, Chaplin has served as a mirror for Jewish theorists of Jewish comedy. Thus, in *The Comic Image of the Jew*, Sig Altman finds the Little Tramp "difficult to 'place' into any other symbolic niche but that of the Jew in the Diaspora." Chaplin's black bowler suggests "those turn-of-the-century photographs showing Jewish peddlers whose black bowlers, substituting for the more traditional black felt hats, are the first concession to 'secularism.'" His "threadbare elegance and precarious dignity," his "amazing agility" and "tendency to kick pomposity in the behind" are, for Altman, all signs of Jewishness. Moreover, Altman writes: "[Chaplin] believes, amazingly enough, in comforting the innocent and helpless and in fighting, mocking, and outrunning the snobs and bullies. And that the latter are none other than those ominous gentiles encountered by the Jew in the gentile world is an interpretation not easy to avoid."

Like Arendt, Altman finds Chaplin an updated Old Testament figure. He is, Altman suggests, the archetypal expression of a "small, dark David-tramp" who triumphs over "the bloated, dough-colored Goliaths." Nor does Altman neglect what Arendt termed Chaplin's Jewish "effrontery." His irrepressible resilience echoes the "élan of Sholem Aleichem's Menachem Mendel, who comes to the city of Odessa in order to become a millionaire without a moment's doubt that he is 'entitled.'" Altman's reading of *City Lights* (United Artists, 1931) goes even further than Arendt's in explicating Chaplin's role as pariah: "The scenes in which the Little Tramp is welcomed as a friend by a drunken millionaire who unceremoniously drops him in the sober light of dawn, are nothing less than "the gist of the Jews' history in Europe."[12]

Indeed, Chaplin's 1931 visit to Berlin provided the occasion for a National Socialist campaign against him. Chaplin was anathema to the Nazis, who denounced him as a "Jewish Communist millionaire" and a "barking dog from London's ghetto." Verbal attacks were followed by demonstrations. After the Nazis came to power in 1933, Chaplin announced that—"for fear of being mistaken for Hitler"—he would henceforth appear without his mustache. Chaplin's films were banned in Germany, but the actor himself continued to figure in the regime's propaganda. In one anti-Semitic tract, his portrait appeared alongside those of Albert Einstein and Max Reinhardt, the caption identifying him as "a little

ABOVE
*City Lights* (1931).

RIGHT
"Goebbels's Inimitable Smile. Chaplin doesn't impress us Berliners. We're accustomed to quite a different comedian of the grotesque!" Anti-Nazi cartoon portraying Charlie Chaplin in the German newspaper *Vorwärts*, March 1931. Chaplin's visit to Berlin was protested by Nazi demonstrators who denounced him as a "Jewish Communist millionaire." After the Nazis came to power in 1933, Chaplin announced that—"for fear of being mistaken for Hitler"—he would henceforth appear without his mustache. Although his films were banned in Germany, the actor figured prominently in the regime's anti-Semitic propaganda.

Jewish acrobat, as disgusting as he is tedious." After his image was prominently included in the 1937 propaganda exhibition, *Der Ewige Jude* (Munich, 1937–38), Chaplin programmatically refused to contradict any statement that he was a Jew, explaining that "anyone who denies this in respect of himself plays into the hands of the anti-Semites."[13]

While working on *The Great Dictator*, the only movie in which he would play an explicitly Jewish character—a humble barber who has an uncanny resemblance to the anti-Semitic dictator Adenoid Hynkel—Chaplin's public identification with Jewish causes grew. In 1939, the *New York Times* reported that the actor had instructed United Artists to pay his European exhibition rentals to an organization aiding Jews emigrating from Central Europe. The following year, he was reported to be among a group that had deposited $6 million in a Milan bank to support refugee Austrian Jews.[14]

Cover of *Di velt fun Tsharli Tshaplin* (The World of Charlie Chaplin) by David Matis, 1959. Matis, a film critic and historian, wrote the first history of Yiddish-language film, published in Yiddish in 1961.

In his book on Chaplin, the Yiddish journalist and film historian David Matis suggests that the actor's perceived Jewishness was a factor of his leftist political sympathies—and was used as ammunition by his political enemies. The question of Chaplin's Jewishness, Matis argues, was raised in 1921, when the star was perceived to be a supporter of Lenin; in 1940, when he was criticized for making *The Great Dictator*; and during the Cold War and the ensuing Red Scare in Hollywood. "The only logical conclusion to be drawn from this fact is that reactionary circles that were always infected with anti-Semitism searched for a way to confirm Chaplin's alleged 'Jewish lineage' with the aim of destroying the artist."[15]

On the other side of the Iron Curtain, however, this supposed lineage was also problematic. The accusations directed against the mainly Jewish "cosmopolitans" of the Soviet film industry included the charge that they had shown altogether too much enthusiasm for the similarly cosmopolitan Chaplin. Indeed, as a true cosmopolitan, Chaplin was suspected of being a Zionist as well as a Communist. In 1948, U.S. Navy intelligence linked him, along with Walter Winchell and Bernard Baruch, to the sale of thirty-six surplus tanks to Haganah forces in Palestine.[16]

Hounded by the FBI, the press, and assorted right-wing pressure groups, Chaplin left America in 1952. The questions of his origins followed him. On first meeting reporters at the Savoy Hotel on his arrival to London, the city of his birth, he was asked about his Jewish background by a writer from the *London Jewish Chronicle*. According to the journalist, Chaplin smiled "sarcastically" at the question, to which he declined to give a straightforward answer. Matis reports that the Israeli press ran several stories during the 1950s on Chaplin's Jewish origins—most fancifully, the account of a man who claimed to have known the future star as a young man in London. Chaplin's parents, he asserted, were Russian immigrants. Their family name was Kaplinski and their son, Charlie, studied in a Talmud Torah.[17]

Source of ethnic pride, political issue, or shorthand for the culture of Hollywood, Chaplin's Jewishness was always a cultural construction. "Most comedians are Jewish," asserted the non-Jewish television personality Steve Allen in 1956. Allen cited forty such comics—including Chaplin, who was thus drafted into the service of another Jewish stereotype. Even Chaplin's non-Jewishness could be used as evidence of a Jewish attempt to pass for Gentile. As late as 1977, Columbia University professor Albert Goldman made the outrageous assertion that "Chaplin was an English Jew who was at pains always to deny or minimize his Jewish origins." Despite this, Goldman continued, Chaplin's "comedy was an abstract of Jewish humor, with the

Chaplin faces execution in *The Great Dictator* (1940), the only movie in which he played an explicitly Jewish character—a "double" for an anti-Semitic dictator.

essential Jewish properties operating in the traditional Jewish manner, the only difference being that the Yiddish tags were removed so as to achieve a 'universal' effect."[18]

Repudiate his heritage as he might, Goldman explains, Chaplin could not conceal "the classic notes and signs of the Jewish comic hero." He "was the apotheosis of the schlemiel," whose Jewish traits included his "vulnerability," his "quick wit" and instinct for self-preservation, his "absurd affectation of dandyism," and, perhaps most significant, his "infatuation with the blond-haired, fair-skinned, voluptuously innocent maidens, whom he courted with eyes brimming with Jewish soul and sentiment." At this point, Chaplin transcends the existential definition of a Jew offered by Jean-Paul Sartre: A Jew is one who is so labeled by the world. According to Goldman's formulation, a Jew is one whose cultural self-denial resembles that of the Jewish non-Jew Charlie Chaplin.[19]

Attempting to dispel the myth of Chaplin's Jewishness in their *American-Jewish Filmmakers*, David Desser and Lester Friedman have pointed out that, if anything, Chaplin was an "essentially Christian filmmaker" whose "redemptive Christian vision" proposed "self-sacrifice and charity as the highest forms of love." To which, I suppose, one might respond that Jews have dreamed of redemption; that Jews, too, are capable of self-sacrifice; that charity is also a Jewish value; and that, in any case, Jesus was a Jew, if not an immigrant comedian.[20]

# VIRTUALLY JEWISH

J. HOBERMAN AND JEFFREY SHANDLER

Charlie Chaplin's mistaken identity as a Jew was largely rooted in his performance of a character that, to many, seemed Jewish. That is, Chaplin's Little Tramp (and Chaplin himself) conformed to conventions of an ethnic "type" already familiar to audiences as a Jew. Such conventions, which include costume, gesture, and dialect, are performative elements; they are enacted, rather than innate, attributes of ethnicity and so can be learned and performed by anyone, regardless of his or her actual identity.

"Playing" Jewish—or Irish, or Chinese, or Yankee, among other ethnic, racial, and regional types—was a stock-in-trade for many American stage actors. By 1880, the vaudevillian Frank Bush, a German-born Christian, had established his niche playing "Luvinsky the Old Clothes Man" and "Abraham Mendel Cohn the Pawnbroker." Blackface, the longest-lived and most disturbing instance of ethnic impersonation in American culture, was also the only one attached to a specific theatrical form—namely, the minstrel show. However, there were roles that required specialists in playing Jews. The actress Nance O'Neil established her career at the turn of the twentieth century by touring as the title characters in stage plays like *The Jewess* and *Judith of Bethulia*. With the advent of motion pictures and phonograph records, new ideas about how to perform various types of characters evolved, at the same time that stereotypes persisted. (Similarly, early radio and the first talking pictures made extensive use of dialect humor.)

Jewish characters in American movies, radio, and television offer a case study of this larger phenomenon. A noteworthy aspect of these performances, frequently dis-

# IRENE WALLACE (Birthplace and dates unknown)

A former vaudeville "Dresden Doll," Irene Wallace was the first female "Jewish" movie star despite, or perhaps because of, her well-publicized Scotch-Irish background.

A profile in the *Motion Picture World* noted that Wallace's work as the Jewish banker's daughter romantically involved with a Russian nobleman in Sidney Goldin's two-reel *Nihilist Vengeance* (Universal, 1913) "stood out so well that it was a surprise to the management." Wallace was next cast as the lead in Goldin's *The Heart of a Jewess* (Universal, 1913), a naturalistic two-reel dramatic comedy of ghetto life that depicted the romantic betrayals and domestic abandonment endemic to immigrant life. As "she arose to the occasion beyond all expectations," the *Motion Picture World* reported: "[The actress] is now looked upon as a star in this particular line and will probably make it a specialty. Miss Wallace has just finished the lead in another big Jewish production entitled *Bleeding Hearts, or Jewish Freedom*

*Granted by King Casimir of Poland.* . . . In due course of time she will no doubt be considered as the leading exponent of Hebraic parts."

In fact, *Bleeding Hearts, or Jewish Freedom Granted by King Casimir of Poland* (U.S.A., 1913)—in which Wallace played the role of Casimir's Jewish queen Esterke—proved to be the actress's last major role. Her career declined precipitously after she wrote an exposé in 1914 detailing the ways in which unscrupulous producers preyed upon innocent starlets. Fired from Universal, she went to work for Selig Polyscope in Chicago. Wallace thereafter disappeared from the historical record, although she left an indelible impression on at least one young filmgoer. In a meditation entitled "The Jew as Movie Subject," published in the February 1930 issue of the film journal *Close-Up*, the American Marxist critic Harry Alan Potemkin attributed the scenario of *Bleeding Hearts* to its star.

—J.H.

Irene Wallace, 1914.

cussed by audiences, is that outside of comedy, Jewish actors rarely played explicitly Jewish characters until the late 1960s. At the same time, some of the best-known Jewish characters were the work of non-Jewish actors. Such "virtual Jews" embody the interplay among perceived ethnic identity, a star's public profile, and a dramatic character's reception. These actors' ability to perform Jews has been variously attributed to their versatility as well as their innate "type," research skills, imagination, or life experience. Thus, when discussing his role as a hasidic *rebbe* in *The Chosen* (Analysis, 1982), Rod Steiger recalled what he learned in his youth as a *shabbes goy*—a Gentile who performs tasks forbidden to observant Jews on the Sabbath.

Television actress Valerie Harper reported that her portrayal of the wisecracking Rhoda Morgenstern (on the television situation comedies *The Mary Tyler Moore Show* and *Rhoda*) was inspired by various New York Jewish and Italian women she knew. Remarkably, Harper's portrayal of Rhoda Morgenstern also provided a role model for Jewish women—in some cases more than twenty-five years after *Rhoda* had its premiere on network television. Jewish studies scholar Vanessa Ochs has characterized Rhoda's self-critique as "Talmudic" and joked that, "If all she could teach me was that a scarf could be worn in multiple ways, *dayeinu* [that would be enough for us]."[1]

The relationship between Jewish characters and the non-Jewish actors who play them may also be symbiotic. In the case of one of the youngest performers in the following selection of non-Jewish performers known for their portrayal of Jews, Nathan (né Joseph) Lane adopted his first name from Damon Runyon's Jewish gangster Nathan Detroit, whom the actor portrayed in the musical *Guys and Dolls*.

# JOHN TURTURRO (Born in New York, 1957)

As Jewish actors like Paul Muni and Edward G. Robinson specialized in playing immigrant Italians (among other ethnic types) during the 1930s, so sixty years later the Italian-American actor John Turturro has appeared as an explicitly Jewish character in a number of movies, most notably *Miller's Crossing* (Twentieth Century Fox, 1990), *Mo' Better Blues* (Universal, 1990), *Barton Fink* (Circle Films, 1991), *Quiz Show* (Hollywood Pictures, 1994), and *The Awakening* (Miramax, 1996; also known as *The Truce*). In the last of these, he starred as the Italian author and Holocaust survivor Primo Levi.

In a 1995 article on Hollywood's "unchosen minority," *Entertainment Weekly* reporter Rebecca Ascher-Walsh juxtaposed Turturro's wry comment, "I'm almost considered Jewish now," with his difficulties being cast for another Jewish role in *Unstrung Heroes* (Hollywood Pictures, 1995): "Frequently, actors who look 'too Jewish' by Hollywood standards—whether or not they are Jewish—are not the first choice to play Semitic characters."

Ascher-Walsh attributed the paucity of "Jewish-looking" actors in Jewish roles to "the ambivalence of [Hollywood's] own executives, many of them Jewish, about seeing Jews represented on the screen," quoting a young Jewish screenwriter who told her that "it's hard for them to make a movie about the kind of Jewishness they've turned their backs on."[1]
—J.H.

John Turturro in *Barton Fink*, 1991.

RIGHT
Poster for *The House of Rothschild* (1934), starring George Arliss, who was also renowned for his portrayals of Benjamin Disraeli in 1921 and 1929.

THE SWORDS OF ALL EUROPE COULD NOT DIVIDE THE HOUSE OF ROTHSCHILD!

All for one and one for all! Five brothers —welded for eternity by a dying father's trust! Standing united against all their enemies — guided by a loving mother's faith!

JOSEPH M. SCHENCK presents

GEORGE ARLISS
in the DARRYL F. ZANUCK production

THE HOUSE OF ROTHSCHILD

BORIS KARLOFF · LORETTA YOUNG
ROBERT YOUNG · HELEN WESTLEY
And a Distinguished Supporting Cast of One Hundred
A 20th CENTURY PICTURE · Released thru UNITED ARTISTS

BELOW
Gregory Peck as King David in *David and Bathsheba* (1951). In *Gentleman's Agreement* (1947), Peck played a journalist who poses as a Jew to research an exposé of anti-Semitism.

ABOVE
Natalie Wood as Marjorie Morningstar. The non-Jewish Wood also played the Jewish stripper and actress Gypsy Rose Lee (née Rose Louise Hovick).

Valerie Harper (right) as
Rhoda Morgenstern, with
Nancy Walker as her mother,
in the television series
*Rhoda* (CBS, 1974–78).
Walker appeared as a *shtetl*
housewife (opposite Zero
Mostel) in the 1959 tele-
cast of the Off-Broadway
play *The World of Sholom
Aleichem*. Harper, who
debuted as Rhoda on *The
Mary Tyler Moore Show*
(CBS) in 1970, had earlier
portrayed a young Jewish
woman in love with a
Gentile on the 1966 comedy
album *When You're in Love
the Whole World Is Jewish*.

Rod Steiger as a Holocaust
survivor in *The Pawnbroker*
(1965). Steiger appeared
as a movie mogul in *The
Big Knife* (1955), a Jewish
character in *No Way to
Treat a Lady* (1968), and
the *rebbe* in *The Chosen*
(1981).

Nathan Lane as Irving
Mansfield, husband of the
author Jacqueline Susann,
played by Bette Midler, in
the film *Isn't She Great*
(2000). Lane also played
Max Prince, a character
based on comedian Sid
Caesar, in the television
version of *Laughter on the
Twenty-Third Floor* (2001).

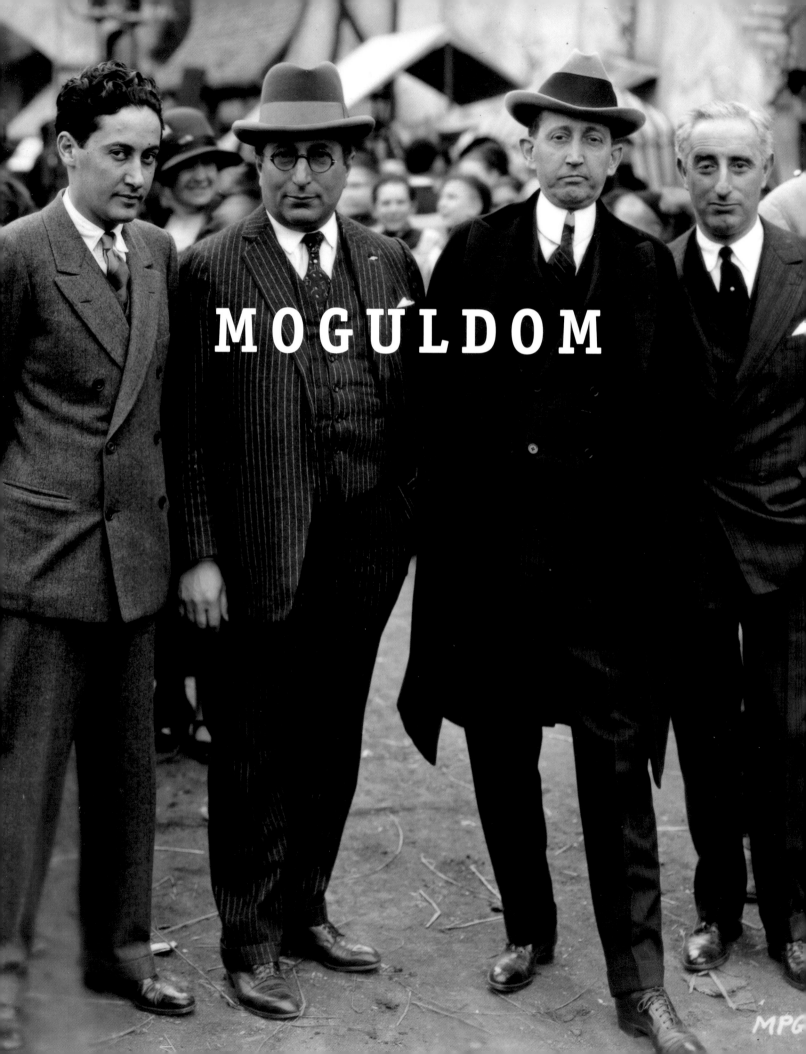

**THE ASSOCIATION** OF IMMIGRANT JEWS WITH AMERICAN MOVIES DATES TO THE NICKELODEON ERA, BUT, LIKE THE MOVIES THEMSELVES, THE NATURE OF THIS ASSOCIATION CHANGED SIGNIFICANTLY ONCE THE BUSINESS OF MAKING, DISTRIBUTING, AND EXHIBITING FILMS BECAME A MAJOR AMERICAN INDUSTRY AND AMERICA BECAME THE WORLD'S DOMINANT PRODUCER OF MOTION PICTURES. By the end of World War I, the American movie enterprise had effectively relocated from the East Coast to southern California and was organized around a half-dozen large studios, most founded and run by Jewish executives of Central and East European origin. While the discussion of Hollywood's Jewishness has encompassed producers, exhibitors, writers, and performers, its focus has more often been on these studio heads, now popularly known as the "movie moguls." Indeed, the public debate over the extent and significance of Jewish involvement in the American film industry, which we term "Hollywood's Jewish Question," has largely coalesced around the moguls and their successors.

This debate has continued from the 1920s to the present, changing its focus and tenor in response to events in both the movie industry and American politics, as well as shifts in cultural sensibility. In addition to what the discussion reveals about the history of American moviemaking and public images of Jews in America, the various attempts to ask or answer Hollywood's Jewish Question offer a revealing history of how twentieth-century Americans have considered the relationship between works of culture and the backgrounds of their creators. As communications scholar Steven Alan Carr observes in his study of Hollywood and anti-Semitism, "by reforming Jewish stereotypes into powerful commentaries on the rise of the media, power, and shifts within American culture," this discussion has structured "an entire way of looking at ethnic agency."[1]

Throughout the history of Hollywood's Jewish Question, there has been more at stake than the welfare of the entertainment industry or the reputation of American Jewry. Central to the discussion, although often implicit, is an awareness of the power inherent in popular entertainment as a force for social change. Hollywood has been feared as a source of both moral corruption and political subversion. Some have attacked the movie industry for its internationalism, others for being the instrument of American cultural imperialism. Consequently, Hollywood's Jews have been stereotyped as both cynical capitalists and seditious radicals.

The first national campaign for movie regulation began in the early 1920s, soon after the industry came to be regarded as the realm of the moguls—and there have been intermittent calls for government control or censorship ever since. While discussion of the Jewish presence in Hollywood has often been coded, enemies of the movie industry have similarly employed the rhetoric of anti-Semitism to articulate positions that might be primarily antimodern, antiurban, anti–New Deal, anti-internationalist, anticapitalist, anti-Communist, or anti-American. Industrialist Henry Ford, who remains one of the most notorious American anti-Semites, was among the first to launch a public attack on Hollywood's Jews. Beginning in 1921, he used his newspaper, the *Dearborn Independent*, to assail Jewish "control" of American theater, banking, organized sports, and other institutions, in addition to the movie industry.

In the late 1930s, isolationist politicians accused the Hollywood studios of manufacturing anti-Nazi and pro-British propaganda as a means of maneuvering the United States into a war to rescue Europe's Jews from Nazism. In 1947, politicians again questioned the loyalty of Hollywood's immigrant founders in the course of investigating another foreign contagion: Communism. Though the original moguls passed from the scene in the 1950s and 1960s, soon after they cooperated with Congress in ridding their industry of its "dangerous" elements, the discussion of Hollywood's Jewishness has not disappeared. The issue resurfaced repeatedly, if obliquely, at the turn of the millennium, in attacks on the movie industry as a purveyor of "secular humanist" values or as the provenance of a cultural "elite."

Hollywood's Jewish Question has not only been posed by anti-Semites; philo-Semites and Jews themselves have entered the discussion, both to defend Jews against attack and to ponder the implications of reading the annals of Hollywood as a Jewish story. Over the years, the saga of the movie moguls has been variously recounted as a foreign conspiracy, a Jewish renaissance ("sans rabbis and Talmud," according to screenwriter Ben Hecht), an American success story, and a tragicomedy of parvenu immigrants' social overreaching. The subtitle of Neal Gabler's influential popular history *An Empire of Their Own: How the Jews Invented Hollywood* (1988) is read as ironic by some and as gospel by others. For American Jews, Hollywood has figured as a complex touchstone, generating wide-ranging responses—sometimes even from the same individual. "To be anti-Hollywood was, in a sense, to be anti-Semitic," claimed Budd Schulberg, son of a pioneer film producer as well as a successful screenwriter. Yet he was also the author of the quintessential Hollywood novel, *What Makes Sammy Run?* (1940)—a book that was itself accused of self-directed anti-Semitism.[2]

Extensive public debate over Hollywood's Jewishness notwithstanding, Jewish filmmakers occasionally used their medium for self-portraiture during the 1920s, producing a number of silent features that dramatized or satirized the Americanization of immigrant Jews. This genre of "melting pot" movies culminated in 1927 with the release of *The Jazz Singer*, a film that would come to mark a major threshold in the history of cinema: the advent of talking pictures. *The Jazz Singer*, however, is noteworthy less for its representation of Jewish life on the Lower East Side than for its distinctive depiction of an immigrant Jewish entertainer—modeled on, as well as played by, Al Jolson—whose adaptation to American ways, including the use of blackface makeup, is shown as integral to his success. (That blackface was also integral to Jolson's persona, as it was to other Jewish performers of that time, poses special challenges in light of the scandalous racism this once-pervasive entertainment convention now signifies.)

In *The Jazz Singer*, the Warner brothers created a kind of collective self-portrait of their fellow moguls, in which traditional Judaism gave way to a new American religion of show business. Inspiring decades of remakes, adaptations, biographies, and satires, the mythic journey portrayed in *The Jazz Singer* has had an enduring appeal in Hollywood, extending beyond the end of the twentieth century.

—J.H./J.S.

# HOLLYWOOD'S JEWISH QUESTION

J. HOBERMAN AND JEFFREY SHANDLER

Adolph Zukor and Ernst Lubitsch. Lubitsch broke into movies in Berlin, playing a series of Jewish comic roles. One of the leading directors of the silent era, he relocated to Hollywood in the 1920s; his early talkies, made for Zukor's studio, Paramount, were celebrated for their sophistication. Between 1935 and 1938, Lubitsch also served as Paramount's production chief—the only working director ever to hold such a position.

*The genii have answered the Wish of the World with the Aladdin's Lamp of the camera and the Magic Carpet of the film. An empire built of the shadow glories has prospered and its boundaries are the limits of the Earth.*

*This empire of the screen has many subjects, slaves, magicians, sheikhs, dancing girls, princesses, grand viziers and emirs. Chief of them all is a certain philosophic little man from Hungary, silent and meek among his millions. His name is [Adolph] Zukor [president of Paramount Pictures], first and last in the alphabet of fame. He has risen, for his day, even as Abou Hassan, from the bazaar to the riches and power of a Caliph Haroun Alraschid in a new Baghdad-on-the-Hudson, capital of Screenland, where dreams come true.*
—Terry Ramsaye, *A Million and One Nights: A History of the Motion Picture through 1925*

MOGUL, noun [Hindi "Mughal," from Mongolian "Mongol," a Mongol]
1. a Mongol; a Mongolian; especially, any of the Mongolian conquerors of India or their descendants.
2. a powerful or important person, especially one with autocratic power.
—*Webster's New Twentieth-Century Dictionary*

## THE INVASION OF THE "ALIEN EX-BUTTONHOLE MAKERS"

The nature of Jewish involvement in the American film industry has been a charged subject of public discussion for almost as long as the industry has existed. Hollywood's "Jewish Question" has involved Jews and Gentiles, anti-Semites and philo-Semites, industry insiders and scholarly observers, clergy and laypeople, fiction writers and journalists; it has ranged from heated invective to coy obfuscation, playful self-mockery to probing analysis. Now over three generations old, it is one of the most extensive, diverse, and contentious public discussions of Jews in America and of Jewishness as an American cultural force.

This topic is rooted in an older, broader discourse. Well before Hollywood was established, political leaders, writers, philosophers, and other intellectuals in Europe and America had begun to debate the "proper" place of Jews in Western society: Could Jews successfully integrate into the mainstream? Could they become loyal citizens of any nation? By the 1920s, the discussion in the United States of what had become known as the "Jewish Question" focused on Hollywood, where many of the most prominent figures were immigrant Jews, including the majority of studio executives. Indeed, the most visible symbols of America's dynamic, expanding motion-picture industry, aside from the films' stars, were the Hollywood studio executives: notably, William Fox (1879–1952), Samuel Goldwyn (1882–1974), Carl Laemmle (1867–1939), Jesse Lasky (1880–1958), Marcus Loew (1870–1927), Louis B. Mayer

(1885–1957), and Adolph Zukor (1873–1976). After the development of talking pictures, they would be followed by younger men: Harry (1881–1958) and Jack (1892–1978) Warner, Harry Cohn (1891–1958), Irving Thalberg (1899–1936), David O. Selznick (1902–1965), and the non-Jewish Darryl F. Zanuck (1902–1979).

Unlike their predecessors in American film production—men like Thomas Edison, D. W. Griffith, and Thomas Ince, who were respectfully referred to as cinema "inventors" or "pioneers"—the "moguls" (as the term implies) were more often seen as autocratic, alien figures. Even when not cast in a sinister light, they were portrayed less as gifted impresarios, who combined financial acuity with an appreciation for talent and a sensitivity to audience sensibilities, than as men who owed their success to a combination of fearsome energy, ruthless ambition, and a shrewd business sense, often forged in the similarly competitive and trend-driven garment industry. (This characterization also had a direct antecedent in the negative image of Jewish theatrical impresarios, who had been denounced as a corrupting element in American theater since the late nineteenth century.)[1]

Anecdotes typically depict Jewish studio executives as vulgar *allrightniks* (American Yiddish for "arrivistes"), whose rapid material rise was not matched by their provincial sensibilities and ham-fisted social style. Thus, a 1925 *New Yorker* profile of "Celluloid Prince" Samuel Goldwyn noted that he "has a valet and dresses and looks like a gentleman, but to hear him speak is a shock. He shouts in a vocabulary of ten words." Nevertheless, the author of the profile conceded, if Goldwyn was uneducated, insensitive, crude, loud, self-promoting, and innately comic, he was nonetheless a "dramatic figure—an inspired buccaneer." The *New Yorker* attributed the immigrant glove-salesman's stunning success in the "mongrel industry" of motion pictures to lessons learned during his Old World childhood: "In Warsaw, Poland, where [Goldwyn] was born in 1882, he must have discovered that the rule of life, in order to live, is not to let live. This philosophy, humanized by a democracy like ours, means outstripping the other fellow by any means possible that does not land one in jail."[2]

From the early 1920s to the present, many observers have argued that the Jewishness of the studio heads and many of their employees entailed shared, inherent characteristics, and that this was somehow instrumental in enabling Hollywood to fashion a new and seemingly universal form of public entertainment for an audience of unprecedented scope. In *A Million and One Nights*, for example, Terry Ramsaye maintained that, scarcely accidental, "it is rather a phase of screen evolution which finds the American motion picture industry, and therefore the screens of the world, administered rather largely by our best and most facile internationalists, the Jews."[3]

Other early historians of Hollywood saw the Jewish role in its creation much less favorably. In his *History of the American Film Industry*, one-time producer Benjamin Hampton disparaged the "ballyhoo artists and spielers" who entered motion picture production through the portal of exhibition: "Showmen of these classes were purveyors of novelties, real or alleged 'genuine new novelties.' They

OPPOSITE
Samuel Goldwyn.

RIGHT
Caricature of Samuel Goldwyn, the "Celluloid Prince," in the *New Yorker*, April 25, 1925.

were perpetual wanderers, descendants in spirit of the mountebanks of previous centuries. . . . Many recruits to the exhibiting branch of the new industry came from New York's East Side, where scores of ambitious young Jews were restlessly searching for access to the sources of wealth and power. They were quick to see the possibilities of the penny arcade and living pictures on the screen."[4]

The largely suspect image of Jews in the nation's entertainment industries was exacerbated by two prevalent currents in American public discourse during the 1920s: nativism and anti-Bolshevism. From the nativists' perspective, Jews—especially those who had recently immigrated from Eastern Europe—were "orientals." Such "Asiatic" foreigners were understood not merely as a distinct religious community, but also as a separate race (a notion that many Jews at the time accepted as well), and were therefore inherently different from white Christian Americans.[5]

For some Americans, orientalism offered a model for relaxing old behavior patterns of strict propriety and finding new ones that might allow for more freely expressed sensuality.[6] American nativists, however, regarded this foreign influence as a destabilizing, corrupting force that threatened the integrity of American culture. That a new industry, as well as a national pastime, was apparently in the hands of recent immigrants of alien background was an urgent cause for concern. Suspicion of Jews as non-Christians and as inassimilable "orientals" coincided with the post–World War I "Red Scare," in which Jewish immigrants were prominently identified with the spread of Bolshevism. This association was fostered by the first English-language translation of the infamous *Protocols of the Elders of Zion*—a forged document, initially printed in Russia in 1905, that purported to expose an international Jewish conspiracy to control the world.[7]

Automobile manufacturer Henry Ford, an ardent nativist and anti-Communist, believed the *Protocols* to be an authentic harbinger of the Bolshevik revolution, and the book formed the basis for much of his own anti-Semitic writing and publishing, which began in the inaugural May 22, 1920, issue of the *Dearborn Independent*. Although Ford was not the first to sound an alarm about what he considered to be the undue and malevolent Jewish influence on American popular entertainment (as well as in banking, politics, and the press), he was the most renowned figure to raise these issues so explicitly and publicly.[8]

The linking of Jews and Communism during the early 1920s contributed to the general rise in American anti-Semitism and—with the Cold War congressional investigations of Hollywood and the subsequent blacklisting of Hollywood leftists—would have enduring consequences in the American film and broadcasting industries. It is not surprising, then, to see Hollywood's Jewish Question addressed at this time as a kind of holy war. In December 1920, the Reverend Wilbur Fisk Crafts—a longtime crusader against vice, prohibitionist, and proponent of federal censorship regulation—sought, in Ramsaye's phrase, "to proclaim a *jehad*," announcing that his watchdog agency, the International Reform Bureau, had resolved to appeal to the United States Congress and the Catholic Church to "rescue the motion pictures from the hands of the Devil and 500 un-Christian Jews." One month later, Crafts expounded his suspicions in "Jewish Supremacy in the Theater and Cinema," an essay that first appeared in Ford's *Dearborn Independent*.

Fear of Jewish influence in the movies merged with ongoing anxieties over the medium's potential to foster indecency and glamorize violence. In April 1921, several months into the period of Prohibition, the *Nation* reported "another one of those

# HENRY FORD

Best known to Americans as the nation's leading manufacturer of automobiles and the inventor of the assembly line, Henry Ford was an ardent and outspoken nativist and anti-Communist who was convinced that American culture was endangered by the corrupting influences of nonwhite races and immigrants. Ford first attacked Jewish control of the film industry in the *Dearborn Independent*, a newspaper published under his supervision beginning in 1919. Similar claims also appeared in a chapter of *The International Jew*, a compendium of essays first issued in 1920 by the Dearborn Publishing Company on what it deemed to be "the world's foremost problem."[1]

In *The International Jew*, Jews are characterized as secretive, clannish, dishonest, exploitative, and seductive. Ford saw Jewish control of American movies and theater as an effort to control popular taste, likening their effect to a narcotic. He imagined that Jews would exploit the movies as a vehicle for subversive propaganda, especially for rehearsing revolution; he understood the film medium itself as a demoralizing force that promoted indecency and lowered aesthetic standards. Significantly, Ford felt the virtues of mass production that he championed in manufacturing to be incompatible with art, which he argued could only be trivialized and cheapened by commercialization. Though Jews and the movie industry are the targets of Ford's attack, his real fears seem to lie elsewhere—fears of the consequences of modernity, as Americans encountered new populations, ideologies, and technologies.
—J.S.

Cover of *Der emes vegn Henri Ford* (The Truth about Henry Ford) by David L. Mekler, published in New York in 1924. This volume denounces Ford as a front for the racist, anti-Catholic, anti-Semitic, anti-immigrant Ku Klux Klan (then at the height of its influence, with a national membership estimated at five million).

From the *Dearborn Independent*, "The Jewish Aspect of the 'Movie' Problem," February 12, 1921, and "Jewish Supremacy in the Motion Picture World," February 19, 1921.

When you see millions of people crowding through the doors of the movie houses at all hours of the day and night, literally an unending line of human beings in every habitable corner of the land, it is worth knowing who draws them there, who acts upon their minds while they quiescently wait in the darkened theater, and who really controls this massive bulk of human force and ideas generated and directed by the suggestions of the screen. Who stands at the apex of this mountain of control? It is stated in the sentence: The motion picture influence of the United States—and Canada—is exclusively under the control, moral and financial, of the Jewish manipulators of the public mind.

Jews did not invent the art of motion photography; they have contributed next to nothing to its mechanical or technical improvement; they have not produced any of the great artists, either writers or actors, which have furnished the screen with its material. Motion photography, like most other useful things in the world, is of non-Jewish origin. But by the singular destiny which has made the Jews the great cream-skimmers of the world, the benefit of it has gone not to the originators, but to the usurpers, the exploiters. . . .

The problem of the immoral show has been neither settled nor silenced. In every part of the country it is intensely alive just now. In almost every state there are movie censorship bills pending, with the old "wet" [i.e., anti-Prohibition] and gambling elements against them, and the awakened part of the decent population in favor of them; always, the Jewish producing firms constituting the silent pressure behind the opposition.

This is a grave fact. Standing alone it would seem to charge a certain Jewish element with intentional gross immorality. But that hardly states the condition. There are two standards in the United States, one ruling very largely in the production of plays, the other reigning, when it does reign, in the general public. One is an Oriental ideal—"if you can't go as far as you like, go as far as you can." It gravitates naturally to the flesh and its exposure, its natural psychic habitat is among the more sensual emotions. This Oriental view is essentially different from the Anglo-Saxon, the American view. And it knows this. Thus is the opposition to censorship accounted for. It is not that producers of Semitic origin have deliberately set out to be bad according to their own standards, but they know that their whole taste and temper are different from the prevailing standards of the American people; and if censorship were established, there would be danger of American standards being officially recognized, and that is what they would prevent. Many of these producers don't know how

modern crusades which in recent years have swept the country." Hollywood was now under widespread attack for its presentation of crime and sex, and thereby for corrupting American youth. The industry's parvenu Jewish leadership was often the target of this assault, sometimes obliquely, sometimes directly. Thus, the editor of the *Brooklyn Tablet*, a Catholic newspaper, characterized the American movie industry as the provenance of "alien ex-buttonhole makers and pressers" who, in their amoral quest for profit, had applied the principles of "the cloak and suit trade" to Hollywood.[9]

Amid talk of extending federal regulation of the film industry, which had been instituted during World War I, no less than thirty-seven state legislatures considered bills to censor motion pictures. Extensive press coverage of popular film comedian Fatty Arbuckle's trial for the rape and manslaughter of a young starlet, the most lurid of several Hollywood scandals of the early 1920s, fanned public outrage. The widespread image of Hollywood as a modern-day Babylon pushed the movie industry toward self-regulation. In March 1922, the studio executives responded to the threat of government censorship by establishing the Motion Pictures Producers and Distributors of America and recruiting United States Postmaster General Will Hays, a prominent Indiana Republican and Presbyterian elder, to be its president.

Given the mandate to police movie morals, Hays developed a production code, which would ensure that "godless" Hollywood would become a bastion of middle-class, mainstream American morality. The "Hays Code," as it came to be known, was widely discussed in terms that characterized this conservative counterrevolution as a clash between racial or religious sensibilities. Hays was humorously referred to

---

filthy their stuff is—it is so natural to them.

Scarcely an American home has not voiced its complaint against the movies. Perhaps no single method of entertainment has ever received such widespread and unanimous criticism as the movies, for the reason that everywhere their lure and lasciviousness have been felt. There are good pictures, of course; it were a pity if that much could not be said; we cling to that statement as if it might prove a ladder to lift us above the cesspool which the most popular form of public entertainment has become.

The case has been stated so often that repetition is needless. Responsible men and organizations have made their protests without results. The moral appeal meets no response in those to whom it is made, because they are able to understand only appeals that touch their material interests. As the matter now stands, the American

Public is as helpless against the films as it is against any other exaggerated expression of Jewish power. And the American Public will continue helpless until it receives such an impression of its helplessness as to shock it into protective action. . . .

Now, there is little wisdom in discoursing against evil in the movies and deliberately closing our eyes to the forces behind the evil. The method of reform must change. In earlier years, when the United States presented a more general Aryan complexion of mind and conscience, it was only necessary to expose the evil to cure it. The evils we suffered from were lapses, they were the fruits of moral inertia or drifting; the sharp word of recall stiffened the moral fiber of the guilty parties and cleared up the untoward condition. That is, evil doers of our own general racial type could be shamed into decency, or at least respectability.

That method is no longer possible. The basic conscience is no longer present to

touch. The men now mostly concerned with the production of scenic and dramatic filth are not to be reached that way. They do not believe, in the first place, that it is filth. They cannot understand, in the second place, that they are really pandering to and increasing human depravity. When there does reach their mentalities the force of protest, it strikes them as being very funny; they cannot understand it; they explain it as due to morbidity, jealousy, or—as we hear now—anti-Semitism. The movies are of Jewish production. If you fight filth, the fight carries you straight into the Jewish camp because the majority of the producers are there. And then you are "attacking the Jews."

If the Jews would throw out of their camp the men and methods that so continuously bring shame upon the Jewish name, this fight for decency could be conducted without so much racial reference.

as Hollywood's "new Czar"; a 1926 profile of him in the *New Yorker* drolly observed that "many pursy magnates, not too long out of the cloak-and-suit and feather-and-hide business, found out new things about Indiana Aryans."[10]

Others doubted Hays's efficacy. The evangelical Reverend Bob Shuler, for instance, dismissed Hays as "the hired man of a bunch of rich Jews, doing politics for them at so much per." Nor did the creation of the Hays Office placate either Reverend Crafts or his successor as head of the International Reform Bureau, the Reverend William Sheafe Chase, an Episcopalian minister in Brooklyn. Chase's career as an antimovie crusader began during the 1906 campaign to close New York's nickelodeons. In the early 1920s, he published *Catechism on Motion Pictures in Inter-State Commerce*, which uses the question-and-answer format of a religious instructional manual to call for federal legislation regulating the content of motion pictures. Warning that "the motion picture industry [was] in the despotic control of four or five Hebrews," he cited Ford's *The International Jew* and *The Protocols of the Elders of Zion* as evidence of a Jewish conspiracy.[11]

Ultimately, Hays outflanked his Protestant critics by forming an alliance with the Catholic Church. Having allowed Catholic clerics as well as prominent laymen to draw up and administer the 1930 Motion Picture Production Code, Hays helped create what the historian Francis G. Couvares has characterized as "an industry largely financed by Protestant bankers, operated by Jewish studio executives, and policed by Catholic bureaucrats, all the while claiming to represent grass-roots America."[12]

# *CATECHISM ON MOTION PICTURES*

From William Sheafe Chase, *Catechism on Motion Pictures in Inter-State Commerce*, 3rd ed. (Albany: New York Civic League, 1922), 115.

*What benefit would come to the Jewish race as well as to the whole world, if the few Hebrews who control the motion picture business would petition Congress for federal regulations?*

The few producers who control the motion pictures are all Hebrews. If they should petition Congress for an effective and just law regulating their business, as the railroads, banks and meat businesses [are] supervised by a Federal Commission, it would be a conspicuous public-spirited act that might begin a movement which would minimize the anti-Jewish feeling which exists in the United States.

This small group of men have secured the control of a most marvelous power for good or for evil in the world. . . . There is a widespread conviction that this power has been and is being used for selfish commercial and unpatriotic purposes, even that it has been prostituted to corrupt government, to demoralize youth, and break down the

Christian religion. There is now a widespread hope that in the engagement of Mr. Hay's [sic] services, these exceedingly powerful Jews have really been incited by an honest purpose to serve the public in a generous and effective way. Yet, thus far, nothing in any large way has been accomplished except in what appears to be another attempt through Mr. Hays to protect themselves cleverly from the increasing wrath of the public by arousing false hopes through promises of reform without law impossible of fulfillment and by appeals for forms of personal and public freedom which are deceptive and selfish.[1]

LEFT
Jesse L. Lasky contemplating a bust of himself.

ABOVE
David O. Selznick, beneath a portrait of his father, Lewis J. Selznick.

The Warner brothers: Harry, Jack, Sam, and Albert.

Jack Warner and Al Jolson, 1936.

ABOVE
Irving Thalberg, Louis B. Mayer, Will Hays, and MGM producer Harry Rapf.

BELOW

Carl Laemmle on his sixty-
seventh birthday, surrounded
by film stars Boris Karloff
(second from left), Vince
Maynard (fourth from left),
Margaret Sullavan (third
from right), and Andy
Devine (second from right),
as well as Carl Laemmle, Jr.
(right), 1934.

BELOW
Jesse L. Lasky.

ABOVE
Marcus Loew (center) with
family, 1924.

ABOVE
Darryl Zanuck, head of
Twentieth Century Fox, with
his studio's biggest star,
Shirley Temple (left), and
daughter Darrilyn holding a
Shirley Temple doll, c. 1935.

## "THE JEWS HAVE THEMSELVES TO BLAME"

*[While] some claim that 80 per cent of the industry is in Jewish hands, . . . Jewishness is at a rather low ebb in Hollywood. Few of either the commercial or the artistic moving picture people will insist on being called Jews or on affiliating themselves with a Jewish movement. Some of America's most popular stars become alarmed when they are reminded of their Jewish antecedents. They will answer you: "No, it is impossible—my birth certificate is a mistake." I most heartily agree with these anaemic creatures that their birth, certificate or no certificate, was a mistake. They are shadows on and off the screen.*

—Benjamin P. Schulberg, quoted in "Zionism in Movieland," *The New Palestine* (1925)

*When Hollywood was still in its infancy, I saw you Jews—my brothers—creep forth from the slums of New York, and from the far flung ghettos of Vilna, Kiev and Warsaw. I saw you leave your huckster carts, your rags and bottles, your tailor's bench, and with the indomitable enterprise that God gave you nurture into being a new industry—the motion picture. . . . But what have you to be proud of? What have you done with this priceless heritage, the motion picture? Have you used it to beautify life? Or have you abused your power, viciously and unscrupulously, with all the hopeless vulgarity of wealth newly acquired. . . . Let me assure you, my brothers, it were far better if you were still sewing on buttons and sorting rags than shamelessly corrupting and befouling the taste of the world.*

—Anonymous author, "A Jew Speaks to the Jews of Hollywood," *The Christian Century* (1931)

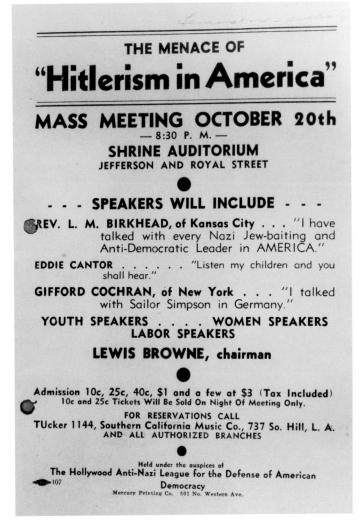

Poster announcing the first meeting of the Hollywood Anti-Nazi League, October 20, 1936.

First voiced in the 1920s, the idea that Hollywood was the seditious product of an immigrant Jewish sensibility inimical to America's "native," Christian majority continued to be articulated in the following decade. Joseph I. Breen—a lay Catholic and former Hollywood reporter who was appointed the head of Hollywood's Production Code Administration in 1934, wrote to a friend at the time that "these Jews seem to think of nothing but money making and sexual indulgence. . . . They are, probably, the scum of the earth."[13]

Breen's rhetoric, albeit expressed in private correspondence, acquired a new resonance in the 1930s, which would witness the Nazis' rise to power in Germany and culminate in the outbreak of another world war. In fact, the discourse surrounding

Hollywood's Jewishness had already begun to change by the end of the 1920s, responding to major developments in the economy, politics, and the film industry itself. The Great Depression that followed the stock market crash of October 1929 prompted many Americans to question the virtues of capitalism and increased radicalism—not the least among employees of the Hollywood studios. In Europe, economic upheavals led to a polarization of political forces, as socialist and Communist activists clashed with fascists and right-wing nationalists. These conflicts would

Members of a committee consisting of fifty-six Hollywood figures who petitioned for an anti-Nazi economic boycott, December 24, 1938. Seated, left to right: Melvin Douglas, James Cagney, and Edward G. Robinson. Back row, left to right: Gale Sondergaard, Helen Gahagan Douglas, Henry Fonda, and Gloria Stuart.

become a cause célèbre in Hollywood, both on and off screen. The advent of "talking" pictures in the late 1920s also prompted a new attention to their scripts, not only among the creators of movies, but also by those—such as the Catholic Church's Legion of Decency—who scrutinized their contents for offensive or seditious elements.

Consequently, the discussion of Jewish influence on the American movie industry came to focus increasingly on political concerns, particularly after the new and stringently enforced Production Code, which closely regulated on-screen criminal and sexual behavior, went into effect in mid-1934. Reflecting a larger inconsistency within anti-Semitic rhetoric, Hollywood's Jews were demonized at both political extremes. On one hand, Jewish studio executives were denounced for cynical, capitalist pandering to the basest elements of the American audience; on the other hand, these studio heads and other Jews who worked in Hollywood, especially screenwriters, were accused of conspiring against the American economic and political order by promoting an international Communist revolution.[14]

During the 1930s, the discussion of Hollywood's Jewish Question centered on the issue of using movies as a means of agitating against Nazism, especially as the United States government initially strove to maintain a policy of neutrality, before lending its support to Great Britain as Europe moved toward war. Individual films became symbolic battlegrounds for waging larger ideological conflicts, and the debates surrounding the production and reception of these films also reveal telling differences between public and private feelings about the Jewish presence in Hollywood.

The Nazi impact on Hollywood was felt soon after Adolf Hitler's appointment as chancellor of Germany in January 1933. The Nazi Party not only purged its own country's film industry of Jews, but in April 1933 demanded the removal of all Jews employed by American film offices based in Germany. The Hollywood studios protested—this amounted to more than half their personnel in the country—but then complied. Meanwhile, the Nazi Party continued to attack America's movie industry as corrupted by Jewish domination and eventually banned all movies featuring Jewish performers from German theaters.[15]

# THE EPIC CAMPAIGN

The Hollywood studios intervened directly in the 1934 California gubernatorial race, mobilizing to defeat the celebrated writer and socialist Upton Sinclair, candidate of the Democratic and EPIC (End Poverty in California) parties. In *Upton Sinclair Presents William Fox*, a biography of the pioneer movie mogul that Sinclair had been commissioned to write, Fox (by then forced out of the studio he founded) strongly criticized the movie industry, going so far as to suggest the possibility of federal regulation. Now Sinclair proposed to revive the local economy by taxing Hollywood.

The movie industry panicked. Joseph Schenck, chairman of the newly established Twentieth Century Fox studio, predicted that Sinclair's election would drive film production from California to Florida. Rallying behind Sinclair's Republican opponent, Frank Merriam, the studios tithed their employees to support Merriam's campaign. Warner Bros. deducted $100 from each worker's paycheck; MGM and Columbia took one day's salary. (The episode is satirized in Budd Schulberg's Hollywood novel *What Makes Sammy Run*?) Some credit these events with radicalizing the industry's hitherto apolitical screenwriters.[1]

In addition to raising money for the Republican candidate, the studios produced anti-Sinclair movies that were widely screened in California theaters. MGM's series of inquiring photographer shorts, "California Election News," were the most egregious in presenting all manner of menacing or crazed Sinclair supporters, including several heavily accented East European Jews. On November 4, 1934, the *New York Times* described one MGM interview with a bearded immigrant:

> *"For whom are you voting?" asks the interviewer.*
> *"Vy I am foting for Seenclair."*
> *"Why are you voting for Mr. Sinclair?"*
> *"Vell, his system vorked vell in Russia, vy can't it work here?"[2]*

Although it was Irving Thalberg who supervised these films, MGM production chief Louis B. Mayer was blamed by Los Angeles attorney H. L. Sacks who, in an open letter to Mayer, wrote that such pictures were "intended to show that while intelligent gentiles are supporting Merriam, Jews express themselves in Hebrew accents as Sinclair supporters because, as they are made to say, 'we won't have to work.'" Sacks warned that were Merriam elected, not only he but "many others of the Jewish race [would] fear that we in America are but one step nearer to cruel and barbarous Hitlerism."[3]

SINCLAIR

DYNAMITER
OF
ALL CHURCHES
AND
ALL CHRISTIAN
INSTITUTIONS

ACTIVE OFFICIAL
OF
COMMUNIST
ORGANIZATIONS

COMMUNIST WRITER

COMMUNIST AGITATOR

THE MAN WHO SAID THE
P. T. A.
HAS BEEN TAKEN OVER
BY THE

BLACK HAND

Issued by
California Democratic Governor's League
M. J. Brown, Secy., 2000 Holly Drive, Los Angeles

The campaign against Sinclair showed that even Jews who were powerful in the movie industry might exploit anti-Semitism. But, as Steven Alan Carr points out in *Hollywood and Anti-Semitism*, Sinclair himself was not above employing Jewish stereotypes, whether attributing an anti-Semitic description of Hollywood producers to Charlie Chaplin in *Money Writes!* (1927) or explaining how, despite his "good Jewish nose," Fox's fellow moguls had joined forces against him.[4]

After the 1934 election, EPIC published Max Knepper's self-described "daring" exposé *Sodom and Gomorrah: The Story of Hollywood*, a mixture of fact and fiction, introduced by Sinclair. Preoccupied with Hollywood's salacious products and sexual amorality, Knepper describes Jewish movie producers—including one depicted as physically repulsive, another blatantly named "Lechstein"—despoiling the innocent American women who flocked to Hollywood in hopes of becoming stars. Taking a populist tone, Knepper writes that "inside their Moorish castles on the top of some Beverly Hills cliff, [the producers] can look down on those in the valley and imagine themselves feudal lords. . . . Or, if their fancy dictates, by establishing a few beautiful women in luxurious apartments about town, they can convince themselves that they are Turkish sultans. . . . Without doubt certain picture executives consider themselves the Napoleons of drama or, perhaps, Mussolinis. (They do not like Hitler.)" Knepper blames Sinclair's defeat on Hollywood and ends his tract promising "federal control is but a matter of time."[5]

—J.H.

Anti-Upton Sinclair handbill from the California Democratic Governor's League, 1934.

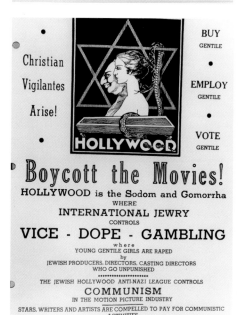

# HEIL! HEIL!

**All Germans and Aryans of Pure Nordic Blood!**

---

## We Have the JEWS on the Run!
### Let Us Keep Up the Good Work!

### DO NOT ATTEND

**Any Theater showing pictures with any of these Jews or Jew Lovers:**

Claudette Colbert is married to a Jew; Norma Shearer was married to a Jew; Margaret Sullivan was married to a Jew; Eddie Cantor is a Jew; Al Jolson is a jew; Sylvia Sidney is a Jew; Ruby Keeler is married to a Jew; and Ricardo Cortez is a Jew.

---

### This is only the Beginning to an End:
#### WATCH ALL FUTURE DEVELOPMENTS

Join any one of our country wide organizations and clubs chartered for the purpose of eliminating the enemy— the JEW from all Industry!

Become a member of this Legion to make this great country of ours safe from the Jew and Russia.

**HEADQUARTERS: San Francisco, California Charter No. 12**

The CCC Camps would make good Concentration Camps for the Jews!

---

Christian Vigilantes Arise!

BUY GENTILE

EMPLOY GENTILE

VOTE GENTILE

## Boycott the Movies!

**HOLLYWOOD is the Sodom and Gomorrha**
WHERE
### INTERNATIONAL JEWRY
CONTROLS
## VICE - DOPE - GAMBLING
where
YOUNG GENTILE GIRLS ARE RAPED
by
JEWISH PRODUCERS, DIRECTORS, CASTING DIRECTORS
WHO GO UNPUNISHED

THE JEWISH HOLLYWOOD ANTI-NAZI LEAGUE CONTROLS
## COMMUNISM
IN THE MOTION PICTURE INDUSTRY
STARS, WRITERS AND ARTISTS ARE COMPELLED TO PAY FOR COMMUNISTIC ACTIVITIES

**ABOVE, TOP**
Anti-Semitic flyer, c. 1936. The Civilian Conservation Corps (CCC) was a New Deal jobs program for young people employed on public works projects.

**ABOVE, BOTTOM**
Anti-Semitic flyer, c. 1937. The juxtaposition of the beautiful Gentile woman with the predatory Jewish man was characteristic of Nazi anti-Semitic propaganda.

**ABOVE, RIGHT**
Illustration from anti-Semitic pamphlet, c. 1937. This type of material was collected by the Los Angeles Community Relations Council, a watchdog organization of Hollywood studio executives to document anti-Semitic activities directed against the moviemaking industry.

How "A Star Is Born"
Ask The Hollywood Jew Who Owns One
# BOYCOTT
## The Jewish Boycotters

### BOYCOTT
Every motion picture starring any member of the
Pro-Communist Hollywood Anti-Nazi League
Destroy Jew Monopoly of the Motion Picture Industry with its Sex Filth Films and Jew-Communist Propaganda

In the United States, Breen and his ecclesiastical supporters saw Hitler's rise as instrumental in their campaign to reform Hollywood. Nazi policies and anti-Semitic agitation had made Jewish studio executives newly vulnerable. "Jewish control of the [film] industry is alienating many of our people," just at the time when "Jews are afraid of things that may possibly happen in this country to them," Los Angeles bishop John J. Cantwell wrote in 1933 to the archbishop of Cincinnati. Shortly thereafter, Hays organized a meeting to discuss the new Production Code with the studio heads. According to Breen's correspondence, the speaker that evening, Joseph Scott, "lashed into the Jews furiously." Scott, a prominent Catholic layman and Los Angeles lawyer well connected to the movie industry, bracketed the studio executives together with Jewish Communists and accused them collectively of ingratitude toward their adopted country that bordered on treason. Given this disloyalty, he argued, the Nazi ideology of anti-Semitism might take hold in America.[16]

Similar threats quashed the first attempt in Hollywood to make a film attacking Nazism. During the summer of 1933, Paramount screenwriter Herman J. Mankiewicz and RKO producer Sam Jaffe announced plans for an anti-Hitler feature, to be called *The Mad Dog of Europe*. Accusing the two men of exploiting a "scare situation," Hays advised them to drop the project. Jaffe eventually sold the idea to agent Al Rosen, who was warned by Breen that such a movie would have an adverse effect: "There is strong pro-German and anti-Semitic feeling in this country [and] because of the large number of Jews active in the motion picture industry, the charge is certain to be made that the Jews, as a class, are behind an anti-Hitler picture and using the entertainment screen for their own personal propaganda purposes."[17]

By the mid-1930s, Breen felt that Hollywood Communists—whom he, too, identified as being primarily Jewish—had launched a campaign to smuggle Communist content into the movies. He was therefore deeply suspicious of the Hollywood Anti-Nazi League (HANL), which was established in 1936. Within a few months, the league enrolled several thousand members, including such stars as Eddie Cantor, Melvyn Douglas, Paul Muni, and Sylvia Sidney, as well as the directors Ernst Lubitsch and Lewis Milestone (all of them Jews). The HANL membership, which was heavily but by no means exclusively Jewish, not only campaigned against Nazism—publishing newsletters, sponsoring radio broadcasts, and organizing meetings, demonstrations, banquets, and the boycott of German products—but also gave vociferous support to the Spanish Republic.[18]

Breen, who sympathized with the Falangist forces led by General Francisco Franco, regarded the league as a conspiracy of left-leaning screenwriters that was "conducted and financed almost entirely by Jews." In December 1937, Breen informed Daniel J. Lord, the Jesuit priest who was the chief author of the revised Production Code, that he was fighting against a movement that strove to "capture the screen of the United States for Communistic propaganda purposes." Texas congressman Martin Dies also attacked the HANL as a Communist front, announcing in the spring of 1938 that the newly established House Committee on Un-American Activities (HCUAA) would conduct an investigation "at which members of the film colony will be afforded an opportunity to reply to charges that they were participating in Communistic activities." (The hearings were in fact not held until late 1947.)[19]

For Breen, the best evidence of a left-wing Jewish campaign in Hollywood was Walter Wanger's production of *Blockade*, released by United Artists. This anti-Franco romance, starring Henry Fonda as a heroic Spanish peasant, was written by John Howard Lawson, a prominent Hollywood Communist. *Blockade*—which the Production Code Administration had approved while Breen was on vacation—opened in June 1938, two weeks after its gala premiere had been canceled, and the film was excoriated by the Knights of Columbus as "leftist propaganda."[20]

That same month, Wanger submitted a script based on journalist Vincent Sheean's memoir, *Personal History*, for Breen's approval. In the screen adaptation (also by Lawson), the hero becomes aware of fascist brutality while covering the Spanish civil war; later, reporting in Germany, he is repelled by the Nazi regime's anti-Semitic policies. He rescues several Jews from persecution and even marries a Jewish woman. Breen informed Wanger that although the script contained no specific violations of the Production Code, such a film would present "grave dangers" for the entire industry with its inflammatory "pro-Loyalist," "pro-Jewish," and "anti-Nazi

ABOVE
Henry Fonda (second from left) with Madeline Carroll in *Blockade* (1938).

RIGHT
Edward G. Robinson (right) interrogates a suspect (Francis Lederer) in *Confessions of a Nazi Spy* (1939).

propaganda." Wanger abandoned the project.[21]

The HANL newsletter reported Harry Warner's plans to produce "important social pictures to combat Fascism" in January 1938, but it was not until the eve of World War II that a Hollywood film would directly attack Nazi Germany. In November 1938—the same month that Nazi filmmaker Leni Riefenstahl visited

Hollywood and the Nazis staged Kristallnacht—Warner Bros. announced their upcoming *Confessions of a Nazi Spy*. Harry and Jack Warner were the only studio heads who openly supported the HANL; the studio had ceased doing business with

RIGHT
Cover of the Nazi exhibition guide *Entartete Musik* (Degenerate Music), 1938. This propaganda exhibition mocked and condemned a wide range of modernist composers, "musical Bolsheviks," and purveyors of "alien music"—including jazz. Like Henry Ford, the Nazis disparaged jazz as the creation of African-Americans and Jews. The cover image caricatures the original poster for German composer Ernest Krenek's popular "jazz opera" *Jonny spielt auf* (1927), grotesquely exaggerating the musician's features and placing a prominent Star of David on his lapel.

BELOW
"American cinema is 95% in the hands of the Jews!" French propaganda poster, 1944.

Germany in 1934. As Breen noted, *Confessions of a Nazi Spy* involved a number of industry leftists and liberals, including refugee director Anatole Litvak, writer John Wexley, and the actors Edward G. Robinson, Francis Lederer, and Paul Lukas. All were Jews, as well as HANL members; Robinson was particularly outspoken, telling the *New York Times* that he "would give [his] teeth to do an American version of [the Soviet anti-Nazi feature] *Professor Mamlock*." *Confessions of a Nazi Spy* was welcomed by other left-leaning Hollywood Jews. Groucho Marx rose at an anti-Nazi meeting to toast Warners as "the only studio with any guts."[22]

The German consul protested to Breen, who passed the letter on to Jack Warner. He not only ignored it but proved impervious to Breen's warning that the film's certain censorship by foreign governments would harm the studio financially. *Confessions of a Nazi Spy* opened on April 28, 1939, three months after Hitler blamed Hollywood's "gigantic Jewish capitalistic propaganda" for Germany's poor relations with the United States. The Legion of Decency, which had defended Riefenstahl during her Hollywood visit, deemed *Confessions of a Nazi Spy* less anti-Nazi than pro-Communist. The popular radio cleric Father Charles E. Coughlin identified the Warner brothers and their star, Robinson, as Jews whose "patriotism [was] only as deep as their hatred of Hitler." Warners hired extra security for the New York premiere of *Confessions of a Nazi Spy*. The movie was picketed at some theaters, and there were isolated cases of violence at certain screenings. In Milwaukee, Nazi

sympathizers torched one theater showing the film. Despite the controversy (or perhaps because of it), the movie performed poorly at the box office.[23]

The Hollywood Anti-Nazi League was thrown into confusion by the 1939

Hitler-Stalin Pact and the subsequent outbreak of World War II, but the American movie industry released several other anti-Nazi pictures in 1940. These included *Four Sons* (written by Lawson) and *The Man I Married*, both produced by Twentieth Century Fox, as well as Charlie Chaplin's *The Great Dictator* (United Artists) and a Three Stooges short, *You Nazty Spy!* (Columbia). Even before most of these movies were released, Dies accused Hollywood Communists of creating an alliance with European refugees and Jewish producers by claiming that "Russia served as a bulwark against the spread of Fascism and anti-Semitism."[24]

Speaking to a closed meeting held late that year, United States Ambassador to Great Britain Joseph P. Kennedy, a former RKO executive, bluntly warned Hollywood executives to cease making anti-Nazi pictures, lest the war against Hitler be blamed on Jews; this, he intimated, was already happening in Britain. The position was soon given public voice, echoing the nativist rhetoric of the 1920s. Addressing a rally of the isolationist America First movement in Des Moines, Iowa, aviation hero Charles Lindbergh maintained that the "greatest danger to this country" lay in Jewish "ownership and influence in our motion pictures, our press, our radio, and our government."[25]

In a national radio address during the summer of 1941, Senator Gerald Nye, a North Dakota Republican and leading spokesman for America First, reiterated the charge that Hollywood, a haven for all manner of foreigners, was agitating for war. "In each of these companies there are a number of production directors, many of whom have come from Russia, Hungary, Germany, and the Balkan countries." The movies, Nye argued, "have ceased to be an instrument of entertainment" and instead now sought "to drug the reason of the American people" and "rouse the war fever."[26]

A month later, the Senate Subcommittee on Interstate Commerce opened hearings on Moving Picture Screen and Radio Propaganda. Nye, the first witness, repeated his charges that the movies had been captured by foreigners: "Unquestionably there are in Hollywood today, engaged by the motion picture industry, those who are naturally far more interested in the fate of their homelands than they are in the fortunes of the United States. I would myself call it the most potent and dangerous 'fifth column' in our country." Nye cited as evidence seventeen "war-mongering" pictures and, pointing out that "those primarily responsible [were] born abroad," suggested that such pictures served the agenda of Hollywood's elite. "Many people seem to assume that our Jewish citizenry would willingly have our country and its sons taken into this foreign war," he stated, adding, "If anti-Semitism exists in America, the Jews have themselves to blame."[27]

Both Harry Warner and Darryl F. Zanuck testified on their own behalf (the latter stressing his Christian background and Nebraska roots). In addition, the studios enlisted Wendell Willkie, Republican presidential nominee in 1940, as their spokesman. Willkie accused Nye and other isolationist senators of attempting to suppress "accurate and factual pictures on Nazism" while deliberately dividing "the American people in discordant racial and religious groups in order to disunite them over foreign policy."[28]

The hearings petered out in October; on December 7, the Japanese air force bombed Pearl Harbor, and the following day the United States entered the war.

## CAUGHT IN THE CROSSFIRE

*Let the glamour show as from far away. Cling to reality, for any departure from a high pitch of reality at which the Jews live leads to farce in which the Christians live. Hollywood is a Jewish holiday, a gentile's tragedy.*
—F. Scott Fitzgerald, working notes for *The Love of the Last Tycoon* (1939)

*I can't talk about Hollywood. It was a horror to me when I was there and it's a horror to look back on. I can't imagine how I did it. When I got away from it I couldn't even refer to the place by name. "Out there," I called it. You want to know what "out there" means to me? Once I was coming down a street in Beverly Hills, and I saw a Cadillac about a block long, and out of the side window was a wonderfully slinky mink and an arm, and at the end of the arm a hand in a white suede glove wrinkled around the wrist, and in the hand was a bagel with a bite out of it.*
—Dorothy Parker, interview in the *Paris Review* (1956)

During the 1930s, Hollywood's Jewish studio executives appear to have been remarkably restrained in response to the mounting attacks directed at them and, more generally, at the Jewish presence in the film industry. But while they were for the most part circumspect in making public rejoinders to American anti-Semitism and (to a lesser extent) to Nazism, they did address these issues privately and more obliquely.

Hollywood studio executives' reaction to the rise of Nazism was far from consistent at first, reflecting individual differences in temperament and experience. Laemmle, the founder of Universal Pictures, was outraged when he learned that his native Laupheim, Germany, had changed the name of Laemmlestrasse to Hitlerstrasse. MGM's Mayer, however, accepted the reassurances of his friend William Randolph Hearst that Hitler's bark was worse than his bite, while Thalberg glibly reported upon returning from a 1934 trip to Germany that "a lot of Jews will lose their lives [but] Hitler and Hitlerism will pass."[29]

Aware of their vulnerable position, Jewish studio executives largely restricted their anti-Nazi activism to behind-the-scenes efforts in the years directly preceding World War II, using their positions to influence other public figures and working tacitly with established Jewish agencies to monitor and combat anti-Semitism. As Carr notes, the idea that the movie industry might be mobilized to effect public opinion or official policy was "completely taboo. Instead, when Jewish film executives opposed anti-Semitism, they placed themselves within a broader discourse of patriotic national identity."[30]

As World War II began, Hollywood's Jewishness emerged as a subject of scrutiny in American fiction. F. Scott Fitzgerald's final, unfinished novel, published in 1941 as *The Last Tycoon*, offers an elliptical, ambivalent portrait of Monroe Stahr, a Jewish Hollywood studio executive (modeled on Thalberg), whose "otherness" is as alluring as it is problematic. Not merely a rehashing of the stereotype of the Jewish parvenu, Fitzgerald's protagonist embodies both the allure of the "American dream" and its demise.

So, too, does Sammy Glick, protagonist of Budd Schulberg's novel *What Makes Sammy Run?* (1941), in which the author offered an excoriating portrait of the quintessential Jewish Hollywood insider.[31] Schulberg portrays Glick's relentless drive as a product of growing up on the urban immigrant street:

There were no rest periods between rounds for Sammy. The world had put a chip on his shoulder and then it had knocked it off. Sammy was ready to accept the challenge all by himself and this was a fight to the finish. He had fought to be born into the East Side, he had kicked, bit, scratched and gouged first to survive in it and then to subdue it, and now that he was thirteen and a man, having passed another kind of bar mitzvah, he was ready to fight his way out again, pushing uptown, running in [his older brother's] cast-off shoes, traveling light, without any baggage, or a single principle to slow him down.[32]

Though more refined than Glick, Stahr is also what Fitzgerald calls a "neighborhood scrapper." Both protagonists are self-made men and, like the movies that they produce, representative of the triumph of American vernacular culture.[33]

For Jewish writers such as Dorothy Parker, S. J. Perelman, Nathanael West, and George S. Kaufman—all of whom, like Fitzgerald, had come to California from New York to try their hand at screenplays—Hollywood's Jewishness figured frequently, if often obliquely, in their fiction and satirical pieces. At times, these references linked the authors' disenchantment with Hollywood to ambivalent feelings about their own Jewishness.

Other Jewish observers chose to respond to Hollywood's Jewish Question by, in effect, erasing it. In 1941, author Leo Rosten published a study, underwritten by the Carnegie Corporation and the Rockefeller Foundation, that sought to debunk the myths of Hollywood as a locus of excess and exotica, and to portray it instead as emblematic of the national culture. In *Hollywood: The Movie Colony, the Movie Makers*, Rosten suggested that the industry be "placed under the microscope of social science like a slide on which we see, in sharper and isolated detail, the organic processes of the larger social body. Pathology illuminates the normal. . . . Let us therefore study the people of Hollywood and the patterns of movie making as one might study the people and practices of Tahiti."[34]

Rosten's study defended Hollywood as central, rather than inimical, to the national culture. The movie industry, he argued, was not beholden to a foreign ideology, nor did it impose an alien credo. On the contrary, Hollywood fed the public's preexisting tastes and was rewarded by the public according to how well it succeeded at this task. Rosten, who would eventually achieve greatest renown for his books on Jewish life (especially

Cover of 1949 paperback edition of Budd Schulberg's *What Makes Sammy Run?* (1941).

*The Joys of Yiddish*, which appeared in 1968), makes almost no mention of Jews in the film industry. Indeed, his one reference to Hollywood's Jewishness focused on the misapprehension of its extent: "There is a widespread assumption that the movie men are foreigners, and even those of old native stock are believed to have 'Jewish' names. Some of the most important people in the movie hierarchy—Darryl F. Zanuck, Y. Frank Freeman, Sidney Kent, George Schaefer, Eddie Mannix, Joseph I. Breen, William Le Baron, Hal Roach, Cecil B. DeMille—are erroneously believed by many to be of the same faith as the mother of Christ."[35]

Mississippi Congressman
John Rankin draped himself
in petitions calling for the
investigation of Communist
infiltration of Hollywood,
1947.

Rosten characterized Zukor, Fox, Goldwyn, and the other "men who built the motion picture industry" as pioneers. Unlike the Vanderbilts, Astors, and other self-made American entrepreneurs, however, these "cellulords" were stigmatized for having risen from modest beginnings. In a footnote, Rosten observed that "in no other industry is humble origin interpreted as a skeleton in the closet rather than proof of admirable success."[36]

Rosten thus implied—but never stated outright—that bigotry, not Jewishness, was un-American. Hollywood's Jewish studio executives were not outside the national mainstream, but the xenophobic nativists who baited them were. This implicit thesis would be elaborated forthrightly in two postwar films on the subject of American anti-Semitism made in the rapidly changing social and cultural climate of the early postwar era: *Crossfire* (RKO, 1947) and *Gentleman's Agreement* (Twentieth Century Fox, 1947).

Following World War II and the revelations of the Holocaust, direct attacks on the Jewishness of Hollywood studio executives and other film industry employees abated, as did American anti-Semitic rhetoric in general. A number of producers were interested in making movies that reflected the lessons of the war. Scenarist Alvah Bessie recalls being hired, along with Howard Koch, to write *The Ghosts of Berchtesgaden*, "a documentary-type thing, which Jack Warner wanted momentarily to make . . . to point out the continuing danger of Fascism and Fascist ideas everywhere in the world, especially in our own country."[37]

Nevertheless, Hollywood's Jewish Question continued to be raised, albeit often more obliquely, as the film industry emerged as a domestic battleground in the early years of the Cold War. On July 18, 1945, Mississippi congressman John Rankin warned Congress that "alien-minded Communistic enemies of Christianity" were "trying to take over the motion-picture industry." Communism, he explained, was "the most dangerous influence in the world today. I am talking about the Communism of Leon Trotsky that is based upon hatred for Christianity. Remember that Communism and Christianity can never live in the same atmosphere. Communism is older than Christianity. It is the curse of the ages. It hounded and persecuted our Saviour during his earthly ministry, inspired his crucifixion, derided him in his dying agony, and then gambled for his garments at the foot of the cross."[38]

The House Committee on Un-American Activities (HCUAA) hearings on Communist infiltration of Hollywood, originally to have begun before the war, were eventually convened in late 1947 under the chairmanship of Representative J. Parnell Thomas of New Jersey and then again, from 1951 to 1953, under Representative John S. Wood of

# CROSSFIRE

Both *Gentleman's Agreement* (Twentieth Century Fox, 1947) and *Crossfire* (RKO, 1947) originated with and were directed by Gentiles. Darryl F. Zanuck, the head of Twentieth Century Fox, was the prime force behind *Gentleman's Agreement*, while RKO producer Adrian Scott fought to make *Crossfire*, which was based on Richard Brooks's novel *The Brick Foxhole* (1965), about a GI who commits a hate crime. After screenwriter John Paxton changed the victim from a homosexual to a Jew, Scott convinced Dore Schary, the new production chief at RKO, to support the project. By some accounts, the decision to change the crime to an anti-Semitic act was made to preempt Fox's amply publicized *Gentleman's Agreement*.[1]

Like *Crossfire*, *Gentleman's Agreement* was based on a novel. Impressed by a *Time* report on Representative John Rankin's referring to Walter Winchell as a "little kike" in a speech that was greeted by applause in the House of Representatives, Laura Z. Hobson (daughter of a onetime editor of the *Jewish Daily Forward*) began writing a story about a Gentile reporter who masquerades as a Jew to report on anti-Semitism in America. Zanuck bought the novel even before publication, announcing that it would be his one "personal production" of 1947. To his displeasure, RKO had already

begun shooting *Crossfire* under the direction of Edward Dmytryk.[2]

Elia Kazan, who directed *Gentleman's Agreement*, would maintain that "lots of rich Jews in Hollywood" did not want the movie made. But, beginning with Zanuck's irate telephone call to Schary, *Crossfire* was subject to far more direct pressure. Joseph Breen demanded script changes to stress the villain's atypicality and ordered that the speeches on bigotry given by the movie's heroic police detective (Robert Young) invoke "all forms of racial and religious intolerance," so as to avoid any charge that the movie was guilty of "special pleading against anti-Semitism."[3]

Moreover, the American Jewish Committee deemed the project a potential threat. In early 1947, AJC representative Dick Rothschild—who, according to an internal memo, felt it "extremely dangerous" to project "the basic idea of killing Jews just because they were Jews" before the American public—attempted to head off the film or at least persuade Schary to change the victim from a Jew to a black. Failing to move Schary, Rothschild went to RKO president Peter Rathvon, also in vain. After *Crossfire*'s release in the summer of 1947, Elliot E. Cohen, the editor of the AJC journal *Commentary*, published an open letter suggesting that despite its good intentions, *Crossfire* could well "reinforce rather than abate the emotions that make for anti-

Semitism." Not only might the movie titillate bigots with the spectacle of a Jew murdered as a Jew, but Hollywood's very attempt to represent anti-Semitism promised unexpected consequences. "There is a time and place for everything, says Ecclesiastes. If we introduced a striptease in an Episcopalian church, the parishioners wouldn't like it. Perhaps a sudden sermon about Jews might fall on deaf ears when we are waiting to see the guns drawn, the detective beaten up, the blood flowing. Do we pay our money to have someone tell us about *Jews?—Somebody* is putting something over."[4]

Both *Crossfire* and *Gentleman's Agreement* (which opened in late 1947) were critically well received, and each garnered multiple Oscar nominations. The eighth highest-grossing film of 1948, *Gentleman's Agreement* beat *Crossfire* for Best Picture and Best Director. That same year, the *Journal of Psychology* published a study with data showing that nearly three-quarters of those viewing *Gentleman's Agreement* maintained the movie had given them a more positive attitude toward Jews. (The remaining 25 percent reported becoming increasingly anti-Semitic.) Ring Lardner, Jr., is the best known of many credited with observing that the moral to *Gentleman's Agreement* was to "never be mean to a Jew, because he might turn out to be a Gentile."[5]

—J.H.

LEFT
Robert Ryan and Sam Levene in *Crossfire* (1947).

ABOVE
Gregory Peck, Dorothy McGuire, Celeste Holm, and John Garfield in *Gentleman's Agreement* (1947).

Demonstration by members of the Hollywood Ten and their supporters, including Lester Cole (third from left, with watch on left wrist); Alvah Bessie (fourth from left); Dalton Trumbo (center, with bowtie); Ring Lardner, Jr. (fifth from right, with glasses); the group's attorney, Ben Margolis (fourth from right, with cigarette); and Herbert Biberman (third from right, with bowtie), 1950. At the time of this demonstration, the Hollywood Ten had been found guilty of contempt of Congress and were about to serve prison sentences.

Georgia. These hearings not only led to the sentencing of ten Hollywood writers to jail for contempt of Congress, but cost dozens of other writers, actors, and directors their careers. The hearings galvanized the entire film industry, placing Hollywood at the center of a national ideological crisis, and they insured maximum publicity for the anti-Communist investigations. (Indeed, the 1947 HCUAA hearings may be considered the opening salvo in a series of congressional probes that would culminate six and a half years later with Senator Joseph McCarthy's investigation of the United States Army.)

The process of rooting out Communist infiltration of the film industry reengaged the discourse of the previous generation's Red Scare, which had linked Jews with Communism. "Indeed, many Jews . . . believed that [the HCUAA] went after Hollywood precisely because it was something of a Jewish preserve," wrote Victor Navasky in his historical analysis of the hearings. Rankin, an influential member of the HCUAA, delivered anti-Hollywood tirades during the hearing, in which he insinuated an easy equation of Jews with Communists. Like the anti-Semitic anti-Bolsheviks of the 1920s, he considered the unmasking of Jews who had changed their names—such as June Havoc (June Hovick), Eddie Cantor (Edward Iskowitz), Danny Kaye (David Daniel Kaminsky), Edward Robinson (Emanuel Goldenberg), and Melvyn Douglas (Melvyn Hesselberg)— tantamount to uncovering a political conspiracy.[39]

Six of the so-called Hollywood Ten—screenwriters, producers, and directors held in contempt of Congress for their refusal to admit or deny Communist affiliation—were Jews: Alvah Bessie, Herbert Biberman, Lester Cole, John Lawson, Albert Maltz, and Samuel Orntiz. Two of the four non-Jews in the group, Adrian Scott and Edward Dmytryk, were associated with the production of *Crossfire*, a film that held particular interest for the HCUAA.[40]

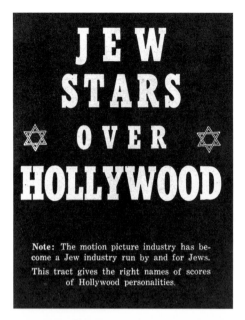

Cover of the pamphlet *Jew Stars over Hollywood*, published by the Patriotic Tract Society, St. Louis, Missouri, c. 1950. "Every motion picture personality mentioned in this article is a Jew. Practically every one of them at one time or another has made a contribution to the destruction of our moral and patriotic stamina. Some have indulged in the pornographic, the lewd and the sensual, while others have indulged in outright Communist propaganda." The same organization also published *Red Stars over Hollywood*.

By presenting anti-Semitism as an expression of unchecked right-wing extremism, *Crossfire* suggested that in the absence of wartime solidarity, the nation faced an internal Fascist threat. Consequently, anti-Communists considered the film to be deliberately inflammatory. According to Myron C. Fagan, the author of *Red Treason in Hollywood*, "the job of creating racial antagonisms and minorities' grievances was handed over to the Hollywood Reds! And they accomplished it to perfection with such films as *Gentleman's Agreement*, *Crossfire*, *Home of the Brave*, *All My Sons*, *Pinky*, *Lost Boundaries*, etc."[41]

The HCUAA investigation of Hollywood created a rift within the organized American Jewish community over how to respond to the hearings, if at all—in other words, whether or not this was indeed a "Jewish Question" that demanded some kind of Jewish answer. In November 1947, Sidney Harmon, a member of the board of the American Jewish Committee, wrote to its president, John Slawson, to propose that the committee charge the HCUAA with spreading anti-Semitism through its handling of the Hollywood hearings. Harmon noted that a majority of people subpoenaed by the HCUAA and sentenced to jail terms for contempt of Congress were Jews; he also invoked the specter of the Holocaust, reminding Slawson that "Hitler had charged the Jews who owned Germany's motion-picture business with being Communists." After waiting over a month to respond, Slawson declined to have the American Jewish Committee take up the issue, characterizing the actions of the HCUAA as a matter not of particular concern for Jews, but "a most important legal problem affecting the rights of all citizens, be they Jews, or Methodists or freethinkers" that was more

John Garfield before the House Committee on Un-American Activities (HCUAA) in April 1951, testifying that he had never been a member of the Communist Party.

appropriately a matter to be taken up by the American Civil Liberties Union.[42]

The HCUAA hearings, the advent of television as a national broadcasting medium, and the antitrust legislation that forced studios to divest themselves of their movie theater chains marked the end of the Hollywood studio era. Also, the studios' founding moguls had almost all retired or passed away by 1960. (The exception was Jack Warner, who lived for another decade.) But the end of this period in American filmmaking did not bring final resolution to Hollywood's Jewish Question. Instead, there were signal shifts in the discourse surrounding the Jewishness of Hollywood, responsive to the increasing public presence of Jews in American culture more generally, as well as changes in the ways in which Americans discussed popular culture and mass media in the final decades of the twentieth century.

*Everyone may have a different view of what [Dorothy Parker's] bagel represents, but if it is the symbolic ordinary Jewish food that the show-business nouveaux riches cling to, it may also symbolize a vulgar strength that repelled Dorothy Parker—and in which she did not share. Hollywood Jews overdressed like gypsies who had to carry it all on their backs, and they clung to a bit of solid, heavy food even when they were no longer hungry, because it seemed like reality. Vulgarity is not as destructive to an artist as snobbery, and in the world of movies vulgar strength has been a great redemptive force, canceling out niggling questions of taste.*
—Pauline Kael, "A Bagel with a Bite out of It" (1971)[43]

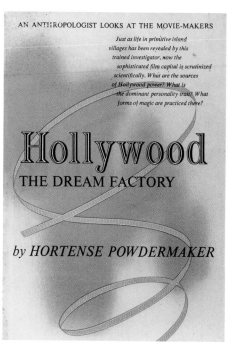

*Was there anything unique about the rising film industry, and the tradition of European Jews, that brought the two together? Impoverished origins and expanding opportunity faced many Americans, but it was the Jews who took over the movies. Although Sammy Glick's ancestors may have suffered more than others, we still must wonder why the same desire to make it did not inspire poor Irish Catholics, Italians, Greeks or others to dominate movie making.*
—Lary L. May and Elaine Tyler May, "Why Jewish Movie Moguls: An Exploration in American Culture" (1982)[44]

In the decades since the end of Hollywood's studio era, efforts to assess the connections between Jews and Hollywood have taken place in a markedly different intellectual and cultural climate. With the waning of McCarthyism and the advent of "the new ethnicity," Jewish difference was no longer treated as either inherently suspect by non-Jews or as a stigma to be obscured by Jews.

During the 1960s, a series of popular biographies and memoirs appeared, notably Bosley Crowther's *Hollywood Rajah: The Life and Times of Louis B. Mayer* (1960), Bob Thomas's *King Cohn: The Life and Times of Harry Cohn* (1967) and *Thalberg: Life and Legend* (1969), and Jack Warner's *My First Hundred Years in Hollywood* (1965). This spate of books, focusing on what was then understood as Hollywood's "golden age," culminated in two histories, both published in 1969, that retold the colorful story of Hollywood in terms of its founders' origins—and in doing so, served to elevate the status of the once-derogatory term "movie mogul."[45]

Reviewing Philip French's *The Moguls* and Norman Zierold's *The Movie Moguls*, the sociologist Norman L. Friedman noted that both books made less of the moguls' Jewishness than their status as immigrants: "Their desire . . . to be fully accepted as culturally assimilated 'Americans,' 'one-hundred per cent Americans,' lent them an enthusiasm for the transmission, idealization, and creation of American popular culture.

ABOVE, LEFT
Cover of anthropologist Hortense Powdermaker's *Hollywood: The Dream Factory* (1950). Powdermaker wrote, "To me the handsome stars with their swimming-pool homes were no more glamorous than the South Seas aborigines exotic. All, whether ex-cannibal chiefs, magicians, front-office executives, or directors, were human beings working and living in a certain way, which I was interested in analyzing."

ABOVE, RIGHT
*New York Times* movie critic Bosley Crowther's 1960 biography of Louis B. Mayer, *Hollywood Rajah*, was the first of the mogul biographies to emphasize its subject's Jewish immigrant origins. Crowther wrote that the age Mayer represented, "the age of great expansion in American films, the age of the motion picture mogul—had passed several years before he died. Many and subtle changes in the film business after World War II had rendered obsolete and archaic the kind of monarchial management for which he stood. The stars could no longer be collected and controlled within his own galaxy."

# THE LAST TEMPTATION OF CHRIST

Conditions under which Hollywood is still construed as an essentially Jewish enterprise may be seen in the controversy that arose around Martin Scorsese's adaptation of Nikos Kazantzakis's novel *The Last Temptation of Christ* (1953).

Scorsese has traced his ambition to make a movie on the life of Christ back to his seeing the biblical extravaganza *The Robe* (1953) as an eleven-year-old altar boy. In 1972, he read the Greek Orthodox author's novel and optioned the screen rights. (The novel, which portrays a human Christ unsure of his divinity, was already controversial, having been placed on the Papal Index soon after its publication.) Paul Schrader, who was raised in the Dutch Reform Church, a Calvinist sect so strict that movies were proscribed, adapted the novel and Paramount Pictures agreed to finance the production, which was to be shot in Israel in early 1983. Soon after the movie was announced, a Protestant group called the Evangelical Sisters began organizing protests directed against Paramount's parent company, Gulf and Western, and by the end of the year, Paramount canceled the project.[1]

Four years later, Scorsese's agent, Michael Ovitz, managed to place a revised version of *The Last Temptation of Christ* at Universal. The picture was shot on location in Morocco in late 1987. Organized protest began to build during the following summer. Ignoring Universal's offer to preview the film in mid-July, a number of religious leaders based

their animus largely on hearsay and an early draft of Schrader's script. Their major target, however, was not Kazantzakis, Scorsese, or Schrader, but Lew Wasserman, chief executive of Universal's corporate owner, MCA. After the Rev. Bill Bright, president of the Campus Crusade for Christ, offered to buy the movie from Universal, so as to destroy it, the Rev. R. L. Hymers, Jr. and two hundred members of his Fundamentalist Baptist Tabernacle picketed Universal Studios. "These Jewish producers with a lot of money are taking a swipe at our religion," Hymers explained as a small aircraft flew over the demonstration pulling a banner that read "Wasserman Fans Jew-Hatred with 'Temptation.'"[2]

On July 20, 1988, one day before Michael Dukakis—soon to be excoriated for his membership in the American Civil Liberties Union—was nominated as the Democratic candidate for president, Hymers and his supporters demonstrated outside Wasserman's Beverly Hills home. A man dressed as Jesus knelt before a wooden cross and was lashed by a "movie producer" in a business suit. Other protesters carried banners reading, "Universal is like Judas Iscariot," and "Wasserman Endangers Israel." That week, the Rev. Donald Wildmon, a Baptist minister from Mississippi, mailed a half-million fliers characterizing Universal as a "company whose decision-making body is dominated by non-Christians," and the Rev. Jerry Falwell predicted *The Last Temptation* would "create

a wave of anti-Semitism." Pat Robertson opined in a letter to Anti-Defamation League head Abraham Foxman that the movie would be seen as "a Jewish affront to Jesus Christ." Syndicated columnist Pat Buchanan accused Hollywood of "assaulting the Christian community in a way it would never dare assault the black community, the Jewish community or the gay community."[3]

Demonstrations continued into August, including one staged outside a synagogue to which Wasserman was thought to belong. Rev. Wildmon wrote to Sidney J. Sheinberg, president of MCA, accusing Universal of a deliberate anti-Christian bias and asking, "How many Christians sit on the board of directors of MCA?" August 9, the same day Wildmon characterized *The Last Temptation* as "blasphemous" on *Nightline*, and Hymers staged a demonstration in which Wasserman was represented nailing Jesus to the cross, the American Catholic church officially condemned the film, which it rated "O" for morally offensive. In Calcutta, Mother Teresa issued a statement suggesting that if U.S. Catholics intensified their prayers, "Our Blessed Mother [Mary] will see that this film is removed from your land."[4]

On August 11, the eve of *The Last Temptation*'s opening, some 25,000 fundamentalist Christians and Catholics rallied outside Universal Studios. Wildmon told the crowd that "Christian-bashing is over. . . . We demand that anti-Christian stereotypes come to an end." Universal released the movie under tight security in nine cites. There were pickets but no incidents, although several Republican members of Congress called it "blasphemous" on the floor of the House.[5]

In late summer, a group of concerned Catholics, including Italian director Franco Zeffirelli, attempted to have *The Last Temptation of Christ* removed from the Venice Film Festival. This effort failed and was tainted by reports that Zeffirelli had characterized the movie as produced by "that Jewish cultural scum of Los Angeles."[6]

—J.H.

Conservative Christians demonstrating against *The Last Temptation of Christ* in front of the home of Universal Studios chairman Lew Wasserman in Beverly Hills. One protester (center, in suit) impersonated Wasserman as another (center, foreground) portrayed Christ.

Through their movies, they presented to the world their own selective perception of aspects of American values and virtues."[46] A parallel pursuit of self-transformation, Friedman thought, was the involvement of Jews in the then-recent revaluation of old Hollywood movies, particularly those of the 1930s, as film art: "Films and film study have become intellectually respectable and chic, and some of the most avid contemporary analysts of film are Jewish-born lower-middle-class youth who have become upper-middle-class literary intellectuals."[47]

The 1970s and 1980s also witnessed portraits of early Jewish filmmakers as celebratory figures of national and ethnic heritage. A 1984 exhibition at the National Museum of American Jewish History honored early film producer Siegmund Lubin as "the man who commercialized the movies" and attributed his early successes to "his incredible adaptability, a particularly Jewish trait painfully acquired through centuries of being the 'outsider,'" a quality he shared with "the legendary Jewish moguls of Hollywood's golden age."[48]

Similarly, Tateh, the patriarch of an archetypal immigrant Jewish family in E. L. Doctorow's bestselling novel *Ragtime* (1975), realizes his entry into America by applying his inventiveness and resourcefulness to the fledgling film industry—itself emblematic of America's spirit of newness and discovery—reinventing himself in the process as "Baron Ashkenazy." Doctorow's idealized producer is not only a born outsider and canny entrepreneur, but also a visionary philosopher:

> In the movie films, he said, we only look at what is there already. Life shines on the shadow screen, as from the darkness of one's mind. It is a big business. People want to know what is happening to them. For a few pennies they sit and see their selves in movement . . . . This is most important today, in this country, where everybody is so new. There is such a need to understand. . . .
>
> When he was alone he reflected on his audacity. Sometimes he suffered periods of trembling in which he sat alone in his room smoking cigarettes without a holder, slumped and bent over in defeat like the old Tateh. But his new existence thrilled him. His whole personality had turned outward and he had become a voluble and energetic man full of the future. He felt he deserved his happiness. He'd constructed it without help. . . . He was a new man.[49]

At the same time, scholarly efforts to assess the Jewish "contribution" to Hollywood continue to rest on assumptions and to revisit questions raised by public discussion of Hollywood's Jewishness first voiced over a half-century earlier. American studies scholars Lary L. May and Elaine Tyler May revisited Hollywood's Jewish Question, remarking that the "uniquely American institution" of Hollywood was created—"oddly enough"—by cultural outsiders, Jews from Eastern Europe. More beneficent than Ford, the Mays rooted the moguls' shared sensibilities in a tradition of "group cohesion" originating in "the shtetl," and a distinctively "expressive heritage," with a predilection for urban culture, entrepreneurship, and upward mobility. Nevertheless, the Mays' approach shares basic assumptions with Ford's: first, that "it was the Jews who took over the movies," and second, that the common ethnic background among the studio chief executives, although an oddity in itself, could explain the advent of an industry "unique to twentieth-century America."[50]

In the most extensive exploration of "how the Jews invented Hollywood," Neal Gabler similarly finds it paradoxical that this quintessential American institution was created by "Eastern European Jews who themselves seemed to be anything but the quintessence of America." Elaborating on the books by French and Zierold, Gabler's *An Empire of Their Own* (1988) traces the careers of the Jewish studio heads from the 1920s to the 1950s, finding in their ethnic origins the fountainhead of Hollywood—not only the business of filmmaking, but also the content of the films made by the studios and the moguls' lifestyles. In this totalizing scenario, Gabler characterizes Hollywood as the Jewish invention of a "shadow America," the idealized vision of assimilationist immigrants who sought to "fabricate their empire in the image of America," even as they would "fabricate themselves in the image of prosperous Americans." The implications of this invention are, as Gabler's title implies, vast and powerful—"ultimately, American values came to be defined largely by the movies the Jews made."[51]

The thesis offered in *An Empire of Their Own*—and elaborated in *Hollywoodism* (1998), the documentary film based on Gabler's book, written and directed by Simcha Jacobowicz and Stewart Stern—characterizes Hollywood film as an intrinsically Jewish contribution to American culture. Jews are not merely credited with inventing a system for making and presenting movies; they are also deemed responsible for fabricating the mythic foundations of Hollywood films that, in turn, have shaped a national consciousness. *Hollywoodism* uses clips from such widely disparate films as *Once Upon a Time in the West* (Paramount, 1969), *Showboat* (Universal, 1936), *Mr. Smith Goes to Washington* (Columbia, 1939), and *Fiddler on the Roof* (United Artists, 1977) to identify championing the underdog, devotion to mothers, and the desire for success as Jewish themes. The documentary is, however, less inclined to claim more problematic aspects of classical Hollywood (for example, the use of racial stereotypes, the willingness to sensationalize sex or violence, or a fondness for sentimentality) as quintessentially Jewish.[52]

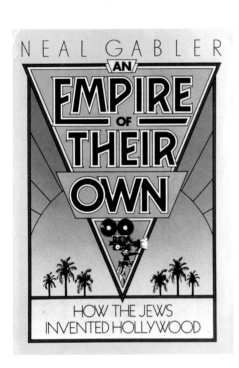

Cover of Neal Gabler's *An Empire of Their Own: How the Jews Invented Hollywood* (1988).

*An Empire of Their Own* and *Hollywoodism* would seem, at first, to confirm Ford's worst fears. Indeed, Gabler's claim that Hollywood was an essentially Jewish invention unintentionally served as fodder for the anti-Semitism of some late-twentieth-century American extremists. The thesis of Hollywood as a manipulative Jewish invention informed the pseudo-scholarship of Afrocentrist Leonard Jeffries, the insinuations of conservative ideologue Pat Buchanan, and the pronouncements of actor Marlon Brando, who told a television interviewer in 1996 that the reason American movies stereotyped all minorities save Jews was that "Hollywood is run by Jews. It is owned by Jews."[53]

"Kings of the Deal," a report on Jewish influence in Hollywood written for the *Spectator* by British journalist William Cashman on the occasion of the creation of the new DreamWorks studio, was not only rife with anti-Semitic innuendo, but invoked Gabler as his authority regarding the clannishness, ostentation, and reverse discrimination practiced by Hollywood's "Jewish network." Called to account, Cashman subsequently cited specific references in *An Empire of Their Own* that he had quoted or paraphrased and wondered about a double standard that permitted Gabler to speak of a "Jewish cabal" but not Cashman himself.[54]

Openly derisive of the movie industry's Jewish moguls, past and present, Cashman missed the pathos that infuses Gabler's account of Hollywood history. For in addition to celebrating Hollywood as a Jewish achievement, both *An Empire of Their Own* and *Hollywoodism* portray Hollywood's Jewish studio executives as victims, both of American anti-Semitism (most fatefully, during the McCarthy era) and of their own embrace of the false god of assimilation into the American mainstream.[55]

While Gabler's premise has alarmed some Jews, who see it as legitimating anti-Semitic accusations of a Jewish conspiracy of international control, others have defiantly embraced the notion of Hollywood as a Jewish terrain. The cover of the August 1996 issue of *Moment*, "the Jewish magazine for the '90s," asserts "Jews Run Hollywood—So What?" Inside, conservative film critic Michael Medved argues that it is foolish to deny the preponderance of Jews in Hollywood and calls on Jews to embrace religious values as guideposts to more responsible filmmaking. Indeed, in his book *Hollywood vs. America: Popular Culture and the War on Traditional Values* (1992), Medved characterized Hollywood (his synecdoche for all popular culture, including the recording and television industries) in terms that might have easily been employed seventy years earlier by its anti-Jewish detractors: Hollywood is a "poison factory"; it celebrates "vulgar behavior, contempt for all authority and obscene language," exhibiting an "anti-religious fury" that "degrades the human spirit."[56]

Others have extolled Hollywood's Jewishness for embodying a quite different ethos. Writing for *Tikkun* magazine in 1995, Paul Buhle champions what he identifies

as the yiddishkeit of left-wing Jews who worked in Hollywood during the studio era, often in opposition to the studio executives, as a defining element in their sensibility—inherently marginal, subversive, adaptable, humanistic. "Consciously or unconsciously," Buhle argues, left-wing Jews who wrote and sometimes directed movies "were reweaving the fabric of the past, their own past, into the present. Yiddish language virtually never appeared in the Hollywood film, but yiddishkeit"—that is, the sensibility of its speakers—"was not absent."[57]

Given the problematic nature of Hollywood's Jewish Question, it is not surprising that the efforts to answer it are themselves rife with problems. They make sweeping generalizations and ungrounded assumptions both about the nature of "the Jews" (itself a problematic construct) and about the complex nature of the American film industry. Filmmaking not only involves an extensive give-and-take among scores of artists and technicians; it also entails a complex negotiation with audiences, whose crucial role in shaping Hollywood as a cultural force is generally absent from the discussion.

What, then, is the enduring appeal of trying to understand the nature of Hollywood by using the Jewishness of its founding executives and others in the film industry as a key? The wide-ranging discussion of Jews and Hollywood suggests multiple possibilities. For some, there may be a desire to root this modern cultural phenomenon in a traditional source, be it as ennobling as an ancient commitment to passing on divine writ or as pernicious as the purported betrayal of a savior. For others, there may be a desire to deal forthrightly with the complex and sometimes coy visibility of Jews, both in the film industry and more generally in American culture. Here, too, the sentiments are mixed: Hollywood can be claimed as a source of Jewish pride or repudiated as a sign of Jewish shame. Given the endurance and elasticity of this discussion, it seems unlikely to abate; rather, it promises to continue to provide a telling index of how Americans draw connections between identity and culture.

ABOVE, LEFT
Former screenwriter and television producer Dori Carter's Hollywood novel *Beautiful Wasps Having Sex* (2000) combines elements of *What Makes Sammy Run?* with *An Empire of Their Own*. One character opines, "Hollywood is the Jewish Mecca. . . . All believers come to pay homage to the glamour god of a perfect WASP life that they themselves invented."

ABOVE, RIGHT
Cover of *Moment*, August 1996.

# ON *THE JAZZ SINGER*

J. HOBERMAN

The archetypal American, so it's been said, rebels against the father's rule; the archetypal Jew accepts the patriarchal order. Jakie Rabinowitz, child of the Lower East Side and son of an immigrant cantor, breaks with a thousand years of tradition to reinvent himself as Jack Robin, an American performer, blacked up and singing about his "mammy from Alabammy" on the vaudeville stage. More than a popular play or the first talking picture, *The Jazz Singer* is the stuff of American Jewish myth— a story that conflates charged issues of patriarchal order, family obligation, secular success, assimilation, and racial identity in one melodramatic package.

For traditional Jews, America blurred accepted distinctions between religion, worldly success, and popular culture. The late-nineteenth-century crowding together of Jews from hundreds of *shtetlekh* on the Lower East Side, and the Darwinian struggle thus engendered among their transplanted *shuln* (synagogues) stimulated liturgical music and promoted a star syndrome already nascent in Europe. During the 1920s, popular Jewish-American entertainers such as Al Jolson and Sophie Tucker were frequently referred to as secular cantors, while the Harlem-based cantor Yossele Rosenblatt not only recorded liturgical music but also performed it on the vaudeville stage, along with secular songs such as "My Yiddishe Mama." The cantorate was a major site for the struggle between the sacred and the secular—one dramatized in the film version of *The Jazz Singer* (1927), which starred Jolson, himself a cantor's son, taking inspiration from his own life.[1]

Jolson was perhaps the greatest of the immigrant Jewish performers who burst upon the American scene in the early decades of the twentieth century. He infused some of the oldest conventions of New World show business—including the blackface makeup that was the central characterization of America's first indigenous theatrical form, and the "mother song" that had given sentimental comfort to three generations of pioneers—with the new ragtime syncopation. Although Jolson never appeared in the Yiddish theater nor sang more than a few Yiddish songs, he had, as the foremost Jewish-American celebrity, a special significance for Jewish audiences and performers.

A ferociously vital performer, Jolson inspired out-and-out impersonation. During his early success, his blacked-up, mammy-singing disciples included not only Eddie Cantor and George Jessel, but also future studio head Harry Cohn, the young Walter Winchell, and Jolson's own older brother, Harry. In his streetwise apprehension of American popular culture, in his fantastic vitality and gangsterish monomania for success, Jolson was cut from the same cloth as the so-called movie moguls. Brash and egocentric, a compulsive gambler and womanizer, yet insecure and apt to wrap himself in the American flag, Jolson was a flamboyant distillation of their composite persona.[2]

In his preface to the film souvenir program, Samson Raphaelson—author of the play from which the movie was taken—recalled that when, as a college student, he first saw Jolson perform, he was overwhelmed and astonished by the religious fervor of Jolson's ragtime. This epiphany was the genesis of his play:

> I hear jazz, and I am given a vision of cathedrals and temples collapsing, and silhouetted against the setting sun, a solitary figure, a lost soul, dancing grotesquely on the ruins . . . Thus do I see the jazz singer.
>
> Jazz is prayer. It is too passionate to be anything else. It is prayer distorted, sick, unconscious of its destination. The singer of jazz is what Matthew Arnold said of the Jew, "lost between two worlds, one dead, the other powerless to be

born." In this, my first play, I have tried to crystallize the ironic truth that one of the Americas of 1927—that one which packs to overflowing our cabarets, musical revues, and dance halls—is praying with a fervor as intense as that of the America which goes sedately to church and synagogue. The jazz American is different from the dancing dervish, from the Zulu medicine man, from the negro evangelist only in that he doesn't know he is praying.[3]

By no means a universal success, the Broadway production of *The Jazz Singer* was dismissed by the *New York American* as "a garish and tawdry Hebrew play." The *New York Herald Tribune* reported that the "almost entirely" Jewish audience complained that many lines were "wholly unintelligible" and that even understanding the play required total "understanding of and sympathy with the Jew and his faith."[4]

The anonymous and conspicuously ambivalent English-language reviewer for New York's largest Yiddish daily, the *Forward*, deemed *The Jazz Singer* "full of false-ness. Reeking with hokum and glorifying the cruelty of parents to their son. . . . And yet it is a moving and thrilling play, a play that caused the vast audience the night I attended to rise and cheer and demand a curtain speech by the principle actor. *The Jazz Singer* is a play by a Jew about Jews and designed for 100 per cent Jewish consumption." Noting *The Jazz Singer*'s basis in the life of Jolson, the reviewer concluded that the play spoke directly to Jews who were estranged from their traditions but uneasy in their assimilation to American life.[5]

In April 1926, Warner Bros.—a small studio whose major asset was the trained dog Rin-Tin-Tin—formed a partnership with Western Electric, creating the Vitaphone Corporation. Over the next few years, Sam Warner would produce scores of one- and two-reel "acts" (mainly solo vaudeville performances) with synchronous sound-on-disc accompaniment. Two months later, at the advice of its then top contract director, Ernst Lubitsch, Warners paid $50,000 for the rights to *The Jazz Singer*.

In August, the first Vitaphone program—eight "talking" shorts (ranging from a speech by industry watchdog Will Hays to the overture to *Tannhäuser* to a song by novelty guitarist Roy Smeck), plus the feature-length *Don Juan*—had its premiere at the Warners' Theatre in New York. Warners' Vitaphone experiment proved successful. A second program opened in October 1926, a third in February 1927. Now Warner Bros. was ready to produce a feature with music and incidental dialogue, protecting its investment with the presence of superstar Jolson.

Appropriately, the film that would sound the death knell for silent film opens on a mournful note. To the accompaniment of a pseudo-Semitic melody, a series of titles identifies the Jews as "a race older than civilization" whose culture is threatened by a new urban music that is "perhaps, the misunderstood utterance of prayer." It is Yom Kippur Eve on the Lower East Side and thirteen-year-old Jakie, son of Cantor and Sarah Rabinowitz, is to chant the Kol Nidre prayer in his father's synagogue. Cut to Jakie performing "My Gal Sal" in a local saloon. Jakie is spotted by Yudelson (Otto Lederer), the film's comic stand-in for the Jewish community, who rushes to report the boy to his father. The cantor (Warner Oland) arrives, drags Jakie by his ear homeward past the pushcarts of Hester Street and, despite Mama's tearful supplications, administers the strap. Tearful Jakie runs away from home, even as his father's Kol Nidre wells up on the soundtrack.

A decade or more passes. In a studio reconstruction of Coffee Dan's, a San Francisco show business hangout of the era, Jolson makes his first appearance as the mature Jakie, now known as Jack Robin. The entire scene is redolent of his liberation from tribal taboo. Jack wolfs down his breakfast of *treyf* (unkosher food), with ragtime ebullience, eyes his Gentile patroness with awe-filled lust, and puts across "Toot, Toot, Tootsie" with lascivious assurance. When called upon to perform, Jack first sings "Dirty Hands, Dirty Face," which is richly evocative of his conflicted patrimony. The song is a mawkish ballad of paternal love in which, alternately maudlin and mocking, the singer revels in the role of father to an incorrigible street urchin who, beneath a grimy exterior, is "an angel of joy." But Jack's inability to sever all connections to his past is made overt in the next musical sequence. While on tour, he is drawn to a hall where the famous Cantor Rosenblatt is giving a concert.

Jack Robin (Al Jolson), formerly Jakie Rabinowitz, singing "Dirty Hands, Dirty Face" in Coffee Dan's.

This ambivalence is further developed when Jack is called to Broadway and triumphantly returns to New York, heading immediately for the Lower East Side, where, as a title informs us, "For those whose faces are turned towards the past, the years roll by unheeded." He finds his mother at home alone, and she embraces him. He then springs to the parlor piano for a strenuous rendition of "Blue Skies." In her only authentic moment in the film, Eugenie Besserer seems utterly flummoxed as Jolson interrupts the song midway to steal a kiss, promise her a new pink dress, offer her a new apartment in the Bronx, and tempt her with a trip to Coney Island, all the while suggestively vamping on the keyboard.[6]

The communion is broken when the cantor/father appears and, catching his wife and son together at the piano, cries "Stop!"—whereupon the film abruptly reverts to silence. In the next title, the cantor denounces the jazz-singing prodigal for his misuse of divine energy. At first, Jack attempts to pacify his father by suggesting that America transcends Jewishness: "If you were born here, you would feel as I do." When his father accuses him of apostasy, a startlingly blunt title appears in which Jack makes explicit Raphaelson's point: "My songs mean as much to my audience as yours do to your congregation!"

*The Jazz Singer* culminates on the afternoon of Jack's Broadway opening, which is, with cosmic inevitability and comic improbability, Yom Kippur Eve. In the middle of the final rehearsal, his mother comes backstage to inform Jack that only by singing Kol Nidre in the synagogue that night can he save his dying father (and, by extension, the Jewish community). Refusing his mother's request, Jack madly rushes onstage and hurtles through the chorus line to intone a fevered incantation of mother worship. He is now, for the first time in the film, the full-blown, iconic essence of "Jolson-ness." Finishing the song to tumultuous acclaim, the dazed and tormented jazz singer returns to his dressing room where, gazing into the mirror, he sees not a blackfaced minstrel but a synagogue filled with praying Jews. Jack realizes he must return to the Lower East Side "before the sun is out of the sky." His producer flatly warns him that if he walks out, he will never again play Broadway. Caught between conflicting commandments, Jack elects to chant Kol Nidre.

This prayer ends the play. The repentant son replaces his dying father as cantor, who had in turn replaced his father, who had in turn . . . a ritual, sentimentalized affirmation of the pain, burden, and eternal nature of Jewishness. For the film, however,

the Warner brothers provided a dream-like reversal in which, back in blackface and back on Broadway, Jack goes down on one knee to sing "Mammy" as Mama herself sits *kvelling* (beaming) in the audience, the fatuously proud Yudelson beside her, and the cantor/father gone forever from the picture.

"Are Jews white?" the scholar Sander Gilman asks. "Or do they become white when they, like Jack Robin, acculturate into American society, so identifying with the ideals of American life, with all its evocation of race, that they—at least in their own mind's eye—become white? Does black-face make everyone who puts it on white?"[7]

As the Warner brothers shot *The Jazz Singer*'s Lower East Side scenes on location and used the Winter Garden Theater (Jolson's "personal kingdom") for the final number, reconstructed the Orchard Street Synagogue on a Hollywood back lot, and included a lengthy interlude with Cantor Rosenblatt in performance, we cannot but be struck by the surplus of authenticity with which they invested the film they would advertise as their "supreme triumph."

*The Jazz Singer*'s souvenir program, which included a useful glossary of the Hebrew and Yiddish words found in the film's intertitles, tersely declares that "the faithful portrayal of Jewish homelife is largely due to the unobtrusive assistance of Mr. Benjamin Warner, father of the producers and ardent admirer of *The Jazz Singer*." This statement, which attempts through paternal approval to legitimize the overthrow of Jewish traditionalism depicted in their film, suggests that the Warners were uneasily aware that the story of *The Jazz Singer* was not only that of Jolson or many of their employees, but also of themselves.

ABOVE
Cantor Rabinowitz (Warner Oland) walks in on Jack Robin serenading his mother (Eugenie Besserer).

RIGHT
Jack Robin comforted by Mary Dale (May McAvoy) backstage.

BELOW
Jack Robin returns to the synagogue to chant Kol Nidre.

OPPOSITE
Cover of souvenir program for *The Jazz Singer* (1927).

PAGES 82–83
Pages from the souvenir program for *The Jazz Singer*.

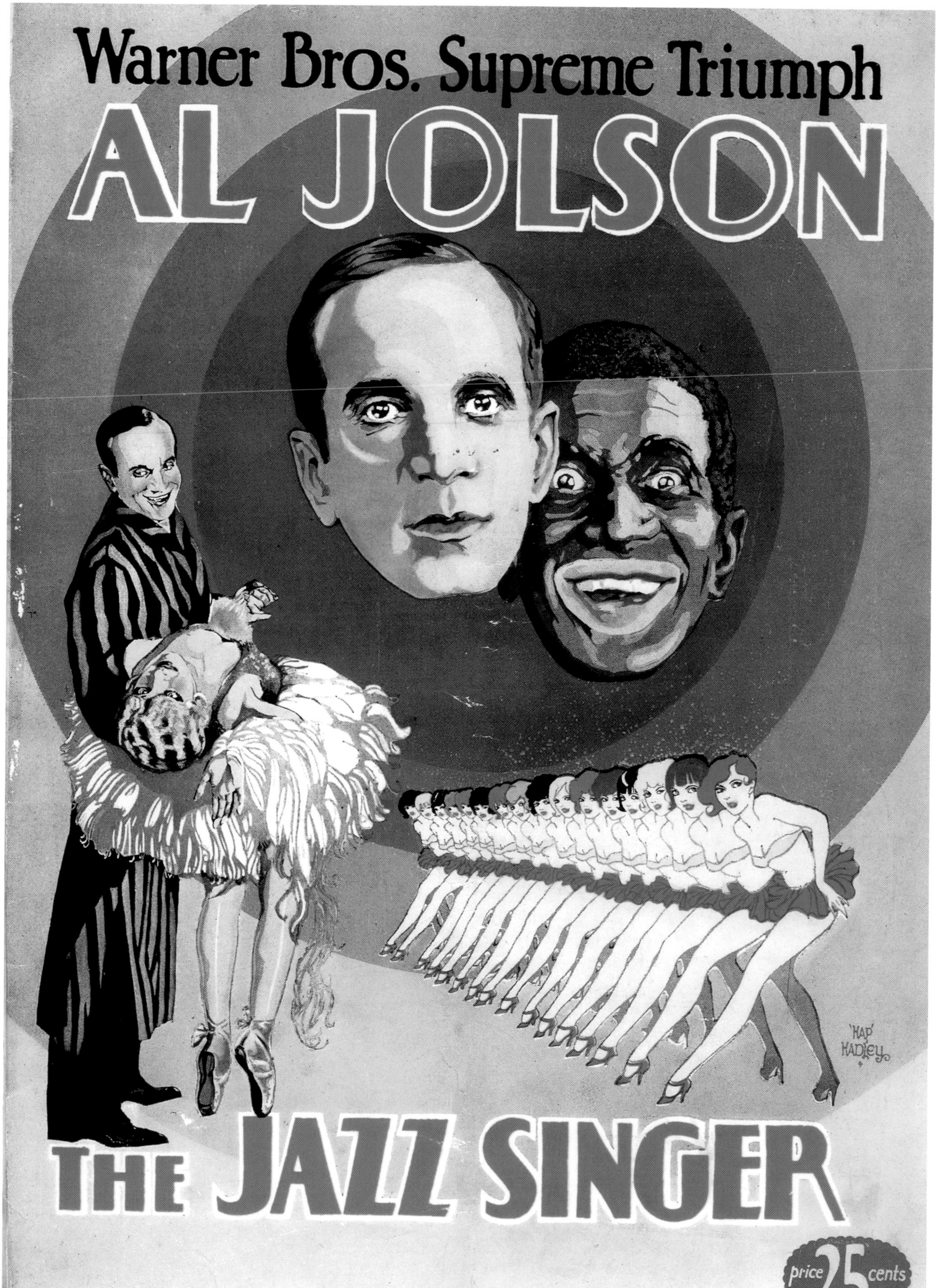
Warner Bros. Supreme Triumph
AL JOLSON
'HAP' HADLEY
THE JAZZ SINGER
price 25 cents

# HOW I CAME TO WRITE "THE JAZZ SINGER"

## By SAMSON RAPHAELSON

WHEN I was a Junior at the University of Illinois, it became very necessary that I should impress a certain young lady. I had a date with her for a certain evening. I wanted to show her the best time to be had in the town of Champaign, Illinois. I borrowed ten dollars and bought two tickets for the one-night performance of Al Jolson in 'Robinson Crusoe' Jr."

I had never seen Jolson before. I had heard of him. I shall never forget the first five minutes of Jolson—his velocity, the amazing fluidity with which he shifted from a tremendous absorption in his audience to a tremendous obsorption in his song. I still remember the song, "Where the Black-Eyed Susans Grow." When he finished, I turned to the girl beside me, dazed with memories of my childhood on the East Side — memories of the Pike Street Synagogue.

I said to the girl, "My God, this isn't a jazz singer. This is a Cantor!"

This grotesque figure in blackface, kneeling at the end of a runway which projected him into the heart of his audience, flinging out his white-gloved hands, was embracing that audience with a prayer—an evangelical moan—a tortured, imperious call that hurtled through the house like a swift electrical lariat with a twist that swept the audience right to the edge of that runway. The words didn't matter, the melody didn't matter. It was the emotion — the emotions of a Cantor.

I said to my friend, "There's a story in this —' a dramatic story."

I went backstage after the performance and I talked to Jolson. He was very busy, but I shall never forget the feeling I had about what a "damn decent guy" he was. I was a youngster deeply stirred by something which undoubtedly stirred him as much as it did me. He sensed that. In those days he had already become the world's greatest entertainer," and a lot of stirred youngsters must have tired to say nothing in particular to him. He behaved as if I were the first. He told me a little of his background.

---

### PREFACE TO "THE JAZZ SINGER"

#### By Samson Raphaelson

HE who wishes to picture today's America must do it kaleidoscopically; he must show you a vivid contrast of surfaces, raucous, sentimental, egotistical, vulgar, ineffably busy — surfaces whirling in a dance which sometimes is a dance to Aphrodite and more frequently a dance to Jehovah.

In seeking a symbol of the vital chaos of America's soul, I find no more adequate one than jazz. Here you have the rhythm of frenzy staggering against a symphonic background — a background composed of lewdness, heart's delight, soul-racked madness, monumental boldness, exquisite humility, but principally prayer.

I hear jazz, and I am given a vision of cathedrals and temples collapsing and, silhouetted against the setting sun, a solitary figure, a lost soul, dancing grotesquely on the ruins... Thus do I see the jazz singer.

JAZZ is prayer. It is too passionate to be anything else. It is prayer distorted, sick, unconcsious of its destination. The singer of jazz is what Matthew Arnold said of the Jew, "lost between two worlds, one dead, the other powerless to be born." In this, my first play, I have tried to crystallize the ironic truth that one of the Americas of 1927 — that one which packs to overflowing our cabarets, musical revues, and dance halls — is praying with a fervor as intense as that of the America which goes sedately to church and synagogue. The jazz American is different from the dancing dervish, from the Zulu medicine man, from the negro evangelist only in that he doesn't know he is praying.

I have used a Jewish youth as my protagonist because the Jews are determining the nature and scope of jazz more than any other race — more than the negroes, from whom they have taken jazz and given it a new color and meaning. Jazz is Irving Berlin, Al Jolson, George Gershwin, Sophie Tucker. These are Jews with their roots in the synagogue. And these are expressing in evangelical terms the nature of our chaos today.

You find the soul of a people in the songs they sing. You find the meaning of the songs in the soul of the minstrels who create and interpret them. In "The Jazz Singer" I have attempted an exploration of the soul of one of these minstrels.

---

But I had already guessed it. I knew there was the spirit of Cantors in him, the blood of Cantors in him.

Five years later in California I wrote the story, I called it "The Day of Atonement." My stories at that time were being published in various magazines. I was a professional writer. I knew most of the editors and they knew me. I said to myself, the first editor that sees this will jump at it. For I felt that it was easily the best story I had ever written. The story turned down by five magazines, Sewell Haggard, editor of Everybody's, bought it. When it appeared I got letters, from my other editors saying, "Why don't you send us stuff like that?" Solomon should have added to a certain remark, "And the ways of an editor with an author."

Mr. Haggard, when he accepted the story, wrote me: "For goodness' sake, don't sell the movie rights on this. You have the makings of a play. Write the play first."

Three years ago I wrote the play. I felt about it as I did about the story. I sent it to Sam H. Harris, who turned it down. I couldn't believe it and wouldn't believe it. I went to his office with genuine concern for Mr. Harris' welfare, fretted him into a state where he handed me over to Al Lewis. Mr. Lewis pointed out certain things in the play which could not be done on any stage. He suggested that if I rewrote it he might be interested. I rewrote it and read it to him. When I finished, there were tears in his eyes. He said, "I'm sorry, but I can't produce this play." I said, "Then why were you crying — because it broke your heart to turn me down?"

I really think Mr. Lewis accepted this play because I wore him out.

If anyone had told me ten years ago, when I first saw Jolson, that he would be in a movie of a play inspired by my seeing him, it would have sounded like a bit of fairy tale to me. At the time this article is being written the motion picture of "The Jazz Singer" has not yet arrived. Jolson, who was so damn decent to me in Champaign, Illinois, in 1916 — Jolson, who came up to me in Stamford after the opening of "The Jazz Singer" two years ago and said, "Boy, if there's anything I can do to make this show a success, just say the word. If it flops, I'll put my own money into it to keep it alive." — Jolson, electric, palpitating, the most American figure in the world today — Jolson's going to be in it. And I'm as eager to see it as if the movie was based on his play, not mine.

# "WARNER BROS. *Present*"

WHEREVER there is a motion picture theatre there is a place set aside for announcements of the program of the day and the days to come. Frequently the movie fan sees a line that arrests his attention. It brings a glow to his face. It is a line prefacing an announcement and it reads:

Warner Bros. Present.

Time was when this line brought no thrill of expectation. That was years ago when Warner Bros. were little known outside the motion picture industry. What happened since then sounds like romance, and would be taken as such if it were not for the concrete facts which accompany a story that might be called: "The Making of A Name."

"PA" WARNER

The story of Warner Bros. opens in Poland in 1885 when Benjamin Warner, chafing under conditions which prevented his children from getting an education, made his way to the land wherein all men are free and equal. Landing in Baltimore, he opened a shop and a few months later sent for his wife and youngsters.

The elder Warner found it no easy matter to feed a family of six, but the youngsters exhibited a sense of responsibility not only to themselves, but to their parents. School sessions over, they hustled for work.

One day news came of a boom in Bluefield, West Virginia. Benjamin Warner went to investigate it, leaving the shop in charge of ten-year-old Harry M. with admonitions that he look after his three brothers, Albert, Sam, and Jack.

After ten years spent in the Monumental City the family moved to Youngstown, Ohio, where Harry and Albert stuck over a shop a sign reading: "Bicycles Repaired." Occasionally Sam would help, but the thing he loved was the theatre. When he got a job at a summer park outside Sandusky, Ohio, Sam was elated.

Motion pictures were coming along at this time and those exhibited at the Sandusky park intrigued Sam. He talked Albert into going in with him on the purchase of "The Great Train Robbery," a two reel classic of its times, and began exhibiting it in that famous country known as "the sticks." The tour was not a success, but oh, what a lot it taught those boys!

Going into Newcastle, Penn., Sam and Albert leased a house contracting for two changes of bill a week. The initial payment was all right, but when told they had to deposit two hundred dollars as a guarantee of good faith, they paled. They did not have it. But Harry came to their rescue,

sold his bicycle shop and found himself also in the movie business.

From this point on one would imagine the young men had easy sailing. Far from it. Having opened an exchange they set about establishing a chain of houses for which they would guarantee to supply the pictures. This was the first plan for a booking exchange. When the whole thing was ready, a combination of the picture producers was instrumental in wiping out their plan and also every dollar they had. It was a terrible blow. The brothers saw that if they were to succeed they would have to produce their own pictures. Harry was to do the financing. It was not long before motion picture exhibitors were showing films that bore the introductory line: "Warner Bros. Present."

A resume of the record of Warner Bros. since that time is illustrative of what can be accomplished by brains, perseverance, and honest business dealings. These men had the will to succeed and refused to allow any little tricks of fate to retard them. Since Warner Bros. produced Ambassador Gerard's "My Four Years in Germany," they have done many big things, including the introduction of John Barrymore as a star in "Beau Brummel," to be followed by "The Sea Beast," "Don Juan," and "When A Man Loves." The Warners introduced Dolores Costello as a star, in "Old San Francisco" for which the public has applauded them. Syd Chaplin's greatest screen successes have been scored under the banner of Warner Bros. Among the other stars identified with the Warner name are Monte Blue, Irene Rich, May McAvoy, Conrad Nagel, Louise Fazenda, Clyde Cook, Warner Oland, and last but not least, that tremendously popular screen figure, Rin-Tin-Tin, the wonder dog of the ages.

It was Harry M. Warner who virtually developed Vitaphone, which is the biggest thing in connection with motion pictures since the birth of pictures themselves. Surely an enviable record. And now comes their supreme triumph, Al Jolson, the greatest comedian of the times, in "The Jazz Singer."

As it was found fitting to open this sketch with reference to Benjamin Warner, it should be fitting to close it with further reference. What became of him as his boys grew to manhood? That he should have gone into motion pictures seems only natural, and for years he proudly guided the destiny of a cosy theatre in Niles, Ohio. It was only the other day that he agreed to retire. Then with his wife he went to Hollywood. Unobtrusively he moved through the Warner Bros. Studios during the filming of "The Jazz Singer." Once there arose some question of the authenticity of a Ghetto scene. He quietly settled it and from that moment his presence was felt and his advice welcomed. From this point, Mr. Warner practically became a technical director of the picture and much of the charm of the home and Ghetto scenes is due to his suggestions. Always eager to listen to their father, the Warners are more eager to do so to-day than ever, so while the public only knows of four Warners there are in reality five, including the quiet figure that takes so much interest in every thing bearing the announcement: —Warner Bros. Present.

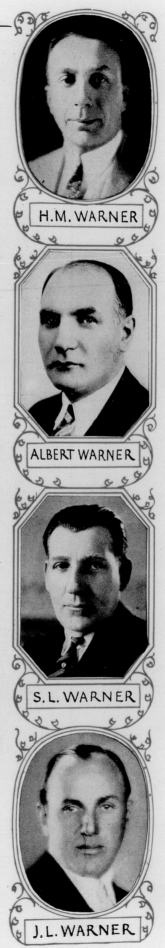

H.M. WARNER

ALBERT WARNER

S.L. WARNER

J.L. WARNER

# THE JAZZ SINGER: A CHRONOLOGY

J. HOBERMAN

**Circa 1886**

Asa Yoelson (Al Jolson), the fifth child of cantor Moses Yoelson and Naomi Cantor Yoelson is born in Srednik, Russia. Brought to America as a child, he grows up in the slums of Washington, D.C.

**1889**

Sholem Aleichem publishes *Yosele Solovey*, a novel about a young cantor's corruption through worldly success. His next novel, *Wandering Stars* (1891), includes a character known as the Lomzer *khazn* (cantor), who comes to America and reinvents himself as the Lomzer Nightingale, singing Kol Nidre "every night in the famous operetta called, by a strange coincidence, *Kol Nidre*."

**1902**

Mark Arnshteyn's Yiddish play *Der vilner balebesl*, based on the story of cantor-turned-opera singer Yoel-David Levinshteyn-Strashunsky (1816–1850), has its world premiere in Lodz—in Polish.

**1904**

Naomi Cantor Yoelson dies. Jolson first performs in blackface.

**1907**

Jolson joins Dockstader's Minstrels, the most important of the remaining blackface minstrel shows.

**1911**

Jolson signs with the Shubert Brothers, becoming the first star of vaudeville and the minstrel show to be legitimized on Broadway.

**April 25, 1917**

University of Illinois undergraduate Samson Raphaelson sees Jolson—then billed as "The World's Greatest Entertainer"—perform in blackface in *Robinson Crusoe, Jr.* at a theater in Champaign, Illinois.

**January 1922**

*Everybody's Magazine* publishes Raphaelson's story "The Day of Atonement," about Jack Robin (born Jakie Rabinowitz), a ragtime-singing cantor's son caught between his Jewish tradition and his desire for show-business success. The story ends with Jack abandoning Broadway to take his dead father's place in the Hester Street Synagogue.

**September 14, 1925**

Raphaelson's play *The Jazz Singer*, an adaptation of "The Day of Atonement," opens on Broadway at the Fulton Theater with sometime-blackface singer George Jessel in the role of Jack Robin. In November, the play moves to the Cort Theater, where it runs through June 5, 1926.

October 7, 1926

Jolson makes his film debut in the Warner Bros. Vitaphone short *Al Jolson in a Plantation Act,* singing three numbers in blackface: "When the Red, Red Robin Comes Bob-Bob-Bobbin' Along," "April Showers," and "Rock-a-Bye Your Baby."

February 11, 1927

*Film Daily* reports that Warners' upcoming version of *The Jazz Singer,* starring Jessel, will be "the first picture into which Vitaphone will be introduced for dramatic effect."

April 18, 1927

Jessel stars in a week-long engagement of *The Jazz Singer* at the Century Theater on Central Park West. Early the following month, the production appears at Werba's Brooklyn Theater.

May 16, 1927

Three weeks before shooting is scheduled to begin, Warner Bros. announces that Jolson has replaced Jessel in *The Jazz Singer.*

October 6, 1927

The Warner Bros. film *The Jazz Singer,* with Jolson in the title role, has its world premiere—one day before Yom Kippur— at the Warners' Theatre in New York. Unlike the play (and the original script), the movie, which runs on Broadway for twenty-three weeks, does not end with Jack Robin chanting Kol Nidre, but rather shows the star back on Broadway and back in blackface, singing "Mammy."

December 19, 1927

Jessel re-creates his starring role in a week-long revival of Raphaelson's "comedy-drama" at the Majestic in Brooklyn. On December 26, the production moves for a week to the Windsor Theater in the Bronx and, on January 16, 1928, reopens for a limited run at Teller's Shubert Theater on Broadway.

December 28, 1927

*The Jazz Singer* has its Hollywood premiere. Frances Goldwyn, wife of Samuel Goldwyn, recalls the night as "the most important event in cultural history since Martin Luther nailed his theses on the church door."[1]

January 1, 1928

*The Jazz Singer* opens in St. Louis, Seattle, and Washington, D.C.

85

May 14, 1928

Raphaelson's play is revived for a week at the Public Theater, on Second Avenue. Although the Public has long been a venue for the Yiddish stage, the production is in English.

August 7, 1928

Jolson signs a three-picture contract with Warner Bros. that not only gives him approval of script, director, and cast, but also includes the unusual option to participate in possible profits.

September 19, 1928

*The Singing Fool*, Warners' partial-talkie follow-up to *The Jazz Singer*, starring Jolson, opens at the Winter Garden on Broadway and goes on to become Hollywood's top-grossing picture up until *Gone with the Wind* (MGM, 1939).

March 26, 1930

Warners' *Mammy*, featuring a new score by Irving Berlin and starring Jolson as a blackface minstrel, opens at the Warners' Theatre.

1930

A Yiddish-language version of Raphaelson's play *The Jazz Singer* is staged in Warsaw with a cantor's granddaughter, Ida Kaminska, in the role of the blackface minstrel Jack Robin.[2]

August 10, 1936

*The Jazz Singer* is broadcast on *The Lux Radio Theater* (CBS) with Jolson in the title role and Yiddish actress Vera Gordon as Mrs. Rabinowitz. Later that year, Warner Bros. abandons plans for a tenth-anniversary remake to star Jolson, with his wife, Ruby Keeler, as Mary Dale and Lionel Barrymore as the cantor.

September 28, 1936

Warner Bros. releases the animated "Merrie Melody" *I Love to Singa*, in which the youngest son of Professor Owl rebels against his father's classical music by becoming a jazz crooner named Owl Jolson.[3]

December 24, 1937

The Eron Pictures film *The Cantor's Son* opens in New York. In this American-made, Yiddish-language anti-*Jazz Singer*, real-life cantor Moishe Oysher leaves his Bessarabian shtetl to become a singing star in America. Having returned for his parents' fiftieth anniversary, he remains to marry his childhood sweetheart and assumes his father's place in the shtetl synagogue.

May 5, 1939

The Twentieth Century Fox production *Rose of Washington Square* opens at the Roxy. A crypto-biography of Fanny Brice, it features Jolson performing several songs, including "Mammy," in blackface.

**October 13, 1939**

Twentieth Century Fox's production *Hollywood Cavalcade* opens at the Roxy. A musical about the silent movie era, it gives Jolson a cameo role, chanting Kol Nidre, in a re-creation of the synagogue scene from *The Jazz Singer*.

Yiddish film *Der vilner shtot-khazn* (The Cantor of Vilna), known in English as *Overture to Glory* (1940). Moishe Oysher (right) as Cantor Yoel Strashunsky succumbs to the spell of Western classical music as performed by Polish composer Tadeusz Moniuszko (John Mylong).

**February 9, 1940**

*Overture to Glory* (Elite Productions), another anti-*Jazz Singer* and the last of the (relatively) big-budgeted American Yiddish talkies, opens in New York at the Cameo Theater. Based on the play *Der vilner balebesl*, it tells the story of a cantor (Oysher) who deserts his family and congregation to become a star in the Warsaw opera.

**January 30, 1945**

*Variety* reports Warner Bros. plans to make a "modernized" *Jazz Singer* starring Paul Muni.

**June 26, 1945**

Warners' George Gershwin bio-pic *Rhapsody in Blue* opens at the Hollywood Theater. Jolson plays himself, singing Gershwin's "Swanee" in blackface.

**November 28, 1945**

*Variety* reports that Warners Bros. has abandoned plans for a *Jazz Singer* remake, which would have starred John Garfield.

**1945**

Cantor Moses Yoelson dies.

**October 10, 1946**

Columbia's *The Jolson Story*, based on Jolson's life (from his childhood through the making of *The Jazz Singer* to an imaginary 1946 comeback) opens at Radio City Music Hall. Larry Parks plays Jolson. Although uncredited in the film, Jolson dubbed the songs. The movie is the third top box-office attraction of 1947 as well as Columbia's highest-grossing release to date.

**June 2, 1947**

*The Jazz Singer* is again broadcast by *The Lux Radio Theater* with Jolson in the title role. Ludwig Donath and Tamara Shayne, who played Jolson's parents in *The Jolson Story*, are featured as the cantor and his wife; Gail Patrick plays Mary Dale.

**February 16, 1948**

Jolson plays himself again in *The Lux Radio Theater* presentation of *The Jolson Story*.

August 17, 1949
Columbia releases *Jolson Sings Again*. The sequel to *The Jolson Story*, it again stars Parks as Jolson, and Jolson once more dubs the songs. The movie ends with the making of *The Jolson Story* and Parks—playing not only Jolson but also the actor who plays Jolson—performing "Rock-a-Bye Your Baby" in the movie's only instance of blackface. It is the highest-grossing movie of 1949.

May 22, 1950
Jolson plays himself yet again in *The Lux Radio Theater* presentation of *Jolson Sings Again*.

October 23, 1950
Jolson dies in San Francisco shortly after returning from Korea, where he gave an estimated 160 shows for U.S. troops.

March 21, 1951
Parks is the first witness to testify before the newly reconstituted House Committee on Un-American Activities. Expected to take the Fifth Amendment, he admits his one-time membership in the Communist Party but pleads not to be forced to give the names of other party members: "Do not make me crawl through the mud like an informer." Parks is threatened with holding Congress in contempt; in a closed-door session two days later, he names a dozen names.

Summer 1951
The National Theater on Second Avenue opens a Yiddish-language version of *The Jolson Story*. In addition to staging Jolson's meeting with General MacArthur in Korea, the play interpolates material from *The Jazz Singer* "improved" to include a tearful reconciliation between father and son. According to Robert Brustein, who played the part of Jolson's announcer, the production employed a Yiddish-speaking Jolson and a blackfaced Jolson-impersonator who mimed to actual Jolson recordings, including "Hatikvah."[4]

December 6, 1951
Warners' *I'll See You in My Dreams*, a musical bio-pic of songwriter Gus Kahn that includes Doris Day's blackface imitation of Jolson, opens at Radio City Music Hall.[5]

December 31, 1952
Warners' remake of *The Jazz Singer* premieres in Miami (it is released on New Year's Eve to qualify for the 1952 Academy Awards). Singer-comedian Danny Thomas stars in the title role as a GI who returns to North Philadelphia, where his father is cantor of a synagogue that their family founded in 1790, determined to break into show

business. Thomas does not perform in blackface—nor is there any other reference made to African-Americans—and his climactic Kol Nidre segues into an onstage rendition of "Living the Life I Love."[6]

**December 25, 1953**
Warner Bros. releases *The Eddie Cantor Story*.

**May 1954**
Columbia re-releases *The Jolson Story* with stereophonic sound. Despite Parks's "friendly" testimony three years earlier, the Brooklyn Fox Theater is picketed by the American Legion.

**March 7, 1956**
Oysher's last (and only English-language) film, the independently produced *Singing in the Dark*, opens in New York. In this post-Holocaust variation on *The Jazz Singer*, Oysher plays a German cantor who loses his family and his memory during World War II. Having made his way to America, he becomes a nightclub singer, but after a blow to his head brings back his tragic past, resumes his identity as a cantor and a cantor's son.

**November 1956**
Jerry Lewis has a top-ten hit with "Rock-a-Bye Your Baby." The single sells 1.4 million copies. The album *Jerry Lewis Just Sings* (which features three other Jolson songs— "I'm Sittin' on Top of the World," "Mammy," and "When the Red, Red Robin Comes Bob-Bob-Bobbing Along") goes to number three on the LP charts.

**February 7, 1957**
Lewis includes a Jolson impersonation in his first one-man show at the Palace Theater on Broadway.

ABOVE, LEFT
Poster for the 1952 remake of *The Jazz Singer*.

ABOVE, RIGHT
Danny Thomas and Peggy Lee in the 1952 version of *The Jazz Singer*. Jerry Golden (Thomas) shows Judy Lane (Lee) portraits of his ancestors, all cantors in the same Philadephia synagogue, dating back to the late eighteenth century.

**October 13, 1959**

NBC's *Ford Startime* broadcasts an hour-long version of *The Jazz Singer*, with Lewis in the title role. In this case, the cantor's son breaks with family tradition to become a singing comedian. Molly Picon appears as the mother; Eduard Franz reprises his role as the cantor in the 1952 remake. Scheduled a day after Yom Kippur, the color telecast concludes with Lewis chanting Kol Nidre in clown-face.

**July 1974**

Plans are announced for a new musical to be based on *The Jazz Singer*, transposing the story from the Lower East Side to Harlem and featuring a black cast. The show is never produced.

A TV GUIDE CLOSE-UP 9:30 28 18 3 STARTIME — Drama

Jerry Lewis in 'THE JAZZ SINGER'

COLOR Joey Rabinowitz' father begs him to carry on the family tradition and become a cantor, but Joey ignores his pleas and enters show business as comedian Joey Robbins.
Oliver Crawford wrote this modernized adaptation of "The Jazz Singer," by Samson Raphaelson. George Jessel starred in the 1925 Broadway version. Al Jolson's 1927 movie version was the first full-length film to feature talking. Ralph Nelson directed tonight's one-hour play. Jerry Lewis sings "Kol Nidre."

**Cast**

| | |
|---|---|
| Joey | Jerry Lewis |
| Ginny Gibbons | Anna Maria Alberghetti |
| Sarah Rabinowitz | Molly Picon |
| Cantor Rabinowitz | Eduard Franz |
| Ed Giddleson | Alan Reed |

*TV Guide* listing for the 1959 *Startime* presentation of "a modernized version" of Samson Raphaelson's play *The Jazz Singer*, starring Jerry Lewis, Molly Picon, Anna Maria Alberghetti, and Eduard Franz (who was reprising his role as the cantor in the 1952 remake of the 1927 film).

**August 1975**

Fifty years after *The Jazz Singer* opened on Broadway, Columbia Pictures re-releases *The Jolson Story* in 70mm.

**October 1977**

The United States Post Office marks the fiftieth anniversary of *The Jazz Singer*'s release with an Al Jolson commemorative stamp.

**Fall 1978**

*Jolson*, a new musical play with British-born Jolson impersonator Clive Baldwin in the title role, has its world premiere at the Paper Mill Playhouse in Millburn, New Jersey.[7]

**Spring 1979**

*Joley*, a new musical dramatization of Jolson's life, runs for eight weeks at the North Stage Dinner Theater in Glen Cove, Long Island, with Larry Kert in the title role. The following year, Kert tours American cities in the one-man show *Al Jolson Tonight!*

**December 19, 1980**

A third version of *The Jazz Singer* opens at the Ziegfeld, with pop star Neil Diamond as an aspiring rock singer. Sir Laurence Olivier co-stars as his father, Cantor Rabinovitch, here a Holocaust survivor. (There is no mother in this version.) Diamond briefly appears in blackface and an Afro wig as a means of performing with a soul ensemble in a black nightclub.[8]

**October 11, 1981**

SCTV parodies the Diamond *Jazz Singer*. A Jewish recording executive (played by Eugene Levy with dreadlocks) opposes the desire of his adopted African-American son (singer Al Jarreau) to become a cantor.

**May 22, 1983**

Kert sings a medley of Jolson songs on the ABC network special "The Parade of Stars," produced at the Palace Theater in New York.

ABOVE
Neil Diamond at the climax of the 1980 remake of *The Jazz Singer*, singing the hit song "Coming to America." Note the scarf, suggestive of a traditional *talis* (prayer shawl).

RIGHT
Poster for *The Jazz Singer* (1980).

July 21, 1988
Michael Dukakis accepts the presidential nomination at the Democratic National Convention in Atlanta, entering the convention hall accompanied by "Coming to America," the anthem Diamond wrote for his version of the *The Jazz Singer*.

October 24, 1991
*The Simpsons* (Fox) broadcasts "Like Father, Like Clown," in which Bart and Lisa attempt to effect a rapprochement between Krusty the Clown and his father, Rabbi Hyman Krustofsky (Jackie Mason), who disowned Krusty when he gave up the rabbinate to become a clown. "If you were a musician or a jazz singer, this I could forgive," the rabbi tells his son. "But a clown?!"

October 23, 1995
*Jolson: The Musical*, based on an original idea by Jolson biographer Michael Freedland, opens at the Victoria Palace in London and subsequently wins the Laurence Olivier award for Best New Musical of 1996. The show portrays Jolson from 1929, covering his stormy marriage to Keeler and subsequent career decline, through the postwar comeback triggered by *The Jolson Story*.

June 1996
Michael Rogin's *Blackface, White Noise* is published: "Anti-Semitism is *The Jazz Singer*'s structuring absence. The visible cost it leaves behind is borne by Jolson as he plays not a Jew but a black."[9]

October 6, 1998
*Jolson: The Musical* opens in Cleveland and tours the U.S. with sometime Yiddish actor Michael Burstyn in the lead. Unlike the British show and the 1997 Toronto production, the American version does not employ blackface.

1998
*The Jazz Singer* places ninetieth on the American Film Institute's list of the one hundred best American movies.

# PUTTING BLACKFACE IN ITS PLACE

MARK SLOBIN

In 1927, the first "talkie," *The Jazz Singer*, appeared, a musical combining antique blackface routines with older synagogue stylings. But it was the electricity of Al Jolson's performance, delivered by the new technology, that seized the public's attention and established him as a Hollywood star. Recently, the pathos of the Jewish performer who needs to blacken up to become an American star has attracted extensive critical response, the best-known of which is probably Michael Rogin's book *Blackface, White Noise: Jewish Immigrants in the Hollywood Melting Pot*.[1]

In this article, I seek to put the Jewish blackface moment of the early twentieth century in a number of entertainment contexts of its time; also included are some reflections on the fate of blackface in more recent decades. As Stuart Hall has written about any snapshot view of popular culture involving blackness, "these moments are always conjectural. They have their historical specificity. . . . They are never the same moment."[2]

### "WHOOPEE"

*The fierce brave is only Mr. Eddie Cantor, as he appears in one scene of the gorgeous Ziegfeld musical comedy at the New Amsterdam. The shadow is, symbolically speaking, the shadow of his former self, for in this show he wears but for a brief time his old familiar blackface makeup. The ladies are not figures on a curtain but are to be seen, very much in person.*

**FAR LEFT**
Double caricature of Eddie Cantor, in the *New Yorker*, January 19, 1929.

**NEAR LEFT**
Eddie Cantor in blackface.

## AMERICAN POPULAR SONG AND ETHNICITY

The United States is the first modern society to express its sense of identity solely through popular—rather than folk or elite—culture. The "minstrel show," an amalgam of entertainments that emerged in the 1830s, was the quintessential expression of identity for a society of Europeans that was eradicating Indians and enslaving Africans while expanding across a continent and preparing to receive large waves of immigrants. Views of minstrelsy have ranged from repulsion against its racism to revisionist analyses of its class- and gender-based comedy. Recently, some writers have even suggested that working-class whites were expressing their own resistance to capitalist domination by channeling their subversive urges into producing and consuming blackface material.[3]

Instead of entering this debate, I want to move on to the larger framework of mixture and invention that the popular song represents and distills, a transatlantic stew of sentiment and commercialism served up to the dispossessed, the uprooted, and the culturally confused. Charles Hamm plays up the complexity of the process by spotlighting Henry Russell as a prime inventor of the American popular song. Russell was "an English-born Jew who studied in Italy, first came to Canada, and then furnished Americans with songs in an Italian musical style, mostly to texts reflecting an Irish type of nostalgia. Of such ethnic mixtures was popular song in America born." The process of objectifying and selling culture was like a vacuum cleaner, inhaling all the available sources. Minstrelsy helped drive the engine of popular entertainment, which also relied on the energy of other ethnic-based sources.[4]

Summing up the situation for the late nineteenth century, Edward Marks, a major song publisher, looked back on the scene from the vantage point of 1927, the year *The Jazz Singer* opened: "A successful song had to be noble, sorrowful, Irish, or all four. Moreover, thirty-six of the hundred and thirty songs [on his list of top hits] came directly from England . . . it was a distinctly British period in the tune business." But earlier, in 1897, when Irish-American entertainer George M. Cohan brought an Irish tune to Marks and his partner, they turned him down flat: "'No more Irish,' Joe and I chorused, for we had seen the ragtime handwriting on the wall."[5]

Despite the flow and flux of trends, the music industry also relied on stable topics, marketable over the decades. One constant was the need for nostalgia in a nation of dislocation. Even back in Russell's time, he succeeded with "one of the most persistent themes of the nineteenth century—nostalgia for youth, home, parents, old friends, lost innocence."[6] It is always easy for entertainers—and politicians—to peddle nostalgia to a country built on mobility and the fast turnover of popular culture. By constant repetition of this topic through the image of the antebellum plantation, minstrelsy overlapped with longlasting American reactionary trends and social anxieties.

Another durable formula common to both minstrelsy and its competitors (and still very much alive in the twenty-first century) is ethnic stereotyping, a kind of pop culture commentary on the integration of immigrants as both producers and consumers. Marks noted the appearance of "first the Irish comic song, then the Italian, and very shortly afterward the Yiddish—the cycle closed in 1920 with 'The Argentines, the Portuguese, the Armenians, and the Greeks.' In each case, the crop of songs followed from ten to twenty years after the main tide of immigration, as the arrivals impressed themselves on the public consciousness."[7]

The successive cresting of immigrant-topic song waves speaks to the main urge that keeps the entertainment machine in high gear as a capitalized and commodified enterprise: the need for stable stars, formats, and structures of feeling to combine with the constant commotion of novelty genres, topical titillation, and new media.

In 1927, *The Jazz Singer* offered new packaging with old contents—minstrelsy and immigrants—just three years after Congress cut off the flow of immigrants to America and two years before the Depression relegated both minstrelsy and ethnic recordings to the realm of obscurity in terms of sales and meaning. By this time, a generation of enterprising, naturalized Jewish-Americans had made their mark on entertainment. Born around 1880, the year the great influx of Eastern Europeans began, they had already invented their own forms of popular culture back in the modernizing Jewish communities of the Russian Empire.

The first datable item of stage music from the fledgling Yiddish theater was written in 1881 in the Romanian city of Jassy, and it consists of "different national songs," including Russian, Romanian, Tyrolean, Chinese, and, prophetically, "Negro." What is crucial here is that this outward-looking and stereotyping impulse, born in the backwoods of Eastern Europe, coincides with the main thrust of American popular entertainment. These energetic Jewish immigrants brought their enthusiasm and skillful eclecticism to New York, where they found it was marketable. Popular culture offered an escalator you could step on at the bottom and take up to a higher economic, if not social, level. It is hardly surprising that Irving Berlin turned his back on the Lower East Side "ghetto," pitched his songs to the popular song studios on Fourteenth Street, and turned out "Marie of Sunny Italy" and "Yiddle on your Fiddle, Play Some Ragtime" as his first hits. Even before Berlin emerged, there was a Sadie Kominsky who wrote mock-black ragtime pieces.

Berlin's generation included a great many street urchins, including Jolson, who rode the popular entertainment machine to better neighborhoods. Often enough, the first stop was coated in black, the color of the burnt cork smudged on them automatically by talent brokers such as the sponsors of the amateur talent show Sophie Tucker wandered into when she came to New York to escape the milieu of her parents' Hartford delicatessen. The ritualized plantation setting and language that revues and vaudeville inherited from minstrelsy suited immigrants well. The pseudo-southern accent covered their poor English.

By looking and sounding conventionally "black," Jews could become, provisionally, "white." In the social reality that lay outside the theater, Jews remained perched between "black" (i.e., racially other) and "white" for some decades to come, alighting on the "white" side in the late 1950s, when institutional quotas and residential exclusion began to ebb. The Irish had undergone a similar process in the nineteenth century, when they rose through the civil and entertainment ranks, starting as an "alien race" and ending in "white" respectability as heads of both theater syndicates and big-city political machines.

## *THE JAZZ SINGER:* BEYOND BLACKFACE

*The Jazz Singer* harnessed the power of blackface and immigration, using the spontaneous combustion of a major national star at the height of his powers to appeal to both an influential Jewish urban audience and a broader American public. The film includes blackface, but not substantially. Jolson's breakthrough live-action songs appear in three scenes, two of which are corkless; only the closing number offers the full minstrel regalia hinted at in the backstage blacking-up scene. Beyond the sparse sound sequences that offer the sizzle of stardom, *The Jazz Singer* is mainly a "silent" film with an orchestral score—a little-remembered fact. There are no fewer than eighty-five musical numbers in the film.[8]

These items look like a checklist of conventions: popular songs, including some by Jewish immigrant songwriters, an arrangement of a Hasidic melody, a Yiddish didactic song and synagogue favorites sung by the star cantor Yossele Rosenblatt, a made-to-order "mother" song co-written by Jolson, and a slew of symphonic excerpts, including snippets of Tchaikovsky, Lalo, and Sibelius. Taken as a whole, this pioneering soundtrack is as encyclopedic as American entertainment itself. The blackface moments we find so startling are inserted into an overarching framework that tells the whole story of sound and sensibility, socially situated.

Blackface is not a unitary tradition, and by 1927, it had floated free of its anchor, minstrelsy and the plantation setting. Surely *The Jazz Singer* relies on the inner vitality that whites associate with blackness to counteract the class and immigrant handicaps of its hero. Yet the real emotional mooring comes from Jakie Rabinowitz/Jack Robin's mother, who benefits from the accompaniment of both Tchaikovsky's *Romeo and Juliet*, which literally underscores the film's Oedipal theme and Jolson's more restrained tribute, "Mother of Mine." The latter is particularly generic, descending from a long line of Irish mother songs, but addressed here to a Yiddish mama. The Jewish mother reciprocates this tribute from American popular culture by embracing her son's blackface turn from his cantorial heritage. For the first time, the Jewish mother and the black mammy are linked. The silver-haired, care-worn lady beams while her son sings about a fictitious black Alabama nanny.

Al Jolson in blackface in *The Jazz Singer* (1927).

This overlap of sensibilities clashes sharply with the most famous contemporary Jewish mother song, "My Yiddishe Mama," released in 1925 with a Yiddish text on one side of the record and an English version on the flip side. Sophie Tucker's big hit uses the Yiddish vernacular to attack its audiences with a wrenching depiction of filial guilt, exposing the gap between a deeply felt immigrant use of the mother theme and Hollywood's generic version. Jolson's "Mother of Mine" represents a kind of standardization that highlights popular culture's clever crafting of sentimental stability. It is designed to reach the widest audience, belying the apparent narrative interest in immigration and ethnicity, with a blackface coating.

Berlin's "Blue Skies" is the most spontaneous number in *The Jazz Singer*, and, like "Mammy," it is sung straight to mother. At the time, Berlin, like his immigrant songwriter colleagues, was felt to have a special sensibility—"the tear in the voice"— that allowed him deeper access to the wellsprings of feeling and creativity. Their music was understood to bubble up from an almost genetic source of deep ethnic/racial/religious feeling. Yet "Blue Skies," like most of his work, was remarkably generic, just as the earliest melodies of nineteenth-century minstrelsy had little to do with vernacular black roots. Berlin came to public attention with "Alexander's

Ragtime Band," a surprisingly non-ragtime sounding song. Written for a nonspecific audience, the vast majority of the Jewish songwriter's output has little contextual grounding, as Hamm points out: "There is no way to tell, from listening to a song by Irving Berlin or any of his contemporaries, whether it was written for vaudeville, musical comedy, the movies, or simply composed for radio play and possibly recording," or to be sung and whistled by people of any generation, country of origin, or social position.[9]

Of course, what is so striking about *The Jazz Singer*, as with all Hollywood sound film until the 1940s, is the absence of an African-American presence. This makes Jolson's blackface seem almost an innocent ingredient in the stew of Jewish ethnic numbers, generic songs, and wallpaper classical underscoring that make up the film's musical mosaic. There is a certain thoughtlessness, vividly expressed in the automatism of his hand gestures while covering his face with blackness—even as he tortures himself over his ethnic identity. His triumphant smile when he sees his minstrel mask in the mirror, quashing all doubts about assimilation, drives home the point of exclusion. Susan Gubar writes that Jakie Rabinowitz, Jack Robin, and Al Jolson himself "appear to suffer the torture they inflict on the black male body."[10] But it is unlikely that Jolson, who brooked no competition from rivals of any race, identified much with the absent blacks of *The Jazz Singer*.

## DISPLACING BLACKFACE

Moments of black-Jewish interaction with entertainment have changed shape with the times. Rogin points to Robert Rossen's *Body and Soul* (United Artists, 1947) as an explicit attempt by left-wing Jewish screenwriters and directors to keep Jewish and black figures in the same social space.[11] In the film, John Garfield plays a Jewish slum boy who has close and traumatic interactions with black boxers as he rises to become the champ. The song "Body and Soul" is consistently used by composer Hugo Friedhofer to underscore emotional scenes. Written by Jewish songwriter Johnny Green, and popularized by Jewish bandleader Benny Goodman and black saxophonist Coleman Hawkins, it can stand in for decades of unspoken collaboration between African-Americans and Jewish-Americans. But what it might have signified as a social statement for the film viewers in the late forties has been lost to our knowledge, over fifty years later.

Left undiscussed is the music that accompanies the opening sequence of *Body and Soul*. The hero awakens after a nightmare about the black boxer he has beaten and injured, and races downtown from his training camp to see his Jewish mother and non-Jewish girlfriend (shades of *The Jazz Singer*). This scene is set to what was eventually called "a jazz score" and is in fact an early appearance of the style, which is usually associated with later films, like Leith Stevens's score for *The Wild One* (Columbia, 1954) or Elmer Bernstein's work on *The Man with the Golden Arm* (United Artists, 1955).

Both Stevens's and Bernstein's writings about their scores, which portray the lives of troubled white Americans, attribute the use of jazz elements to either generalized big-city "hysteria and despair"[12] or "exhibitionistic . . . confused and wondering," inarticulate youth.[13] This justification glosses over any possible audience identification with the African-American sources of the music. But Shelly Manne's frenetic (white) drumming in *The Man with the Golden Arm* might well have struck a "black" chord with viewers accustomed to explicit indexing of these components in earlier films. (For example, a 1930s Betty Boop cartoon, featuring the Louis Armstrong orchestra, cuts back and forth between the live black drummer and the animated image of a cannibal banging a cooking pot.)

It is in these attenuated, ventriloquized ways that the traditions of blackface have lived on, much longer than the obvious displays of blackface from the 1930s to 1950s by non-Jewish stars like Mickey Rooney and Fred Astaire. A common continuation of the Bernstein approach comes in the frequent narrative move of white people who spontaneously break into Motown songs whenever they need to truly bond, which happens continuously across the film and television landscape. Usually we see constrained white families or groups of buddies that need to break the ice with each other by invoking the sounds of soul at key narrative junctures—in shows or films that have no visible or important characters of color. This kind of everyday, exclusionary incorporation of blackness tends to be the current form of reference to the older issues this essay addresses.

More recently, the Motown move might be replaced by rap. In a mindless television movie, for example, we see a teenage nerd pumping himself up to accost pretty girls at a party by carrying on an interior rap monologue. His blacking up is purely mental, but voyeuristically visualized for the viewer. This internalized mimicry is yet another ingenious method of displacing blackface.

Even the techniques of outright ethnic ventriloquism have hardly vanished from American media, as Patricia

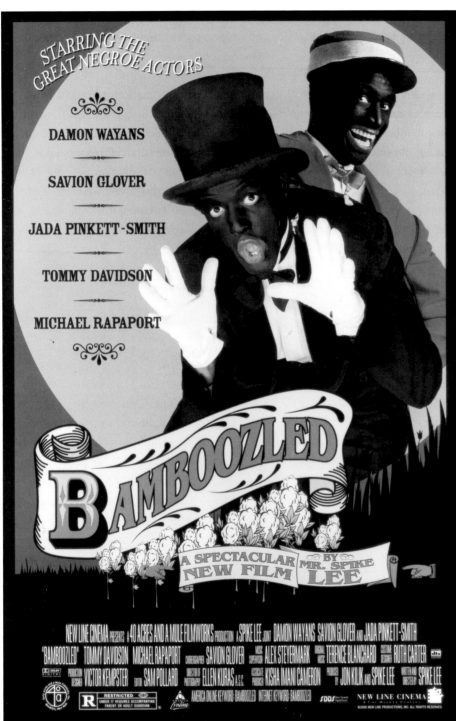

Poster for *Bamboozled*
(2000).

Williams points out in a scathing analysis of the "lovable" character Jar Jar Binks in *Star Wars Episode I: The Phantom Menace* (Twentieth Century Fox, 1999).[14] Blackface may have been ruled out of order in today's entertainment, but the use of "spaceface" in sci-fi vehicles shows just how far the tentacles of old showbiz monsters can reach across the years. Both exclusionary incorporation and blatant caricature are long-term descendants of the older forms of American entertainment.

Significant differences do separate past and present practices. Jolson's grease-paint was external, while the more recent forms are internal. As an exterior marker, by Jolson's later film days in the early 1930s, blackface had become outdated. In one of those films, a quartet of musicians pursues him from the recording studio through the streets of the city, imploring him to abandon "Mammy." They are splashed by a passing truck, turn black, and end up backing up his triumphant minstrelsy.

The scene is designed to make Jolson look like what we would call today a pop music dinosaur: stubbornly anachronistic and proud of it. Film discourse on stage and screen had moved to newer, more sophisticated stylings, such as the early all-white Hollywood musical or the all-black neo-plantation films that began as early as 1929 with *Hallelujah* (MGM). In the 1930s, the southern white playwriting duo of DuBose and Cora Heyward penned both *Mamba's Daughters* and *Porgy* about the colorful life of Carolina African-Americans. The latter work was raised to new dramatic and musical heights by George Gershwin, whose status grew from Jewish songwriter to operatic composer by imitating the vernacular song of a black community. The move that began in the 1950s toward internalized coding of white settings and characters, leading from the jazz score through Motown mouthings, seems perhaps even more thorough as a process of ethnic erasure.

In 2000, Spike Lee made an audacious move, bringing old-fashioned, excruciatingly literal blackface back to public attention. In his film *Bamboozled* (New Line), a cynical African-American television writer produces a blackface show performed by African-Americans, which becomes a national hit, only to bring death and disaster to the principals. Lee skewers everyone, including the Jewish industry types that rationalize the return of minstrelsy. Brilliant and caustic as its premise and production numbers are, *Bamboozled* was critically treated more as an oddity than a sensation, and vanished quickly from the screens. As Paul Gilroy argues forcefully in *Against Race*, we have moved into a "post-race" phase where bodies—even black ones—figure more as tools of consumerism than as political pawns.[15]

Still, we should recoil reflexively and retrospectively at any display—however covert—of the minstrel mask and closely scrutinize its Jewish wearers of earlier decades. We should also see the blackface moment that culminated in *The Jazz Singer*, along with its metamorphoses since then, as part of a durable structure of race-conscious sentiment, crafted through music, that became integrated into American life over many generations of entertainment. Its traces have been painted over, but not erased.

# AN AMERICAN AT HOME, A JEW ON THE AIR

**THE PASTIME** OF INDIVIDUAL HOBBYISTS IN THE FIRST
DECADES OF THE TWENTIETH CENTURY, RADIO BECAME A WIDELY POPULAR NATIONAL BROADCAST MEDIUM BY
THE EARLY 1930S. THE 1930 CENSUS REPORTED THAT 46 PERCENT OF FAMILIES IN AMERICA HAD A RADIO
RECEIVER; 67 PERCENT OF AMERICAN HOMES HAD RADIOS BY 1935 AND 81 PERCENT BY 1940. During the hardest years of the Great Depression, media historian Erik Barnouw notes, "millions sat spellbound nightly" as they listened to popular comedic and musical broadcasts.[1]
The virtual community created by radio was simultaneously intimate and national in its impact, as Gerald Nachman recalls in *Raised on Radio*: "From this small box . . . I learned much of what I knew about honor, romance, justice, evil, humor, manhood, motherhood, marriage, women, law and order, history, sports, and families. I was told how life was meant to unfold and what America was all about. As I stretched out listening to it, night after night for a decade from my young boyhood into my midteens, the world seemed—sounded, rather—intimate, manageable, and coherent yet at the same time vast and mysterious and thrilling."[2]

While radio flourished at the same time that Hollywood was transformed by the advent of "talking pictures," the two media are a study in contrasts. Movies transformed the nature of public entertainment, creating a new pastime and a novel setting; radio brought an important innovation to private life, reshaping domestic spaces by linking them with a vast, virtual public sphere. Whereas Hollywood gave pride of place to creating long, narrative features, radio emphasized variety, broadcasting a great diversity of musical and spoken presentations that ranged from sporting events to religious sermons, soap operas to quiz shows, newscasts to dance-band concerts. The film industry was financed by ticket sales; radio's income was generated more indirectly by selling advertising time to sponsors of its broadcasts. And while the film industry generally avoided direct governmental regulation, broadcasters had to comply with regulations mandated by the Federal Communications Commission and other agencies.

Although Jews figured prominently among the ranks of radio's creators—including network chiefs William Paley (CBS) and David Sarnoff (NBC)—the medium was not subject to the same degree of public scrutiny during its heyday in the 1930s and 1940s as a "Jewish" invention. Production of many nationally aired series was based in New York, providing numerous Jewish writers and performers working in vaudeville and legitimate theater with access to a public forum of unprecedented scope. Radio enabled performers such as Jack Benny, Gertrude Berg, George Burns, Fanny Brice, Eddie Cantor, and Ed Wynn to reach a national audience.

The Jewishness of these artists, however, generally played no direct role in their radio performances, even though it often informed their stage work more explicitly.

Brice, for example, was renowned for comic, Yiddish-inflected dialect routines on stage; on radio, she became best known as the precocious Baby Snooks. On their comedy variety shows, Burns and Benny offered carefully honed performances of "themselves" as performers. Benny surrounded his on-air persona with a cadre of comic ethnic sidekicks, including the Jewish figures Mr. Kitzel and Shlepperman. The outstanding exception was Berg, creator and star of *The Goldbergs*, a genial situation comedy about Jewish family life in the Bronx. From the late 1920s through the mid-1950s, Berg's creation would be the most widely known Jewish family in America, first on radio, then on film, stage, and television. The forthright, if circumscribed, performance of Jewishness on *The Goldbergs* would prove an anomaly on television. During the same years that the series was telecast, Jewish talents both behind and before the camera on comedy-variety programs such as *Texaco Star Theater* (later known as *The Milton Berle Show*) and *Your Show of Shows* would make only the most occasional, coy reference to Jewishness. Several decades would pass before the latter series would be claimed publicly as a landmark of American Jewish comedy.

Family gathered around
the radio, c. 1950s.

While major Jewish performers seeking to build a national following generally left their own ethnicity off the air, Jewish and other ethnic identities were a staple of radio comedy and drama, following the precedent of vaudeville and the legitimate stage. In this auditory medium, dialect was the key to signaling ethnic types and became the foundation for a distinctive form of language play that was the basis for the medium's humor. "Linguistic slapstick," Susan Douglas observes, "asserted that America was as vibrant, pliable, inventive, absorptive, defiant, and full of surprises as its language. And it claimed that that vibrancy came from the bottom up, not from the top down."[3]

Though dialects, names, and other markers were used to signal various ethnic groups on radio, they were also understood as something that anyone could learn to imitate and reproduce. As central as ethnicity was to radio comedies, the medium also intimated that these identities were performative rather than innate. On radio, Irish-Americans portrayed Italians, Italian-Americans played Jews, Jewish-Americans played Greeks, and, perhaps most famously, two white men portrayed the most popular African-American characters on the airwaves in *Amos 'n' Andy*.[4]

As Yiddish expressions and inflections served as ethnic signals on mainstream American radio, Yiddish-language programming flourished on several stations in major American cities. Along with Yiddish-language films made in the United States during the 1930s and 1940s, these broadcasts constituted alternative media that spoke to immigrants in their native language. During these decades, Yiddish film and

radio bore witness to the language's gradual shift from the vernacular of hundreds of thousands of recent arrivals from Eastern Europe to a language of heritage, used in performances of nostalgia as well as parody.

Beginning in the mid-1930s, broadcasters also explored radio's potential as a medium for "high" drama. Radio plays, such as those produced for CBS by the Columbia Workshop, sought to demonstrate that radio drama could effectively present topics of serious social concern to general audiences. Among the genre's most accomplished authors was Norman Corwin. Scripts that he wrote during World War II—*They Fly through the Air* (1939), *We Hold These Truths* (1941), *On a Note of Triumph* (1945)—celebrated American democracy while reviling fascism.

American radio became a site of concern for American Jews when they were targeted by one of the most popular radio personalities of the 1930s. At the beginning of the decade, Father Charles E. Coughlin developed a national following for his populist, anti-Communist radio sermons, aired weekly on CBS. When Coughlin's exhortations against American banks and the financial policies of the Roosevelt administration grew explicitly anti-Semitic in the late 1930s, his broadcasts became the subject of a landmark campaign by American Jewish leaders against defamation in the media.[5]

On radio, the Coughlin case was exceptional in its scope; however, it epitomized a disquieting expression of anti-Semitism in the American public sphere. The networks responded to the challenge posed by Coughlin's controversial broadcasts by instituting ecumenical religious broadcasting that provided a forum for a diversity of viewpoints and that emphasized shared ethical values among America's religious communities over denominationalism. This prompted the Jewish Theological Seminary to collaborate with NBC during the mid-1940s to produce the series *The Eternal Light*, which would eventually prove to be one of the most enduring venues for the presentation of Judaism on the airwaves, broadcasting on radio and, later, television for over forty years.

—J.H./J.S.

# THE MEDIA THAT "SPEAK YOUR LANGUAGE": AMERICAN YIDDISH RADIO AND FILM

J. HOBERMAN AND JEFFREY SHANDLER

During the middle decades of the twentieth century, alternative Jewish media flourished in the United States, distinguished from mainstream film and broadcasting by the language used: Yiddish. The mother tongue of most Jewish immigrants from Eastern Europe, Yiddish was also spoken, or at least understood, by many of their American-born children. Though only briefly popular and addressed to a limited community, Yiddish films and radio broadcasts are among the most expressive achievements of immigrant Jewish popular culture, and they shed light on the range and influence of American mainstream entertainment.

The forty feature length American Yiddish talkies and numerous short subjects made between the advent of sound and the end of World War II constituted the largest corpus of films made in the United States for an American audience in a language other than English.[1] Catering largely to an immigrant public, Yiddish films provided an American ethnic community with its own cinematic universe. In these films, everyone—cantors, seamstresses, psychiatrists, police officers, judges, Negro servants, Polish aristocrats, Ukrainian peasants, and even anti-Semites—not only speaks Yiddish but inhabits an imaginary world in which Yiddish is the predominant, sometimes the sole language and where Yiddish-speakers' sensibilities are central, not peripheral. At the same time, these films aspired to emulate the aesthetics of Hollywood film genres—musical comedies (*Zayn vaybs lyubovnik* [His Wife's Lover], High Art Pictures, 1931), contemporary issue films (*Der vanderender yid* [The Wandering Jew], Jewish American Film Arts, 1933), and prestigious literary adaptations (*Grine felder* [Green Fields], Collective Film Producers, 1937)—while offering variations on the intergenerational melodramas that were the mainstay of the American Yiddish stage (*Vu iz mayn kind?* [Where Is My Child?], Menorah Productions, 1937).

Poster for the 1937 American Yiddish talking picture *Vu iz mayn kind?* (Where Is My Child?). Yiddish talkies more often centered on intergenerational conflict than romantic love.

Maurice Schwartz, in costume, directing the Yiddish talking picture *Tevye* on location outside Jericho, Long Island, 1939. Schwartz played the title role in this film, the most expensive Yiddish talkie produced in the United States.

The quintessence of immigrant culture, American Yiddish films demonstrate the distinctive cultural creativity of a community intensely negotiating the disparities between "Old" and "New" Worlds. Though modern in form, these films are often unabashedly nostalgic in content. This is especially true of the films made on the eve of World War II, as the future of the East European Jewish way of life that they celebrate seemed increasingly imperiled. The most lavish and perhaps best remembered of American Yiddish films, *Tevye der milkhiker* (Tevye the Dairyman, Maymon Films, 1939), anticipated the Broadway musical *Fiddler on the Roof* in adapting Sholem Aleichem's popular stories of Tevye, a simple Jew living in a Ukrainian village at the turn of the century. Released only a few months after the Nazi invasion of Poland, the film was made from the vantage point of American Jews, who were casting a wary eye toward the future of their East European relatives.

Similarly, Yiddish radio was, in its heyday, one of the most popular forms of alternative-language broadcasting in the United States. As early as 1923, the Yiddish journalist (and future Socialist city councilman) B. Charney Vladek attempted to enlist the *Jewish Daily Forward*'s editor, Abraham Cahan, and even RCA's David Sarnoff in the creation of a Yiddish-language radio station in New York City.[2] Within a few years, stations in New York, Philadelphia, Chicago, and other cities

There's
Freedom in
the Newton
Hills---for
Jewish and
Ukranian
Actors,
Monks,
Nudists and
Nazis

A Dramatic Moment in the Jewish Folk Motion-Picture with Music, "The Singing Blacksmith," Which Was "Shot" Near Newton, New Jersey.

Between Scenes Leah Noemi Does a Little Knitting Atop a Modern American Car Parked on the Old Russian Set.

Anna Appel, Famous Character Actress of the Jewish Theatre, Portrays the "Matchmaker" in the Motion Picture Version of David Pinski's "Jacob, the Smith."

# Hollywood in Miniature

ONLY five miles from Camp Nordland, the Nazi stronghold in New Jersey, members of a Jewish acting company made a moving picture in their own tongue. For this convincing proof that freedom of belief, ideals and artistic expression exist in our democracy, you need only have taken a trip to the region around Newton, the county seat of Sussex County, New Jersey.

As might have been expected, farmers and dairymen were going about their usual Summer tasks, with only a passing interest in the Nazis or the Jewish actors. You might have come across numerous followers of the fine art of fishing, tourists and campers, and a colony of sun-worshippers who believe in getting a tan all over at a nudist camp. The replica of the Russian peasant-village-before-the-Revolution where scenes were being filmed for the Jewish movie, is near the Shrine of the Little Flower at the Monastery of the Benedictine Order. And the cinematographers and sound men who did the technical work of recording the dialogue and singing and action of the Jewish actors all answer to definitely Irish names!

There's freedom in "them thar hills" around Newton!

We weren't particularly interested in either the Nazis or the nudists but we were curious about the Little Hollywood that's sprung up in Jersey, so we sent a colorphotographer (name of Flanagan!) to get some shots of the Jewish actors at work. The pictures on this page are a few he brought back. He also brought back the information that the film is being produced by the Collective Film Producers, Inc., who last year made the successful "Green Fields." This year's picture is titled "The Singing Blacksmith" and is based on a novel by David Pinski called "Jacob the Smith."

Edgar G. Ulmer directed the cast of more than 50 headed by the star, Moishe Oysher, and including such favorites of the Jewish stage as Anna Appel, Paul Baratoff, Miriam Rissell, Max Vodnoy, Florence Weiss, Leah Noemi and Michael Goldstein. There might be another Paul Muni among them!

Miriam Rissell Touches Up Her Lips for the Next Scene. The Sign Behind Her Tells Us That She Is Standing in Front of a Dry-Goods Store in the Make-Believe Village.

A Horse from a Jersey Farm Gets a New Harness and a Part in the Russian Story Being Filmed. Veteran Actor Max Vodnoy Gives Him an Encouraging Pat As He Steps Before the Camera.

OPPOSITE
A production story on the Yiddish talking picture *Yankl der shmid* (Yankl the Blacksmith; known in English as *The Singing Blacksmith*), published in the Sunday supplement of the *New York Mirror*, September 18, 1938.

RIGHT
Yiddish stage and film star Molly Picon on the set of the 1929 Vitaphone short *A Little Girl with Big Ideas*, produced by Warner Bros. Although Picon ordinarily spoke unaccented English, here she employed a heavy Yiddish accent.

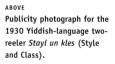

ABOVE
Publicity photograph for the 1930 Yiddish-language two-reeler *Stayl un kles* (Style and Class).

ABOVE
Scene from the 1939 Yiddish talking picture *Mayn zindele* (My Sonny). On the wall are photographs of leading Yiddish stage personalities, including Molly Picon.

with large Jewish populations offered regular broadcasts in Yiddish: news reports, soap operas and other dramas, religious programs, musical and comedy shows. These stations were a marginal presence within the spectrum of radio broadcasting, often found at the extreme ends of the dial and transmitting at a much lower wattage than network stations, therefore reaching a much more localized audience. Sometimes they also shared their place on the dial with other stations, and this led to some striking juxtapositions. The most famous Yiddish radio station, New York's WEVD, once split its on-air time with WBBR, which was owned by the Jehovah's Witnesses.[3]

Yiddish radio announcer Zvee Scooler.

WEVD was one of the first stations to bring Yiddish to the American airwaves. It was founded in 1926 to disseminate the same socialist message received by the readers of the *Jewish Daily Forward*, which acquired the station in 1932. (The station's call letters pay tribute to Socialist Party leader Eugene V. Debs.) Known for decades as the "station that speaks your language," WEVD also presented programming in Spanish, German, Italian, Turkish, and Japanese. With the advent of additional New York–area stations airing Yiddish programming during the 1930s, radio became an important venue for a variety of performers, especially musical talents, both sacred and secular. The latter included Yiddish stage artists Molly Picon, who had her own series on WMCA, and Zvee Scooler, whose weekly commentaries in verse on current events earned him the title of WEVD's *grammayster* (master of rhyme). Yiddish radio also became an important vehicle for presenting the virtuousity of Jewish instrumentalsts, such as the klezmer clarinetists Dave Tarras and Naftuli Brantwein.

While Yiddish radio was essentially a secular undertaking, cantorial singing proved a popular staple of its music programming, presenting the cantor's art in broadcasts that blurred traditional boundaries between the sacred and the secular. Among a number of cantors who took to the ether, Moyshe Oysher, an international star on the Yiddish stage and leading man in several Yiddish musical films, became a fixture of Yiddish radio in the 1930s, where he was known as *der maysterzinger fun zayn folk* (the mastersinger of his people). Radio proved an especially important venue for *khazntes*, or "lady cantors," who could perform on stage or on the air, but not in synagogues.

# RADIO OR PHONOGRAPH?

The advent of new media technologies had a defining impact on American family life throughout the twentieth century. The English-language section of the *Jewish Daily Forward* noted the effect on Yiddish-speaking immigrants and their American-born children in a 1924 article debating the respective virtues of the radio versus the phonograph. At the time, Yiddish-language broadcasting hadn't yet begun, so the choice between the two media had profound cultural as well as linguistic implications that separated the two generations.

L. Honors, "Radio—Phonograph: That's the Bone of Contention in Jewish Families These Days," *Jewish Daily Forward*, August 3, 1924, p. 3.

The radio, to my mind, is the most Jewish of all instruments. It does a great deal of talking. And, though one may not see the talker, he can easily imagine him standing near the microphone, waving his hands up and down and shouting his lungs away. A most enjoyable occupation, since no one can stop him. For that matter, a most harmless instrument, as it can easily be shut off.

But, as with most inventions and machineries, the radio has brought unhappiness to many a poor home. Indeed, it is a new source of jealousy, futile longing, broken hearts and broken pocketbooks. . . . In many a poor family, the problem now arises as to what to buy, a phonograph or a radio. The price is about the same; the benefits are not.

So the whole family gathers round the famous table and takes up the burden of the problem.

During the discussion, the following interesting division may be noticed. On one side are the heads of the family, the father and mother. Siding with them are the older children, those who were born on the other side, who have received their training and education in Russia, in Germany, in Austria, in Hungary, or in Roumania. They talk English more or less fluently, but they converse in a still better Yiddish or Russian or German. They enjoy a Yiddish or Russian show, they have a taste for the best in literature, they have an ear for music. They vote for a phonograph.

Opposed to them is the new generation, the boys and girls who were born and brought up in this country. Physically well developed, they have a natural urgency for every intemperance that will afford a release for their superabundance of bodily energy. Noise, sports, exciting dancing, adventure, danger—whatever makes for immediate action, for vigorous motion draws their hearts and fires their imagination. They have no taste nor desire for the subtle, the fine, the nuances. Gloom, thoughtfulness, intellectual considerations are not for them. These are the children of a young and vigorous soil, and their faculties are young and pulsating. Their vote is cast for the radio. . . .

Both sides admit in the discussion that the proper thing to do is to get both a radio and a Victrola. The former keeps one in touch with the daily world, the latter affords an opportunity to listen to the world's classics as often as one desires. The older generation could listen to their heart's content to Jewish tunes and pieces by Jewish comedians. The younger set could get in touch with any broadcasting station and open floodgates of noise and merriment and dance themselves into physical exhaustion.

Much of American Yiddish radio was in fact bilingual, mixing Yiddish and English within the same program—sometimes within a single sentence. The Barry Sisters, a singing duo who began their career as the Bagelman Sisters, performed an extensive bilingual repertoire of popular tunes on their program, *Yiddish Melodies in Swing* (WHN, 1939–55), which "takes old Jewish folk songs and mixes them in the smart uptown fasion of Yiddish swing."[4]

The disparities between the original Yiddish lyrics and their English versions evince a playful sense of movement back and forth between tradition and modernity, as well as between "majority" and "minority" cultural sensibilities. In contrast to the dialect humor heard on network American broadcasts—in which Jews, as part of a range of American ethnic types, were mocked from a nativist perspective[5]—the bilingual humor of American Yiddish performers demonstrated their sense of mastery over the challenge of integrating into the American mainstream while maintaining ties to their distinctive immigrant heritage.

Following the practice of mainstream broadcasting, most Yiddish radio programs were underwritten by sponsors, including both businesses catering specifically to Jewish consumers (for example, Manischewitz Matzo Company) and national concerns, such as Planters Peanut Oil, St. Joseph Aspirin, and Campbell's Soup. Yiddish-language commercials for these products epitomize a sense of Jewish immigrants' "at-homeness" in America, signifying their identity as a consumer market.

World War II transformed American Yiddish radio, providing it with a new subject of interest as well as new performers and audiences. In the late 1930s, Horowitz Margareten Co., a manufacturuer of kosher foods, sponsored WMCA's *Jewish Refugee Theater*, which featured peformances by artists fleeing Nazi persecution in Europe. After the war, broadcasts organized by the United Service for New Americans aired on both Yiddish- and English-language stations presented profiles of survivors of the Holocaust.

Unlike the undercapitalized and risky Yiddish film business, the relatively inexpensive and flexible medium of Yiddish radio endured during the postwar years, providing scattered listeners with a virtual public gathering place, where Yiddish remains to this day—at least symbolically—the lingua franca. In 1960, thirty-three radio stations in the United States carried Yiddish programming.[6] Today, regular Yiddish broadcasts continue to be heard on stations in such cities as Washington, D.C., Cleveland, Portland (Oregon), and Boston, in addition to New York. These programs serve a diverse audience that includes orthodox Jews, older immigrants (especially recent arrivals from the former Soviet Union), as well as younger American-born Jews drawn to the "revival" of klezmer music and Yiddish culture.[7] Although the Forward Association sold WEVD to ABC in 2002, *The Forward Hour*, which debuted on this station in 1932, continues to air weekly, making it one of the longest-running radio programs in the history of broadcasting.

# "THE YIDDISH DIALECT"

On American radio, ethnicity was performed through sound. Actors could master dozens of dialects that inflected English according to conventions, established on the vaudeville stage, of how different ethnic communities spoke. The following is an excerpt of instructions for performing a Yiddish dialect, which marked Jewish characters in radio comedies. Note how stereotypes of behavior and temperament are linked to conventions of speech patterns.

From Lewis Herman and Marguerite Shalett Herman, *Foreign Dialects: A Manual for Actors, Directors and Writers* (New York: Theatre Arts Books, 1943), 392–413, passim.

## THE YIDDISH DIALECT

Yiddish, though a hybrid language, is a common means of communication in the older Jewish settlements of Europe. Jews born and educated in these foreign communities and emigrating to new lands will often carry with them the Yiddish language or its accents. For this reason, the Yiddish a Jew speaks varies radically according to what country he was born and brought up in. . . . It would be impossible, however, to treat all these national variations and that is why the rules given in this chapter are broad generalities. Nevertheless, if the rules are used as suggested, a credible and characteristic Yiddish dialect can be achieved.

In the same way, it would be difficult to give a thumbnail sketch of the Yiddish character without omitting a great deal of vital material. It is enough to say that the Yiddish character is as varied as its speech.

The Yiddish husband is primarily a good family man. Although the Talmud places the wife in an inferior position in a Jewish household (and few modern Jews now read the Talmud), she is not a drudge as is the German housewife. The family relationships between parents and the children are perhaps as salutary as any in the world. Jewish parents will sacrifice everything for their children's education and welfare. And Jewish children seldom completely forsake their parents.

The Jew rarely drinks liquor. It is customary to sip wine on the holidays, but he almost never becomes intoxicated. In spite of the lack of this usual method of conviviality, he is warm-hearted and quick to make friends. His extreme sentimentality is evidenced by his love of pathos in melodrama, music, and literature.

## THE YIDDISH LILT

As in the Irish, the Cockney, and the Swedish, the Yiddish lilt is one of the most important factors in the dialect. With the substitution of a few vowels and consonants, the use of a few variations in syntax, and the lilt, a Yiddish dialect can be portrayed quite successfully.

Much of the sing-song in the Yiddish lilt can be attributed to the influence of Talmudic scholars and singing cantors. It was these Talmudic scholars who, in the course of their studies, resorted to the Socratic form of questions and answers. The long, involved and formalistic religious argument—often violent but always essentially devotional—has obviously had its effect on Jewish secular life (the relish of argument for argument's sake, the answering of a question with another question) and especially on Jewish speech (the distinctive sing-song lilt). . . .

The pitch of Yiddish speech is much higher than in American and the falsetto is reached many times, especially under the stress of emotion. That is why the Yiddish dialect should have a wide pitch range which, at times, reaches almost incredible, squeaking peaks. But it seldom descends to the lower registers. This wide pitch range accounts for the nasality in the speech which occurs when the high notes are produced in falsetto through the nose, instead of from the throat and chest. The emotional coloring does not, however, speed up the tempo of the speech, as might be expected. . . .

## TYPICAL PHRASES

The color of a dialect is affected by the sentence structure and by certain typical phrases. Yiddish has a great many odd expressions that identify it. For example, an expression of contempt would be voiced by repeating a word immediately after it was spoken by another person and then adding a rhyming word beginning with "shm," as in:

"di pEEkshUH vUz bEHt.""AH! bEHt-shmEHt!"
(The picture was bad.)(Ah! bad-shmad!) . . .

Other typical expressions are: . . .

"mEHik lAHik EHn EHktUH."
(Make like an actor.) . . .

"voot bi AH shEHim fU di nEHibUHz"
(would be a shame for the neighbors) . . .

"shAHrAHp vEEt di frAsh tUk!"
(Shut up with the fresh talk!)

# GOLDBERG VARIATIONS: THE ACHIEVEMENTS OF GERTRUDE BERG

DONALD WEBER

"The Great Gertrude" is how the famous critic of popular culture, Gilbert Seldes, styled Gertrude Berg in 1956. On radio in the 1930s and 1940s, on Broadway, in the movies, and, from 1949 through 1956, on television, she was the most familiar and easily the most recognizable icon of the Jewish matriarch in the American popular imagination. Berg's career was truly remarkable, not only because of the variety of entertainment media she succeeded in mastering, but because she was the constant, creative force behind the microphone. From the beginning of the radio version of *The Goldbergs* (initially titled *The Rise of the Goldbergs*), Berg was the series's only writer—authoring thousands of scripts over the years—producer, and star; she was its guiding light. In the history of twentieth-century American entertainment, there is perhaps no equivalent figure who has incorporated such a range of abilities or achieved such continuous success. There is probably no woman in American popular culture who has assumed, auteurlike, all the creative and commercial responsibilities Gertrude Berg managed to perform in a career spanning thirty-five years.[1]

The story of Berg's achievement on radio and television also allows us to examine—thanks to the rich cache of primary materials from the Berg Papers housed at Syracuse University Library—how her original idea of portraying American Jewish family life to America was received by audiences (both Jews and non-Jews) across the nation. At first, radio executives were wary of a series highlighting the trials and tribulations of an "ethnic" family dreaming of success in America; they worried that the sound of Jewish dialect would offend their listeners' ears. The American public, however, immediately embraced the show when it premiered in November 1929, a month into the Great Depression. *The Goldbergs* enjoyed enormous popularity by the early 1930s (rivaling that of *Amos 'n' Andy*). Letters poured in, often written to Berg in care of the show's Chicago-based sponsor, Pepsodent Toothpaste, about the inspirational agency of her "family." A letter from 1931 captures immediate impact of *The Goldbergs*: "We certainly admire the ideals this family stand [*sic*] for, and the way they reach the inner and higher feelings of us all. In our estimation they are doing more good than all the World Peace Conferences put together. The Goldbergs are to the mind what Pepsodent is to the mouth—they both leave a clean, wholesome feeling not to [*sic*] soon be forgotten."

Perhaps the clearest expression of the show's positive national reputation, in June 1932 (less than three years after its debut), the vice president of Pepsodent reported to Berg that *The Goldbergs* had received

3,302 letters during the month of May *alone*, with 2,838 "compliments on the episodes; only eleven were objections."[2]

Why did *The Goldbergs* generate such an enthusiastic popular response? Why did Berg's portrait of Jewish family life deeply touch the American public in the 1930s? How did the series change over time, from a daily radio series to a 1948 Broadway play *Me and Molly* (running 156 performances), to the feature film *Molly* (Paramount, 1951) to the well-remembered (for those of a certain age) television show *The Goldbergs* (1949–56)?

Cover of *The Rise of the Goldbergs* (1931), a collection of short stories "translated" from the first season of *The Goldbergs* on the radio. The book's introduction was written by Eddie Cantor.

Gertrude Berg's life story and experience were far removed from the Yiddish-inflected world of Tremont Avenue in the Bronx, where she situated her radio family in the 1930s. Born in East Harlem in 1899, Berg attended Wadleigh High School and, for a while, Teacher's College of Columbia University, where she took some writing courses. Contemporary profiles in both Jewish newspapers and show business publications report that Berg spoke English without any accent (early in her career she read Yiddish commercials in transliteration) and had received little in the way of Jewish religious training. Her connection to the Old World of immigrant Jewish life was limited, indirect, filtered mainly through her grandparents' more observant ways and through her occasional trips downtown to the Lower East Side, a still vibrant scene she would often visit in search of inspiration for her shows. "It's Molly!" pushcart peddlers would cry out along Orchard Street in the early 1950s, in recognition of the most famous Old World Jewish mother in American culture.

"I know the streets and I love to shop there," Berg explained to a reporter, along for the photo-op of Berg on Orchard Street. Journeying from her richly appointed rooms on Park Avenue (contemporary profiles situate Berg in uptown comfort, surrounded by high culture symbols of bursting bookcases and modern paintings), Berg walked the East Side streets listening for dialects and searching for bargains.[3]

As for the original Goldberg family, Papa Jake was modeled on her own businessman father, also named Jake. In the summers, her father ran a small Catskills hotel in Fleischmanns, New York, where Berg first entertained Jewish audiences with the skits that would launch her show business career. The children, Samily and Rosily as they were affectionately called on radio, were inspired by her own children, Cherney and Harriet. Uncle David, the only member of *The Goldbergs* who continued to speak with a pronounced Yiddish accent into the 1950s on the television series, survives as a representative of the older generation, along with Tante Elka and various secondary characters.[4]

Berg was often asked to account for the enormous popularity of her show, to explain why her warm vision of ethnic family life captured the public's heart in the 1930s. Some years later, in an article for *Everywoman's Magazine* entitled "Why I Hate the Term 'Soap Opera,'" Berg reflected on the success of *The Goldbergs*: "A good radio serial is one which strikes an affinity with its audience by presenting problems with which listeners, as ordinary people, are familiar. . . . When *The Goldbergs* went on the air for the first time, there was a feeling that it might not go across, because it was too down-to-earth, and that what people wanted was escapist material. . . . Through showing how other people live, a radio serial utilizes its medium, the networks, as a powerful channel for the dissemination of progressive ideas, tolerance, and understanding."[5]

Although it may not be representative, a sampling of listener responses to the radio version of *The Goldbergs*, drawn from the Gertrude Berg Papers, provides us with a palpable sense of how some of the millions of Americans who regularly tuned into its daily fifteen-minute broadcasts related to the program. "Visiting with the Goldbergs" is how a woman and her eighty-four-year-old mother writing to Berg from Maine in 1932 described their ritual evening encounter with Molly Goldberg. The daughter reports: "I heard of a household in a nearby city where no telephone calls are answered between 7:45 and 8:00 because *The Goldbergs* are on the air."[6] *The Goldbergs* on radio thus appears, at least based on this account, to have become a surrogate family for its listeners, enveloping households across the country with the familiar sounds of middle-class experience and the comforting messages of middle-class ideals.

A youthful Gertrude Berg featured on the cover of *Billboard* magazine, October 20, 1934.

For some historians, the 1930s was an anxious time when people often sought soothing narratives to salve the prevailing economic uncertainties. (Think of the appeal of all variety of visionary-millennial movements—political, religious, and social—that characterized this decade.)[7] In this respect, *The Goldbergs* became, at a certain level, a source of cohesion for its worried listeners, perhaps offering some redemptive hope in the figure of Molly Goldberg, the stabilizing matriarch guiding her own family through turbulent times.

Berg was genuinely surprised by the overwhelmingly positive reaction to her imagined Jewish family. She had sought, in creating *The Goldbergs*, to adjust some of the negative stereotypes about Jews she felt had been fostered in the American popular imagination. In this respect, Berg drew on, adapted, and eventually softened the various traditions of "ethnic" humor from vaudeville (the long line of "German" comedy teams, exemplified by Smith and Dale), the dialect stories of Montague Glass ("Potash and Perlmutter" and "Abe and Mauruss"), and, in Berg's own view, the vulgar dialect humor of the mid-1920s cartoonist Milt Gross (above all, in his sketch collections *Nize Baby* and *Dunt Esk!!*). Of course, dialect humor itself incorporates a long line of practitioners, artists who created by various phonological and lexical markers the conventions of "ethnic" expression itself, and Berg may best be situated within this tradition of dialect art. Thus Berg's own *performance* of what has been called the "Jewish voice" was itself a construction, a self-conscious act of expressing what she understood to be the urgent, heartfelt concerns of her Jewish-American, New World citizens.

Consider, for example, a portion of one of Berg's first dialogues, which she performed for Edward R. Murrow on an episode of *Person to Person* in the mid-1950s, and which she reprinted in her 1961 autobiography, *Molly and Me*:

> Jake: Molly, your soup is feet for a kink.
> Molly: You mean a President. Ve're in Amerike, not in Europe.
> Jake: Oy, Molly, soon ve'll be eating from gold plates.
> Molly: Jake, d'you tink it'll taste better?
> Jake: Soch a question.[8]

This exchange already delineates the psychological core of Berg's central characters: Jake (played originally on radio by James G. Waters, the star, only a few years earlier, of the huge Broadway hit *Abie's Irish Rose*), always seeking a fuller material existence; Molly, always tempering his impulsive, excessive desires with a down-to-earth reality check designed to remind him—and, of course, her listeners—about the spiritual and moral costs of acquisition.

Or consider this excerpt from another early radio script of *The Goldbergs*, dated February 1930, titled "Sammy's Bar Mitzvah":

> Mollie: You know, Jake, ull de pipple vhat goes arount saying dat in life is more
>    troubbles den plezzure is ull wrong—I tink so.
> Jake: Bot everybody says so—even de beegest writers.
> Mollie: Oy, dat's because dey didn't found out de secret.
> Jake: Aha! So you found it, ha?
> Mollie: Yes, Jake. Dun't leff. Maybe I'm a plain peison, and I dun't ridd vhat de
>    high writers is writing, bot by myself I found out de whull secret.
> Jake: So tell me too.
> Mollie: You see, Jake, it's true vhat in life is lots of trobbles. Bot de come, dey're
>    here, you go through vid dem, and findished.
> Jake: Nu, so dat's de secret?
> Mollie: Not yat. Bot de goot tings, de plezzures, is never findished. Dey're ulvays
>    vid you—if not outside, den inside.
> Jake: How's dat?
> Mollie: Because ull you got to do is cloise your eyes—vhat am I talking?—not
>    even cloise your eyes—only tink, and ull de nicest fillings, de best experi-
>    ences in your life is beck again, and even more lovely den before. You can
>    live it ull over again! . . .
> Jake: Your secret can't vork for everybody, Mollie. Maybe unly far drimmers like
>    you.
> Mollie: Nu, be a drimmer! Dat's de secret, see?[9]

In this wonderful exchange, we hear a heavily Yiddish-inflected English (again drawing, perhaps, on the stage conventions of an earlier German-Jewish theatrical style), designed to address the emotional needs of its audience less than a year into the Depression. Molly's voicing—really revoicing—of the dreamer's unflappable progressivist vision surely must have reverberated in the hearts and minds of listeners across the country. And if Mollie's homespun rhetoric of dreaming had an impact,

Marquee of the Chicago
Theater, 1934, announcing
"The Goldbergs, All in
Person on Stage, Radio's
Beloved Family."

its effect on her audience may be connected to her own identity as newly arrived American visionary: Molly Goldberg as a *greenhorn* sage recapitulating, indeed incarnating, the country's innermost ideals of historical optimism and resilient, self-reliant striving.

Thus, at one level, the radio *Goldbergs* contained a sediment of national ideals, a rich deposit of folk wisdom unearthed by attentive listeners in the 1930s.[10] Molly, in this respect, looms as an immigrant keeper of the national dream, her dialect-driven English the source of collective inspiration. No longer outsiders, the radio Goldbergs strive to join the consensus, with Molly the symbolic representative of the country's heart, expressing the ideological-mythic ideals of the dominant culture. In contrast to the raw, unsavory dialect art of Milt Gross and the vaudeville "Jew" comics, Berg conjures an unparodic linguistic radio stage of ethnic voices: In the profoundly unironic world of Molly Goldberg, the immigrant's "drimm" does, in fact, equal the American dream.

Berg and the cast of the CBS radio program, *The Goldbergs*, late 1930s. Everett Sloane, second from left, played Sammy Goldberg from 1936 through 1939, when he departed for Hollywood with Orson Welles and was replaced by the first Sammy, Alfred Ryder. Roslyn Silber (center) and James R. Waters (right) were the original Rosie and Jake.

At still another level of feeling, *The Goldbergs* mined the memories of its Jewish listeners. For some, the show even appears to have assuaged shame and anxieties over social marginality and cultural difference; for others, it helped release long-suppressed or simply forgotten ethnic feelings. In the radio series, Berg broadcast shows depicting the family's observance of the High Holidays and Passover, a practice that continued through the early 1950s on television. Berg consulted religious authorities on the "authenticity" of these shows.

In the case of the "Passover Show" on radio, broadcast April 3, 1939, we overhear the family singing—in Hebrew—from the Haggadah when a rock crashes through the window of the Goldbergs' home. This is Berg's striking allusion to Kristallnacht, and one of the few times the show allows history to intrude into the family's life. There were also some episodes that mentioned family members or friends trying to escape from Eastern Europe before the Holocaust.

To these visibly "Jewish" occasions many of her listeners responded with gratitude for Berg's performance and recognition of Jewish liturgy and ritual. After hearing the Yom Kippur show of October 1935, one listener from the midwest wrote to thank Berg on behalf of the two Jewish families in town: It "touched our hearts as it was so real and reminded me of years gone by." A young woman from Los Angeles, responding to the same broadcast, admitted to being "a modern Jew of the younger generation, but [the Yom Kippur show] certainly gave a tug at my heart strings." After listening to the Yom Kippur show of 1943, a Jewish educator from Cleveland thanked Berg because "this series from your facile pen has done more to *set us Jews right* with the 'goyim' than all the sermons ever preached by the Rabbis" (emphasis in original). And after the first *Goldbergs* Yom Kippur show aired on television in 1949, a young woman felt moved to respond, "I admire your courage to depict our Jewish life in such a beautiful way."[11]

From the beginning, Berg's representations of Jewish faith and observance, however abridged or attenuated on the radio, inspired a certain pride in her Jewish listeners. In the process Berg herself became an emblem of nostalgia, a figure associated with the incarnation of ethnic memory. Berg was in her early forties, but she was felt to be of the older generation. Writing in 1942, the assistant superintendent of the Guild for the Jewish Blind invited Berg to visit with her residents. "You seem to be their favorite, especially among the old folks, who adore you and love your program," the administrator explained. "You symbolize for them the lives that they have lived."[12]

In 1934, after the success of the initial radio *Goldbergs*, Berg had a syndicated column in the Jewish press titled "Mamatalks," which served out morsels of homey philosophy, written not in Molly's fractured dialect, but in Berg's own perfect English.[13] "Molly" quickly became a national commodity. In 1944, her new sponsors, Proctor and Gamble, sought to put out, presumably as an advertising device, a "good-will booklet" on the history of *The Goldbergs* to coincide with a comic strip based on the series that was to appear in the *New York Post*. Writing to her sponsors about the strip, Berg assured Proctor and Gamble that she "would have the final say on what was done" and "would naturally see that characters represented would be in every way lovable and lifelike and would permit no caricatures."[14] The comic strip began to appear in June 1944, revisiting the themes of an earlier *Goldbergs* plot titled "Mama Saves the Day." The cartoon panels often concluded with a box titled "Mama Says" and with a fitting moral tag, for example, "Every day a little is some day a lot."[15]

After the second *Goldbergs* run on the radio, Berg took a break from that medium and began writing what eventually opened in late February 1948 on Broadway as *Me and Molly*, another variation of the Goldberg family saga in America. This time, however, the story is set not in the present, but rather in 1919, at the threshold of the family's rise in economic status. In his *New York Times* review, Brooks Atkinson recognized the distinctive quality of Berg's vision of (Jewish) American life: "Even those who tossed it away as trash were compelled to respect some quality in it. For basically it is authentic, not only of the Goldbergs in the Bronx, but of middle-class people all over America who are trying to bring up their children well and live respectable lives. 'Me and Molly' strikes an American average. . . . The real quality of 'Me and Molly' lies in its recognition of familiar things."[16]

Of course, terms like "authentic," "average," and "familiar" resonate as the key, if these days contested, words in Atkinson's appreciation. Despite its ethnic particularity, *Me and Molly* is, more or less, a predictable narrative of Americanization. It staged the moral and economic crisis afflicting a Jewish family in 1919, striving for middle-class respectability in a new apartment in the Bronx. As cartoon illustrations of the period show, the crucial moment in the Goldbergs' transition involves the purchase of a piano—symbolic of their class and cultural arrival—pulled through the window. The matriarch-heroine, as always, saves the day, solving the chronic problem of her bitter husband's longing to run his own dress business by anticipating the need for ready-to-wear dresses sized proportionately so that all women can find a dress according to her body shape. Looking forward, Molly prophesies great things for the family. (The final scene of *Me and Molly* has the Goldbergs moving into a larger apartment in the building.) Looking back, Jewish audiences in 1948 participated in the evocative nostalgia conjured by Berg, the story of *their own* American journey, from steerage to the middle class.

Playbill for *Me and Molly* (1948), the Broadway stage version of *The Goldbergs*.

With the mild success of *Me and Molly*, Berg turned next to the new medium of television. In January 1949, she moved her "family" from radio and Broadway to the small screen, when *The Goldbergs* premiered on CBS, co-starring Philip Loeb as Jake (Loeb had also played Jake on Broadway).[17] Berg also co-wrote a script for a movie version of *The Goldbergs*, which appeared (to substantial commercial success) in March 1951 as *Molly*, starring the entire television cast. *The Goldbergs* on television was hugely popular as well, and Berg received the Emmy Award for Best Actress in 1950.

The story of *The Goldbergs* on television is important, since its relatively short tenure (1949–56) reflects a number of key moments in television history itself. Briefly, *The Goldbergs* can be situated among a cohort of "ethnic" family shows like *Mama* (CBS, 1949–56), about a Scandinavian family in turn-of-the-century San Francisco; *Bonino* (NBC, 1953), a short-lived series about Italian-American life starring Ezio Pinza; *Life with Luigi* (CBS, 1952), with actors such as Carroll Naish and Alan Reed (later the voice of Fred Flintstone) impersonating Italian-American characters; and

Berg on the set of the 1951 Paramount feature film, variously known as *The Goldbergs* and *Molly*.

*Amos 'n' Andy* (CBS, 1951–53), which, like *The Goldbergs*, made the transition from radio to TV. In addition *The Goldbergs* can be linked with early variety shows like *Texaco Star Theater* (NBC, 1948–56) and *Your Show of Shows* (NBC, 1950–54), both of which drew heavily on vaudeville traditions and parody (in fact, Berg made a number of guest appearances with Milton Berle as "Molly").[18]

In its first two television seasons, *The Goldbergs* revisited familiar plots and situations from its radio days. Berg surrounded the family with a vibrant assortment of Jewish relatives and neighbors (played by famous Yiddish theater actors like Menashe Skulnik—who for a while had played Uncle David on radio—Joseph Buloff, and David Opatoshu, as well as emerging actors such as Anne Bancroft, Harvey Lembeck, and Arnold Stang). Some of the shows were set in Pincus Pines, a version of Berg's father's Catskills hotel. In some of the early episodes that survive on kinescope, the Goldbergs even perform vaudeville-like sketches.

The set of the televised version of *The Goldbergs* (CBS), c. 1950.

What is notable about the early television episodes of *The Goldbergs* (1949–51) is how richly connected to the affective world of Jewish America these shows truly are: Berg's pointed use of dialect and Yiddish speech inflections, the plots that depict the hopes and dreams of the Jewish community (domestic and religious), the show's generally *heymish* (cozy) feel. Above all, what marks the high quality of these earliest television *Goldbergs* is the fiery presence of Loeb, an actor highly regarded in the serious New York theater scene, who is terrific as the Goldbergs' discontented paterfamilias. In one 1949 episode, "The Rent Strike," he portrays an outraged Jake defiantly refusing to pay his Bronx landlord's rent increase. In the end, Molly saves the day, softening the landlord by baking a birthday cake for him. "A landlord is also a person," Molly declares. The gift of food and Molly's generous heart overcome the threat of a Bronx tenement rift and the potential of class conflict.[19]

In the summer of 1950, however, Loeb's name appeared in *Red Channels*, a publication that listed those actors and writers who, it was claimed, had various affiliations with left-leaning organizations. Among the subversive activities that Loeb was accused of supporting was a group calling for the integration of baseball. According to most accounts, Berg tried to keep Loeb on *The Goldbergs*, but the pressure from General Foods, the show's sponsor, proved too great. Loeb was taken off the series (Berg paid his salary over the next year), and the program went off the air until the winter of 1952. Loeb was

The original cast of the television version of *The Goldbergs* shows off a family portrait. Left to right: Arlene McQuade, Philip Loeb, Gertrude Berg, and Larry Robinson.

blacklisted for the remainder of his professional life. On September 1, 1955, he swallowed an overdose of sleeping pills after checking into the Hotel Taft. The Loeb affair attracted a sizeable amount of press in 1952. Berg followed Loeb's fate intensely, keeping a scrapbook filled with various clippings about the event.[20]

In retrospect, Loeb's blacklisting and eventual suicide represent the complicated encounter of *The Goldbergs* with an alternate (Jewish) history, specifically, a political history of dissent and social activism that had no place within the corporate-run television landscape of the early 1950s. What kind of Jewish world did *The Goldbergs* ultimately inscribe? Most plotlines avoided head-on discussions of world politics, concentrating instead on family and neighborhood activity with an occasional crime or adventure to liven up the action. In a 1956 profile in *Commentary* titled "The Real Molly Goldberg"—with the show in its final year, the television family transplanted from the Bronx to cozy suburban Haverville (and a new Papa Jake)—Berg explained that sensitive subjects could not be represented on television. "You see, darling," she said in her unaccented English, "I don't bring up anything that will bother people. That's very important. Unions, politics, fundraising, zionism, socialism, inter-group relations, I don't stress them. . . . After all, aren't such things secondary to daily family living? The Goldbergs are not defensive about their Jewishness or especially aware of it." Berg continued, "I keep things average. I don't want to lose friends."[21]

Or, to be frank, corporate sponsorship. After all, most early television, as George Lipsitz has shown, had a complex relation to the emergent world of commodity culture that characterized early 1950s America. The powerful sponsors of "ethnic" television shows often appropriated the moral authority of immigrant memory—through the unimpeachable example of figures like Mama and Molly—to legitimate the contemporary scene of "acquisition." In the case of *The Goldbergs*, Molly appeared as the primary salesperson for General Foods, urging her audience to buy, for example, Sanka coffee. In fact, Berg's alter ego became, by the middle of the decade, a promoter of various products, from *The Molly Goldberg Cookbook* (1955) to a line of dresses for larger women, which Berg herself helped sell in various department stores around the country.

Finally, however, in the wake of the Loeb blacklisting, *The Goldbergs* began losing its necessary relation to the energizing springs of ethnicity itself. By the 1955–56 season, the show, now titled *Molly*, feels awkward, straining under the weight of wacky plots, with relatively little connection to things recognizably "Jewish." The pronounced dialect tones of the radio show (recall the rich exchange of the 1930 "Bar Mitzvah" episode) disappear after 1952. So do episodes depicting Jewish rituals, including Jewish liturgy. Ironically, the Goldberg family's move to antiseptic Haverville looks forward to the emergent world of network television when, by the end of the decade, national syndicates eventually took over the omnipotent role of individual sponsors as the country became geographically connected, "wired" by the laying of coaxial cables, coast to coast. In radical contrast to figures of ethnic memory like Molly and Mama, by the late 1950s, pipe-smoking, WASP men displace Old World women, and suburban fathers seem to know best.

Despite the end of her legendary television show, Berg—true to her endlessly ambitious nature and enormous popularity—continued to perform on stage and television. In the mid-1950s, she was featured in such made-for-TV dramas as *Paris and Mrs. Perlman* (*Alcoa Hour*, 1956), about a widow from the Pittsburgh suburb of

*Red Channels*, published by American Business Consultants, exposed the "Communist front" associations of one hundred fifty-one people working in radio and television. Among them were such prominent Hollywood stars as John Garfield and Judy Holliday, both subsequently subpoenaed by the House Committee on Un-American Activities. Philip Loeb's lengthy dossier in *Red Channels* notes, among other things, that he signed a petition to discontinue the Dies Committee; sponsored a 1938 fund drive for the Yiddish worker's theater Artef; supported the End Jim Crow in Baseball Committee, the North American Committee to Aid Spanish Democracy, and the Negro Labor Victory Committee; and was a member of the Non-Partisan Committee for the Re-election of Congressman Vito Marcantonio.

Gertrude Berg, producer.

Squirrel Hill and her romance with an attentive Frenchman; *Mind over Mama* (*Elgin Hour*, 1955, directed by Sidney Lumet), about an overbearing mother; and *The World of Sholem Aleichem* (1959), playing a version of "Molly" in fin de siècle Russia. Berg also appeared in the Broadway hit *A Majority of One* (1959), for which she received the Tony Award ("Molly in Japan," is how one reviewer summed up *Majority*),[22] and the now obscure television series *Mrs. G. Goes to College* (CBS, 1961–62), about an older women who returns to college (the show co-starred her *Majority* co-actor Sir Cedric Hardwicke). Berg's last performances were in *Dear Me, the Sky Is Falling*, which opened on Broadway at the Music Box in March 1963. She co-wrote the story, which is about an overbearing mother whose daughter consults a psychiatrist, with Leonard Spigelgass, who also penned *A Majority of One*.

Thus, from 1929 until her death in 1966, Gertrude Berg achieved a commanding, indeed, beloved presence in the imagination of millions of Americans. "She is a great force in whatever she does," Gilbert Seldes recognized in 1956, "and in this, the primary business of giving life to imagined people, she is incomparable."[23] With the character of Molly Goldberg, Berg created and ultimately inhabited a role that the American public embraced, without a trace of irony, for over thirty-five years. That she was able to sustain such a character for so long, performing variations on Molly Goldberg to the delight of the American public, is surely a testament to her many memorable achievements in the realm of entertainment.

# THE GOLDBERGS: A CHRONOLOGY

J. HOBERMAN

**November 20, 1929**
*The Rise of the Goldbergs* premieres on NBC's Blue radio network as a fifteen-minute show and is aired sporadically through May 23, 1931. Originally, the show concerns the family's ascent from Hester Street to Park Avenue. With the onset of the Great Depression, the Goldbergs relocate to the East Bronx.

**July 13, 1931–July 6, 1934**
Sponsored by Pepsodent, *The Rise of the Goldbergs* is broadcast by NBC six evenings each week, immediately following *Amos 'n' Andy*. In mid-1934, shortly before the show is cancelled, the Goldbergs leave the Bronx for the rural town of Lastonbury, Connecticut, where Jake takes a job managing a mill.

**1934–36**
*The Rise of the Goldbergs* cast tours the vaudeville circuit.

**April 17–December 25, 1935**
Gertrude Berg writes and appears in *The House of Glass*, a weekly half-hour radio serial about a hotel in the Catskills.

**January 13–July 10, 1936**
*The Goldbergs* (as the show is retitled) is revived by CBS radio as a late afternoon serial, broadcast five days a week from 5:45 to 6:00 PM, under the sponsorship of Colgate-Palmolive.

**September 13–December 31, 1937**
*The Goldbergs* returns briefly to NBC.

**January 1, 1938–March 30, 1945**
Sponsored by Procter and Gamble, *The Goldbergs* moves back to CBS as a daytime drama. The family remains in Lastonbury.

ABOVE
Comic-strip version of *The Goldbergs* in the *New York Post*, June 6, 1944.

RIGHT
Jigsaw puzzle depicting the Goldberg family at home.

**February 26, 1948**
*Me and Molly*, written by Berg, opens on Broadway at the Belasco Theatre and runs for 156 performances, through July 10, 1948. The action is set in the Bronx; the cast includes Philip Loeb, David Opatoshu, and Eli Mintz. "No wonder the Goldbergs have been popular on the radio," Brooks Atkinson writes in the *New York Times*. "Mrs. Berg is a real human being who believes in the people she writes about and is not ashamed of their simplicity."

October 18, 1948

Berg makes her television debut as a Bronx housewife on NBC's *Chevrolet on Broadway*, along with Minerva Pious (Mrs. Nussbaum on Fred Allen's radio show).

A *Life* magazine feature on Berg, April 25, 1949, celebrated *The Goldbergs'* arrival on television. The caption below the photograph read, "Ten years of Goldberg scripts tower over creator, Gertrude Berg. A hotel owner's daughter, Mrs. Berg got ideas for *The Goldbergs* from grandmother, had terrible time convincing sponsors her show would not offend either Jews or non-Jews. She has always acted Molly in the show—and acts much like her in real life, too."

*Variety* speculates some could find the actresses' Yiddish accents objectionable and wonders "whether Chevy and NBC are wise in projecting such racial stereotypes," adding that a set of a synagogue interior might also be considered "in bad taste."

January 10, 1949

*The Goldbergs* has its television premiere as a thirty-minute situation comedy, sponsored by Sanka and shown on Monday nights on CBS. The family now lives in the Bronx, at 1030 East Tremont Avenue, apartment 3B.

September 2, 1949–June 24, 1950

*The Goldbergs* returns to CBS radio and the Bronx. Sammy and Rosalie are again children; as on the simultaneously shown television series, Jake is played by Broadway actor Philip Loeb.

Summer 1950

Loeb is named in *Red Channels* as an actor with Communist "affiliations." Berg declines to fire him. *The Goldbergs* is dropped by its sponsor, General Foods (the manufacturer of Sanka), and cancelled by the CBS network after the season ends in June 1951.

March 7, 1951

*Molly*, directed by Walter Hart and also known as *The Goldbergs* (Paramount), opens at the Paramount Theatre in New York. The movie stars the TV Goldbergs: Berg, Loeb, Larry Robinson, and Arlene McQuade. Eduard Franz, who will play the cantor in the 1952 remake of *The Jazz Singer*, appears as Alexander Abel, Molly's wealthy, now aged, former suitor.

February–July 1952

*The Goldbergs*, with Harold J. Stone as Jake, returns to television on NBC, sponsored by the network's corporate owner RCA. The fifteen-minute show runs three nights a week through July. According to Berg, *The Goldbergs* goes off the air at the end of the season when she declines to be rescheduled opposite *I Love Lucy*.

On the set of the Goldbergs' Bronx apartment, c. 1950. Note the juxtaposition of the Old World samovar and New World portrait of George Washington.

**May 26, 1953**

Gertrude Berg and Arlene McQuade appear as Molly and Rosalie Goldberg in an hour-long skit on *The Texaco Star Theatre* (NBC), opposite host "Uncle" Milton Berle, who would later maintain that he was interested in using Berg as a recurring character on the show.

**July–September 1953**

After a year's hiatus, *The Goldbergs* has a second tour on NBC, on Friday evenings, as a half-hour summer replacement. Robert H. Harris now plays Jake.

**April–October 1954**

*The Goldbergs* is revived by the DuMont network to fill the Tuesday evening slot vacated by Bishop Fulton Sheen's *Life Is Worth Living*.

**1955–56**

Relocated from the Bronx to suburban Haverville, and known alternatively as *Molly*, *The Goldbergs* appears on television for the last time, as a half-hour syndicated telefilm.

**October 4, 1961–April 5, 1962**

Berg returns to CBS as Sarah Green, a widow who decides to pursue higher education, in *Mrs. G. Goes to College*. The cast includes Sir Cedric Hardwicke, who played opposite Berg in the 1959 Broadway production *A Majority of One*. Midway

Poster in Rockefeller Center announcing the return to television, "by popular request," of *The Goldbergs* to NBC, 1953.

through its single season, the program is moved from Wednesday to Thursday evenings and renamed *The Gertrude Berg Show*.

**Autumn 1961**
Berg revives Molly Goldberg in a series of commercials for SOS scouring pads: "Yoo-hoo, Mrs. Bloom. Have you tried the new SOS? With soap, it's loaded."

**March 2, 1963**
*Dear Me, The Sky Is Falling*, a play adapted from a story co-written by Gertrude Berg, opens on Broadway at the Music Box Theatre and runs for 145 performances, through July 11. Berg stars as New Rochelle housewife Libby Hirsch, with Howard Da Silva as her husband. "The name of the play is different, but the character is essentially the same and so is the basic apparatus," Howard Taubman writes in the *New York Times*.

**1965**
Berg records an LP record, *How to Be a Jewish Mother: A Very Lovely Training Manual* by Dan Greenburg.

**September 14, 1966**
Gertrude Berg dies in New York at the age of sixty-six.

**November 1, 1973**
The musical *Molly* opens on Broadway at the Alvin Theater. Set in the Bronx during the Depression, this adaptation of *The Goldbergs* centers on Molly's attempt to put her family back on an even keel after Jake loses his tailoring job. The songs (by Jerry Livingston and the team of Leonard Adelson and Mack David) include "There's a New Deal on

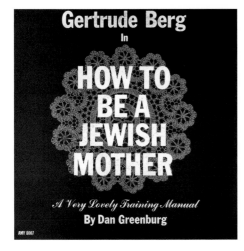

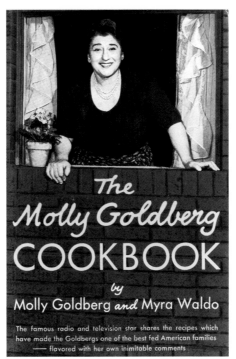

**ABOVE**
Album cover of *How to Be a Jewish Mother* by Dan Greenburg, narrated by Gertrude Berg, 1965. In one of her final performances, recorded before a live audience in Chicago, Berg parodied the archetypal Jewish mother she invented and embodied for decades.

**RIGHT**
Cover of *The Molly Goldberg Cookbook* (1955). Traditional Jewish-American recipes were framed by homey anecdotes in the voice of Molly Goldberg.

the Way," "The Tremont Avenue Cruise-wear Fashion Show," and "Go in the Best of Health." Directed by Alan Arkin, *Molly* stars Kaye Ballard in the title role, with Eli Mintz re-creating his TV characterization of Uncle David. It runs for sixty-eight performances, including previews.

127 **THE GOLDBERGS: A CHRONOLOGY**

# FATHER COUGHLIN

The Nazi regime's first large-scale, mandated assault on Jews, their property, and houses of worship throughout Germany and Austria took place on November 9–10, 1938. Known as Kristallnacht (Night of Broken Glass), this was a threshold event in Nazi policies toward Jewish citizens of the Reich. Less than two weeks later, Father Charles E. Coughlin—among the most popular radio personalities in America at the time, and the best-known Catholic cleric heard regularly on the nation's airwaves—delivered one of his most controversial radio broadcasts. An effort to rationalize Nazi anti-Semitism while denouncing it, Coughlin's remarks provoked widespread protest from American Jewish groups, including the American Jewish Committee, the American Jewish Congress, B'nai B'rith, and the Jewish Labor Committee. Coughlin not only relativized the Nazis' persecution of Jews against the legitimacy of Nazi anti-Communism (foreshadowing revisionist Holocaust historiography of the 1980s), but he also found the extensive attention paid to Kristallnacht in the news media suspiciously disproportionate, insinuating undue Jewish influence at work.

—J.S.

From Father Charles E. Coughlin, "Persecution—Jewish and Christian," radio speech, Sunday, November 20, 1938.

At long last, a calloused world has come in personal contact with a persecution which it understands. At long last, it appears that the better sympathies of an indifferent citizenry are aroused to protest against the mad injustices now being meted out to a minority people resident abroad. . . .

Thus, I shall ask an intelligent audience composed of intelligent Christians and intelligent Jews, "Why is there persecution in Germany today? How can we destroy it?" . . .

To be effectual in our discussion, . . . it is necessary to record the following facts. Although cruel persecution of German-born Jews has been notorious since 1933—particularly in the loss of their citizenship—nevertheless, until last week the Nazi purge was concerned chiefly with foreign-born Jews. German-citizen Jews were not molested officially in the conduct of their business. The property of German-citizen Jews was not confiscated by the government although a few synagogues and stores were destroyed by mob violence. . . . Until this hour no German-citizen Jew has been martyred for his religion by government order although restrictions were placed upon Jewish professional men.

While it is true that foreign-citizen Jews resident in Germany were disparaged and expelled, it is likewise true that many social impediments were placed in the pathway of Catholics and Protestants by the Nazi government—impediments which are revolting to our American concepts of liberty. But despite all this, official Germany has not yet resorted to the guillotine, to the machine gun, to the kerosene-drenched pit as instruments of reprisal against Jew or Gentile. . . .

In all such countries Jews are in the minority . . . but a closely woven minority in their racial tendencies; a powerful minority in their influence; a minority endowed with an aggressiveness, an initiative which, despite all obstacles, has carried their sons to the pinnacle of success in journalism, in radio, in finance and in all the sciences and arts.

Thus, with these facilities at their disposal, no story of persecution was ever told one-half so well, one-half so thoroughly as the story of this . . . reprisal which culminated in a series of persecutions. Perhaps, may I resubmit, this is attributable to the fact that Jews, through their native ability, have risen to such high places in radio and in press and in finance; perhaps this persecution is only the coincidental last straw

which has broken the back of this generation's patience. . . .

[L]et us pause to inquire why Nazism is so hostile to Jewry in particular, and how the Nazi quality of persecution can be liquidated. . . . Nazism was conceived as a political defense mechanism against communism and was ushered into existence as a result of communism. And, communism itself was regarded by the rising generation of Germans as a product not of Russia, but of a group of Jews who dominated the destinies of Russia. . . .

Official information emanating from Russia itself informed the world that communism, while barbarously opposed to every form of Christianity, made it a crime for any comrade to utter a single word of reproach against the Jews. Uncontradictable information gleaned from the writings and the policies of Lenin proved indisputably that the government of the Soviet Republics was predominantly anti-Christian and definitely antinational. More than that, the 1917 list of those who, with Lenin, ruled many of the activities of the Soviet Republic, disclosed that of the twenty-five quasi-cabinet members, twenty-four of them were atheistic Jews. . . .

I speak these words, certainly holding no brief for Germany or for Nazism. Simply as a student of history, I am endeavoring to analyze the reason for the growth of the idea in the minds of the Nazi Party that communism and Judaism are too closely interwoven for the national health of Germany. . . .

Therefore, I say to the good Jews of America, be not indulgent with the irreligious, atheistic Jews and Gentiles who promote the cause of persecution in the land of the communists; the same ones who promote the cause of atheism in America. Yes,

be not lenient with your high financiers and politicians who assisted at the birth of the only political, social and economic system in all civilization that adopted atheism as its religion, internationalism as its patriotism and slavery as its liberty. . . .

My fellow citizens, I am not ignorant of Jewish history. I know its glories. I am acquainted with its glorious sons. I am aware of the keen intellectuality which has characterized its progress in commerce, in finance, in all the arts and sciences and,

particularly, in the field of communications.

But I am also aware that every nation from time immemorial has listed in its hand the lash of persecution to strike the back of Jews. . . . Since the time of Christ, Jewish persecution only followed after Christians first were persecuted—persecuted either by exploiters within their own ranks, as in the Middle Ages, or by enemies from without, as in our own days—the days of communism.

Many historians—in fact, the vast majority of them—maintain that the Jews were persecuted because of their social philosophy. Parallel with their persecution has been the persecution of Christians—not for their social philosophy but for their religion. . . . Between the years 1917 and 1938 more than twenty million Christians were murdered by the communistic government in Russia. Between these same years. . . . $40 billion—at a conservative estimate—of Christian property was appropriated. . . .

Alas! the news of Christian persecution came to our shores. Alas! the press and the radio were almost silent. Alas! this present government made friends of these murderers by recognizing their flag! . . . Why, then, was there this silence on the radio and in the press? Ask the gentlemen who control the three national radio chains; ask those who dominate the destinies of the financially inspired press—surely these Jewish gentlemen and others must have been ignorant of the facts or they would have had a symposium in those dark days—especially when students of history recognized that Nazism is only a defense mechanism against communism and that persecution of the Christians always begets persecution of the Jews. . . .

Thanks be to God, both the radio and the press at length have become attuned to the wails of sorrow arising from Jewish persecution! May these notes rise in rapid crescendo until a symphony, not of hate but of love, not of protest but of determination, fills the heart of every human being in America.

Father Charles E. Coughlin began broadcasting on local stations in the Midwest in the mid-1920s. During the Great Depression, he drew large audiences with his impassioned, politically charged speeches, heard nationally over the CBS network.

# RELIGION, DEMOCRACY, AND RADIO WAVES: *THE ETERNAL LIGHT*

JEFFREY SHANDLER

The first major use of broadcasting by an American Jewish religious movement began in 1944, when the Jewish Theological Seminary (JTS)—the intellectual center of Conservative Judaism—initiated *The Eternal Light*, a half-hour radio series produced in conjunction with NBC. *The Eternal Light* continued to be heard on radio through the late 1980s. The series also appeared on NBC television beginning in 1952 and lasted through the late eighties, constituting the longest-running regular presence of Jews as a religious community on American airwaves. Over the years, *The Eternal Light* presented hundreds of broadcasting hours in the form of dramas, concerts, documentaries, panel discussions, and interviews. In its heyday, during the forties and fifties, the radio series was heard by some six million listeners across North America.[1]

*The Eternal Light* epitomized American Judeo-Christian ecumenism of the post–World War II era. At this time, all three major commercial networks sponsored ecumenical broadcasts as part of their public service programming. *The Eternal Light* was aired on Sundays on a rotating basis with Protestant and Catholic programming. This was, in fact, one of the first and most popular enactments of American religious pluralism of the period. Within this forum, *The Eternal Light* had a double agenda: first, reaching out to Jews, especially the unaffiliated or geographically isolated; and second, promoting understanding and

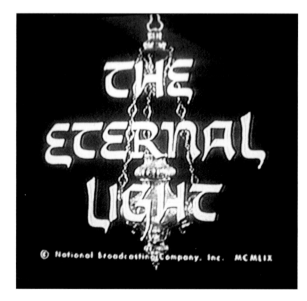

NEAR RIGHT
Title image for the NBC ecumenical television series *The Eternal Light*, 1959.

FAR RIGHT
Cover of a Jewish Theological Seminary promotional brochure for *The Eternal Light*, c. 1950. The number of listeners claimed by the producers of the radio program—six million—was perhaps also meant to evoke the number of Jews who lost their lives during the Holocaust.

Television production of *Kasrilevka on the Mississippi*, an original play dramatizing a fictional encounter between Yiddish writer Sholem Aleichem and Mark Twain (1955), produced by the Jewish Theological Seminary for the NBC ecumenical series *Frontiers of Faith*.

ABOVE

Actor John Garfield, playwright Morton Wishengrad, orchestra conductor Milton Katims, and producer Milton Krents rehearsing an *Eternal Light* broadcast, 1940s.

RIGHT

RCA president David Sarnoff (left) and Jewish Theological Seminary Chancellor Louis Finkelstein in an NBC broadcasting studio, 1940s.

tolerance of Jews among non-Jews. In this respect, *The Eternal Light* resembled contemporary efforts by the Anti-Defamation League and other American Jewish organizations to combat anti-Semitism through public education.

The earliest *Eternal Light* broadcasts were all original dramas. This was both a remarkable innovation in Jewish religious culture, in which drama has been largely an alien mode of expression, and a pioneering venture in broadcasting. "Serious" radio drama was still a novelty. The first *Eternal Light* scripts were a series on synagogues around the world of historical interest—beginning with *A Rhode Island Refuge*, a play by Morton Wishengrad about Newport's Touro Synagogue, which focused on the famous letter that George Washington wrote to this congregation in 1790 extolling the United States's commitment to religious toleration. This debut broadcast typified *The Eternal Light*'s emphasis on demonstrating the compatibility of Jewish and American values.

*The Eternal Light* was also distinguished by an aesthetic of respectability. The producers of the series used broadcasting to enable Jews to pay a virtual Sunday social call on their non-Jewish neighbors; therefore, they wanted to be on their "best behavior." *The Eternal Light*'s lofty prose, delivered by stentorian performers, offered a striking alternative to the portrait that early American radio otherwise offered of Jews, typically as comic characters who spoke in a malopropistic, Yiddish-inflected dialect.

Although JTS was primarily concerned with addressing its non-Jewish audience, *The Eternal Light* also created a new American Jewish Sunday-morning ritual. Listening to these broadcasts became an important rite of civil religion for Jews across the nation. It was, after all, the one moment in the week when Jews appeared regularly, forthrightly, and with dignity as a religious community in the public forum of American broadcasting. In one of his semiautobiographical novels, Philip Roth recalls the place of the radio series in a Sunday routine duplicated in many American Jewish homes during the early post–World War II years: "Fifty-two Sundays a year, for most of my lifetime, my father went out to the corner for the smoked fish and the warm rolls, my brother and I set the table and squeezed the juice. . . . Then, after my parents had read the Newark Sunday papers and listened on the radio to 'The Eternal Light'—great moments from Jewish history in weekly half-hour dramatizations—we two boys were rounded up and the four of us set off in the car to visit relatives."[2]

The very different presence of Jews in American broadcasts today is indicative of how much American sensibilities about the public enactment of difference have changed since this model of religious pluralism flourished in midcentury. Then David Sarnoff, president of RCA, could claim, as he did on the occasion of the tenth anniversary of *The Eternal Light*, that "radio waves, which are a manifestation of an 'Infinite Reason,' . . . do not discriminate against race, religion or creed. Freedom is their essence—and they enter the homes of Protestants, Catholics and Jews alike."[3]

# NORMAN CORWIN

Late in 1944, CBS radio commissioned Norman Corwin, one of the leading radio dramatists of the day, to write *On a Note of Triumph*, a one-hour broadcast celebrating the Allies' victory in Europe. Corwin's script incorporated quotations from actual news bulletins, correspondence, and political speeches. The narration was performed by Martin Gabel and the music was composed by Bernard Herrmann. In this excerpt, Corwin briefly mentions Jewish suffering at the hands of the Third Reich as portending the full extent of the evil of Nazism.

From Norman Corwin's radio drama *On a Note of Triumph*, aired on CBS, May 8, 1945.

*But what do we know now that we didn't know before? What have we LEARNED out of this war?*

For one thing, Evil is not always as insidious as advertised
But will, upon occasion, give fair warning, just as smoke announces the intention of flame to follow. . . .

Never has disaster had so many heralds as this war:
Cassandra spoke from every lecture platform, and the notices were posted high and low:
A cabinet minister resigned at Downing Street, protesting;
A President cried, "Quarantine!"
Moscow sent food and guns to Barcelona;
A housewife in Duluth boycotted German goods. . . .

Signs and portents?

It was no furtive tapping on the window sill at night,
But clamorous pounding in the public square,
Blow after blow, like a monstrous dropforge,
Beating into shape the time to come.
And the time came, and the prophecies matured:
The storm arrived, and was no surprise to the barometer:
The Jew who had cautioned. . . .
*The Nazis are not against the Jews alone—that's just a sham. If you let them carry on this way, they'll be the death of Christians, too.*

. . . he saw gentiles die as well, and sighed,
And foraged for bullets in the cellars of the Warsaw ghetto.
Yea, and the time came, and it developed that Cassandra and the Jew were right and that the Cliveden set was wrong:
Fire and brimstone, dropping from the sky, were educational:
There were tongues in torpedoes; sermons in bombs; books in the running battles.
Whatever was learned, was learned the hard way,
Between blood transfusions and last rites.

# PHILIP ROTH ON NORMAN CORWIN

The writer Nathan Zuckerman—a recurring character in the novels of Philip Roth—shares many traits with his creator, including a 1940s adolescence in Newark, New Jersey. In Roth's 1998 novel *I Married a Communist*, Zuckerman recalls the impact that Norman Corwin's radio play *On a Note of Triumph* had on his nascent aesthetic.

From Philip Roth, *I Married a Communist* (New York: Houghton Mifflin, 1998), 38–39.

My subject was the lot of the common man, the ordinary Joe—the man that the radio writer Norman Corwin had lauded as "the little guy" in *On a Note of Triumph*, a sixty-minute play that was transmitted over CBS radio the evening the war ended in Europe (and then again, at popular request, eight days later) and that buoyantly entangled me in those salvationist literary aspirations that endeavor to redress the world's wrongs through writing. I wouldn't care to judge today if something I loved as much as I loved *On a Note of Triumph* was or was not art; it provided me with my first sense of the conjuring *power* of art and helped strengthen my first ideas as to what I wanted and expected a literary artist's language to do: enshrine the struggles of the embattled. (And taught me, contrary to what my teachers insisted, that I could begin a sentence with "And.")

The form of the Corwin play was loose, plotless—"experimental," I informed my chiropodist father and homemaking mother. It was written in the high colloquial, alliterative style that may have derived in part from Clifford Odets and in part from Maxwell Anderson, from the effort by American playwrights of the twenties and thirties to forge a recognizable native idiom for the stage, naturalistic yet with lyrical coloration and serious undertones, a poeticized vernacular that, in Norman Corwin's case, combined the rhythms of ordinary speech with a faint literary stiltedness to make for a tone that struck me, at twelve, as democratic in spirit and heroic in scope, the verbal counterpart of a WPA mural. Whitman claimed America for the roughs, Norman Corwin claimed it for the little man—who turned out to be nothing less than the Americans who had fought the

patriotic war and were coming back to an adoring nation. The little man was nothing less than Americans themselves! Corwin's "little guy" was American for "proletariat," and, as I now understand it, the revolution fought and won by America's working class was, in fact, World War II, the something large that we were all, however small, a part of, the revolution that confirmed the reality of the myth of a national character to be partaken of by all.

Including me. I was a Jewish child, no two ways about that, but I didn't care to partake of the Jewish character. I didn't even know, clearly, what it was. I didn't much want to. I wanted to partake of the national character. Nothing had seemed to come more naturally to me, and no method could have seemed to me any more profound than participating through the tongue that Norman Corwin spoke, a linguistic distillation of the excited feelings of community that the war had aroused, the high demotic poetry that was the liturgy of World War II.

History had been scaled down and personalized, America had been scaled down and personalized: for me, that was the enchantment not only of Norman Corwin but of the times. You flood into history and history floods into you. You flood into America and America floods into you. And all by virtue of being alive in New Jersey and twelve years old and sitting by the radio in 1945. Back when popular culture was sufficiently connected to the last century to be susceptible still to a little language, there was a swooning side to all of it for me.

Radio playwright Norman Corwin directing a CBS broadcast in May 1945.

# "THE VANISHING JEW"

Henry Popkin's "The Vanishing Jew of Our Popular Culture: The Little Man Who Is No Longer There" examines the absence of Jewish representation in movies and broadcasting during the years following World War II, relative to the number of Jewish performers active on stage and screen less than two decades earlier. From our current perspective, Popkin's essay serves as a signpost of American Jewish self-scrutiny at midcentury, demonstrating how intellectuals have traced the dynamics of Jewish representation in entertainment media as an indicator of larger concerns.

The author was a twenty-eight-year-old drama critic when his essay was first published in *Commentary* during the summer of 1952. Throughout the late 1940s and early 1950s, this influential journal regularly printed articles assessing popular culture as measures of signal shifts in American Jewish life following World War II. Thus, Popkin's piece appeared soon after Irving Kristol's "Is Jewish Humor Dead? The Rise and Fall of the Jewish Joke" (November 1951) and prompted a rejoinder from one of his subjects, Sam Levenson, who wrote "The Dialect Comedian Should Vanish" (August 1952). It is Popkin's essay, however, that has been cited most often for its analysis of how a minority regards its public image.

Wide-ranging in his scope, Popkin gathers dozens of examples to illustrate his argument that during the middle decades of the twentieth century, recognizably Jewish figures had all but completely disappeared from public view in American popular culture—and that, in large measure, this was as a result of Jews' own apprehensions about the consequences of visibility. "The Vanishing Jew" is itself a product of its own anxious time; implicit in Popkin's essay is the notion that any sort of Jewish representation is bound to be problematic. As striking as Popkin's thesis, however, are those examples of Jews in American public culture that the writer did not see or, perhaps, chose not to cite: images of Jews as victims of Nazi terror or as founders of the new State of Israel, Jews as Hollywood moguls or as left-wing screenwriters. Popkin had nothing to say about the impact of congressional red-hunting on the career of the recently deceased movie star John Garfield (or of *Red Channels* on the cast of *The Goldbergs*), let alone the fears regarding anti-Semitism precipitated by the trial of convicted atomic spies Julius and Ethel Rosenberg, who were appealing their death sentence to the U.S. Supreme Court as this issue of *Commentary* was on the newsstands.

Fondly invoking actors and personalities such as George Sidney, Willie Howard, and Lou Holtz, who were still in the public eye during Popkin's adolescence, "The Vanishing Jew" attests to the persistence of Jewish concern with visibility as it evinces a shift in sensibility with regard to how Jews ought to be visible. Indeed, another oft-cited article on this topic—N. L. Rothman's "The Jew on the Screen," which first appeared almost twenty-five years before "The Vanishing Jew"—attacks as prancing buffoons the same performers Popkin regards with nostalgia.[1]

The dialect comedians that Popkin celebrated did, in fact, vanish from popular memory as well as popular culture. A quarter century after Popkin's article appeared, Albert Goldman—another professor with an interest in popular culture—published an essay in which he maintained that "until the 1950s there was never any Jewish humor in the American media," and that "far from exploiting their identity as Jews, most comics did everything in their power to disguise the fact they were Jewish."[2]
—J.H./J.S.

From Henry Popkin, "The Vanishing Jew of Our Popular Culture: The Little Man Who Is No Longer There," *Commentary* 14, no. 1 (July 1952): 46–55.

In Auden and Isherwood's play *The Dog Beneath the Skin*, a modern knight-errant bound upon a sacred quest encounters a sinister financier named Grabstein. Grabstein has cornered the rubber market, started a war in Spitzbergen, and "practically owns South America"—no one could possibly mistake him for anything but a satirical composite of every absurdity of the anti-Semitic imagination.

In 1948, however, when the group, the Interplayers, presented a lively production of *The Dog Beneath the Skin* in New York, Grabstein became a ruddy, white-haired Englishman named Mansfield, and with the loss of the archetypal quality of the Jewish "international financier" the character became quite pointless. The unusual element in this case was the fact that it involved an avant-garde play and a sophisticated little theater audience. For what may be called "de-Semitization" is by now a commonplace in the popular arts. There has grown up an unwritten law that makes the Jew the little man who isn't there. This law originates not in hate, but in a misguided benevolence—or fear; its name is "sha-sha" (Yiddish for hush-hush) At its most effective, the taboo banishes all Jewish characters, all Jewish names, the word "Jew" itself. If we pretend that the Jew does not exist, the reasoning goes, then he will not be noticed; the anti-Semite, unable to find his victim, will simply forget about him.

The policy of concealing Jews has itself been so well concealed that it is seldom mentioned in print. One of the rare discussions of it occurs in Ben Hecht's *A Guide for the Bedevilled* (1944). Hecht writes: "The greatest single Jewish phenomenon in our country in the last twenty years has been the almost complete disappearance of the Jew from American fiction, stage, radio and movies."

The source of this phenomenon, as of so

many others in Jewish life today, is Hitler. When Hitler forced Americans to take anti-Semitism seriously, it was apparently felt that the most eloquent reply that could be made was a dead silence: the American answer to the banishment of Jews from public life in Germany was the banishment of Jewish figures from the popular arts—in the United States.

The process has not been so thorough as Hecht suggests. In the comic strips, Harry Hershfield's *Abie the Agent* and the dialect strips of Milt Gross continued to be published despite Hitler; still, when Hershfield eventually did give up his comic strip history of the Jewish businessman, he is said to have promised to revive it when times were "better" for the Jews. . . .

A similar situation prevails in the comic books. "Comic" publications specializing in real-life stories have featured illustrated biographies of Irving Berlin, Bernard Baruch, Mordecai Noah, Judah Touro, Daniel Mendoza, Selman A. Waksman, and others, often with the hand of "Jewish defense" showing all too plainly, but the more numerous, more popular, and less inhibited comic books get along without Jewish characters altogether.

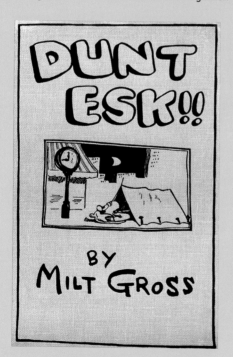

Cover of *Dunt Esk!!* (1927),
written and illustrated by
Milt Gross.

In pocket reprint editions of novels, now selling in astronomical numbers all over the country, the process of "de-Semitization" has had a growing effect. The reasoning behind this policy is that these inexpensive reprints are more likely than the original editions to fall into the hands of readers who will discover anti-Semitism, perhaps where it does not exist, and will either sympathize or be offended—equally undesirable reactions. Thus, in the Avon Books reprint of Irving Shulman's novel of juvenile delinquency in Brooklyn, *The Amboy Dukes*, every trace of Jewish reference is eliminated. Bar Mitzvah becomes "confirmation," and remarks about kosher meat are deleted; Goldfarb becomes Abbott, Semmel becomes Saunders, etc., etc. And yet the novel would seem to have little power for harm—in its original form it says no more than that Jews, like other groups in America, have the problem of juvenile delinquency.

It was more logical for the same publisher to "de-Semitize" Jerome Weidman's *I Can Get It for You Wholesale* in its pocket edition. The Avon editors have toned down the more striking Jewish names and Jewish references: Meyer Babushkin is renamed Michael Babbin, Pulvermacher becomes the more euphonious Pulsifer, the hero's mother calls him Hershie instead of Heshie (does this make him less Jewish?) and feeds him pancakes instead of *blintzes*. Perhaps, in view of the enormous and uncritical audience reached by pocket editions, these changes were justified, since the principal impression conveyed by the novel is of the total depravity of its emphatically Jewish main character: Harry Bogen may be said to add a new chapter in moral corruption to the ancient stereotype of the merciless sharp trader, where the boys of *The Amboy Dukes* are only petty criminals of the type familiar among all groups in slum neighborhoods. But once concealment is accepted, publishers prefer to play safe. There lies the danger. . . .

In the performing arts, the Broadway theater suffers least from self-consciousness of this sort. Partly this is because the dramatist retains considerable control over his work;

a more important fact is that plays are written for the adult theater-going audience of New York, where playwrights and the public are reconciled to the existence of the Jews and think their stage representation neither exotic nor obscene. In fact, a Jewish character in a Broadway play or revue often seems as much a local reference as a statement about the topography of Columbus Circle. . . .

To be sure, our growing reticence about Jews may have deeper effects, whose extent it is impossible to measure. Sometimes, one suspects, there is a kind of pre-censorship, often unconscious, that does its work inside the mind of a playwright. Arthur Miller's *All My Sons* and *Death of a Salesman* might be cases in point; in spite of their vaguely Protestant and "Anglo-Saxon" atmosphere, both plays strike some familiar Jewish chords in their treatment of business life and family relations and often in the cadences of their dialogue. George Ross makes an interesting detailed case for *Death of a Salesman* as an essentially Jewish play in his article "'Death of a Salesman' in the Original" (*Commentary*, February 1951).

The Jewish dialect comedian who once flourished in the theater, the movies, radio, and, more recently, in television, is likewise disappearing. Some specimens of the type were seen briefly on Broadway in the two Yiddish-American revues aimed at the Jewish market, but the best of the tribe live in semi-retirement, like Lou Holtz, or are dead, like Willie Howard and George Sidney.

The tradition of these comedians goes back to at least the turn of the century, when David Warfield's black-bearded, derby-wearing peddler fixed the general outlines; for years, young Jewish comedians were invariably billed as "the second David Warfield." Like Warfield, many of these were on some occasions "Dutch" comedians, but the differences between the Jews and the "Dutch" were minimal. "Dutch" meant, of course, German, and George Jean Nathan has pointed out the interesting fact that a great deal of "Dutch" comedy became Jewish during the First World War because of the unpopularity of everything German;

Gertrude Berg and the cast
of the CBS radio program
*The Goldbergs*.

Those Jewish comedians who remain still make occasional appearances on the stage and on television, and they have been heard over the radio. The movies have been almost entirely closed to them for nearly twenty years. (A rare exception was the recent appearance of Smith and Dale in the movie *Two Tickets to Broadway*.) The principal reason for the difference is the fact that radio and television sprang up in the shadow of Broadway, in the mainstream of a freer tradition that could still recognize and present foreigners and foreign accents without excessive self-consciousness or reticence. Lou Holtz and Willie Howard made frequent guest appearances with Rudy Vallee; such characters as Schlepperman and later Mr. Kitzel have appeared on the Jack Benny program; Fanny Brice did "Jewish" monologues (before she became completely identified with Baby Snooks); and there have been Fred Allen's Mrs. Nussbaum, Henry Burbidge, *The Goldbergs* (not all of the actors were comedians, but Menashe Skulnik and Arnold Stang would surely qualify). *Potash and Perlmutter* and *Abie's Irish Rose* were the basis of mercifully short-lived dramatic serials, and there was once a comedy series about a detective named Cohen who had an assistant named Dr. Wasserman.

But the fog of concealment has been creeping over these areas too. At least one Jewish radio comedian seems to have fallen victim to the complaints of hypersensitive listeners: according to Alistair Cooke, Lou Holtz had to go off the air when his act was, incredibly, accused of being anti-Semitic. Apparently, most of the leading Jewish "dialecticians" have been objects of complaint at one time or another, and—to mention a more directly cultural factor—the Jewish comedian in his best embodiments is in any case out of step with the industrialized techniques of gag files and joke conferences that now rule.

On television, to be sure, there has been a kind of renascence, and perhaps we may hope it will endure, though one suspects that the chief factor has been simply television's gargantuan need for material. Smith and Dale have made guest appear-

another war has now accelerated the disappearance of that comic vein. The first full-length Jewish-dialect comedy to win wide popularity was *Potash and Perlmutter*, produced in 1913, the longest-running play of its season; its sequels came just in time to profit from the anti-German feeling of the war years. In any case, however, the Jewish comedians and their plays soon found a large audience. . . .

Hoffman's comedies, the Potash-and-Perlmutter plays, and such other examples of the genre as Anne Nichols' *Abie's Irish Rose* are little more than commercial attempts to capitalize on comic dialects. What art most of them had seems to have been imparted by the actors. George Sidney, Harry Green, Alexander Carr (who created the role of Mawruss Perlmutter), and their fellow comedians of the revues, Willie Howard, Lou Holtz, Fanny Brice, and Smith and Dale, were all expert performers. . . . Most of these actors were at their best when they used their own material, Smith and Dale in *Dr. Kronkheit*, Harry Green in *The Cherry Tree*, Lou Holtz and Willie Howard in their Sam Lapidus and Pierre Ginzburg routines.

ances, *The Goldbergs* has become a popular dramatic series, Menashe Skulnik briefly had his own program, and the new medium found its own Jewish comedian in Sam Levenson. (The main reason for considering Milton Berle a Jewish comedian is his occasional use of such a phrase as "for two cents plain." The querulous, skeptical city types played by Arnold Stang have a better claim to a place in the Jewish comic tradition.) Some of these actors have been sadly handicapped by a lack of materials; Skulnik in particular was victimized by the threadbare skits that were written for him. Only Levenson has exhibited a fresh and personal flair in his adaptations of Jewish stories and his discourses on family life. But even he is so strongly aware of the hostile forces of "shasha" that in the preface to his book *Meet the Folks* he anticipates his critics by disclaiming some of the traditional elements of Jewish humor. One of the least persuasive disavowals is his rejection of stories about the "little Jew." I for one cannot see why such stories are, as Levenson puts it, "fundamentally anti-Semitic"—would we be somehow better or more sympathetic if we were a race of giants? Levenson goes on to assure his readers that he has "tried to keep the stories within the great Hebrew-Christian tradition

of the goodness and the dignity of man." Fortunately Levenson is not as good as his word. The stories in *Meet the Folks* are not all concerned with oversized models of goodness and dignity.

Whatever may happen in the future, one fact is encouraging: in television, as in radio during its heyday, there prevails what might be called the New York idea, that Jewishness is not freakish or embarrassing and there might as well be Jewish comedians as any other kind. Hence one finds that sort of Jewish reference, whether comic or not, that stands in refreshing contrast to the rest of our antiseptically "Aryanized" popular culture: a Yiddish phrase spoken, a Jewish dialect or intonation, an identifiably Jewish ironic quality, or—to get away from comedy— a "detective" play about a dress business run by a Mr. Alpert in the garment district, another about the return of the prodigal son on the Seder eve, and adaptations of Elmer Rice's *Counsellor-at-Law* and Samson Raphaelson's *The Jazz Singer*. All of this expresses no attitude. Breaks no lances against anti-Semitism; it only recognizes one fact of experience: that the Jews do exist.

The blight has fallen most heavily on the movies. It was not ever thus. Time was when

Groucho Marx in *Animal Crackers* could sing "My name is Captain Spalding the African Explorer," and add under his breath, "Did someone call me *shnorer*?" And when James Cagney could find a moment to make a proud display of his knowledge of Yiddish. In her recent autobiography *Red Ribbon on a White Horse*, Anzia Yezierska tells how Samuel Goldwyn brought her to Hollywood to work on the silent movie version of her story of Jewish life, *Hungry Hearts*; she was dismayed at being joined by Montague Glass, author of *Potash and Perlmutter*, who was commissioned to turn *Hungry Hearts* into a "Jew-play" with a happy ending. *The Cohens and the Kellys*, in 1928, was one of the biggest box-office hits, and its heroes accordingly had further film adventures in Paris, Africa, Atlantic City, and Hollywood; in addition, there were film versions of *Potash and Perlmutter*, *Welcome Stranger* (less attractive than the original) and *Abie's Irish Rose*. And no one who knows the history of the movie needs to be told that the first talkie (actually part talking and part silent), *The Jazz Singer*, featured Al Jolson as a Jewish boy who was being brought up to be a cantor, but left the synagogue to become a popular entertainer.

If the scripts were usually uninspired, there were actors, on the screen as on the

Chico, Zeppo, Groucho, and Harpo Marx in *Animal Crackers* (1930).

Vera Gordon as Mama Kantor and Bobby Connelly as the young Leon Kantor in the silent version of *Humoresque* (1920).

duced in 1931 with John Barrymore, and *Oliver Twist* in 1922 with Lon Chaney and again in 1933 with Irving Pichel, no protests seriously threatened the films' distribution, even though the villains were visibly Jewish. There were tear-jerkers about Jews—*Symphony of Six Million* (with Ratoff), *No Greater Love* (with Carr), and the silent *Humoresque*. There were screen adaptations of plays, including *Counselor-at-Law* (with John Barrymore), *Once in a Lifetime* (with Ratoff), *The Last Mile* (with Stone), *Kibitzer* (with Green), *The Yellow Ticket* (with Elissa Landi as the Jewish heroine), and *Street Scene*, in all of which the Jewish characters were preserved intact. A few pictures—for example *The House of Rothschild*—defended the Jews against anti-Semites. . . .

Then came the great retreat. By 1935 most of the Jewish comedians had vanished from the screen. Harry Green was in seven movies in 1934 and none in 1935; since leaving Hollywood he has spent most of his time in England, appearing occasionally on Broadway and making two movies in 1940. George Sidney retired from movie-making in 1935, reappearing just once more in 1937 and also acting on Broadway. Gregory Ratoff and George E. Stone became less identified with Jewish parts, and Ratoff ultimately came to be a director. Alexander Carr's story was the saddest. He was very busy in Hollywood till 1934; after that he couldn't get a part. At the end of 1938 he turned up in New York to entertain at a Jewish night club, returned to Hollywood in 1940 to appear in Preston Sturges's *Christmas in July*, and died in 1946, having made only one picture in the last twelve years of his life. . . .

Often the changes have taken the form of eliminating Jewish villains—a practice which may be defensible as good public relations practice in behalf of the Jews, but might well have boomerang effects if it should appear that Jews were the sole beneficiaries. Italians still furnish most movie gangsters, and this emphasis has been particularly obvious since the Kefauver hearings; other nationalities also make visible contributions to the ranks of villains. How-

stage, who sometimes rose above their material, especially after talking pictures brought more of the stage comedians to Hollywood. In Hollywood, George Sidney repeated his early stage success, and so did Harry Green, who had been one of the "second David Warfields" of years ago. Gregory Ratoff was identified with Jewish roles; as late as 1932 it was announced that he would play the lead in Samuel Ornitz's novel of Jewish life, *Haunch, Paunch, and Jowl*, but the picture was never made. George E. Stone made a career of playing young Jews. In the late 20s and early 30s these four, along with the veteran Alexander Carr, were among the busiest comedians and character actors. The monologists and revue comedians never got very far in pictures, possibly because they could not make their comic antics conform to the dull stereotypes of movie characters and the dubious logic of movie plots; Willie Howard, like Smith and Dale, was assigned principally to making short features.

But comedians were not the only Jewish types to be seen in the movies of that earlier period. When *Svengali* was pro-ever, when *Kind Lady* was filmed in 1936, the French antique dealer, a by no means unsympathetic character, had his named changed from Rosenberg to Roubet; in the latest movie version of this play he is called Malaquaise. Similar examples are numerous. . . .

More disturbing than the disappearance of one Jewish character here and another there, is the absence of recognizable Jews in films that *require* their presence. Elliot Paul and Luis Quintanilla, in their study of Hollywood conventions, *With a Hays Nonny Nonny*, suggest that a Hollywood producer might film the Biblical story of Esther as a tale of Nazi oppression of the Czechs: "It would be bad for the public to get the idea the Nazis are persecuting Jews. . . . In the eyes of the producers, it is even worse to show a Jew in clover than one in the soup up to his eyes. The solution is not to show him at all. He becomes a Czech or some kind of Central European the 40,000,000 [moviegoers] can view impersonally."

By this sort of logic, Hollywood frequently excluded the issue of anti-Semitism from movies attacking the Nazi movement. A few films did show anti-Semitism as a part of Nazism, following the novels or plays on which they were based with at least a reasonable fidelity: *The Mortal Storm*, *Tomorrow the World*, *Address Unknown*. But only a few years before, reports had come out of Hollywood that the issue of anti-Semitism was eliminated from the script of *Three Comrades* over the protests of the authors of the screen play, one of whom was F. Scott Fitzgerald. And the British-made *Mr. Emmanuel*, generally regarded as the first movie to attack Nazi anti-Semitism, was thought so revolutionary that it was publicized with such slogans as "A daring picture on a daring subject" and "Have you got the nerve to see this picture?"

Even plays and novels telling stories of Jewish life were "de-Semitized." In John Howard Lawson's *Success Story*, filmed in 1934 as *Success at Any Price*, Ginsburg became Martin and Glassman became Griswold, with Douglas Fairbanks Jr. and Colleen Morrow acting these leading roles,

which had been played on Broadway by Luther and Stella Alder; a happy ending helped to prettify the proceedings. Later, when Irwin Shaw's parable of tyranny and revolt, *The Gentle People*, was filmed under the title *Out of the Fog*, the Jewish tailor Goodman turned into an Irish tailor named Goodwin. Abel Kandel's novel of Jewish life, *City for Conquest*, was made the basis of a movie of Irish life. The play *Home of the Brave* dealt with the psychological problems of a Jewish soldier; the movie made him a Negro, burdened with precisely the same problems. (At about the same time, seeking to make a movie about anti-Semitism, Hollywood picked up a novel called *The Brick Foxhole* which was about the murder of a non-Jewish homosexual, and turned it into *Crossfire*. Go know!) . . .

Pushing further into the area of distinctively Jewish subject matter, the movie makers watered down the Jewish elements of the New York garment industry in the greatly altered film version of Jerome Weidman's novel *I Can Get It for You Wholesale*. The movie also cleaned up the personal ethics of the book's principal character (besides changing him into a woman: Harry Bogen became Harriet Boyd). Even the Borscht Belt and the Old Testament have not escaped. In *Having a Wonderful Time*, based on Arthur Kober's play, the Catskill vacationers became, as the disappointed Frank S. Nugent put it in the *New York Times*, "alle goyim." Typical campers were Douglas Fairbanks Jr. and Ginger Rogers; Stern became Shaw, Kessler became Kirkland, Aaronson was Armbruster, Sam Rappaport was Emil Beatty, and, in short, it seemed most unlikely that this particular summer hotel should really be located in the Catskills. Likewise, neither Hebrews nor Israelites are ever mentioned in De Mille's *Samson and Delilah*; instead, Samson persistently reminds us of his loyalty to the Tribe of Dan; we never hear of any larger social unit to which Dan belonged. The makers of *Quo Vadis* could be a little bolder, perhaps because they proceeded on the assumption that a movie with a Christian theme and offering Peter and Paul as its only Jewish characters has by its very nature disarmed

the (nominally Christian) anti-Semite. *Quo Vadis* shows us a Paul not unlike the anti-Semite's traditional concept of the large-nosed, black-bearded Jew, and has him identify himself as a rabbi. "Despise him if you dare," the incipient anti-Semite is implicitly admonished, "but remember that this Jew is Saint Paul."

Beyond the more conscious desire to avoid inciting anti-Semitism, another motive that operates less consciously in suppression of Jewish elements in films is simply the desire to prettify, to depict life without discordant, heterogeneous elements. Jews are an intrusion; they do not belong to the pretty picture. Their presence is suppressed just as other odd, unsightly things are suppressed. Thus in *Golden Boy*, the hero's distinctive physical mark was changed from crossed eyes to curly hair for the same reason that the name Gottlieb was changed to Lewis— for beauty's sake. Similarly, in *The Glass Menagerie* Garfinkel's delicatessen was changed to Schultz's for the same reason that Mrs. Wingfield was made to speak of "stomach trouble" instead of "cancer of the stomach."

When the unsightly Jews must be present, if is often felt necessary to conceal their peculiarities in a cloud of other peculiarities: Jews may be strange, some films seem to say, but other people are strange too—strangeness itself is made a form of the familiar. Often the Irish seem to offer the handiest camouflage. Thus in *The Lost Weekend* Don Birnam must walk along Third Avenue desperately seeking a pawnshop where he can sell his typewriter. In the novel he discovers from two Jews "in their Sunday-best" that all pawnshops are closed for Yom Kippur, and that ends the conversation. In the movie he cries: "What about Kelly's and Gallagher's?"—a rather unlikely question. "We've got an agreement," he is told. "They keep closed on Yom Kippur and we don't open on St. Patrick's"—the inference being that closing on St. Patrick's Day is a regular practice among Americans of Irish descent. Here, as in such plays as *Abie's Irish Rose* and *Two Blocks Away*, the

John Garfield (left) and
Lilli Palmer (right) in *Body
and Soul* (1947).

though he is called Corporal Jake Feingold").
In most of these films, the characterization
of the Jewish figure is fairly perfunctory,
but no more or less so than the characterization of most of the other service men.
Wayne Greenbaum, the clever ironic City
College graduate played by Sam Levene in
*The Purple Heart*, is probably the best portrait in the gallery; most of the others are
virtually interchangeable. . . .

One more detective movie deserves to be
mentioned here: *Where the Sidewalk Ends*,
from a screen play by Ben Hecht, who, as
his *Guide for Bedevilled* testifies, has a
special interest in the return of the Jew to
the movies. Hecht goes at this task with a
vengeance, presenting a sympathetic detective named Klein, who is the embattled
hero's best friend; Klein's wife Shirley, who
conforms to a popular but well-intentioned
stereotype of being superficially ungenerous
but proving ultimately to have a heart
of gold; an unregenerate gangster named
Sid Kramer; a dress manufacturer named
Friedman who seems pleasant enough but
who unjustly discharges the heroine when
she becomes involved in a murder; and a key
witness, a Mrs. Tribaum, who is a friendly,
elderly widow. This movie is in fact not very
good, but it does succeed in putting across
the revolutionary (for Hollywood) idea that
the Jews simply are there in the community,
capable of the same strengths and the same
weaknesses as others. (Another common-
sense natural treatment of Jewish characters
that deserves mention is *Body and Soul*, a
movie about a Jewish prize fighter.)

message of "tolerance" comes to us at second hand, and the Irish, whose acceptance
is taken for granted, are made buffers for
the Jews: Jews are a bit peculiar, so the
argument seems to go, but they are after all
no more outlandish than the Irish.

This "buffer system" seems also to supply the logic behind those "cross section"
films where Jews are self-consciously presented as "part of America," engaged with
their fellow Americans in some common
task. In recent years the common task has
often been World War II, and with extraordinary regularity the typical "service picture"
would present Americans united in military
action but showing their diverse backgrounds in their accents, their names, and
their recollections of home. Along with the
Texan, the man from Brooklyn, the Americans
of Irish, Italian, and Slavic descent, occasionally a Negro, there might be a Jew. Such
pictures as *A Walk in the Sun*, *The Purple
Heart*, *Guadalcanal Diary*, *Air Force*, *Action
in the North Atlantic*, *Sands of Iwo Jima*, and
*Bataan* all belong to this category of "minority" abstractions, and they all admit the Jew
into the cross section (of *Bataan*, the *New
York Times* reviewer observed: "Thomas
Mitchell plays his usual Irish iron-man, even

In *It's a Big Country*, one of the most
ardently inoffensive of the "cross section"
films, there is a "Negro episode" in which,
instead of a professionally acted story, we
see newsreel clips of Negro dignitaries, while
the spoken commentary tells us that these
are "Americans" in every walk of life; the
word "Negro" is not used—one would never
guess from the sound track what the episode
is about. As one might expect after this
display of discretion, the "Jewish episode"
never mentions Jews. An American soldier
home from Korea calls on the mother of a

friend who has been killed in action. The mother is hospitable until she learns that the soldier's name is Maxie Klein, but her hostility changes back to friendliness when he reads a letter from her son in which the son urges the necessity of having "allies." Klein is of course a satisfactorily neutral name; the mother never mentions the cause of her hostility, and Maxie never refers to it. The letter he reads is at a respectful, discreet distance from the subject at hand. One wonders how many of those the film wished to influence for the better even got the point of this episode.

*Crossfire* and *Gentleman's Agreement*, though they presented their messages more clearly, suffered likewise form an excess of discretion. Bent on showing that Jews are just like everyone else, these films so neutralized their Jewish characters as to deprive them of all reality. Indeed, in *Gentleman's Agreement*, it will be recalled, the main "Jewish" character is simply a Gentile who calls himself a Jew so he can write a series of articles called "I Was Jewish for Eight Weeks." And *Crossfire* simply failed to characterize fully the Jewish victim of prejudice; evidently the makers of the movie were so concerned to enlist everybody's sympathies on his side that they feared the results of endowing him with any specific traits other than a vague benevolence. They did not allow Sam Levene to give the typical performance he has sometimes been permitted to give, even in the movies, apparently because they did not want it said that he was "too Jewish."

It is certain that the important role played by Jews in the movie industry, and some sensitivity about the large financial rewards the industry has brought them, have, especially since Hitler, contributed to the establishment of the "tradition" of suppression, evasion, and sugar-coating that I have described. There has also been pressure from Jewish organizations, often more energetic than effective. And there has been support from the Hays code, which went into effect in 1934 and which provides that no religion shall be ridiculed; under the code, Jews are

Robert Mitchum, Robert Ryan, and Robert Young in *Crossfire* (1947).

regarded as members of a religious group. The avowed intention of the policy has been laudable: to combat anti-Semitism. But there is in it also a great deal of stuffiness, timidity, and plain lack of imagination, which, when it is allowed to predominate, produces a culture of stereotypes and uniformity.

We are entitled to ask, too, whether the policy does not even defeat its primary purpose. Do not these restrictions and concealments make the Jew, in the eyes of the anti-Semite or the potential anti-Semite, more menacing and mysterious than ever—a figure so powerful that he can cause his image and his very name to vanish when it serves his purpose? The disappearance of the Jew from the popular arts inevitably inspires the question, especially among the prejudiced: what does he have to hide?

If the creators of our popular culture believe in a world in which the Jew exists, let them show such a world. Let the Jew come back, not as apologist or walking object lesson, not as a generalized focus for sentiments of tolerance or as a public-relations representative of his people, but the man himself in all his concreteness— his strengths and his weaknesses—the human being he used to be.

# OUR *SHOW OF SHOWS*

### J. HOBERMAN AND JEFFREY SHANDLER

*Your Show of Shows* was one of the first major programming successes of the American television industry. This ninety-minute comedy-variety program (originally known as the *Admiral Broadway Revue*) aired live every Saturday night for five seasons on NBC (1950–54). The program's creator, Max Liebman, found inspiration for *Your Show of Shows* in theatrical revues that he and other producers had presented both on Broadway and at resort hotels on the outskirts of New York.

The series offered its viewers the equivalent of a brand-new Broadway revue each week—a program of music and dance sequences alternating with comedy sketches.

While *Your Show of Shows* was hailed for pioneering advances in the quality of television production and for helping introduce opera singers, ballet dancers, and other performing artists to the general American public, the series is best remembered today for its inspired comedy. Many critics consider it to have set the standard for comedy writing and performing against which television variety and situation comedy programs are measured to this day. A number of the writers who worked on *Your Show of Shows* or its successors, *Caesar's Hour* (NBC, 1954–57) and *Sid Caesar Invites You* (ABC, 1958)—including Woody Allen, Mel Brooks, Selma Diamond, Larry Gelbart, Carl Reiner, and Neil Simon—went on to write, direct, produce, and perform in an extensive list of television situation comedies and talk shows, comedy recordings, Hollywood films, and Broadway plays.

Sid Caesar's writers, c. 1956. Front row: Gary Belkin, Sheldon Keller, Michael Stewart, and Mel Brooks; back row: Neil Simon, Mel Tolkin, and Larry Gelbart.

While many of those involved in *Your Show of Shows*, both before the camera and behind it, were Jews, the series made only occasional, passing references to Jewishness in its comedy, such as the use of Yiddishisms in sketches. For example, the show's parodies of foreign films included a Japanese film "starring *gantze mishpochoh* (whole family) . . . , *gehaktekh leber* (chopped liver), and *shmateh* (rag) . . . and a Gallic romp set in a *boîte* named *La Fligl* (The Chicken Wing)."[1] As literary scholar Irving Howe suggested, this practice may have served the writers as "a wave to the folks back home . . . an inside joke."[2] Indeed, the show was not discussed in the mainstream press as having any connection to Jewishness, at least not directly. Thus, one reviewer in the *New York Journal-American* wrote that producer Max Liebman's "years of dipping into entertainment borscht gives the program a definite flavor, experience, adaptability, and taste."[3]

It was only a generation later that the series's writers and performers revisited *Your Show of Shows* as a fountainhead of the comedic talents of American-born

## The Forgotten Closet

In the 1950's, the site of the famed "writers' room" (**A**) was a warren of production and writing spaces, including the office of Max Liebman, the television producer. Today it is a three-room, unoccupied corner suite on floor 6M of the City Center building. To reach the closet where he stashed a trove of documents, a visitor must now walk past the elevators (**B**), down a corridor, through a ladies' room (**C**) and into another corridor (**D**) to the closet (**E**). But before walls were added years later (**F**), the closet was easily accessible from the writers' room.

children of Jewish immigrants from Eastern Europe. They have appeared repeatedly on television talk shows and in documentary films, celebrating the inspiration derived from their shared sensibility as American Jews growing up in New York during the Depression and coming of age during World War II. In one such interview, Reiner recalled that the series's head writer, Mel Tolkin, would often exhort them, "'Gentlemen, we've got to get something done! Jews all over America will be watching Saturday night!' We assumed only Jews watched this. Of course, it wasn't so. . . . We were very aware that we were Jewish, and we wanted to make sure that America understood our humor."[4]

Several of these writers have turned to their early days working on *Your Show of Shows* as inspiration for more recent works. Reiner drew on his experience as a writer for the series in his autobiographical television situation comedy *The Dick Van Dyke Show* (CBS, 1960–66), originally intending to play the lead role of Robert Petrie himself.[5] The behind-the-scenes world of *Your Show of Shows* was re-created in the comedy *My Favorite Year* (MGM, 1983), produced by Mel Brooks's Brooksfilms. And in 1993, Neil Simon paid homage to the show and its creators in his Broadway play *Laughter on the Twenty-Third Floor*, adapted for television in 2001.

ABOVE
On November 14, 2000, this map accompanied a front-page story in the *New York Times* announcing the discovery of a treasure trove of lost scripts from *Your Show of Shows*: "The Egyptians may have King Tut's tomb, but now New Yorkers have Max Liebman's closet."

RIGHT
Mel Brooks (standing), Woody Allen, Mel Tolkin, and Sid Caesar.

Sid Caesar and Imogene
Coca as Samson and Delilah
in *Your Show of Shows*.

BELOW
Carl Reiner (left) directing
George Segal and Rob
Reiner in *Where's Poppa?*
(1970).

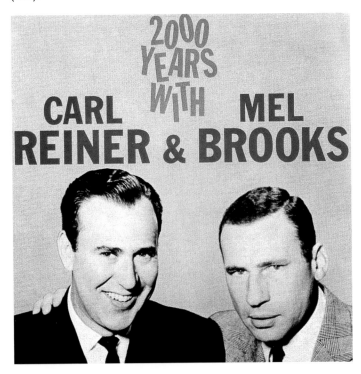

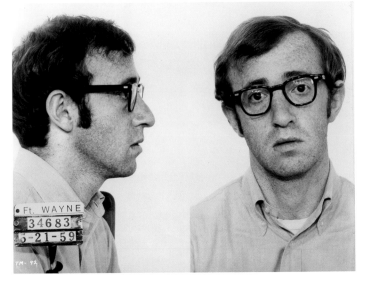

ABOVE
George Burns and Walter
Matthau as aging vaudevil-
lians in the film version of
Neil Simon's *The Sunshine
Boys* (1975).

ABOVE
Mug shot of Virgil Starkwell,
played by Woody Allen in
his 1969 film *Take the
Money and Run*.

*The Dick Van Dyke Show* (CBS, 1960–66), with Rose Marie, Morey Amsterdam, and Dick Van Dyke as the writing staff for the "Allen Brady Show." Carl Reiner based the situation comedy on his experience as a writer for *Your Show of Shows.*

*My Favorite Year* (1982) recreated the backstage world of *Your Show of Shows*, with Joseph Bologna (third from left) as Stan "King" Kaiser, based on Sid Caesar.

Advertisement for the television version of *Laughter on the Twenty-Third Floor* (2001), Neil Simon's homage to *Your Show of Shows*, featuring Nathan Lane as Max Prince, a character modeled on Sid Caesar.

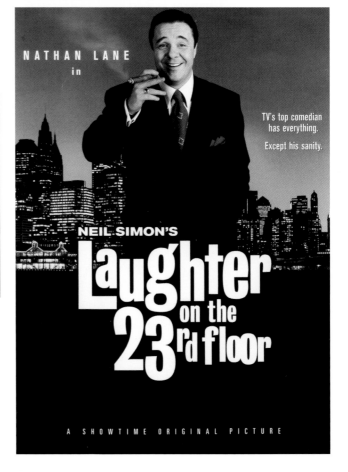

STAR GALLERY

**IT SHOULD BE NO SURPRISE** THAT THE MOST
EXTENSIVE AND VARIED DISCUSSION OF JEWS AND THE ENTERTAINMENT
MEDIA CENTERS ON FAMOUS PERFORMERS. ACTIVELY ENCOURAGED
BY PRODUCERS, PUBLICISTS, AND THE PERFORMERS THEMSELVES, THE
PUBLIC'S INTEREST IN MOVIE STARS HAS BEEN A PROMINENT FEATURE OF
THE AMERICAN FILM INDUSTRY FROM ITS EARLIEST DAYS.

Celebrities have loomed large in radio and television as well. The discourse surrounding stars extends beyond the consideration of their artistic virtuosity to a fascination with their entire being. The offstage lives of the stars—their homes, what they wear and eat, with whom they are intimately involved, and the social causes they may espouse—are no less compelling than their onstage work.

As a star's persona infuses his or her performances, each new role resonates with the accumulation of previous performances, official publicity, and unofficial gossip. In this way, a star becomes a "text," to be studied and discussed by the public. As Richard Dyer argues in *Stars*, his classic analysis of the subject, stardom is a social and ideological phenomenon with intimations of the miraculous. At once fictional representations and actual people, stars effect a "magical reconciliation" of seemingly contradictory states.[1] Thus, while some stars verge on mythic archetypes (the vamp, the Latin lover, America's sweetheart, the bitch goddess, the teen heartthrob, the good bad boy), stars can also seem familiar, even intimate presences. For their fans, stars can become objects of worship, of obsession, of inspiration; they engender complicated, intense relationships that are almost always completely imaginary.

The Jewishness of the Jewish star often becomes part of this relationship between star and audience—especially, though by no means exclusively, for Jewish audiences. (Anti-Semites may be as eager to unmask hidden or suspected Jews as Jewish fans are to lay claim to stellar co-religionists.) The discussions of stars' Jewishness are as complex and multivalent as the larger discourse on Jewish identity over the past century. Often the debate is at odds with what stars themselves (or rather, their publicists) have to say about being Jews—which usually is nothing at all. Indeed, during the earlier decades of the twentieth century, most Jewish stars would do whatever was necessary to obscure their origins, variously altering their names, accents, noses, hair, and personal histories. Often, therefore, talking about a star's Jewishness constitutes an act of cultural subversion, not only undoing the efforts of an industry to conceal or transform it, but also transgressing conventional boundaries of what is deemed appropriate for public consideration in the American mainstream.

This "Star Gallery" samples the discourse around the Jewish stars of American film and broadcasting, from the era of silent movies to the present. The selection, by no means comprehensive, is intended to demonstrate the great range of opinions about Jewishness inspired by a wide variety of stars. Along with figures such as John Garfield and Barbra Streisand, whose open acknowledgment of their Jewishness has figured prominently in discussions of their lives, work, and identities, the gallery includes less obvious examples, such as one of Hollywood's first cowboys, Bronco Billy Anderson. There are, in addition, several unusual cases: converts (Marilyn Monroe, Sammy Davis, Jr.), cartoon characters (Betty Boop, Superman), and a young woman whose dreams of a Hollywood career were unrealized but have been extensively imagined by others (Anne Frank).

Some pieces in the Star Gallery are reprinted from press reports, memoirs, or other vintage sources. Others reflect the personal engagement of contemporary writers with Jewish stars or are the editors' syntheses. Not surprisingly, these texts often tell us more about their authors and their personal concerns with Jewishness than they do about what being a Jew might mean to the stars in question. As is often the case with stars, the performer serves as a catalyst for the audience member's self-projection.
—J.H./J.S.

Montage illustrating a profile of Theda Bara, "Vampire Woman," in *Theatre* magazine, November 1915.

Theda Bara
1885–1955
Born as Theodesia Goodman
Cincinnati, Ohio

The first movie star to have an image fabricated through a full public relations build-up, Theda Bara burst upon the scene as the exotic, kohl-eyed, cigarette-smoking, implacable vamp (from the word *vampire*) in the Fox production *A Fool There Was*. Released in January 1915, the movie grossed some $3 million, more than ten times the studio's entire income for the previous year.

William Fox had purchased the rights to Porter Emerson Brown's stage play *A Fool There Was* and, on the advice of the play's producer, cast an unknown in the role of the femme fatale. Fox publicists invented Bara's background as well as her name and the newly minted star signed a three-year contract prohibiting her to marry, take public transportation, act in the theater, go to a Turkish bath, pose for photographs, or close the window curtains on her limousine. She was to always appear heavily veiled and was allowed out only at night. Journalists were initially told that she spoke no English.[1]

"Always I have been a Charlatan," Bara wrote in a 1919 article. "For years, my emotional display has been accredited to my Arab blood. Such is the fame of Charlatanism that dark hair and eyes have been interpreted as positive proof that I was nursed on camel's milk in a chief's tent, with my baby face turned to the East." In fact, she was the daughter of a Polish Jew who immigrated to Ohio, married a Swiss-born woman, and became a small-scale clothing manufacturer. Theodesia Goodman grew up in the middle-class, largely Jewish neighborhood of Avondale, attended the University of Cincinnati for two years, then moved to New York in 1905, hoping to go on the stage. According to her biog-

rapher Ronald Genini, the future vamp played secondary roles for a Lower East Side Yiddish theater in 1910 before breaking into movies as an extra.[2]

Fox cast Bara as a specifically Jewish character in her second feature, *The Kreutzer Sonata* (based on Yiddish dramatist Jacob Gordin's adaptation of a work by Leo Tolstoy), but, after *A Fool There Was*, her image was set for all time. Occasionally billed as "The Wickedest Woman in the World," Bara appeared in thirty-eight films over the next four years, playing Carmen, Cleopatra, Madame Dubarry, and Salome—as well as the Devil's Daughter, the Serpent, the Vixen, and the Tiger Woman. Her salary, supposedly $75 per week for *A Fool There Was*, reached $4,000 before her popularity faded in 1919.[3]

Like the movies in general, Bara promoted the pleasure principle. According to Terry Ramsaye, her pictures "made money at the box office [in about the same proportion that] they made trouble with the censors." The actress embodied the foreign, oriental, sybaritic aspect of motion pictures; some suggest that her persona was specifically Semitic. In *Evil Sisters: The Threat of Female Sexuality and the Cult of Manhood*, Bram Dijkstra calls Bara "the American male's fondest nightmare: a sexual woman whose motives for seduction were not strictly economic, but 'organic' as well." She was the invasive other of everyone's fears: Salome, Judith, Astarte; Lilith, the lustful, primal Eve who stole semen from sleeping men; Lamia, her daughter, the serpent queen. Semitic, masculinized, she was also "Shylock, Svengali, Dracula: Arab Death."[4]

Nine years after Bara's last screen role—parodying her image in the 1926 Hal Roach comedy *Madame Mystery*—the actress volunteered a self-characterization as "just a nice Jewish girl."[5]

—J.H.

Bronco Billy Anderson
1882–1971
Born as Max Aronson
Little Rock, Arkansas

The original movie-star cowboy, as well as one of the cinema's first continuing characters, Gilbert M. Anderson wrote and directed himself in some 375 "Bronco Billy" movies between 1907 and 1914. An Arkansas-born traveling salesman, Max Aronson arrived in New York at age eighteen, changing his name to Gilbert Maxwell Anderson in hopes of becoming an actor. After playing several roles (and being thrown by a horse) in Edwin Porter's epochal 1903 western *The Great Train Robbery* (Edison), Anderson became a production assistant at Vitagraph. Now a filmmaker, he moved west to Pittsburgh, then Chicago—there cofounding the Essenay company in 1907—and finally California. Although among the first (some say *the* first) to make movies in Los Angeles, Anderson established a production base at Niles Canyon, near San Francisco, where he specialized in westerns.

The Bronco (originally Broncho) Billy character, an outlaw turned hero, was introduced in *The Bandit Makes Good* (Essanay, 1907) and gained tremendous popularity over the course of a boom that, by 1910, saw one out of five American-made movies devoted to "wild west" subjects. A few of these, including two movies entitled *The Yiddisher Cowboy* (Lubin, 1908, and American, 1911), were comedies featuring incongruous Jewish protagonists. Bronco Billy, however, had no ethnicity. Max Aronson's world-famous alter ego was an icon. Hollywood journalist Ezra Goodman described him as "a good-bad man [who] never changed the stolid expression on his face or the costume he sported. He rode a pinto horse and rescued young ladies, but never kissed them." Anderson retired Bronco Billy in 1915 (the same year he lured ascendant star Charles Chaplin away from Mack Sennett's Keystone for a brief stint at Essenay); he revived the character in 1919 to little success.[1]

On the occasion of Anderson's death, Harry Golden wrote of his childhood admiration for the star who "helped the imagination escape the Lower East Side. . . . Immigrant boys didn't troop to see Bronco Billy Anderson because we wanted to grow up and become actors or because we couldn't stand our home life. We went to see Bronco Billy because he taught us the attitudes we most admired in the new world. . . . The early Westerns conferred upon us our first ideals of American manhood: speak the truth, shoot straight and save the wagon train."

"What we didn't know," Golden added, "was that Bronco Billy Anderson's name was Max Aronson and that the horse he rode was a saddle mounted on a sawbuck."[2]
—J.H.

ABOVE
**Bronco Billy Anderson (center)** in *Broncho Billy and the Gambler* (1914).

Fanny Brice
(center) in *My Man* (1928).

Fanny Brice
1891–1951
Born as Fania Borach
New York

**FANNY BRICE**

"I believe it's because I'm Jewish that I have been a steady climber on the stage," Ziegfeld star Fanny Brice told the readers of the *Jewish Tribune* in 1928. "Not that my success has been brought by imitations of Jewish types, but the versatility with which I have been credited is peculiar to the Jews. There is no need of my giving historical justification for my statement, as scholars have long determined that a variety of experiences, and a constantly changing environment have produced adaptability in the Jew, rarely possessed by other people."[1]

The eighteen-year-old Fanny Brice found herself as a popular performer with a comic specialty song, "Sadie Salome, Go Home"—the tale of an adventurously stage-struck Jewish-American girl—written for her by Irving Berlin. Brice performed the song with a Yiddish accent although she herself was the daughter of Hungarian and Alsatian immigrant parents and had grown up middle class in an ethnically mixed Newark neighborhood.

The success of "Sadie Salome" catapulted Brice into the 1910 *Ziegfeld Follies*, where she also sang a "coon" song. Gilbert Seldes would approvingly bracket Brice with Al Jolson as an example of the "demonic" in the American theater. But, unlike Jolson, Brice was explicitly Jewish, both in her use of Yiddish-dialect humor and her stage personae. As provided for her by Berlin, her stock character was the nice Jewish-American girl in an unlikely situation.

(She satirized Theda Bara in the 1916 *Follies* and again in 1920, singing "I'm a Vamp from East Broadway.") Brice's signature torch song, "My Man," which she first sang in the 1921 *Follies*, was understood as a reflection of her tormented marriage to the gambler and con artist Nick Arnstein.

At the height of her career, Brice was the most famous Jewish woman in America; her well-publicized cosmetic surgery in 1923 prompted Dorothy Parker to wisecrack that "Fanny Brice cut off her nose to spite her race." (In her 1980 autobiography, Molly Picon writes that Brice ceased to be funny after she had her nose "fixed.") Nevertheless, Brice continued to specialize in Jewish humor. Herbert Goldman cites Brice's popular 1927 recording, the dialect monologue "Mrs. Cohen at the Beach," as a significant precursor to the persona that Gertrude Berg would develop several years later in *The Rise of the Goldbergs*.[2]

In 1928, Warner Bros. signed Brice for its second full talkie, *My Man*. But, unlike the same year's smash Jolson vehicle, *The Singing Fool*, *My Man* was a box-office failure, something *Variety* blamed on the star's "Hebrew jesting." A second feature, *Be Yourself!* (made for United Artists in 1930 and including several songs written for Brice by her new husband, the showman Billy Rose), proved scarcely more successful. Brice consequently reinvented herself as an ethnically neutral radio star, playing the character Baby

Snooks for eleven seasons beginning in 1937–38.

Brice's life story has become a show business myth. The Twentieth Century Fox film *Rose of Washington Square* (1937) was loosely based on her marriage to Arnstein, with star Alice Faye singing "My Man." (Unhappy with the movie, Brice sued the studio for damages and won an out-of-court settlement.) A decade after her death, Brice's son-in-law, Ray Stark, engaged Isabel Lennart to write a bio-pic. Due to a lack of studio interest, the material was first produced as the Broadway musical *Funny Girl*, which featured Barbra Streisand and opened on March 26, 1964. A film version (released by Columbia), again with Streisand, was made in 1968. "The projection of Fanny Brice's rise from the pushcart-laden Lower East Side to Ziegfeld stardom and a baronial Long Island estate, avec Rolls-Royce, is achieved in convincing broad strokes," per *Variety*.[3]

*Funny Girl* elevated Streisand to the peak of American show business while reducing Brice to a footnote. For the cultural critic Camille Paglia, "Streisand's greatness [was] that she was able to inject the madcap Fanny Brice persona with all the sensuality and glamour of the great stars." Unlike Brice, Paglia noted, the aggressively ethnic Streisand refused to alter her "Jewish" nose.[4]

—J.H.

# "Plastic Surgery for the Stage"

Fanny Brice's rhinoplasty was performed by Dr. Henry J. Schireson in her apartment at the Ritz-Carlton in Atlantic City, New Jersey, during the summer of 1923. According to Dr. Schireson, Florenz Ziegfeld opposed the surgery, explaining that while he could get all the "classic beauties" he wanted, Brice was unique. "There are a hundred pretty girls with nice noses for every place in the chorus—and they're all alike. This nose cannot be replaced or imitated. It's a million-dollar nose."[5]

The operation merited no less than four items in the *New York Times*, including the following editorial, which appeared on August 16, 1923. Neither the editorialist nor Brice herself explicitly identifies her nose as a mark of Jewishness; rather, they discuss it as a signifier of taste, temperament, and class. Likewise, the surgery is likened to urban renewal and is understood as artistic, rather than an ethnic "transformation."
—J.H./J.S.

From an editorial in the *New York Times*, August 16, 1923, 14.

Miss Fannie Brice has just had her nose condemned and torn down, and is about to erect a high-class modern structure on the site. To speak of this operation in terms of engineering is only to reflect the language of the dispatches from Atlantic City, where the great event took place. One might think it the greatest engineering feat since the building of the Panama Canal. Miss Brice says, or at any rate is quoted as saying: "I look in the mirror and I say to myself that this is the nose that God gave me, and I tell myself how well it has served me, and how faithfully. But then, in noses as in life, one wearies of the too familiar. Charm lies in the unexpected. Besides, I am tired of having to fit my hats to the curse of my nose rather than the needs of my temperament."

Ah, well, Progress, the Time Spirit, will be served. An age that scrapped the Madison Square Presbyterian Church when it outlived its usefulness can hardly pause for an actress's nose. Terms of a real estate transaction are appropriate, for it appears that the real reason for the reconstruction of the nose was not the desire to buy hats for the temperament, but to act in plays of a different type. In other words, it was a change in the character of the district— just as in the case of the Madison Square Presbyterian Church—which required the demolition of the old structure and the erecting of a new one.

Miss Brice, already successful in homely comedy for which the old nose was an asset, now wants to branch out. In the drama of the drawing room the nose might distract attention from the play, like Robert Edmond Jones's setting for "Macbeth." Other artists would accept this limitation and go on doing comedy; Miss Brice boldly decides to abolish the inhibitory nose. It is a perilous undertaking, artistically if not surgically. Yet everybody will hope that the purpose which its owner has in mind will be attained. Certainly no great harm can be done, for unlike some other comedians Miss Brice carries her talent inside her head and not on the frontal elevation.

An interpretative artist, of course, is able to do things that a creative artist couldn't attempt. Miss Brice thinks that she can change her style by changing her nose. Hurrah for the intrepid Fannie, whose motto is "All for art and a nose well lost."

Fanny Brice and Hume Cronyn in *Ziegfeld Follies* (1946).

Eddie Cantor
1892–1964
Born as Edward Israel Iskowitz
New York

The most resilient of Jewish variety performers, Eddie Cantor was the child of Russian immigrants, deserted by his father after his mother's death, and raised in poverty by his maternal grandmother—whose name, Kantrowitz, shortened and Americanized by a Lower East Side public school, became the basis for his own.

Cantor was a professional entertainer by age fourteen, working his way through vaudeville and burlesque as a blackface comedian until he was hired for the 1916 edition of the *Ziegfeld Midnight Frolic*. Featured in the next three editions of the *Ziegfeld Follies*, Cantor joined Fanny Brice as the only Jews among the Follies' mainstays. Although Cantor persuaded Florenz Ziegfeld to allow him to perform without burnt cork, blackface remained intrinsic to his identity. (The 1925 *Ziegfeld Follies*, in which Cantor did not appear, included a number, "Eddie Be Good," in which twenty-four chorus girls blacked up to look like the absent star.) Nevertheless, as his biographer Herbert Goldman describes it, Cantor's "persona was unmistakably Jewish—pushy, slightly nebishy." Indeed, Cantor "openly proclaimed his Jewishness in jokes and Yiddish ad-libs on the stage."[1]

A Broadway star throughout the 1920s, Cantor relocated to Hollywood with the coming of talking pictures, appearing in the first two Ziegfeld productions to be filmed, *Glorifying the American Girl* (Paramount, 1929) and

*Whoopee!* (United Artists, 1930). In both, Cantor's persona is openly ethnic. *Glorifying the American Girl* includes a skit in which he plays Moe the Tailor (a character he introduced in the *Follies* a decade earlier), a near-demonic Lower East Side immigrant Jew who uses a "ghetto" hard sell that verges on physical violence to outfit the innocent mark who has wandered into his shop. In *Whoopee!*, a million-dollar vehicle produced by Samuel Goldwyn and promoted as a "genuine $6.60 Broadway production," Cantor stars as a hypochondriacal New Yorker who goes West for his health. The press book characterizes him as a "Jewish cowboy" while promising "laughs, giggles, gurgles, [and]

roars run riot," when he begins "to cut up as a Jewish Indian." Indeed, in attempting to sell a blanket, Cantor's Jewish Indian lapses into Yiddish.[2]

*Whoopee!* was a hit in New York and other, mainly northern, cities where Ziegfeld companies regularly toured, but its urban "sophistication" (like that of the talkies in general) was not universally appreciated, particularly in the hinterlands, where audiences sometimes resented the show-biz sharpies who displaced their favorite stars. As the Atlanta-based trade journalist Ernest Rogers correctly pointed out in *Variety*, there was no reason to assume that "a film which was a smash on Broadway" would perform as well on Peachtree Street.

EDDIE CANTOR

"Names like Eddie Cantor, George Jessel, Sophie Tucker et al. may mean money when put in front of a Broadway house; but in Atlanta, they've got to sell their stuff or miss the trade." As detailed by Henry Jenkins, Cantor's on-screen persona underwent a marked de-Semitization—as did his subsequent, far more successful movies.[3]

In the meantime, the entertainer opened up a second front in 1931 as the first established star to host his own network radio show. Goldman argues in his biography that Cantor used radio to redefine the nature of stardom. Through constant references to his wife and five daughters, Cantor "made himself a 'member of the family' to millions of Americans in a way that no performer had ever sought to be. . . . Cantor's use of his own family as radio props—allowing him to share his own private life with millions of Americans—made his private life a public one as well. Through Cantor's influence, the line between celebrity and actor became gradually blurred, and stars were finally perceived not as simply top-of-the-line actors but as public figures."

Goldman also considers Cantor to be "the first great performer-'humanitarian.'" Cantor had been an Actors' Equity activist since his stint in the *Follies*; years later, he attempted in vain to persuade Darryl Zanuck to buy the rights to the union musical *Pins and Needles* as a vehicle for himself. With radio, he took on new causes. In *Raised on Radio*, his history of the medium's American heyday, Gerald Nachman calls Cantor "the master, if not the originator, of the heartfelt appeal, which planted the first seed of celebrity do-goodism. . . . Before there were mawkish Jerry Lewis telethons, there was

Eddie Cantor on radio asking you, in his imploring manner, to give generously to the March of Dimes, the Heart Fund, the Boy Scouts of America, the National Myopia Society, or whatever charity tugged at his heart that week."[4]

Indeed, Cantor invented the March of Dimes (at the behest of Franklin Delano Roosevelt, who referred to him by name as his "good friend" on the occasion of his own Thanksgiving 1938 radiocast). According to Goldman, Cantor raised an estimated $1 billion for charity and, for many Jews, seemed the epitome of *yiddishkeit*, "a blend of model citizen and personal humanitarian, with a folksy, self-deprecating humor that belied his total faith in himself, his people, and his God. He made one feel good to be a Jew."[5]

Nor did Cantor neglect Jewish causes. He denounced Hitler as the "number one gangster of the world" and organized a drive to get five hundred Jewish children out of Nazi Germany. Cantor was also an early supporter of Israeli statehood. In 1939, he attacked the radio priest Father Charles E. Coughlin as an anti-Semite and, as a result, lost his sponsor, the R. J. Reynolds Tobacco Company. (Eleven years later, Cantor denounced Joseph McCarthy, only months after the Wisconsin senator made national headlines by declaring that the U.S. State Department was riddled with Communist agents.)

Adapting to yet another medium, Cantor hosted NBC's *Colgate Comedy Hour* on television for four seasons (1950–51 through 1953–54). During the course of his February 17, 1952, show, he used his trademark handkerchief (a prop often waved behind him as he skipped offstage) to mop the brow of guest

performer Sammy Davis, Jr., then a member of the Will Mastin Trio. When NBC was bombarded by racist hate mail, Cantor rose to the occasion by inviting the Mastin Trio to be on his next program. Davis, according to *Variety*, "walked away with the guesting honors, repeating the socko work he did on Cantor's last previous show." Cantor even reiterated his gesture, again wiping the perspiring Davis's face.[6]

Like Al Jolson, Cantor was the subject of a sentimental bio-pic, although it was less successful. He recorded twenty songs which star Keefe Brasselle lip-synchs in *The Eddie Cantor Story*, released by Warner Bros. on December 23, 1952.

—J.H.

# SYLVIA SIDNEY

Sylvia Sidney
1910–1999
Born as Sophia Kosow
New York

Born in the Bronx, Sylvia Sidney became an icon of 1930s slum dramas. She made her screen debut in the 1931 adaptation of Elmer Rice's stage play *Street Scene* as the Jewish hero's Irish girlfriend. *Variety* called her "persuasive" in a role for which she was "particularly fitted, typifying as she somehow does here, the tragedy of a . . . girlhood cramped by sordid surroundings. Even her lack of formal beauty intensifies the pathos of her character."

A budding exotic, Sidney was next cast as Cho-Cho-San in Paramount's version of *Madame Butterfly* (1931). An article in the December 5, 1931, *Picturegoer Weekly* speculated on the actress's unusual looks: "There's Bohemia in her own blood. Or, rather, Romania, which is the next state to it and near enough unless you're a stickler for accuracy. Sylvia's father was Romanian and her mother was Russian. She claims that makes her the Balkan gypsy she longs to be!"
—J.H.

Sylvia Sidney in *City Streets* (1931).

Harpo, Groucho, and Chico Marx with director Sam Wood during the filming of *A Night at the Opera* (1935).

Chico
1887–1961
Born as Leo Marx
New York

Gummo
1892–1977
Born as Milton Marx
New York

Harpo
1888–1964
Born as Adolph Marx
New York

Zeppo
1901–1979
Born as Herbert Marx
New York

Groucho
1890–1977
Born as Julius Marx
New York

No other American performers have engendered more wide-ranging speculation on the Jewish origins of their art than the Marx Brothers. The sons of Simon and Minnie (née Schoenberg) Marx, Jewish immigrants from Alsace and Germany, the five Marx Brothers—Chico, Harpo, Groucho, Gummo, and Zeppo—evolved their distinctive personae in vaudeville and on the Broadway stage before making a series of films that have remained among the most enduringly popular comedies of the Hollywood studio era. These include *The Cocoanuts* (Paramount, 1929), *Animal Crackers* (Paramount, 1930), *Monkey Business* (Paramount, 1931), *Horse Feathers* (Paramount, 1932), *Duck Soup* (Paramount, 1933), *A Night at the Opera* (MGM, 1935), and *A Day at the Races* (MGM, 1937).

Although the Marx Brothers—particularly the Italian-accented Chico—often appear as immigrant characters (and a 1932 *Time* cover story on the brothers characterized Groucho as "the prototype of Hebrew wisecrackers"),

specifically Jewish references, even oblique ones, seldom appear in their movies. Most famously, Groucho rhymes "explorer" with *shnorer* (Yiddish for *beggar*) in the song "Hooray for Captain Spalding," performed in the opening scene of *Animal Crackers*. This film also includes Chico's exposure of a pretentious poseur as "Abie the fish man" from Czechoslovakia. Such allusions may owe their presence less to the Marx Brothers themselves than to the team's screenwriters, notably George S. Kaufman and S. J. Perelman.[1]

The Marx Brothers said little about their Jewishness in memoirs or elsewhere. "We Marx Brothers never denied our Jewishness," Groucho maintained late in life. "We simply didn't use it." Groucho is nevertheless the source for the most oft-cited anecdote on this topic. Referring to the Hillcrest Country Club—founded by Los Angeles's German Jewish community in the 1920s, when they were barred from the city's other social clubs—he

OPPOSITE
Al Hirschfeld (American, b. 1903). *The Marx Brothers*, 1935. Collage with sheet music, silk, felt, steel wool, fur, cotton, string, ink, and opaque white, 17 1/4 x 15 1/4 in. (43.8 x 38.8 cm). National Portrait Gallery, Smithsonian Institution, Washington, D.C. © Al Hirschfeld. The Margo Feiden Galleries Ltd., New York.

ABOVE, LEFT
*Marxists*, French photographer Frédéric Brenner's gathering of Groucho impersonators, was taken in New York in 1994. This photograph was later published in his book *Jews/America/A Representation* (1996).

ABOVE, RIGHT
Andy Warhol (American, 1928–1987). *Ten Portraits of Jews of the Twentieth Century (Marx Bros.)*, 1980. Silkscreen print, 40 x 32 in. (101.6 x 81.3 cm). The Jewish Museum, New York, Promised gift of Lorraine and Martin Beitler.

allegedly commented, "I wouldn't want to be a member of any club that would have me."[2]

Nevertheless, film critics, scholars of Jewish-American culture, and others have repeatedly mined the Marx Brothers' oeuvre for markers of a cultural sensibility that can be identified as Jewish. This has prompted the film historian Lester Friedman to ask rhetorically whether an artist "from a Jewish home" is "automatically endowed with Jewish humor, wit, or pathos." Friedman suggests that the practice of attributing the Marx Brothers' humor to their essential Jewishness may be a form of projection or cultural narcissism, the result of conflating cultural "representations with intuited attitudes."[3]

Indeed, such assertions ultimately tell us more about the desire of various observers to situate the Marx Brothers in Jewish culture than they do about how Jewishness may have informed their artistry—if at all. (Described by one critic as the "symbolic embodiment of all persecuted Jews for 2,000 years," Groucho is said to have responded:

"What sort of goddamned review is that?")[4] Rather, these comments demonstrate the range of the observers' own notions of the culture—from ancient, sacred writ to modern immigrant institutions—that informs Jewish cohesion.[5]

—J.H./J.S.

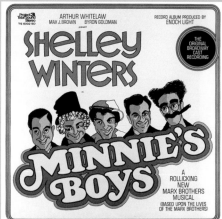

TOP, LEFT
"The Yippies are Marxists.
We follow in the revolutionary tradition of Groucho,
Chico, Harpo and Karl."
Photo collage from Jerry
Rubin's *Do It!* (1970).
Groucho, who lived through
the Marx Brothers revival
and Jewish humor boom of
the 1960s, ultimately
came to be seen as a pop
culture patriarch.

TOP, RIGHT
Original cast album of the
1970 Broadway musical
*Minnie's Boys*. Shelley
Winters starred as stage
mother Minnie Marx.

BOTTOM, LEFT
Playbill for the 1980
Broadway musical *A Day in
Hollywood, a Night in the
Ukraine,* which imagined
the Marx Brothers in a
screenplay based on Anton
Chekhov's one-act farce,
*The Bear.*

BOTTOM, RIGHT
Come-as-your-favorite-
Marx-Brother party scene in
*The Way We Were* (1973),
with Robert Redford (left)
as a Groucho and Barbra
Streisand (center) as Harpo.

# On the Jewishness of the Marx Brothers

## Sig Altman

"A less symbolic and more direct relationship to Jewish ambiguity [than Charlie Chaplin] may be discernible in the slouching, bespectacled, cigar-puffing figure of Groucho Marx. He too is out to deflate pomposity and defeat villainy, yet he is also a recognizable Jewish con man. His con game, however, is primarily one of identity. . . . He is obviously not what he claims to be, but he has few illusions about the acceptance of his claims. . . . That resigned acceptance, that passive amusement in being defeated by others, coming as it does from one affecting all the mannerisms of the go-getting 'shrewdie,' sums up the comedy of Groucho and conceivable that of a certain ironic type of Jew still not fully at home in the secular Western world, ambiguous, yet skeptical of the value of his own ambitions."[6]

## Patricia Erens

"[The Marx Brothers' comedy] reflects a Jewish urban attitude toward life, a sense of street-smart language learned on the Lower East Side, and linguistic tours de force derived from Talmudic debates."[7]

## James Yaffe

"The true tradition is being preserved. . . . The torch, which was carried by Sholem Aleichem, was passed on to the Marx Brothers; nothing could be more Jewish than their desparate zany insults, designed to deflate their pompous enemies but eventually making nothing but trouble for themselves."[8]

## Joel Rosenberg

"The zany, anarchic energy of the Marx Brothers, their subversive wordplay and dizzying non-sequitur, suggest a kind of Melting Pot meltdown. . . . Its roots perhaps go back to the centuries-old traditions of the *Purimshpiel* [Yiddish Purim play], itself a parody of assimilation, which grew from the great biblical tale of assimilation, the Book of Esther."[9]

## Ruth Perlmutter

"The Marx Brothers are always poised for attack: wit their weapon, vulgarity their mask, and cruelty their protection against emotional involvement and ethnic vulnerability. The incarnation of the expression *épater les bourgeois*, they are the surrealist brothers of the typical 30s American-Jewish rebel. Like the narrator of [Mike Gold's novel] *Jews Without Money*, they replace the Torah and the prayer shawl, but inimitably—with impiety, subversion, and putdown."[10]

## Charles Musser

"[In *Animal Crackers*] the Marx Brothers are Jewish hustlers insinuating themselves into WASP high society, itself shown to be a model of corruption and doubtful respectability, without this elitist group realizing what is happening. This comic premise is an aggressive assault on the exclusionary policies being applied to Jews by WASP-dominated universities, country clubs, and other public and private institutions."[11]

## Esther Romeyn and Jack Kugelmass

"The plots of the Marx Brothers' movies typically revolve around immigrant schemes to make fast money and gain entry into the exclusive worlds of class and culture. . . . Chico's virtuoso trick piano playing and his brother's dexterity at the harp (especially evident in *A Night at the Opera)* sabotage the exclusivity of high culture—a subversive strategy that reappears in the performances of numerous other Jewish comedians."[12]

## Albert Goldman

"If Chaplin distilled the self-pitying comedy of the schlemiel, the Marx Brothers brought to intense focus the other great mode of Jewish humor: the anarchic mockery of conventions and values, which crumble to dust at the touch of a rudely irreverent jest. 'Subversive' was the word for the Marx Brothers, as it has been the word often since employed both as condemnation of and tribute to the work of Jewish humorists who refuse to be trammeled by the conventional pieties."[13]

## Mark Winokur

"It is as if the [Marx] Brothers are attempting to found a *landsmannschaft*, an organization consisting of 'individuals from the same village (shtetl) or region in the Pale.' The *landsmannschaft* was an attempt to maintain a recognizable bond apart from sanctioned identities; as an attempt to help the immigrant fit in, it emphasized a memory and history separate from American memory and history. . . . In a world of tight collars and constricting belts, it was an ephemeral return to the more comfortable, if rougher, robes and tunics of the shtetl."[14]

## Irving Howe

"Even silliness, the Marx Brothers showed, had a point. In their films the disassembled world is treated with total disrespect, an attitude close to the traditional feeling among Jews that the whole elaborate structure of gentile power is merely trivial. The gleeful nihilism of the Marx Brothers made a shamble of things, reducing their field of operations to approximately what a certain sort of East Side skeptic had always thought the world to be: *ash un porukh*, ashes and dust."[15]

• • •

Finally, some have suggested that the Marx Brothers might have been seen as "too Jewish" even in Hollywood. In his collective biography of the brothers, Simon Louvish writes that Irving Thalberg "was a Marx fan" who, in order to bring the brothers to MGM, had to overcome Louis B. Mayer's reluctance "possibly caused by Mayer's loathing of anything in pictures that might draw attention to his Jewish immigrant origins."[16]

—J.H./J.S.

Betty Boop
Created in New York, 1930

### *Bubbie* Boop

Recently, I was invited to give a talk on Betty Boop at a meeting of the newly formed Berkeley Hadassah Young Women's Group.[1] I had been traveling to academic conferences on both film and Jewish studies with a version of this paper for a couple of years, presenting the Fleischer Brothers' Betty Boop cartoons in relationship to the animators' Lower East Side, Yiddish-American background. The cartoons are replete with references to Jewish culture and—as in *Betty Boop's Bamboo Isle* (1932), where Samoan natives greet Betty with a clearly enunciated "*shalom aleichem*!"—unlikely characters who speak a smattering of Yiddish.[2]

Saving the best for last, I always concluded my presentation with evidence that Betty herself is clearly Jewish. In a 1931 cartoon, *Minnie the Moocher*, a plot straight out of the Yiddish cinema of that time introduces us to a conflict between Betty's Eastern European parents and Betty herself, a thoroughly American flapper. Watching her famous figure, Betty refuses to eat the food that would turn her into a proper *yidishe mame* (Jewish mother), and leaves home, taking her first steps out into the world as a sexy, sassy, Jewish-American woman, the star of her own show. This revelation produced huge grins and discussion in a hall full of Jewish history scholars at Hebrew Union College in Cincinnati. Finally, Riv-Ellen Prell, known for her work on the position of women in Judaism, remarked with a smile that she would have felt differently (implying: better) about being a Jewish woman if she had known Betty Boop was Jewish.[3]

Before Riv-Ellen's comment, I hadn't thought much about Betty as a role model for Jewish women. In fact, she seems singularly unsuited to the position. Betty Boop is all about short skirts, round breasts, and her garter; in fact, she spends a good deal of time in her cartoons undressed. I revisited the cartoons with Dr. Prell's comment in mind before speaking to the Hadassah group made up of young —twenties and thirties—professional Berkeley feminists. Armed with all the evidence of Betty's Jewishness I could muster—her Lower East Side home in *Any Rags* (1930) and *Minnie the Moocher* (1931), her strong Brooklyn accent and her Yiddish dream in *Betty's Lifeguard* (1934)—I posed the question to the group: Is Betty Boop a positive role model for Jewish women?

In her favor, we screened cartoons that put Betty in control: *Betty Boop for President* (1932), *Judge for a Day* (1935), and *Betty Boop's Trial* (1934). Betty was the only female cartoon star of the 1930s, and story lines like these placed her in positions of power in a world that looked much like the real one: urban, complicated, dirty, and occasionally dangerous. In contrast, Mickey Mouse, that other big thirties cartoon star, lived in a world almost devoid of politics or the difficulties of real American life. The argument against Betty as exemplary Jewish woman pointed out that her presidential platform was one of providing free jazz and cabarets to the citizenry, that she frequently relies on sex appeal to get what she wants, and that the only clearly Jewish characters in the films, her parents, are made distinctly unsympathetic.

I would add to this that almost all Betty's early story lines involve her getting into trouble because of a man and her later ones (after the Hays Code forced her to lose her garter and lengthen her skirts) involve her inability to make good decisions about her future (often necessitating a rescue by her post-Code boyfriend, the strapping Fearless Freddie).

Through it all, though, Betty remains independent, single, and self-sufficient. She comes to symbolize the new American of the thirties, male or female, tutored in the difficult life of immigrant urban enclaves, but capable of succeeding in any American context, even the presidency. Betty is clearly a male fantasy, animated to show off her carefully drawn "tits and ass," but like real Jewish women, she exceeds her expected boundaries, performs roles unaccustomed to women of any creed, does it loudly and in front of an audience of millions, and leaves in 1939 much beloved and sorely missed, ripe for her recent revival. One young Hadassah member gave as her ultimate argument for adding Betty to our pantheon of foremothers: "She's so glamorous!" A glamorous, sexy, active Jewish woman who could be our grandmother—not such a bad ancestress, *nu*?[4]

—Amelia S. Holberg

Max Fleischer & Mae Questel.

Betty Boop and her sidekick Bimbo, flanked by their creator, Max Fleischer, and the Bronx-born vaudevillian Mae Questel, one of several women who provided her distinctive voice. Questel (1908–1998) spoke for Boop from 1931 until the character's retirement in 1939. She subsequently played specifically Jewish roles on stage and screen, including the skeptical Mrs. Strakosh in *Funny Girl* (1968) and, most famously, the great Jewish mother in the sky in Woody Allen's segment in the anthology film *New York Stories* (1989).

Cover of the first issue of *Action Comics*, June 1938, introducing the character of Superman.

**No. 1**                    **JUNE, 1938**

ACTION COMICS

**S U P E R M A N**

Superman
Created in Cleveland, Ohio,1934

A refugee boy sent by his doomed parents to America to escape the catastrophe that would destroy their world, Superman was a one-person diaspora created by Jerry Siegel (1915–1996) and Joe Schuster (1915–1992), childhood friends from Cleveland, during the summer of 1934.

Cartoonist Jules Feiffer described the origins of this first superhero of Siegel's adolescent fantasies as "a first generation Jewish boy of Russian stock, planted in the Midwest during the birth of native American fascism, the rise of anti-Semitism, the radio broadcasts of Father Coughlin."[1] Rejected by syndicated comic strips, Superman found his métier in the new media of comic books. His first appearance—six months after Kristallnacht—in the June 1938 issue of *Action Comics* marked the beginning of a pattern that would last for over half a century. Secretly the nearly invulnerable "Man of Steel," Superman maintained a public identity as the "mild-mannered reporter" Clark Kent.

Jeff Salamon has linked Superman's dual nature to the Zionist Max Nordau's 1898 call for a new generation of physically imposing *Muskeljuden*: "While Superman represents Nordau's ideal Jew, Clark Kent is the anti-Semitic stereotype Nordau was trying to replace—bespectacled, a coward, and in love with but unable to arouse the interest of Lois Lane, the shiksa of his dreams. . . . Moreover, his job—journalist—is a perfect example of the 'parasitical' occupations European Jews had been accused of holding since the birth of capitalism."[2]

Feiffer, by contrast, regards Superman as the "ultimate assimilationist fantasy," suggesting that Siegel's accomplishment was "to chronicle the smart Jewish boy's American dream. . . . It wasn't Krypton that Superman really came from; it was the planet Minsk."[3]
—J.H.

Bess Myerson,
Miss America 1945.

Bess Myerson
Born 1924
New York

Ever since she became the first Jewish woman
to win the Miss America pageant, in 1945,
Bess Myerson has loomed large in Jewish-
American public culture. Her victory, historian
Edward Shapiro claims, "signaled the postwar
movement of American Jews into the American
mainstream."[1]

   Throughout Myerson's long career in
the public eye—as a television personality,
public official, political figure, author, Jewish
community activist, and the subject of several
scandals—her status as a model of Jewish-
American womanhood and her iconic value as
the epitome of Jewish "at-homeness" in America
have accrued complex, sometimes highly
ambivalent meanings. In taking the measure
of Myerson's public life in her 1990 book
*When She Was Bad*, journalist Shana Alexander
reflects on the intersection of Myerson's
background as the daughter of Yiddish-speaking immigrants, growing up in the Sholem
Aleichem Houses in the Bronx during the
Depression, with her place in American popular culture, which experienced signal shifts in
the years immediately following World War II:

*The non-Jewish world heard of* schlock *with the
advent of the big TV game shows in the early
1950s.* Schlock *was the merchandise the shows
gave away, all the refrigerators and "dining-
room suites" and trips to Hawaii; the toothy TV
"hosts" who handed the free stuff out became
known as* schlockmeisters.

   *But many non-Yiddish-speaking people
about Myerson's age had become aware of the*

word schlock *a few years earlier, in the 1940s,
when the word was often associated with the
bathing-beauty contest held each September in
Atlantic City. At about the same time, young
women first became aware of another exotic,
exciting word,* sharkskin, *that being what the
beauties wore—white one-piece* sharkskin
*bathing suits. They became aware of "American
beauty roses" because that's what the contes-
tants carried as they paraded the Boardwalk.*[2]

The night before Myerson, a talented pianist
who had recently graduated from Hunter
College with a degree in music, won the title
Miss New York City, the organizer of the
Miss America pageant, Lenora Slaughter,

approached her to suggest that she change
her name to Betty Merrick. Myerson refused
and, despite the pressures that were allegedly
brought on the pageant and its judges, was
anointed Miss America. According to Alexander,
Myerson suffered through the first weeks
of her reign, which began with several appearances on Atlantic City's tawdry Steel Pier
and continued with a vaudeville tour in which
she did four shows a day, "always in her
bathing suit." Alexander writes:

*As winter came on in 1945, something hap-
pened that saved Bess Myerson's soul. She
was invited by the Anti-Defamation League
of the B'nai B'rith to tour the nation's high*

Bess Myerson and Allen Funt as hosts of the TV show *Candid Camera*, 1966.

schools speaking out against religious and racial intolerance of all minorities, not only Jews. As a beautiful young woman of working-class background, she was just the sort of person who could most readily capture people's attention, the league believed, and work to change the institutionalized prejudice that still held the nation in its grip.

Bess loved the assignment. It appealed to her sense of idealism, and her need to do something useful. Until her stint as Miss America ended, Myerson spent about half of her time speaking on racial, religious, and political tolerance to high school students, Kiwanis clubs, Rotary clubs, women's groups, 4-H groups, and anyone who would listen. She received $25 per performance.

"You can't be beautiful and hate," her standard speech began, "Because hate is a corroding disease and affects the way you look. . . . You can't hide it—ever. It shows in your eyes. It warps your expression. It affects your character, your personality." It was a weird Dorian Gray theory of personality devel-

opment, a curious amalgam of moralism and narcissism, which may be why it went over so well with her young audiences. . . .

By now, her celebrity as Miss America had made Bess Myerson the special heroine not just of the Sholem Aleichem Houses, but of all the Jews in America. In an incredible accident of timing, she had won her title in the same year that the shocking facts and sights of the Nazi concentration camps and their systematic extermination of six million Jews became known to the world. At that horrendous moment in human history it seemed somehow redemptive that here, in America, a Jewish girl should have been chosen fairest in all the land.[3]

Beginning in the late 1940s, Myerson appeared frequently as a pianist on New York television, eventually getting her own show. By 1952, she was the host of a network game show, *The Big Payoff*, and subsequently became a regular panelist on the long-running *I've Got a Secret*. In the late 1960s, Myerson became New York's celebrity

Commissioner of Consumer Affairs and, as Alexander notes, was a passionate fund-raiser for the State of Israel. Alexander writes:

Bess began to refer to herself publicly as "Queen of the Jews." The reference was to the biblical Queen Esther, the beautiful savior of the Persian Jews whose story Jews celebrate on the holiday of Purim. Of course there has always been more than a touch of self-mockery in the sobriquet, but many people did not pick it up, so that later in life, when Bess was no longer so popular, so admired, so adored, much of the public scorn directed against her was in retribution for her chutzpah.[4]

In early 1999, filmmaker Bill Condon announced plans for a Bess Myerson bio-pic to be called *Queen of the Jews*.[5]
—J.H./J.S.

Paul Muni
1895–1967
Born as Muni Weisenfreund
Lemberg, Austria

The son of Yiddish actors who immigrated from Galicia to New York's Lower East Side, Paul Muni appeared on stage from early childhood. He rivaled Maurice Schwartz as the leading actor in Schwartz's Yiddish Art Theater, leaving that company in 1926 to appear in the English-language Broadway production of *We Americans*. Muni made his movie debut three years later, starring in a number of Warner Bros. prestige films throughout the 1930s. Although Muni specialized in playing ethnic and historical characters—most famously an Italian-American gangster, a Chinese peasant, a French novelist, and a Mexican political leader—he appeared on-screen in a Jewish role only in his final film, *The Last Angry Man* (Columbia, 1959). When he died, the *Jewish Daily Forward* proclaimed Muni "the most successful actor from the Yiddish theater to cross over to the English-language stage and movies." The following week, the Yiddish journalist Moyshe Krishtol reflected on the actor's double career and multiple identities. Krishtol assured the *Forward*'s readers that the authentic artist was named Weisenfreund, his proper home was the stage, and his true language was Yiddish.

—J.S.

**From Moyshe Krishtol, "Paul Muni, Muni Weisenfreund,"** *Jewish Daily Forward*, September 2, 1967, pp. 4, 8.

I never called him by the name that made him world-famous—Paul Muni—but by the name that made him beloved to me—Muni Weisenfreund. Like everyone else, I was amazed by his truly monumental creations on the stage and by his performances in such roles as Louis Pasteur, Emil Zola, and his last great role as Clarence Darrow (in *Inherit the Wind*) —performances that will remain models for generations to come.

But when I think about this remarkable master, what first comes to mind are his per-

formances as Kopl in Sholem Aleichem's *The Grand Prize*, Ivan Ivanovich in Sholem Aleichem's *Hard to Be a Jew*, the publicity man in Khone Gottesfeld's *When Does He Die?*, Osip in Gogol's *Inspector General*, and other roles that he performed in the Yiddish Art Theater, performances that I can still savor to this day.

No doubt this has a lot to do with me—how I reacted, when I had these experiences at the time, in the 1920s, when I saw Weisenfreund in these roles. It was a romantic time in the Yiddish theater, in Yiddish literature, and in Jewish life in general (and everyone was so

young then). That may be true, but none of the other Yiddish actors of that time—and there were such wonderful artists among their ranks —has left me with the kind of feeling I have every time I think about Weisenfreund and his various roles, which literally make me feel warm inside. And I don't have that feeling for "Paul Muni," that is, for the roles that he created in English, whether on stage or in the movies, with the exception of, perhaps, his performance as Clarence Darrow, which possessed a bit of the flavor of his Yiddish roles. . . .

Whatever role Muni played—a Russian Orthodox priest, a Jewish tailor, an Italian gangster (*Scarface*), a French scientist (*Pasteur*) —he gave himself over to the role completely. He learned everything that he could about the person that he was to perform, sought to live his way into the character, working long and

Theater entrance promoting the Paul Muni vehicle *The World Changes*, 1933.

hard. When he finally stepped onto the stage, he was that character, that person, whom he performed down to the smallest detail, a model of perfection. He did not rely on his great talent, on his many years of success, on his skills; every role was a challenge that demanded his full attention, his complete concentration. . . .

The last years were very hard for this great performer. Before his so-called "comeback" in *Inherit the Wind* several years passed where he did nothing. The movie industry knows no bounds when it wants to elevate someone. When the movie producers saw that they could make millions with this actor, they gave him the greatest promotion and called him nothing less than "Mr. Paul Muni." No other

actor was given such honors. But after a short while—after he had great successes and couldn't find suitable roles (he didn't want to appear in just any film)—the movie bosses decided that Muni was finished, that he was a "has-been," and that they didn't need him any more. That is the way things are, it seems, only in the movie industry, which literally swallows people and then spits them out. The fact is that this "has-been" had such a great success in *Inherit the Wind* that some consider it to have been his greatest role. But I'm not sure that Kopl in *The Grand Prize* wasn't a greater work of art, though it was a much smaller role.

—Translated by Jeffrey Shandler

Judy Holliday configured as classic Hollywood cheesecake.

# JUDY HOLLIDAY

Judy Holliday
1922–1965
Born as Judith Tuvim
New York

The daughter of immigrant, Yiddish-speaking intellectuals, Judy Holliday grew up in Sunnyside Gardens, an early model housing project in Queens, New York. Although she is said to have had an IQ of 172, Holliday never attended college and began her performing career as a teenager at Unity House, the International Ladies Garment Workers Union adult summer camp in the Poconos, where she met Adolph Green. Holliday later teamed with Green and Betty Comden as the Revuers, a group of topical entertainers who appeared during the early 1940s at Max Gordon's racially integrated downtown clubs, Café Society and the Village Vanguard.

Holliday changed her name after a brief Hollywood foray and became a Broadway star as the comic, street-smart gangster's moll in the 1946 hit *Born Yesterday*. She nevertheless had to fight for the role when Columbia made the movie version, released in 1950. Studio boss Harry Cohn famously disparaged her as "that fat Jewish broad," until Holliday won an Oscar as the best screen actress of 1950. (George Cukor, who directed *Born Yesterday*, had used Holliday's supporting role in his 1949 *Adam's Rib* [MGM] as a screen test to convince Cohn. "A better realization on type than Miss Holliday's portrayal of a dumb Brooklyn femme doesn't seem possible," *Variety* wrote.)[1]

A supporter of progressive causes who had signed a *Variety* ad in support of the Hollywood Ten, Holliday was listed in *Red Channels*; soon thereafter she was investigated by the FBI and was intermittently picketed by the Catholic War Veterans. William H. Mooring, a critic syndicated in twenty-two diocesan newspapers, attacked *Born Yesterday* as crypto-Marxist, "the most diabolically clever political satire I have encountered in almost thirty years of steady film reviewing." March 26, 1952, only a year after winning an Oscar, Holliday was subpoenaed to testify before the U.S. Senate Subcommittee to Investigate the Administration of the Internal Security Act. Will Holtzman opens his 1982 biography of Holliday with a detailed and somewhat melodramatic description of this testimony:

The senator turns things over to his staff director, Richard Arens, a lawyer with a hard jaw and a no-nonsense monotone straight out of Gangbusters. "Name?"

"Judy Holliday."

"Your name is Judy Holliday as a stage name, is it?"

"Yes," her voice flutters.

"A professional name?"

"Yes," she says firmly but diffidently.

"What other name have you used in the course of your life?"

"Judy Tuvim. T-u-v-i-m." Translated liberally it is Hebrew for "holiday." Arens asks as though Holliday were not a stage name but an alias. He seems especially eager to establish that she is Jewish.[2]

Although she named no names, Holliday was cleared to make five more movies before her untimely death, including *Bells Are Ringing* (MGM, 1960), co-written by her erstwhile Café Society comrades, Comden and Green.
—J.H.

Judy Holliday looks askance at William Holden (right) as Broderick Crawford hovers in *Born Yesterday* (1950).

John Garfield.

JOHN GARFIELD

John Garfield
1913–1952
Born as Jacob Julius Garfinkle
New York

**Golden "Boychik"**

Throughout his Hollywood career, from his 1938 debut in *Four Daughters* until his death in 1952, John Garfield was known as an urban "tough guy," "rebel," and "outsider" in the Warner Bros. stable of actors that also included James Cagney, Humphrey Bogart, Edward G. Robinson, and George Raft. After appearing in a series of "B" features, Garfield ascended to "A" level stardom with *Pride of the Marines* (Warner Bros., 1945) and *The Postman Always Rings Twice* (MGM, 1946), followed by *Nobody Lives Forever* (Warner Bros., 1946), *Humoresque* (Warner Bros., 1946), *Body and Soul* (United Artists, 1947), *Gentleman's Agreement* (Twentieth Century Fox, 1947), *Force of Evil* (MGM, 1948), *We Were Strangers* (Columbia, 1949), *Under My Skin* (Twentieth Century Fox, 1950), *The Breaking Point* (Warner Bros., 1950), and *He Ran All the Way* (United Artists, 1951). At the time of Garfield's death of a heart attack, he had been the victim of anti-Communist black-listing, having refused to identify publicly friends who were Communists and being suspected of harboring "un-American" left-wing sympathies himself.

There was, however, another component of Garfield's public image, highly significant for some American spectators, while completely ignored by the mainstream press: his Jewishness. This public neglect was, in itself, doubtless no surprise to most American Jews, since such attention was rarely—if ever—deliberately drawn to a star's Jewishness. During the studio era of Hollywood, characters originally identified as Jewish were routinely stripped of this distinction. Similarly, stars' names and biographies were altered to accommodate the perceived wishes of the Gentile mainstream.[1] In this and parallel practices around stars of other backgrounds, Hollywood demonstrated clear "ethnic strategies for assimilation."[2]

Nevertheless, Warner Bros. did generate publicity about Garfield's Jewishness and directed it exclusively at American Jews by way of syndicated columnists of the Jewish-American press. (Many American Jews were already familiar with young "Jules," especially theatergoers in New York, who had followed his career on stage with the Group Theater, where he appeared in *Waiting for Lefty*, *Awake and Sing*, and *Golden Boy*.) Thus, advertisements run in the *Philadelphia Jewish Times* and the *Los Angeles B'nai B'rith Messenger* for two of his films specifically mention his Jewishness: "John Garfield, young Jewish actor, portrays one of the leading characters in the widely acclaimed film" (for the 1938 Warner Bros. film *Four Daughters*) and "Another Jewish Actor Rises to Stardom" (for the 1939 Warner Bros. movie *They Made Me a Criminal*).[3]

These and similar local Jewish news papers also routinely ran syndicated stories on Garfield's future roles—some of which never materialized, including a film entitled *Concentration Camp* and a movie about Israel—as well as reports on the actor's participation in Hollywood's Yom Kippur services and his work on behalf of the United Jewish Appeal for Refugees and other Jewish charities.[4] Syndicated columnist Dick Chase reported not only on his name change, but also on rumors that his father was "a cantor in a Bronx synagogue and that Jules himself used to sing in a choir on Sabbath mornings." Jews were also informed of his friendship with Jewish celebrities; his assistance on *We Will Never Die*, Ben Hecht's 1943 pageant memorializing Jewish victims of Nazism; and his support for Jews seeking to establish a state in Palestine.

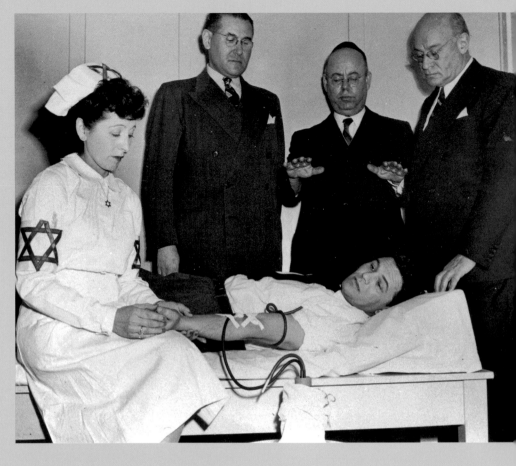

John Garfield gives blood for the Magen David Adam (Red Star of David). In the final years of his career, Garfield was a prominent supporter of Jewish causes.

They should "provide themselves with machine guns—and use them!" Garfield is said to have stated.[5]

Moreover, Garfield's significance for American Jewish audiences was tied to some of the roles he played at the height of his film career: Paul Boray in *Humoresque*, Charlie Davis in *Body and Soul*, and David Goldman in *Gentleman's Agreement*. These performances suggest Garfield's gradual emergence as a performer of Jews on screen. Boray's Jewishness, explicit in Fannie Hurst's novel about a poor immigrant's son who becomes a concert violinist, is obscured in the film version of *Humoresque*. Though Davis is nominally identified as a Jew in the Depression-era boxing drama *Body and Soul*, this is not central to his character or the film's plot. Finally, in *Gentleman's Agreement*, a film about exposing anti-Semitism among America's elite, Goldman is not only explicitly Jewish; his Jewishness is central to his presence.

Jewish film audiences forged their own readings of all three films. Years before the release of *Humoresque*, Jews were reportedly "looking forward with great interest to the new screen production of this opus."[6] Many regarded the film's Lower East Side setting and the accents of the actors playing Garfield's parents as signifiers of the film as Jewish. In her study of Jewish images in American film, Patricia Erens links Garfield's star presence with the character of Paul Boray, who is self-described as "outside, always looking in," which she identifies as "the classic Jewish position."[7]

In *Body and Soul*, Jewish audience pride in Garfield as a Jewish star is replicated within the film's narrative. Toward the end of the film (significantly, perhaps, Garfield's first independent feature), boxer Charlie Davis is visiting his mother's Lower East Side home before one of his final bouts, when a delivery man named Shimin Rushkin (portrayed by a Jewish comedian of the same name) arrives with groceries. He tells the Davises how important Charlie's successes in the ring are to his fellow Jews. After making a toast "to the future retired champeen of the world," Shimin explains why he is betting on Charlie to win the fight: "It isn't the money. It's a way of showing. Over in Europe, the Nazis are killing people like us just because of their religion. But here, Charlie Davis is champeen."

Whereas the Jewishness of Garfield's role in *Gentleman's Agreement* was a given, it provided Jewish audiences with an opportunity to analyze the significance of both the character of Dave Goldman and Garfield's presence in the role. Significantly, the discussion often focused on the issue of Jewish distinctiveness, which is so critical to the argument of the film: "The stated purpose of the film is to destroy that lethal commonplace which categorizes the Jews in special ways apart from oth-ers," noted one columnist. "Garfield [wasn't] supposed to betray any traits commonly labeled as 'Yiddish.'"[8]

Such remarks suggest an awareness both of the film's significance as a watershed in the public presence of American Jewry and of the problematic nature of acceptance into the cultural mainstream at the price of concealing difference. Thus, when Garfield died five years after the release of *Gentleman's Agreement*, one local Jewish-American paper asserted his Jewish origins, subverting years of Hollywood obfuscation, as they mourned his passing: "Jules Garfinkle—to give him his right name—had a good Jewish schooling and spoke and read Yiddish fluently."[9]

—Samuel J. Rosenthal

LEFT
"Another Jewish Actor Rises to Stardom." Advertisement in the *B'nai B'rith Messenger* for the 1939 film *They Made Me a Criminal*, starring John Garfield.

ABOVE, TOP
Joan Crawford and John Garfield in *Humoresque* (1946).

ABOVE, BOTTOM
John Garfield's character bleeds to death as co-star Shelley Winters looks on, in his final film, *He Ran All the Way* (1951).

LEFT
Shelley Winters,
c. 1951.

BELOW
Larry (Lenny Baker) is given
a lunch fit for a growing boy
by his mother (Shelley
Winters) in *Next Stop,
Greenwich Village* (1976).

# SHELLEY WINTERS

Shelley Winters
Born 1922 as Shirley Schrift[1]
East St. Louis, Illinois

No actress since Gertrude Berg has been more associated with the Jewish mother than Shelley Winters. Winters, however, was a Jewish mother for the 1960s: blowzy, strident, and generally overwhelming. She was born in East St. Louis (where her mother, Rose Winters, once sang with the city opera) and moved to Brooklyn as a child. Her father was a haberdasher who, convicted of arson, served a year in Sing Sing prison. A teenage beauty queen (Miss Ozone Park) and garment center fashion model, Winters appeared in a summer stock production of *Born Yesterday* playing the role created by Judy Holliday. She was signed by Holliday's studio, Columbia, and initially typecast as a sultry blond, a good "bad" girl.

Winters's ambitions as an actress led her to study at the Actor's Studio in New York. She appeared opposite John Garfield in his last feature, *He Ran All The Way* (United Artists,1951) and eight years later won an Oscar as Mrs. Van Daan in *The Diary of Anne Frank* (Twentieth Century Fox, 1959), a part for which she gained twenty-five pounds. Winters would never return to glamour roles. She played the Lower East Side madam Polly Adler in *A House Is Not a Home* (Embassy Pictures, 1964) and, beginning with *Enter Laughing* (Columbia, 1967), a series of more respectable, if no less formidable, Jewish mothers in *Wild in the Streets* (American International Pictures, 1968), *Buona Sera, Mrs. Campbell* (United Artists, 1968), *The Poseidon Adventure* (Twentieth Century Fox, 1973), *Blume in Love* (Warner Bros., 1973), and *Next Stop, Greenwich Village* (Twentieth Century Fox, 1976). In 1970, she took a break from movies to play the Marx Brothers' stage mother in the musical *Minnie's Boys*.

Although Winters had mainly played the Jewish mother of Jewish sons, from 1991 through 1996 she had a recurring role as Roseanne's grandmother "Nana-Mary" Harris on the situation comedy *Roseanne*.[2]

—J.H.

Shelley Winters as the
President's Jewish mother in
*Wild in the Streets* (1968).

Danny Kaye
1913–1987
Born as David Daniel Kaminsky
New York

I was five years old when I first heard Danny Kaye sing. It was 1954 and I was spending the afternoon at my grandparents' apartment on Chauncy Street on the fringe of Brooklyn's East New York. Later that afternoon, when my father returned, he brought an album of six 78 rpm records with a two-color, stiff cardboard cover and separate brown paper sleeves for each record. He placed the first record on the small box phonograph, and out of the cloth-covered speaker came this curious male voice that shot from baritone to falsetto with no warning and managed to scat more words in a single breath than seemed possible. The album was a grab bag of Kaye's hits— "The Babbitt and the Bromine," "Minnie the Moocher," "The Princess of Pure Delight," "The Fairy Pipers," "Molly Malone"—and I listened in rapture. This voice—expressively hysterical, unrestrained, childish but sophisticated—was unlike anything I had ever heard. Even more intriguing was the cover photograph of this funny-looking man, making a face and flinging his arms and hands about in the most unmasculine fashion. I didn't have words for it then, but as a gangly, nonmasculine boy who already knew he hated sports, I felt drawn to this person. In retrospect, I see that he was probably my first crush.

As I grew up, I saw every Danny Kaye movie when it was released and never missed them when they were on TV. What struck me most in these films was how often Kaye played

dual roles. The sheer joy he took in multiple self-inventions—a trick I was learning myself as I became increasingly aware of being gay in the 1950s and early 1960s—was inspirational. While I always retained my youthful fondness for Kaye, I didn't think seriously again about him until I began to examine ideas about Jewish masculinity, sex, and gender. Of course, I knew of biographer Donald Spoto's assertion that Kaye and Laurence Olivier had had an affair (a fact that seemed possible, if unsubstantiated), but overt homosexuality struck me as somewhat beside the point when thinking about Danny Kaye. There had been hints of it throughout his life. He received rave reviews for his first major Broadway role as a flighty gay photographer in Moss Hart's 1941 musical *Lady in the Dark*, and his very public estrangements with wife Sylvia Fine have been interpreted as a marriage of convenience becoming very inconvenient. But the intensity generated by his theatrical persona was about the elusiveness of authentic identity: what he was hiding.

After scoring successes on Broadway and

in New York nightclubs, Kaye went to Hollywood in the early 1940s. But Danny Kaye was not a "natural" as a Hollywood star. Enormously, if idiosyncratically, talented, he lacked what Hollywood had defined as "It"—sex appeal. His public persona was high-strung, flighty, epicene to the point of outright nelly: certainly not romantic, leading-man material. But Kaye, with the help of Fine who collaborated with him on his films, found an ingenious solution: the creation of alter egos that allowed the performer to counterbalance his "gay" persona with more masculine ones. Kaye's screen work from the 1940s to the 1960s presents us with dazzling examples of how—through doubling —Kaye manipulated and calibrated his gender affect and (perceived) sexual identity.

In movie after movie, Kaye played characters who, through various plot devices, split in two: one ineffectual, fearful of women, Casper Milquetoast; the other a more dashing, heterosexually inclined male. In *Wonder Man* (Samuel Goldwyn Company, 1945) he plays twins: one a ladies' man, the other a

PAGES 178–80
Danny Kaye in multiple roles in *The Secret Life of Walter Mitty* (1947).

bookish librarian. In *The Kid From Brooklyn* (RKO, 1946) he portrays a mild-mannered milkman whose alter ego is a vicious prize-fighter; in *The Secret Life of Walter Mitty* (RKO, 1947) he is a timid accountant with an active fantasy life as a series of brave heroes. The invention of this dual Danny Kaye was a stroke of genius, and his early films were highly effective in displaying his incredible talents. These pictures were enormously popular and he repeated the formula less successfully in *The Inspector General* (Warner Bros., 1949), *Knock on Wood* (Paramount, 1954), *On the Double* (Paramount, 1961), and *The Man from the Diner's Club* (Columbia, 1963).

Kaye's constant use of double, even multiple, roles in films was not only a calculated response to dealing with his "gay" persona, it had a deeper resonance in his career and life. Not only was Kaye "too gay," but he was also "too Jewish." Kaye's personal and theatrical roots were decidedly Jewish. Kaye was born David Daniel Kaminski on January 18, 1913, in the East New York section of Brooklyn. His parents and two older brothers came from the Ukrainian town of Ekaterinoslav, and the family spoke Yiddish at home. Kaye dropped out of high school, and by the summer of 1929 he had a summer job as a *tummler* at White Roe, a Jewish resort in the Catskills where he would return for several years between odd jobs. In 1934, he toured as a comic with a dance act to Asia, where he perfected what would be known as his signature "git-gat-gittle" nonsense rapid-patter talk, a form of "speech" many critics see as coming directly from Yiddish.

But Kaye did not continue the Jewish theatrical traditions in which he began and often responded negatively to other Jewish performers who preserved those conventions. Even in his early professional stage career, Kaye never "played Jewish," a pose that Hollywood mandated he maintain. Signed by Samuel Goldwyn for a series of musical comedies, Kaye began his career in the shadow of Goldwyn's fear that Kaye looked "too Jewish." The studio dealt with this by dyeing his red hair blond (claiming it made his nose look smaller) and requiring that he legally change his name to Danny Kaye.

Hollywood's concern over Kaye's ostensible Jewishness shaped his image, rendering him relentlessly and blandly non-ethnic in all of his early films. This assimilated makeover dovetailed with Kaye's inability to convey a masculine, or even heterosexual, romantic image. The conflation of overt Jewishness and non-normative masculinity was not a new phenomenon. Historically, Jewish actors in Hollywood were caught in a bind since Jewish men were viewed by many in the Gentile culture as less than normatively masculine. As a result, actors who were identified as Jewish were not considered for romantic leads, though they were commonly accepted as comics: Jack Benny, George Burns, Eddie Cantor, the Marx Brothers. Performers such as John Garfield, Paul Muni, and Edward G. Robinson were repackaged as non-ethnic to appeal to a broader audience.

Danny Kaye was caught at the dead center of this cultural crisis. When Kaye emerged as a Hollywood star in the 1940s, Sam Goldwyn attempted to package him as a direct successor of Eddie Cantor, who had starred in a series of noted Goldwyn musicals in the 1930s. Not only was Kaye's extraordinarily manic performance style reminiscent of Cantor's—he was known as the Apostle of Pep—but he also mirrored that performer's ambiguous gender presentation. Presenting a fey, almost presexual form of masculinity, Cantor's characters, while never overtly homosexual, usually ran from any serious heterosexual involvement. In the Broadway and Hollywood performance culture of the 1930s, Cantor's gender ambiguity could be seen as an integral expression of his clearly Jewish male persona. Kaye's first film, *Up in Arms* (RKO, 1944), was a remake of Cantor's *Whoopee!* (United Artists, 1930), and most of Kaye's future roles continued to mirror the "feminized" characters that Cantor had made famous. Timid, hypochondriacal, hysterical, and often frightened of heterosexual relationships, these characters were schlemiels, but never objects of ridicule. Rather, Cantor often used them as a humorous, but concise, critique of normal, accepted masculine behaviors.

The problem that Kaye faced as a Hollywood star was that he needed to be less Jewish and more "masculine" than Cantor. It was easy to diminish all specifically Jewish references. But changing his gender effect was more difficult, since his nontraditionally masculine inflection was essential to his character and performance. Here Kaye's doubling worked brilliantly. His doppelganger characterizations can be viewed on a number of levels. Are Kaye's fey characters "gay" and the more masculine ones "straight?" Or are we looking at the difference between characters who are closeted and those who are out? And how much of this is being enacted by Kaye on a conscious level? Was this an inside joke that Kaye, however he saw his own sexuality, was playing on his audiences?

And does it mean that Fine was a prime architect of Kaye's film persona? Was she in on the joke? When Kaye's films are at their best, as in *Wonder Man* (RKO, 1945) or *The Court Jester* (Paramount, 1956), they still function as dazzling examples of how wit and intelligence can present complicated ideas about gender and sex in an extraordinarily entertaining fashion.

But as the 1950s became the more sophisticated 1960s, Kaye's film career was sideswiped by history and the approaching sexual revolution. Except for the brilliant *Court Jester*, most of his films after 1947 failed at the box office. Part of the problem was that audiences wearied of the repetitiveness of the plots. More important, Kaye's career was damaged because, as a performer, he had removed the possibility of erotic or romantic energy from his characters. Trapped between mainstream culture's demand for nonmasculine Jewish performers and his own desire to escape from it, Kaye created characters that were neutered, emotionally anemic. The situation was so evident that Goldwyn, when asked what was wrong with Kaye's career, announced, "Nobody wants to fuck Danny Kaye."

Yet Kaye's career continued. His incredibly popular shows at London's Palladium and the Palace in New York during the 1950s, as well as his successful television variety show a decade later, made him one of the country's most beloved entertainers. Here he was able to be himself without the constraints of being a romantic leading man.

His presentations of Jewishness and of "playing Jewish," however, were more problematic. Except for a few roles—as a Jewish businessman in war-torn Paris in *Me and the Colonel* (Columbia, 1958) and a Holocaust survivor in the made-for-TV film *Skokie* (CBS, 1981)—he rarely portrayed Jewish characters or dealt with Jewish themes. Kaye was often overtly hostile to Jewish material. He once accused Alan King of being a "Jew comic" and turned down the chance to originate the role of Tevye in *Fiddler on the Roof* because it was "too ethnic." Sometimes this antagonism ventured into realms of the absurd. When asked by a newspaper reporter about how "Jewish" his performance as Noah in the 1970 musical *Two by Two* was going to be, Kaye responded: "Actually, when you talk about Noah, there really were no religions then. It's really about a universal group, not any one ethnic thing."

How connected were Kaye's concerns about being an overtly Jewish and not very masculine, even nelly, male performer? Certainly in the context of 1940s and 1950s Hollywood, he would never have had a chance to succeed unless he eradicated his Jewish background and made some concessions to becoming a credible romantic interest. While we might now wince at his animosity toward promoting a public Jewish persona, we can also understand it as a deeply entrenched defensiveness about his own identity. This was, after all, the decade that brought us the execution of the Rosenbergs and the targeting of Jewish performers by the House Committee on Un-American Activities. It was also the beginning of the gay rights movement in the United States, as well as a time of unprecedented assault on gay people by the government, the legal system, and the medical establishment.

In a very visceral way, Kaye was trapped by history and culture. His flamboyant, unconventionally masculine persona placed him directly in a clear tradition of American Jewish comics. However, this did not fit the new, more overtly sexualized masculinity of the 1950s. By rejecting this tradition and attempting to pass by being both schlemiel and romantic ladies' man, he fabricated an intriguing and complex hybrid of Jewish masculinity.

"Was Danny Kaye gay?" is always the first question asked whenever I have lectured on Kaye and his "hidden" queer and Jewish identities. I have no idea. Given the complicated, sometimes conflicted internal lives we all have, maybe Kaye did not know the answer to that question either. But, on one level, it does not matter. What does matter is that when he was at his best, he spoke to audiences, probably through the lens of his own confusions, and they—as I did as a child and as a young gay man—responded.

—Michael Bronski

*Modern Screen*, November 1956. While giving pride of place to Marilyn Monroe's conversion, the magazine's cover also promotes stories about the private lives of Elizabeth Taylor, another famous Hollywood convert to Judaism, and Janet Leigh, then married to Tony Curtis (né Bernard Schwartz).

## MARILYN MONROE

Marilyn Monroe
1926–1962
Born as Norma Jean Mortenson
Los Angeles
Converted to Judaism 1956

**From "Marilyn Enters a Jewish Family" by Susan Wender, which appeared in the November 1956 issue of *Modern Screen*.**

*Entreat me not to leave thee and to return from following after thee; for whither thou goest, I will go; and where thou lodgest I will lodge; thy people shall be my people; and thy God my God . . .* —Ruth I:16–17

At the end of June, 1956, Marilyn Monroe, in the presence of Arthur Miller and his family, and the Rabbi Robert Goldburg, affirmed her acceptance of these age-old Biblical words. On the following pages, *Modern Screen* takes great pride in presenting the warm and beautiful story of how Marilyn, the orphan girl without roots, has found peace and security in the Faith of the man she loves.

It was a cloudy day, but the little chapel of the synagogue was lit with the soft, subdued radiance of a pale summer sun filtered through stained glass. Inside, a girl named Marilyn Monroe sat quietly in a center pew, looking down at her white-gloved hands. Her golden hair, brushed back and smoothed, curled out at the ends beneath a tiny veiled hat. Her dress was demure and simple, her face scrubbed beneath the dusting of powder and light lipstick.

On her left sat her mother-in-law and her father-in-law. From time to time the elder Mrs. Miller raised a hand to pat at her hair. Her husband fingered the prayer book in the rack before him, drawing it out from time to time to turn the pages and linger over old, familiar prayers.

On Marilyn's right a tall, thin man consulted his watch, glanced at his bride, then reached out a large hand to cover her small one. She turned to him and smiled. There was no fear in her smile, not even a trace of nervousness. It was one of the most important moments of her life, this short time of waiting until the Rabbi would enter and begin the ancient conversion ceremony that would make her a Jew for the rest of her life. . . .

When she was a little girl, she had no family, she had no home. Her mother was—away. Her father was a man she never knew. Her home was a foundling home sometimes, or else it was a house in which a family lived, and she, the boarder, the ward of charity, stayed. Sometimes they were good to her, sometimes they were not. It didn't matter much, for they were strangers all.

In the foundling home, she was taught to say prayers. Supposedly she said them to God, but as far as she knew, she said them to the matron who came to listen and look cross if a word were left out. They didn't make much sense to her anyhow. She asked for blessings and to be good. With or without the prayer, she was good. With or without it, there was no blessing. What did it matter if a word was left out? This God, whoever He was—He was a stranger too. . . .

Time passed, and the authorities in charge of her life took her away from . . . [one] home and put her into another, and another, and back to the foundling home, and then out again. . . . Sometimes one or another of the families she lived with took her to church, and she heard about God again. Sometimes He . . . was terrifying and awesome. Sometimes He was a gentle God, loving and kind, helping instead of punishing. At first she tried to make sense out of it, but she couldn't. No one else seemed to have trouble knowing who God was, only she. She asked no one; she was unaccustomed to asking questions. People preferred that she do as she was told and be quiet. She never stayed long enough in one place to go to Sunday School, to meet a minister. In the end, she decided that God was as the rest of the world—a friend to others, a stranger forever to her.

When she was sixteen she married a boy, and thought she was going to have what she had never had—a family of her own, a warmth all around her. But it turned out that he was just a boy, not a father and mother and a whole world. Just a boy, with not too much to give, at that. Or maybe she asked too much of love, having starved for it for so long. Eventually, his was one of the homes she left.

Nine years later her name was Marilyn Monroe, and under that name, she married again. This time she married a man, not a boy. His name was Joe DiMaggio, and as far as Marilyn knew, he was the first person in the world who ever needed her.

Like her, he was lonely. Like her, he was famous, and surrounded by people who offered their time, presence, laughter—but seldom their love. They would open, she thought, as she had thought before, the whole world to each other.

And again, she was wrong. Her new husband was a quiet, moody man to whom real

# THE TWO WAYS LIZ TAYLOR RUINED HER MARRIAGE

# modern screen

DELL NOV. 20c

marilyn
enters a
Jewish
family

## JANET LEIGH: My Feelings During Childbirth

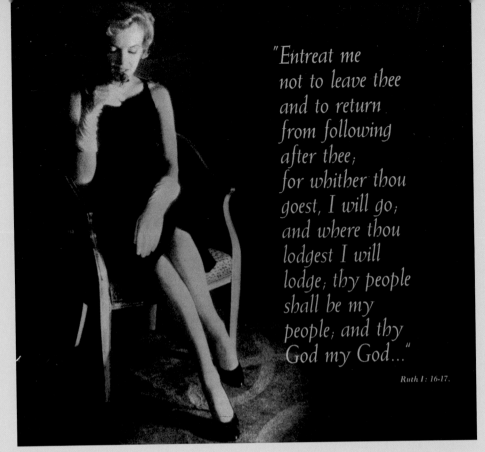

"*Entreat me
not to leave thee
and to return
from following
after thee;
for whither thou
goest, I will go;
and where thou
lodgest I will
lodge; thy people
shall be my
people; and thy
God my God...*"

Ruth 1: 16-17.

warmth was foreign. Before they were married, he introduced Marilyn to his family, his sister, the San Francisco house in which he had lived. She thought they were to be her relatives, with all the meaning that word had for her. He was fond of his family. But he felt no clinging need to know them intimately as Marilyn did. She suffered at the loss.

They were married in a civil ceremony. They could not have a religious one; Joe, a Catholic, had incurred the displeasure of his church by divorcing his first wife. . . .

It was a marriage that could not last.

When it was over, she went to New York. She needed to learn to live. . . . For a long time she had been reading. Poets, great novelists, books of philosophy, books on art and music. She had grown accustomed to the laughter and the wisecracks that came when she told anyone; she didn't mind too much. It was good for her career, she supposed. Even if it weren't, she'd go on reading. Somewhere in the books were the answers she sought.

While she was looking for herself, she found Arthur Miller.

Five years before, she had met him at a Hollywood cocktail party. They had talked for a while—at least, he had talked, and she had listened. What he thought of her she did not know, but to her he was a giant, a man of mind, a man who knew the answers to questions, a man she could worship. But only from afar. . . .

When she came to New York to recover from the blow her marriage had been to her, she met him again. He was separated from his wife. And she—she was the unexpectedly bright Miss Monroe, the only person in a room-

ful who knew what she was talking about when, amid giggles, *The Brothers Karamazov* was mentioned.

"It's very strange," he told her, "that you should be so interested in Dostoevsky. As a matter of fact, he's one of my favorites . . ."

Marilyn smiled at him. "Not so strange," she said. "You told me that back in 1951."

That wasn't all she remembered. He was interested in social welfare, so was she. He loved bike-riding—she had always wanted to learn. He liked parties that were more than dancing—and at those parties Marilyn turned up, holding a vodka-and-orange-juice, scarcely sipping it, listening, always listening. One evening he drew her away from the group. "You never say anything," he accused.

Her large eyes turned on him honestly. "I'm afraid," she said. "There are so many of them, and they know so much . . ."

So he took her away from the crowds and together they discovered who she was—a shy, beautiful girl with a lot to say, when she could find the courage to say it. Time after time she sent him into peals of helpless laughter with a well-timed crack. "Why don't you talk like that at your press conferences?" he'd gasp.

"Oh, they'd just say my agent wrote it."

He took her bike-riding, and when she fell on the famous behind, she rose up again, giggling. He met her for lunch in Manhattan, and found her hidden behind scrubbed face and loose blouse, chatting with drugstore waitresses and newsdealers. He came to depend more and more on seeing her, on hearing her comments on his work, getting her opinions of his friends. . . .

But it was when he took her home that they fell in love.

Home, to Arthur, was a frame house in Flatbush, Brooklyn. Not much of a place to look at, he told Marilyn. His mother told her more about it while Marilyn sat on a kitchen chair and watched the busy, capable fingers preparing dinner. Once the Millers had been wealthy, and lived in a lovely place in Manhattan. Then came the Depression. Everything went. They were barely able to manage the move to Flatbush. Arthur was a good boy. Always wanting to help. He delivered bagels before school to earn some money. Bagels—"Here, I'll show you," Mrs. Miller exclaimed, producing one from a bag in the oven. A hard, round, roll-like affair with a hole in the middle. Had Marilyn ever had one? With cream cheese and lox?

Marilyn said yes, she had. Lots of her show-business acquaintances were Jewish; she'd eaten lox and bagels with them.

Oh, well, then she knows about Jewish food and things. Not that the Millers kept a Kosher home, with no pork or rump steak or shrimp allowed in it; not that they didn't have cream in their coffee when they had it with meat. But still, they were not completely unreligious. For years her old father had lived with them, and for his sake they had kept the dietary laws. It did no one any harm, and in many ways it was good. It reminded them that they were Jews. It was good to know who you were. And being Jewish—well, when people like you were in trouble, or when something good happened, you could share a little of it with them, you could feel at one with them. Did Marilyn understand?

Yes, she understood.

At dinner Mrs. Miller and the quiet man who was Arthur's father reminisced. . . . Remember the time Artie couldn't get into college because his high school grades were so low? The Millers turned, seriously, to Marilyn. You see, they told her, in a Jewish family, the education is the most important thing. More important than money or position. To a Jewish

family the thought that the son will be a doctor or a lawyer or a teacher or a writer—that is what makes you hang on through bad times, gives you courage to live. So when Artie suddenly wanted be a writer—well, they were pretty shocked, because he was always the one playing ball or tinkering with a motor, . . . but if Artie wanted to study—more power to him, he should have every penny they could scrape together. So two years after he got out of high school Artie had both the money and the guts at the same time; he went up to Michigan University and talked them into letting him in. Then he won every prize for creative writing they had to give. Proud? Were they proud? They beamed on him all over again. Marilyn, listening, watching as they told her the story, knew that nothing would ever make them as proud again.

Dinner over, they carried the dishes into the kitchen. "Let me help," Marilyn begged, and Mrs. Miller handed her a towel. Drying the dishes, listening to the chatter, she was supremely content. The arm her hostess put around her when they went back to the living room, the smile Artie's father turned in her direction when she wandered over to the bookcase to look at the titles,—they all

seemed so natural, homey, right. "You never want to move?" she asked.

"No, we thought of it once or twice. We could afford it now; Artie makes a good living, my husband does all right. But you know you get close to your neighbors, you see the same people for twenty years, your children grow up in these rooms, you belong to the temple—why should you leave? For a fancier neighborhood with fancy strangers? You understand?"

"Oh, yes," Marilyn said. She understood. When they said goodnight finally and walked down the block to Arthur's car, she held his arm, looking about her. Down the block she could see the outline of a temple. Here and there a porch light gleamed faintly on a mezuzah nailed to a door jamb—a sign, put up by the residents, that they were Jews, obeying the commandment to keep the work of God nailed to the entrance of their homes that they might remember it always. Inside the mezuzah, Artie's mother had said, was a tiny scoll beginning with, "Thou shalt love the lord . . ."

"It all comes back," she said slowly, "to being Jewish, doesn't it?"

Arthur took his pipe out, "All what?"

"Knowing who you are. Being content. Everything."

He grinned. "Well, a lot of people who aren't Jewish know who they are and they seem pretty happy."

"I suppose." She was silent for a while. "But your family—they say they aren't religious, really. But still—it's always there, being Jewish—a sort of constant beauty in the background."

He looked at her. "Being Jewish is not

שְׁמַע יִשְׂרָאֵל יְהוָה אֱלֹהֵינוּ

HEAR O ISRAEL THE LORD OUR GOD

יְהוָה אֶחָד

THE LORD IS ONE

## CERTIFICATE OF CONVERSION

This is to record that _____

having sought to join the household of Israel by accepting the religion of Israel and promising to live by its principles and practices was received into the Jewish Faith

on _July 1, 1956_

corresponding to the Hebrew date _22nd Tammuz, 5716_

at _Lewisboro, New York_

_Rabbi Robert E. Goldburg_
SIGNATURE
_Kermit Miller_
SIGNATURE
_Walter H. Grumm_
SIGNATURE
_Arthur Miller_

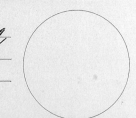

**THY PEOPLE SHALL BE MY PEOPLE AND THY GOD MY GOD**

BOOK OF RUTH

COPYRIGHT, 1955 BY UNION OF AMERICAN HEBREW CONGREGATIONS

always a beautiful thing. It can be one of the roughest things in the world. People—"

"I know. But even suffering can be a good thing, if you don't do it alone, if you share it with people who believe in the same things, who understand. . . . Her voice drifted off into the night. Holding hands, he drove her back to the city. . . .

"Teach me to cook," she begged his mother.

"You can cook. You made a very good steak and a nice salad."

"Oh, that." Marilyn waved her hand. "I mean—the kind of things you make. What Arthur likes."

"Well, I don't know where to start." Marilyn thought. "Gefülte fish?" . . .

And Marilyn, delighted, flew about the kitchen, producing failures and successes, most of which were devoured, indiscriminately, by Art's kids.

Over one such dinner they discussed the wedding. Should they try to elude the reporters—or invite them? Who should witness the ceremony? Who should perform it, a judge or a j.p.? Arthur and his father debated. Marilyn sat silently.

Arthur turned to her. "What do you say, honey?"

She blushed. "I think I'd like to have a Rabbi."

"A Rabbi? You mean you want a religious wedding?"

"Yes, I thought it would be—nice. I wanted a blessing on the marriage."

Arthur was uncomfortable. "Well, I thought of it of course, and the folks would love it —but the thing is—a Rabbi can't marry

us because you aren't Jewish." He paused. "Of course, if you _were_ Jewish—"

There was a long pause. Then a voice, "Do you—would they—is there any way I could become a Jew?"

"Well, if you want to, there is."

"Want to," she said "_want to!_ I've been wanting to talk to you about it for so long! I thought after we were married I could—but I didn't know if anyone could just—become. I thought it was—closed."

"_Closed,_" he said, laughing. "Nope, not at all. We have to call a Rabbi, that's all, and give you instruction. Then there is a conversion ceremony and they ask you questions— that's it. If you're sure. You know you don't have to. Our marriage will be perfectly legal without it, and it doesn't matter to me. You

have to be sure. You have to have thought about it."

She looked at him. "I haven't thought about anything else," she said. "With the possible exception of you."

They phoned a Rabbi, Dr. Robert Goldburg of New Haven. Yes, he would give the instructions and perform the ceremony. No, no trouble at all.

In her room that night, Marilyn lay awake. Her mother-to-be had kissed her and cried. Her father-to-be had folded her in his arms. The warmth around her was to be hers, not only by right of marriage, but by right of faith. Whatever was to come, she would share with them, and they with her. Never had she felt so much that she was coming home.

The next day tragedy struck. They went

for a drive, briefly. On the way home a reporter followed them, driving wildly to catch up to the car far ahead. Looking out the window as Arthur's car climbed the winding road, Marilyn saw the car below crash and spin. They got help and went home. "It's got to stop," Marilyn said.

"How do we stop it?"

She sighed. "Give them what they want. Get married."

They made arrangements quickly for a brief civil ceremony. When it was over, Arthur took her aside. "Honey, you know we are married now, even in the eyes of my religion. If you don't want to go through with the conversion, you don't have to."

"I want to be a Jew," she said, "as soon as possible. I want it now, before we go to England. I want to be married again, in temple. This doesn't change anything. I only want it more."

The Rabbi came to the house. All that day and all that evening he told Marilyn what it meant to be a Jew. Her husband was a "Reform" Jew, so she needn't keep Kosher, nor sit apart from him at services, as she would if they were Orthodox. She would light candles on Friday night to welcome the Sabbath, which lasted until sundown Saturday, but need not restrain from touching money or riding on that day. She would be, he told her, as Jewish as she wanted to be. He gave her the *Old Testament* to read. At the end of the evening, he took Arthur aside. Usually, he said, the conversion ceremony followed a much longer period of instruction. He knew there was no time for that, since they were due to leave for England. He understood Mrs. Miller's desire to be married again in the religious ceremony. She could return for more instruction when they came back. He would make an exception—the conversion would take place the next day and the second marriage promptly thereafter.

Arthur came back to Marilyn, who was waiting anxiously. "You'll do," he said.

And so, on that pale morning, Marilyn sat in the chapel, remembering.

A door opened and the Rabbi came in, "Marilyn," he said gently.

She rose and stood before him. Quietly the service began.

"Is it of your own free will that you seek admittance into the Jewish fold?"

"Yes."

"Do you renounce your former faith?"

She had had none; she renounced her lack of faith. "Yes."

"Do you pledge your loyalty to Judaism? Do you promise to cast in your lot with the people of Israel amid all circumstances?"

It is good, she remembered, to suffer—if you share it with others . . . "Yes."

"Do you promise to lead a Jewish life?"

She thought of her new family, holding each other close in a bond of love. "Yes."

"Should you be blessed with children do you agree to rear your children according to the Jewish faith?"

Her children, who would forever know who they were, who would have an answer to their questions. "Oh, yes," she said.

The Rabbi smiled at her. "Repeat after me" he said, and together they spoke the ancient words of the convert. . . .

He read her the words of Ruth. Behind her she could hear the rustle as her family rose in their places and began to read aloud, "Let us adore the everliving God and render praise unto Him who spread out the heavens and established the earth . . ." They were praying—praying for her!

The Rabbi took her hand and gave her solemnly a name chosen from the Bible—a name she keeps entirely to herself. "With this name as token you are now a member of the household of Israel and have assumed all its rights, privileges and responsibilities." . . .

It had been a long road, a hard road. But with shining eyes and a blessing upon her, Marilyn had come home.

# SAMMY DAVIS, JR.

Sammy Davis, Jr.
1925–1990
New York
Converted to Judaism c. 1956

## The Cat Upstairs

The story of Sammy Davis, Jr.'s religious conversion was a classic in many Jewish homes of
the 1960s. It usually began with the retelling
of the widely reported car accident in November
1954 that cost Davis his left eye and nearly his
life. With regularity, my own mother would
repeat the story to my sister and me, spinning
it into a cautionary tale about a life-altering
incident that humbled a sinner. As the entertainer lay dying in a Las Vegas hospital, a
Jewish friend placed a mezuzah in his hand.
When he ultimately pulled through, Davis
looked back on his compulsive and unrepen-
tant life with horror. And the mezuzah, which
he had clutched so fervently that it left an
imprint on his palm, was the omen of the Jewish
spirituality that would soon be imprinted on
his soul and become his salvation.

The real story, as Davis told it years later,
had less to do with a mezuzah (actually given
to him years before the crash) than with the
despondency he felt after his recovery. "I
knew that I had to make the audience believe
I was nice, humble, warm—any number of
things which I once had been but was no
longer," Davis wrote of his despair. In the
months and years after the accident, he
searched for ways of coping with a life driven
by professional, but not spiritual, fulfillment.
That search led him to rethink the meaning of
God—"The Cat Upstairs," as he called him—
and the power of organized religion.

It was the Jews, he concluded, who were
the most "swinging bunch of people." By that
he meant that the Jewish people had what it
took: the vitality, generosity, self-possession,
intelligence, and perseverance to survive
thousands of years of persecution and have
a profound effect on the world. The Jews were
black people's true comrades and role models
in the civil rights movement; they could
empathize with the black man's burden, he
reasoned, because they had once been slaves
themselves. While Davis tended to idealize
Jews in much the same simplified way he saw
the rest of the world, his religious transformation was in no way careless or shallow. It
required years of prayer, introspection, and
learning.

Davis's superstar status, however, turned
his conversion to Judaism into something
more public, a headline grabbing act that
served as a lightning rod for American attitudes about race and religion in the early
1960s. Neo-Nazi "storm troopers" picketed one
of his performances in Washington, D.C.: "Go
back to the Congo, you kosher coon," read one
of their signs. African-American writers feared
that his conversion—along with his disinter-
est in black theaters and nightclubs, affairs
with white women, association with the otherwise all-white "Rat Pack" (which included
Frank Sinatra, Dean Martin, Joey Bishop, and
Peter Lawford), and marriage to the Swedish
actress May Britt in 1960—was yet another
sign of his selling out of black America. "We
are sorry to be the ones to remind Mr. Davis
of his obligation to the Negro community,
but even sorrier for the necessity to do so,"
concluded one editorial in a black newspaper

entitled "Is Sammy Ashamed He's A Negro?" As
Davis himself admitted, even some of his own
friends, black and white, suspected that his
conversion was nothing more than a publicity
stunt designed to curry favor with powerful
Jewish producers.

Becoming a Jew was undoubtedly more of
an asset than a liability for Davis in an entertainment industry that was more liberal and
considerably more Semitic than the rest of
America. Davis had experienced virulent, ugly
bigotry in his career. But he also believed that
his extraordinary gifts as a performer insulated
him, to some extent, from the institutional
racism of show business: "It was as though my
talent was giving me a pass which excluded
me from their prejudice," he wrote in 1965.
To a limited extent, he was right. In military
training in Cheyenne, Wyoming, in the mid-
1940s, Davis was kicked and beaten by white
soldiers, stripped naked, and painted with
racist slurs. On nightclub stages a few years
later, as the singing, tap-dancing, and impersonating lead dynamo of the Will Mastin Trio,
he was cheered by white patrons, despite the
fact that he was forbidden to sleep, gamble,
or dine in many of these establishments.

As a black man in a still largely racist
industry, Davis most strongly identified with
those pioneers of the 1920s and 1930s, such
as Eddie Cantor and Al Jolson, who struggled
against anti-Semitism to forge a place in the
mainstream for Jewish entertainers. Two
decades later, he strove to emulate them, to
become the first black superstar. Ironically, it
was Cantor who gave Davis his first mezuzah,
which he had eyed with curiosity in Cantor's
dressing room after the two performed together.

As Davis implied, in his best-selling autobiography *Yes I Can* (1965), it was during this sacred exchange that his affinity for Judaism first became clear.

But Davis's identification with his Jewish idols could also border on the perverse. A recording of Davis doing the Jolson standard, "Rock-A-Bye Your Baby with a Dixie Melody," at the Coconut Grove in 1963 suggests both a sly parody and a self-hating appreciation of a man who had regularly performed the song in blackface. Declaring, tongue-in-cheek, that the old chestnut was the "most sung song in America," Davis uncannily impersonated a range of hip entertainers interpreting it. It was upsetting to hear Davis's imitations of Nat King Cole, Louis Armstrong, and Billy Eckstein (whom he jokingly called "Epstein"), black stars who probably would have left show business rather than endure the humiliation of singing the song in public. But it was his dead-on impersonation of Jolson that was most disturbing, reeking as it did of the abasement of an elegant black man impersonating a white man performing a grotesque caricature of a black man.

Ultimately, Davis's conversion to Judaism represented a reversal of the traditional appropriation of blackness by the earlier generation of Jewish entertainers. Jolson's performances in blackface or George Gershwin's *Porgy and Bess* simultaneously played on white people's fascination with blackness and sent an indirect message of support for civil rights in an entertainment industry that had banished all but the most abject and stereotypical depictions of black people. Even blackface had seemingly well-meaning intentions, easing white audiences into proximity with blackness and helping to make possible the presence, albeit not always positive, of black performers in the mainstream. But white audiences always knew that Jolson's "blackness" was no deeper or more dangerous than the shallow layer of insidious stereotypes, burnt cork, and greasepaint that concealed his pale skin.

In marking himself as a Jew, Davis refigured this relationship, overlaying an illusion of "whiteness" onto his dark body. It allowed the entertainer, intentionally or otherwise, to comfort his liberal, white, and often Jewish fans by openly affiliating with an "ethnic" group that mirrored back to them their own upstanding whiteness. Davis's Jewishness may have made him almost white in some people's eyes. My mother, for example, who usually referred to black people as *schwartzes*, would not hurl the slur at him. Yet, throughout most of his career, Davis was usually seen by the media and the public as a black entertainer, despite his unshakable credentials as a Jew.

Ten years after his death, Davis's music is experiencing a popular and critical revival; his Jewishness, however, remains largely undiscussed in the critical writing on his work. The astonishingly gifted entertainer has still not found a place in the pantheon of Jewish show-business icons of the twentieth century.

In retrospect, the accusation that Davis transformed himself into a Jew in order to be more acceptable to white people seems unfair. His detailed account of his conversion to Judaism in *Yes I Can* demonstrated the seriousness of the crisis that led him to passionately turn to the Jewish faith. It was this very passion, exemplified in the eyes of liberal Jews by his outspoken commitment to social justice—he was a strong supporter of Israel as well as a vocal antiracist and advocate for the poor—that led many of his Jewish fans to feel betrayed by his shift towards the political right in the early 1970s. A much reproduced photograph of Davis hugging Richard Nixon at the 1972 Republican Convention stunned and disheartened Jews and blacks alike.

And yet, even this incident underscored the complexity of Davis's motivation. Was his embrace of Nixon evidence of a sycophantic flirtation with the party in power and, thus, an abandonment of the principals of Jewish social justice? Was it a sign of Davis's need to be all things to all people—on the one hand, campaigning for a reactionary President who shamelessly flattered and courted him and, on the other, donating large amounts of time and money whenever Jesse Jackson asked him to support one of his black-empowerment initiatives? Or was it the acting out of a bitter man who had been disinvited from John F. Kennedy's inauguration because the President-elect feared that the presence of Davis and his white wife might infuriate his racist, but politically useful, Southern guests? The downturn in the quality of the singer's work—his uncool "The Candy Man" was at the top of the charts at the time—further eroded Jewish confidence in Davis's sophistication and idealism. My liberal, opera-singer mother was appalled: "I can't believe that washed-up *schwartze* hugged that son-of-a-bitch," she said on the morning the picture was published. It was the first time that Davis's race meant more to her than his religion.

—Maurice Berger

Sammy Davis, Jr., as demolition expert Josh Howard in
*Ocean's Eleven* (1960).

Sammy Davis, Jr., presents
Archie Bunker (Carrol
O'Connor) with a "peace
and love" medallion on an
episode of *All in the Family*,
1972.

Sammy Davis, Jr., as Sportin'
Life and Dorothy Dandridge
as Bess in *Porgy and Bess*
(1959). According to Davis,
he informed the film's producer Samuel Goldwyn that
he would not work on Yom
Kippur. "Directors I can
fight," the surprised
Goldwyn is said to have
exclaimed. "Fires on the
set I can fight. Writers,
even actors, I can fight. But
a Jewish colored fellow?
This I can't fight."

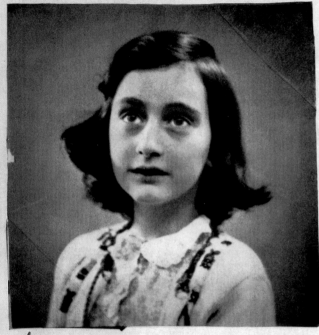

LIFE

## WHAT HAPPENED AFTER END OF ANNE FRANK'S DIARY
### EXCLUSIVE STORY TELLS OF HER TRAGEDY

Dit foto,
ik m
wen
altij
te zi
Dan
ik nog wel een ka
om naar Hollywood

ANNE FRANK ON PAGE FROM HER DIARY

REG. U.S. PAT. OFF.

AUGUST 18, 1958 **25** CENTS

LEFT
Anne Frank on the cover
of *Life* magazine, August 18,
1958.

ANNE FRANK

Anne Frank
1929–1945
Frankfurt, Germany

*This is a photograph of me as I wish to look all the time. Then I might still have a chance of getting to Hollywood. But at present, I'm afraid, I usually look quite different.*
—Anne Frank, *The Diary of a Young Girl*, entry for October 10, 1942

During the past half-century, the life of Anne Frank, who died in March 1945 in the Bergen-Belsen concentration camp at the age of fifteen, has been portrayed on American radio, film, and television more frequently and prominently than any other Jew in modern times. Within a few months of the publication of her wartime diary in English in 1952, dramatizations of it were aired on American radio and television. Frances Goodrich and Albert Hackett's official stage version of *The Diary of Anne Frank*, which premiered on Broadway in 1955, was later released as a Hollywood film and produced twice for television.

Over the decades, numerous documentary films and telecasts on Anne Frank have extended the scope of the diary to examine her childhood and family background, chronicle her final months as a prisoner in German concentration camps, and evaluate her significance as an icon of Dutch Jewry. Television has also occasionally reflected on how Anne has become a powerful figure in the American imagination—most notably in the dramatization of Philip Roth's novella *The Ghost Writer* (1979), in which a young American Jewish writer is convinced that he has discovered Anne alive and living incognito in New England in the late 1950s. Whatever young Anne's aspirations for Hollywood might have been, she could doubtless never have imagined achieving such extraordinary posthumous celebrity.

—J.S.

# Anne Frank in American Broadcasting and Film: A Selected List

"Anne Frank: The Diary of a Young Girl"
*Frontiers of Faith*, NBC, 1952
The first American dramatization of Anne Frank's diary, scripted by Morton Wishengrad, was telecast on November 16.

"Anne Frank: Diary of a Young Girl"
*The Eternal Light*, NBC, 1952
This radio drama based on the diary, written by Meyer Levin, was aired on December 14.

*The Diary of Anne Frank*
Twentieth Century Fox, 1959
The film version of Frances Goodrich and Albert Hackett's play was directed by George Stevens, with Millie Perkins as Anne.

"Who Killed Anne Frank?"
*The Twentieth Century*, CBS, 1964
A news documentary on Nazi war criminals, narrated by Walter Cronkite.

"The Legacy of Anne Frank"
*The Eternal Light*, NBC, 1967
This documentary features an interview with Anne's father, Otto Frank.

"The Diary of Anne Frank"
*Sunday Night at the Theatre*, ABC, 1967
The first television production of the play by Goodrich and Hackett, featuring Diane Davila as Anne.

"The Heritage of Anne Frank"
*Directions*, ABC, 1972
ABC News London Bureau chief George Watson journeys to the building in Amsterdam where Anne Frank and her family were hidden during World War II.

*The Diary of Anne Frank*
Showtime, 1977
A second production of the Goodrich and Hackett play for television, featuring Melissa Gilbert as Anne.

"The Holland of Rembrandt and Anne Frank"
*The Eternal Light*, NBC, 1981
The broadcast presents Holland—a refuge to Sephardic Jews who fled the Spanish Inquisition during the fifteenth century and to European Jews fleeing Nazi persecution in the twentieth century—as seen through the eyes of the Dutch artist Rembrandt and the words of Anne Frank.

"The Ghost Writer"
*American Playhouse*, PBS, 1984
A dramatization of Philip Roth's novella.

*The Man Who Hid Anne Frank*
A&E, 1988
A documentary on the Frank family's experiences while in hiding, which includes interviews with the people who hid them.

*The Last Seven Months of Anne Frank*
PBS, 1989
Public television broadcast of a Dutch documentary, featuring interviews with women who recall Anne Frank's final months in concentration camps.

*Anne Frank Remembered*
PBS, 1989
Four high school students from the Holocaust Center at Bronx High School of Science discuss reading Anne Frank's diary with Bill Moyers.

*The Attic: The Hiding of Anne Frank*
CBS, 1988
Based on Miep Gies's account of hiding the Franks and their friends in the Secret Annex, featuring Mary Steenbergen as Miep.

*Anne Frank Remembered*
Sony Pictures Classics, 1995
Academy Award–winning documentary, directed by Jon Blair, featuring Glenn Close reading excerpts from Anne's diary.

"Anne Frank: The Missing Pages"
*Investigative Reports*, A&E, 1998
Documentary report on the recent discovery of five pages from Anne's diary that her father had removed because of their harsh portrayal of his relationship with Anne's mother.

*Anne Frank*
ABC, 2001
Four-hour miniseries, based on Melissa Muller's biography of Anne Frank, featuring Hannah Taylor Gordon as Anne.

RIGHT
Mr. Dussell (Ed Wynn),
Anne Frank (Millie Perkins),
Mrs. Frank (Gusti Huber),
Peter Van Daan (Richard
Beymer), Mr. Van Daan
(Lou Jacobi), Margo Frank
(Diane Baker), and Mrs. Van
Daan (Shelley Winters) in
*The Diary of Anne Frank*
(1959). Winters won the
Oscar for Best Supporting
Actress.

RIGHT
Promotional material for
*The Diary of Anne Frank*
(1959).

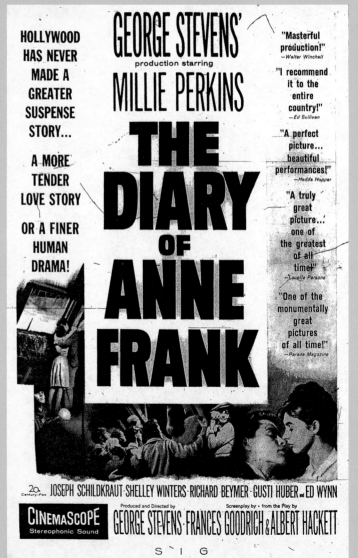

"Hollywood"

From the musical *Yours, Anne* (1985)
Words by Enid Futterman
Music by Michael Cohen

Isn't Hollywood divine
If I were there
I'd walk on air
I'd light up and shine
Whirling around
I'd never touch the ground

Wouldn't Hollywood be grand
If I were there
And Fred Astaire
Extended his hand
I watch him take mine
I watch our fingers entwine

Lovely
He thinks I am lovely
He smiles at me
He bows to me

Suddenly we start to dance
A perfect pair
A love affair
So rich with romance
Spinning around
We never make a sound

Wouldn't Hollywood be grand
If I were there
And Fred Astaire
Were holding my hand
Wouldn't Hollywood be simply . . . grand

# BARBRA STREISAND

GLAMOUR WOUNDS

## Glamorous *Jewesses*

**Rhonda Lieberman on The Way We Are**

On the problem of the actor—

*And it is really high time to ask: What good actor today is not—a Jew? . . . Finally, women. Reflect on the whole history of women: do they not have to be first of all and above all else actresses?*

—Friedrich Nietzsche, *The Gay Science*, 1882

In his book *Spurs* or *Nietzsche's Styles*, Jacques Derrida works Uncle Friedrich's Jew-woman moment to comment upon "truth's abyss, as non-truth." He points out that while "truth" can only be a surface, or in quotation marks, it still flirtatiously tempts us to lift her veil and possess her.

### The Jew is the Thing

Now that middle America has gone into recovery, *The Prince of Tides* recently offered filmic fast-food for the inner child. The world emerges as a disappointing landscape populated by those who are in denial and those who are in recovery; one suspected that that is the way we are but why does it seem so smarmy here? The film is beautifully shot, and the narrative occurs over the traumatized body of Nick Nolte's twin sister—a gifted poetess and Holocaust survivor-wannabe(!). As absent cause driving the narrative, she is kept offscreen—literally recovering in a mental ward from a botched suicide attempt. Barbra Streisand is her immaculately groomed therapist, determined to crack her case through Nick Nolte, who is elected by the dysfunctional family to be his sister's "memory"—the witness of the nasty family-trauma material. The only encounter with trauma is a nonencounter: as "witness" to trauma, the subject is split from herself—she cannot have access to the nasty blotch inaugurating her symptom or personality. The film literally dislocates the sister's trauma in Nolte. This is all well and good. As the soigné cosmopolitan *Über*-Jewess shrink, however, Babs ultimately cannot compete with Nolte's goyish connection to his native soil. Therapists shouldn't have affairs with their patients, but that is the least offensive aspect of the film. After she

Barbra Streisand, 1968.
Photo: Photofest. **Friedrich Nietzsche**. Photo: New York Public Library Picture Collection.

*Artforum*, January 1993.

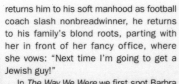

returns him to his soft manhood as football coach slash nonbreadwinner, he returns to his family's blond roots, parting with her in front of her fancy office, where she vows: "Next time I'm going to get a Jewish guy!"

In *The Way We Were* we first spot Barbra spotting another blond nodding off at a bar: Robert Redford. She takes him home where he throws up and crashes into a drunken stupor. In the middle of the night he makes love to her, still drunk, while she remains alert and vigilant. In the morning he remembers nothing. Throughout the film he has something like 20 cocktails. We see him in his WASP milieu maintaining his cool with alcohol, while the activist Jewess cheers him on to engage in the world in an affirmative way. Barbra, as supportive Jewess and muse, seems to stand for his mushed-up libido. I was keyed into the Jewish/WASP encounter or rather nonencounter when I saw *The Way We Were*. What struck me was the configuration of the WASP as the sleeping object of history and the Jew as the vigilant, suffering, and somehow tackier subject. Nevertheless the Jewess functions as the lure who can lead the WASP "back" to his numbed desire.

So what's with the WASP-Jew conjunction over the inner child? The fantasm goes like this: equipped with a hot line to suffering, the Jew enjoys a privileged relation to the WASPS' trauma and therefore can heal or at least witness or at least package it for them. Ralph Lauren and Calvin Klein have demonstrated that no one can imagine and merchandise the fantasy scene of WASP plenitude better than a Jew. In the Barbra films, WASP plenitude emerges as a glossy traumatized shock layer significantly numbing the WASP sensorium and robbing him of subjective experience; he is a blond object to be rescued by the Jew from his own sorry condition.

Jews fill a public service. They simplify things for people—in the anti-Semitic (Western) imaginary, the fantasm of the Jew supports a black-and-white world divided between discrete ethnic "identities," i.e. "Jew" and "non-Jew." To paraphrase Lacan, Jew-essence is impossible. Like Truth, like "Woman," the *essence* of the Jew does not exist, yet the traumatic fantasy of WASP plenitude is supported and witnessed by the desiring gaze of the Jew. The Jew emerges as a codependent "expert" on and potential healer of WASP trauma: the cool surface congealing, like a photo, over the shock data of tawdry family histories. . . . In the masquerade of

the social symbolic, which is in effect "reality," Jews have a hot line to pathos. They've taken over this realm of affect and people envy them for this.

## The Way We Were

In the award-winning 1965 TV special *My Name is Barbra*, Babs is fabulous in a souped-up Empire-waisted glamour gown with a sailor-suit neckline. Coded as virtuosic child sophisticate, she frolics through elaborate crane shots with a full orchestra in black tie. In case we have any doubts about her sassy ingenue status the next sequence borders on kiddie porn: Babs in a modified sailor-suit, anklets, and patent-leather Mary Janes, her glamorous Babhood indicated, however, by the heavy Egyptoid makeup of the period. When she sings in baby talk, swinging her legs from an oversized nursery table, the effect is alarming. Why, you may ask, the child thing? As cross between woman-child and urban sophisticate, Babs is the uncanny power Jewess, a scary composite figure hovering between the insatiable needs of the child and the calculating eye of the expert consumer. In a telling segment, she is loosed on the sumptuous sales floor of Bergdorf's, singing a "poverty" medley, including "secondhand Rose." Embodying the formidable avatar of Jewess in her excessive, insatiable desire for goodies, she appears with her big nose in absolutely flawless outfits, delighting and disturbing all of us as singing surrogate for the sublime disproportion between our desires and our capacity to satisfy them.

Let Babs be a lesson to us all. We love the early Babs because she was the desiring subject who somehow didn't fit onto the scene of glamour plenitude. No matter how sumptuous the mise-en-scène, the nose would puncture the fantasy. The "what is wrong with this picture" effect was endearing: embodying glamour divided from itself, glamour and its own lack-in-being. The avatar of the pampered Jewess prevails in our cultural imaginary: Donna Karan and Joan Rivers both radiate the smooth patina of the shopping maven. But whereas the supermodel seems preternaturally worthy of commodities because she seems more like them, more like an object, the Jewess emerges as their tortured consciousness, the suffering subject. Shut out from total identification with the commodity, she is doomed to witness the trauma of their inarticulate power. The unitary trait, that little bit of the real representing the mark of ethnicity—like a Jewish nose—sets them apart from total identification with the commodity signifier, e.g.,

they will always read as JAPs in Chanel. But *The Prince of Tides* denies this symbolic reality. As the polished queen of the film, Barbra truly becomes the JAP Nightmare. Reaching the goal of Total Princesshood, she becomes grotesque: our sympathy with her as a desiring subject turns to shit. Having "entered the Fantasy," she smarms through the film as a maudlin melancholic subject in mourning for her sense of humor.

## Impossible Jew-Essence

Embodying difference from herself, the flip side of self-identity, the power Jewess operates in the cultural imaginary as a low-end Derrida: she is philosophically dangerous, or at least a threat to the concept of "being" as it is traditionally understood. The Jewish diva is always a limit case, a diva in quotes: it is impossible not to see her *acting out* the part of diva. Yma Sumac, the singing "Incan princess" and esteemed kitsch goddess, was such a raving simulacrum that an apocryphal myth spontaneously generated about her "origin"—as Amy Camus, a self-styled Jewess from Brooklyn. According to Holly Woodlawn, the Warhol "superstar": "She made me want to become an Egyptologist." Rhoda Morgenstern obeyed the law of no Jew-essence in reverse: as Mary Tyler Moore's Jewess sidekick she was played by a *shiksa*—Valerie Harper.

With the exaggerated boobies and bawdiness of a drag queen and immunity to even remedial glamorization, Bette Midler exemplified the Jewess as sublime grotesque body. Exulting in lapses of taste as a bouncing bundle of Jewess vitality and wit, the early Bette achieved a kind of Hegelian self-overcoming in which "Spirit" in the form of voice and self-consciousness triumphed with gusto over physical packaging—the inverse of the supermodel effect. It was no accident that her earliest supporters were real drag queens. As the Divine Miss M., she seemed to be a second-order drag queen, simulating a drag simulacrum of a woman. Her destiny seemed scripted by the hand of Fate: as a Jewish girl from Hawaii she was born to be inappropriate. As a lesbian simulacrum of a drag simulacrum of a woman, Sandra Bernhard is the zesty Jewess of the '90s. Nietzsche saw "truth" as a woman, a Jew, a literary man—all adepts at histrionics and masquerade; truth is a simulacrum, who whines. As one Jewish lady would put it so memorably: "There is no there there." So shalom Andy Warhol! Oy. □

Rhonda Lieberman teaches at the School of the Art Institute of Chicago.

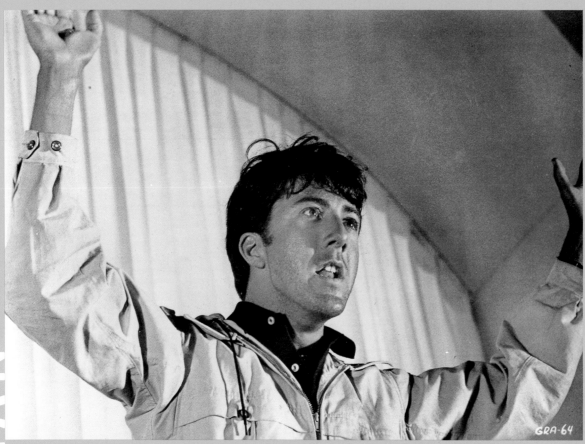

LEFT
Dustin Hoffman in
*The Graduate* (1967).

BELOW
"Dusty and the Duke."
Illustration by Milton Glaser
for the cover of *Life*
magazine, July 11, 1969.

# DUSTIN HOFFMAN

Dustin Hoffman
Born 1937
Los Angeles

Making his film debut as the eponymous protagonist of *The Graduate* (Embassy), Dustin Hoffman struck some as a new sort of Hollywood hero. Six weeks after the movie opened in December 1967, *New York Times* film critic Renata Adler characterized Hoffman's Benjamin as "a shy, inhibited intellectual (probably Jewish) who has never played on any team in his life."[1]

Adler did not mention Hoffman's short stature, prominent nose, and nasal voice. Still, her readers were quick to respond. One letter to the editor, written by Susan Applebaum and Ellen Bendow of New York, accused the critic of imagining Jewish stereotypes. "There is nothing about [Benjamin's] name, or anything that he or any of the other characters say, that would imply this [Jewishness] is so."[2]

By contrast, the future Hollywood writer Bruce Vilanch, then an editor at the *Ohio State Daily Lantern* in Columbus, supported Adler's

observations: She has "rightfully detected a good deal of Jewishness in the film's attitude." Vilanch went even further to suggest that, by the end of the movie, Ben had become a "mensch." For his part, Hoffman added his own ethnic subtext to the material, years later describing his audition for the part opposite the "uptight WASP goddess" Katharine Ross, who played Mrs. Robinson's daughter Elaine, as a "Jewish nightmare." The enormous success of *The Graduate* elevated Hoffman to stardom and ushered in the brief period of the ethnic Jewish matinee idol and youth icon in the forms of George Segal, Elliott Gould, Richard Benjamin, Charles Grodin, and Gene Wilder.[3]

Hoffman's subsequent roles include a number of specifically Jewish parts and several Jewish historical figures: Lenny Bruce in *Lenny* (United Artists, 1974), Carl Bernstein in *All the President's Men* (Warner Bros., 1976), and Dutch Schultz in *Billy Bathgate* (Touchstone, 1991). He played Jewish everyman "Babe" Levy in *The Marathon Man* (Paramount, 1977), a movie in which he was tortured by Laurence Olivier's Nazi dentist, and memorable

Hollywood producer Stanley Motss in *Wag the Dog* (New Line, 1997). Hoffman's stage roles include both Shylock and Willy Loman, the crypto-Jewish protagonist of Arthur Miller's *Death of a Salesman*.[4]

—J.H.

Cast of the TV series *Roseanne* (Roseanne, Sara Gilbert, Lecy Goranson, Michael Fishman, and John Goodman).

was played by a Jack Benny whose "real life" was less familiar to the public. A husband and a father, Benny was quite well known for his personal generosity and philanthropic activities. George Burns and Gracie Allen, a real-life married couple who had developed a married-couple act in vaudeville, also played entertainers and used their own names on their radio and TV shows. Both *Jack Benny* and *Burns and Allen* were among the highest-rated shows on both media for decades.

Similarly, Roseanne had spent years touring comedy clubs and appearing on cable TV shows developing the character of Roseanne, a sarcastic redneck *hausfrau*. Her self-deprecating monologues, including her tag line, "I'm a domestic goddess," produced a nationally familiar character. Like Jack Benny (né Benny Kubelsky) and George Burns (né Nathan Birnbaum), Roseanne is a Jewish performer who fixed her name and self-consciously constructed an American—as opposed to a Jewish-American—persona in order to cultivate a transdemographic audience in the mass media. All three created not only public masks, but also fictional domestic sitcom milieus that in no way indicated Jewish background, culture, or religion. None used phonetic or phonemic Yiddishisms in their acts, in the style of Jewish-American comics such as Milton Berle, Sid Caesar, or Joan Rivers, much less Jackie Mason or Lenny Bruce. Yet, in each case, the "middle-American" sitcom setting they constructed can be seen as part of the performer's reconstruction of self from a culturally marginal Jewish-American personality into an unhyphenated American.

There is a particular significance in this

## Roseanne
Born 1952 as Roseanne Barsky
Salt Lake City, Utah

The stand-up comedy regeneration of the 1980s, marked by the grand openings of chains of franchised "comedy clubs," produced a new wave of stars, one of whom was Utah-born Roseanne Barr (née Barsky). Like many of her most successful colleagues—Jerry Seinfeld and Ellen Degeneres among them—she soon learned that in the gold-rush media environment of the 1990s, the stand-up stage, even for its greatest artists, was little more than a bohemian affectation in terms of the prevailing bottom lines of big-time show business. Prime-time television was where the money was. The networks, however, had long abandoned stand-up comedy in favor of its relatively sappy narrative cousin, situation comedy. What was an acerbic wit to do?

*Roseanne* (ABC, 1988–97), like *Seinfeld*, *Ellen*, and the others, was a rehabilitation of a mythic persona that the comic had developed on the comedy-club circuit. The stand-up had

to step into a prefabricated proscenium and become the central focus of a dramatic *mise-en-scène*. Narrative was never the strong point of the sitcom. The genre's concept of order is too simplistic: its absence is too rarely upsetting, its facile restoration too little in doubt. The savvy of *Roseanne* and other stand-up personacoms is that they accept this fact and invest their energies elsewhere. Like a newspaper comic strip, *Roseanne* concentrated its efforts not so much on plot as on manufacturing a "Roseanne consciousness" and lending it to the viewer to share the Roseanne "take" on all that passes before her in the world of the show.

This approach was actually a revival of an ancient sitcom technique that could be traced back to *The Jack Benny Show* (CBS, 1950–64; NBC, 1964–65) and *The George Burns and Gracie Allen Show* (CBS, 1950–58). The sitcom character Jack Benny was familiar to a mass audience of tens of millions: a cheapskate bachelor living in Beverly Hills and working as a professional entertainer with his own radio, and later, TV show. The role of "Jack Benny"

# Found Fulfilment.

Promotional postcard for the Kabbalah Centre featuring Roseanne, 1990s.

# KABBALAH.

*juif manqué* technique for Jack Benny and Roseanne. Unlike many Jewish-American comedians, they grew up far away from the New York neighborhoods where Jewish-American identity offered a feasible cultural alternative. The immediate demographic circumstances of Jewish kids in Waukegan, Illinois (Benny), and Salt Lake City (Roseanne) demanded different strategies than were called for in the schoolyards of Brooklyn or the Lower East Side. If Benny teased the "cheap Jew" stereotype by playing the role of a non-Jewish pennypincher with nonchalant impunity, Roseanne subverted another powerful stereotype—the Jewish mother—and did so in an even more radical fashion.

Much of the power of the stand-up Roseanne arose from the character's raw mean-spiritedness and brazen laziness, qualities that set her in polar opposition to the self-sacrificing mother and tireless *balebuste* (housewife) portrayed, for example, by Gertrude Berg on *The Goldbergs* for twenty-five years on radio and TV. The stand-up Roseanne was lewd and crude, a mother who punished her children by telling them that they were really adopted and, furthermore, that she was thinking of giving them back. She didn't mind sending them out to play in traffic. Instead of homemade chicken soup and matzoh balls, Roseanne feeds her *mishpokhe* (family) meat by-product hot dogs and barbecue flavor Doritos—and they had better like it.

The stand-up Roseanne, however, was something less than compatible with the mitigating generic constraints of situation comedy. Resolution of twenty-two minute comic narratives seems to depend on unambiguous professions of love and support, not exactly the stuff from which convincing bile is brewed. The sitcom *Roseanne* was constantly put to the test in its early episodes by the hyper-sentimentality of the genre. As in *The Honeymooners* (CBS, 1955–56), no matter how much domestic animus is generated, all roads lead back to "Baby, you're the greatest." Roseanne, at first, seemed determined to challenge this monolithic generic convention.

Contemptible characters, however, are difficult to pull off in situation comedy, especially in title roles. Don Rickles found this out during the 1970s, when at the peak of his popularity as a stand-up, he endured a succession of failed sitcoms, unable to find a way of wedging his popular mean-spirited rank-out humor into a genre that coheres around overplayed demonstrations of tepid warmth. Much to her credit, in time Roseanne came to this realization. The sitcom demanded a Roseanne Conner who would have to be too good to be true to the stand-up Roseanne. Firing producers and writers with the dispatch of a George Steinbrenner, she remodeled the show.

The "domestic goddess" jokes could be told, but they could not be acted out. They were rhetorically demoted into distanced wisecracks laughed at not only by the audience, but also by Roseanne Conner's family, thus giving assurance to all that this was no Clytemnestra about to devour her young. Though bad (meaning unloving) mothers are not compatible with situation comedy, Roseanne demonstrated that bad-mouthed mothers can be, as long as they are not abusive in any lasting way. The social and cultural resentments of the character remained. They became the vinegar to counterbalance the sitcom's structural overdose of saccharin. As was the case with *Jack Benny* and *Burns and Allen*, a fully trimmed tree graced the living room for the Christmas show.

—David Marc

HOWARD STERN

Never before has
a man done so much
with so little.

PRIVATE PARTS

Poster for Howard Stern's
autobiographical film
*Private Parts*, 1997.

HOWARD STERN

Howard Stern
Born 1954
New York

### The King (Jew) of All Media

Howard Stern has long been described as one of the most unlikely—and enduring—pop-cult figures in American show-business history. His phenomenal rise over the past two decades from irritating toilet-mouth radio deejay in the Reagan era to grunge spokesman-cum-best-selling author-cum-Hollywood maven is remarkable and continues to disturb the broadest spectrum of political and cultural elites. It would be difficult to unearth in the twenty-first century an American media celebrity as universally reviled as Howard Stern. He is also a *pintele yid*.[1]

Howard's personality is familiar to most Jewish suburban families. He is the goofy, obsessive-compulsive child who is certain to disrupt any dinner gathering with an endless stream of smart-aleck interruptions, wacky, never appropriate invective, scatological anec-dotes, and nonstop chatter.

In typical WASP households, such chil-dren are reprimanded, silenced, or banished from the evening's repast. Jewish-American families normally tolerate boorish adolescent behavior and even reward it—but only if the juvenile in question exhibits a respectable laugh-provoking ability.

Humor is among the most important

constructs (and sexually enticing components) in Jewish culture. A physically unattractive Jewish boy (like Woody Allen) or girl (like Joan Rivers) with a strong comic persona can still be considered good marriage material. Sociological studies maintain that American Jews are five times more likely to advertise their humorous qualities in newspaper personals than Gentiles. Jewish lesbians are nine times more likely to do so than their Protestant and Catholic sisters. Inversion, irony, comic presentations of self, political rants, over-the-top complaining, and generally unfettered insulting discourse all lead to Jewish success in the staid bed- and boardrooms of America. Hardcore joking is said to have replaced Yiddish as the secret language of the Jews and helped boost them up the rungs of the social ladder.

Howard is an unusual case in point. Born in 1954, he came of age during the "Yiddishization" of American comedy in the Ed Sullivan/ Great Society era. But, for the most part, Howard's comic models did not spring from homogenized Borscht Belt stand-up via Sunday night television or Lenny Bruce records. Instead, nine-year-old Howard borrowed from the Saturday morning panorama of insipid/transgressive childhood entertainments: *The Howdy Doody Show*, *Rocky and Bullwinkle*, pro wrestling, and *Captain Kangaroo*. The results were dirty puppet shows that he mounted for friends and family in his Long Island basement rec room.

Young Howard also begrudgingly followed his father, a radio engineer, into the mock creation of an older amusement format: the radio show. Here, like the solo puppeteer and cartoon animator he had been, the talk-show host could control both the content and the total means of expression through his vocal persona, editing, and added technical effects. The vehicle of radio also hid the boy's ungainly Hebraic body. In a sense, Howard had reverted to a discarded and more secretive presentation of Jewish comedy: the 1930s radio show. Like Jack Benny, Milton Berle, George Burns, Eddie Cantor, Alan Funt, and Harry Richman, Howard could parody and expose the world without physically exposing himself. Oddly enough, the megalomaniacal Howard would most closely resemble another early Jewish radio giant with whom he had no familiarity: Molly Goldberg (Gertrude Berg). (*The Howard Stern Show* today is a virtual recapitulation of *The Goldbergs* with the substitution of stuttering and eubonics for greenhorn-inflected Yid-English and multicultural Bronx accents. And both radio *balebustes* [housewives] have spent much of their airtime energies settling inane family quarrels and listening to banal advice from neighbors and other nudniks.)

Howard's climb to stardom began in the late 1980s, after he teamed up with Robin Quivers, a black female sidekick and the voice of reason. Unlike other hot-talk radio hosts or shock-jocks, Howard's politics were unpredictable and rarely fell into acceptable left/ right columns. For instance, when a caller challenged Howard's tirade for the reintroduction of capital punishment in New York State ("A Volt for a Jolt"), the bad-boy acknowledged the man's basic thesis: Many people executed by the state in America were later found to be innocent. Howard even went further than his listener-protester; most executed convicts were probably blameless of the crimes that doomed them, but they were guilty of so many other crimes that we don't know about that they deserved to die. It was perfect Jewish "brat" wisdom.

In 1992, the FCC fined Infinity Broadcasting, Stern's boss, $600,000 for violation of the national obscenity code. Howard confessed on the air that he masturbated to pictures of Aunt Jemima and comically seethed about the size of his penis, claiming it was so inadequate that he needed two bodyguards to shield it from view whenever he used a public urinal.

The mid-1990s marked a great change in traditional American broadcasting. The severing and reattachment of John Bobbitt's penis, the O. J. Simpson trial, Marv Albert's weird sexual antics, and the Monica Lewinsky scandal inescapably altered the vocabulary and etiquette of hard news and analysis. Howard proved to be only a few years ahead of his time.

The 1990s also saw a "counter-assimilationist" trend among Jewish-Americans. For the first time since the 1920s, Jews in Hollywood extolled their backgrounds by consciously creating positive Jewish types (or casting Jewish actors to play them) in sitcoms and action thrillers. Even the characters in *Seinfeld* stopped celebrating Christmas.

In 1998, Howard Stern, who billed himself for decades as a "half-Jew" (the other half supposedly Italian) suddenly proclaimed his full Israelite ancestry. It startled many of his twenty-four million fans. But few Jewish parents with mini-Howards in their midst were surprised. By partially denying, and then reaffirming, his roots, Howard was merely acting out his tribal script.

—Mel Gordon

# ADAM SANDLER

Adam Sandler
Born 1966
New York

"The Chanukah Song," which comic actor Adam Sandler first performed on *Saturday Night Live* in December 1994 and recorded a year later, is not so much a Jewish "Jingle Bell Rock" as an amulet against alienation and an anthem of Jewish pride: "When you feel like the only kid in town / Without a Christmas tree / Here's a list of people who are Jewish / Just like you and me."[1]

This childishly sung doggerel places Sandler in the tradition of such Yiddishizing troubadours as Mickey Katz and Allen Sherman. But they had addressed largely Jewish audiences and, if they made a joke of their own Jewishness, they did not expose Hollywood's non-ethnic Jewish stars. Sandler's open cultural narcissism—identifying a list of Jewish celebrities without fear that this might be a problem—dispenses with the underlying subject of American Jewish comedy, namely uneasiness with the Gentile world.

Neither edgily neurotic nor verbally agile, devoid of social criticism and overt *shikse*-lust, Sandler's comedy seemed to confound the prevailing stereotypes for Jewish-American stand-ups. At the end of *The Counterlife*, Philip Roth imagined a Jew "without Judaism, without Zionism, without Jewishness . . . just the object itself, like a glass or an apple."[2] So the overgrown teenager Sandler presented himself, much to the pleasure of many young American Jews. When, in late 1996, the students of a Manhattan Jewish day school were polled on their Jewish heroes, the actor finished second (behind Jerry Seinfeld but ahead of Howard Stern and God, who placed fourth).[3]

As the millennium approached, *New York* magazine reported that "for a small but passionate army of young women," Sandler was "a Jewish love god." Some equally passionate young Jewish men, meanwhile, have argued for Sandler's intelligence. "Is Adam Sandler the Most Important Living Jewish Commentator?" the national Jewish student magazine *New Voices* asked in late 1999. Inside, Harvard sophomore Benjamin Dreyfus offered a line-by-line exegesis of Sandler's "Goat Song" as an allegory of Jewish history, complete with illustration by Marc Chagall.[4]

—J.H.

STAND-UP JEWS

**THE FINAL DECADES** OF THE TWENTIETH CENTURY AND THE FIRST YEARS OF THE NEW MILLENNIUM HAVE WITNESSED A FLOWERING OF JEWISH-AMERICAN CULTURAL ACTIVITY UNRIVALED IN SCOPE AND FORTHRIGHTNESS. IN POLITICAL ACTIVISM AND SCHOLARSHIP, POPULAR CULTURE AND "HIGH" ART, GROWING NUMBERS OF AMERICAN JEWS HAVE STOOD UP TO BE SEEN *AS JEWS.* This new Jewish visibility began in the 1960s, following decades of Jews promoting their integration into the American mainstream and coyly encoding the presentation of Jewish difference. Jewry's newfound self-assertion in the American public sphere coincides with that of other groups—African-Americans, women, gays, and lesbians, in particular. Indeed, Jewish participation in the "new ethnicity" of the 1960s and 1970s often resembled these concomitant developments in identity politics and culture, and sometimes coincided with them (especially in the work of some feminist and gay activists). At the same time, though, how and why American Jews "stand up" is responsive to their particular place in this nation's annals of culture, as it is to their distinctive social, political, and economic trajectory in America.

There may be no better demonstration of this phenomenon than the efflorescence of Jewish-American self-portraiture in the nation's entertainment media, beginning with a new generation of Jewish stand-up comedians, who began to reach national audiences in the early 1960s on television variety programs and comedy albums. These were soon followed, in the late 1960s and early 1970s, by a spate of "Jewish new-wave" films. They featured young Jewish performers who refused to change their names, noses, or hair to conform to the conventions of Hollywood stardom; some of these films also boasted forthrightly Jewish names in their titles: *Portnoy's Complaint* (Warner Bros., 1972), *Bye Bye Braverman* (Warner Bros., 1968), and *Sheila Levine Is Dead and Living in New York* (Paramount, 1975).

In the 1990s, American television witnessed an upsurge of situation comedies about Jews, epitomized by the tremendously popular series *Seinfeld* (NBC, 1990–98). These films and broadcasts not only situated Jews prominently and forthrightly in the American cultural mainstream, they also served a host of Jewish performers, writers, directors, and producers as vehicles for self-exploration. Frequently, this took the form of communal satire, which positioned Jews (especially Jewish men living in New York) as archetypes for a national audience.

The distinctive course of contemporary Jewish-American culture has also been shaped by modern Jewish experience beyond this nation's borders—especially the catastrophe of the Holocaust and the establishment of the State of Israel. Here, too, American entertainment media have played important roles in enabling both Jews and non-Jews to imagine these remote chapters of history. The film *Exodus* (United Artists, 1960), which marks the culmination of Hollywood's treatment of the early days of Israel, recounts the story of the state's creation in the idiom of American nation-making epics. At the same time, *Exodus* offered American audiences a pioneering vision of Jews asserting their right to be seen as equal to, yet different from, others. American-made dramatizations of the Holocaust—especially *The Diary of Anne Frank* (Twentieth Century Fox, 1959), *Judgment at Nuremberg* (United Artists, 1961), the *Holocaust* miniseries (NBC, 1978), and *Schindler's List* (Universal, 1994)—have become the most popular and influential representations of the Nazi persecution of European Jewry to be seen internationally, while frequent telecasts dealing with the Holocaust have played a strategic role in situating it as a fixture of the American moral landscape.

As much as recent involvement of American Jews with the entertainment media has broken new ground, there have also been striking reiterations of earlier phenomena. Jewish religious broadcasting, largely dormant since the mid-twentieth-century heyday of *The Eternal Light*, has re-emerged as an important, albeit quite different, cultural force in the telecasts and videos produced by Lubavitcher hasidim. Finally, the Jewishness of Hollywood and its significance as a cultural and political force once again became a subject of contentious public discussion during the final decade of the twentieth century, when David Geffen, Jeffrey Katzenberg, and Steven Spielberg created DreamWorks Studio, and Bill Clinton, both as candidate and as president, established unprecedented ties with leading figures in Hollywood.

—J.H./J.S.

# *EXODUS:*
# REAL
# TO REEL TO
# REAL

DEBORAH DASH MOORE

*If only there had been a camera at the time of Moses, . . . for the Exodus. In our own time there has been another exodus and this time a camera was present.*
—Opening narration of Meyer Levin's documentary film, *The Illegals* (1947)

*We saw history made before our eyes; we saw it but could hardly believe it. . . . In the end nothing came of the plan to make a picture. What we had seen was so much larger than life it would have looked like pure propaganda. No one would have believed it.*
—Fred Zinnemann, on observing Israel's War of Independence, in *An Autobiography: A Life in the Movies* (1992)

World War II was over. Returning servicemen, many still in uniform, filled the streets. When a dashing young man arrived in Los Angeles, veterans were crowding bus platforms and train stations on their way home. Friends said Reuven Dafni, tall and handsome, with dark hair and a thin mustache, looked just like Errol Flynn. Dafni, a war hero who had parachuted behind Nazi lines in a desperate effort to rescue Hungarian Jewry from annihilation, was heading for Hollywood. Unlike returning American veterans, Dafni wasn't looking for work. For him and his fellow Haganah operatives on a secret mission in the United States, the war was not over.[1] In fact, their war was just beginning.

The struggle to rescue the surviving remnants of European Jewry and to bring them illegally to Palestine in defiance of British gunships and White Papers started as soon as the shooting stopped. Dafni came to win over Hollywood Jews on behalf of the armed struggle for a future Jewish state. In the dream factories of America's preeminent town of images, Dafni personified a new ideal type of young Jew: a fearless man of action. His own military exploits and good looks enhanced his persuasive eloquence. A young generation of producers, directors, and writers, many of them veterans of American military service, found Dafni's message irresistible.

That message was simple, but powerful: homeless for centuries, Jews needed a home of their own. They could not return to live in the graveyard that was Europe. Their home in Palestine, promised by Great Britain in the last war, was now denied to them. Britain had betrayed its pledge for the sake of Arab oil. Therefore, Jews had no choice but to fight British perfidy though illegal immigration. Arab opposition to Jewish settlement, stirred up by outsiders, would disappear once a Jewish state became a reality. American Jews, unscathed by World War II, were not asked to risk their lives in this war. No, they need only contribute their wealth—and, if they were willing, their reputations—to purchase guns and military supplies. Palestinian Jews would do the rest; they would fight, in producer Dore Schary's words, "for peace and security in the homeland."[2]

Dafni's appeal inspired a few moviemakers to use their skills to convey the Zionist message. Robert Buckner filmed *Sword in the Desert* (Universal), a fast-paced action movie, right after the establishment of the State of Israel. It opened in 1949 and starred the Jewish actor Jeff Chandler as a daring underground leader. His romantic counterpart, a defiant radio broadcaster named Sabra, announces boldly to her British captors: "I am still a Jew, and this is my country. You have no rights here, moral or legal, and therefore no authority over me." Echoes of the American Revolution reverberate in her rhetoric. Nonetheless, *New York Times* movie critic Bosley Crowther deplored such "frank idealization of the struggle of Jews" to secure their "homeland" and censured

DESIGNED BY SAUL B.

OTTO PREMINGER PRESENTS
PAUL NEWMAN · EVA MARIE SAINT
RALPH RICHARDSON · PETER LAWFORD
LEE J. COBB · SAL MINEO · JOHN DEREK
HUGH GRIFFITH · GREGORY RATOFF
JILL HAWORTH IN "EXODUS"

MARIUS GORING · ALEXANDRA STEWART · MICHAEL WAGER · MARTIN BENSON · PAUL STEVENS · BETTY WALKER · MARTIN MILLER
VICTOR MADDERN · GEORGE MAHARIS · JOHN CRAWFORD · SAMUEL SEGAL · SCREENPLAY BY DALTON TRUMBO · BASED ON THE
NOVEL BY LEON URIS · MUSIC BY ERNEST GOLD · PHOTOGRAPHED IN SUPER PANAVISION 70, TECHNICOLOR® BY SAM LEAVITT · TODD
AO STEREOPHONIC SOUND · ART DIRECTOR RICHARD DAY · A U.A. RELEASE · PRODUCED AND DIRECTED BY OTTO PREMINGER

the movie's "crude ridicule of the British." Jews emerged triumphant at the "humiliating expense" of British soldiers, a "potentially disturbing" portrayal of recent historical events in the context of the Cold War.[3]

The producers, writers, and directors who saw a moral drama in Israel's struggle for freedom did not share Crowther's distaste for bashing America's closest ally as the Cold War intensified. Progressive moviemakers seized on Israel's battles as extensions of their own liberal creed. For them, Zionism was "a popular revolution," a progressive cause that was also a safe one in a time of fear in Hollywood.[4]

The consensus adopted by movie versions of Israel's history simplified reality, giving it a single trajectory, idealizing its participants, and emphasizing its American resonance. In its focus on Palestine's frontier conditions, the drama of Israel's establishment had no room for offscreen events in American living rooms, meeting halls, and synagogues, or even in Washington's corridors of power. American Zionists played no role, not even a supporting one, in the imaginations of Jewish-American moviemakers. Instead, Jewish writers, directors, and producers transformed ideological rhetoric into compelling images, Zionist politics into Israeli national myths, Middle Eastern history into an American epic, and biblical metaphors into current events. To do this, they drew upon mythic elements in America's imagined past. With its successful revolution against the British, the United States provided a compelling model for telling the screen story of the birth of a new nation, especially to an American audience.

Although Stanley Kramer's film *The Juggler* (Columbia), starring Kirk Douglas as a psychologically damaged Holocaust survivor escaping to Israel, failed to reap box office rewards in 1953, it did feature the young state as heroic, Jewish response to Hitler's extermination program. This connection reappears in the only one of these movies to make millions—*Exodus*. Like the novel on which it was based, *Exodus* was extraordinarily popular. When it opened in December 1960, *Exodus* had the largest advance sale of any movie to date, some $1.6 million.[5] The picture, with a production budget of $3.5 million, grossed $13 million.[6]

Both novel and movie owe their origins to Hollywood's Jewish politics. Key figures, all Jews, include Schary, a liberal producer at MGM and Louis B. Mayer's heir apparent, who wore his social conscience on his sleeve; Leon Uris, a young novelist and screenwriter with a radical childhood, who saw action in the Marines during the war; and Otto Preminger, an independent producer and refugee from Nazism who gravitated toward liberal politics in his choice of movies.

Dov Landau (Sal Mineo) in prison.

Schary wanted to make a movie on Israel. When Uris approached MGM with a proposal to write a novel on Israel that would become a movie, he received a commission. But by the time Uris returned from researching his epic in Israel, Schary had lost his position at MGM. With Schary's departure, support for the project disappeared. At this point, Preminger entered the scene. Preminger was given Uris's manuscript; he "started reading it after dinner and couldn't put it down." When he finished, he knew he "wanted to make that film."[7] Playing upon MGM's fears of an Arab boycott, Preminger purchased the film rights to Uris's manuscript in 1957. He paid only $75,000, a small sum given the novel's subsequent popularity, which rivaled *Gone with the Wind* in sales.

*Exodus*, the novel, appeared in 1958. It became a bestseller a month after publication and stayed on the charts for an entire year, including nineteen weeks as number one. Its vision of the creation of the State of Israel influenced an entire generation of American Jews. In preparation for writing, Uris logged thousands of miles conducting interviews and shooting photographs in Israel. When the Sinai campaign interrupted his research, he covered the 1956 war as a correspondent. "It was a revelation to me," he explained to an interviewer. "We Jews are not what we have been portrayed to be. In truth, we have been fighters."[8] Uris intended to show the truth. He saw his own image reflected in his vision of the new Jew.

Critics tried to understand why *Exodus* so captured the Jewish-American imagination. One suggested that it "is actually an *American* book, which portrays Israel *through American eyes*." American Jews want to read this novel "because it seems to tell them a *new kind of story* about *a new kind of Jew*." These new Jews "have stopped running, hiding, scheming or pretending. They are Jews who fight, who die, who love and who *triumph*."[9] David Boroff called the book "the suburbanite's dream novel" with "its vicarious heroism, for surrogate strong men. The experience in Israel provides this for the American Jew." Yet Boroff admitted that when he lectured on *Exodus*, "inevitably, there is the well-intentioned man who relates that after the book came out, his UJA campaign met its quota after years of struggles and reverses."[10]

The novel reached Americans of all stripes, even State Department officials. One who preferred to remain anonymous confessed that "*Exodus* revealed what I suspected. The State of Israel is a remarkable revival of the ancient Hebrew nation." Spelling out his meaning, he admitted that he sympathized with "Israelis like Ari Ben Canaan," the novel's hero. This willingness to accept characters as representative types speaks to the novel's historical verity. Ignoring the fact that the book and its characters were fiction, the official concluded that such men as Ben Canaan showed that "Israel is a nation of farmers and fighters, real people. They are not like the Jews here who are so materialistic and money-mad."[11] Such a distinction between Israeli and Jew disturbed the novelist Philip Roth. He saw a dark side to the notion that "the Jews can take care of themselves." For him, *Exodus* threatened "to remove from the nation's consciousness . . . the memory of the holocaust itself, the murder of six million Jews, in all its raw, senseless, fiendish horror."[12]

Preminger brought his own interpretation to the novel. Though Uris had written other screenplays and wrote the novel with a film version in mind, Preminger "very quickly realized he [Uris] couldn't write" Preminger's kind of movie. Preminger wanted to make "an American picture, after all, that tries to tell the story, giving both sides a chance to plead their side." He worked hard to balance his characters, including a British general sympathetic to the Jews to contrast with an officer who is "frankly anti-Semitic." Preminger explained, "we tried to make this [anti-Semitism] humorous and entertaining."[13] Uris found anti-Semitism neither humorous nor entertaining. Like Buckner, Uris portrayed the British as the enemy.

Instead of Uris, Preminger hired the blacklisted writer Dalton Trumbo and worked with him to shape a screenplay quite different from Uris's novel. In fact, Crowther critized Preminger and Trumbo for having "considerably temporized in exposing the adversaries."[14] Others disagreed, complaining that "the film unequivocally blames the Arabs." *Time* magazine resented the sympathetic portrayal of the Irgun, claiming that "the picture goes on to sanctify the Jewish terror." Then, in a provocative flourish, the reviewer concluded that "the kind of blind hatred that excuses the Jewish terror was also used to excuse Nazi extermination camps."[15] To add to the controversy surrounding the movie, Preminger decided to give Trumbo credit in his own name on the finished film. Preminger's announcement before the filming began helped to break the blacklist.[16] The movie symbolically marked the end of the painful postwar era of anti-Communist investigations. When it was released, American Legionnaires picketed theaters in protest.[17]

The physical authenticity of scenes on location in Israel and Cyprus contributed to the sense that *Exodus* was the genuine article, a true slice of reality. Press coverage of the filming detailed the use of actual cells in the Acre prison where Jews were held and executed by the British. Hundreds of Israelis worked as extras. Almost every scene, except those at the youth village that was built for the movie, was shot at its original location.[18] Preminger explained that this was "necessary to show that we really tried to tell the truth, and we just didn't make up a story."[19] Many American Jews first glimpsed Israel's landscape in the movie.

*Exodus* evokes the Bible in its title, sweep, and extraordinary length, which exceeded three-and-a-half hours of running time. (At a preview, the comic Mort Sahl is reported to have yelled, "Otto, let my people go.")[20] Critics have seen the movie as a variant on American westerns and war movies or as a modernized version of the biblical epics of Cecil B. DeMille. Lester Friedman calls it "a Hollywood Western played out in the desert instead of on a prairie, a tale of brave men overcoming the dangers of a wild frontier to bring law, order, and civilization to a new land."[21] By drawing upon a genre familiar to Americans, *Exodus* gave Israel a persona. The movie placed the figurative "white hat" on Israel's head, certifying the state, its leaders and citizens, as "good guys."

The central theme of *Exodus* links the creation of the Jewish state with the rescue of Holocaust survivors. But unlike *Sword in the Desert*, which ignores the refugees except as objects of rescue, or *The Juggler*, which focuses on one survivor's painful process of healing, *Exodus* shows pitiful victims transformed overnight into brave pioneers. Guided by the Haganah—embodying Jewish military might and cunning—a ragtag group of refugees turn themselves into a self-disciplined people's army. (A very clean one, too, despite difficult conditions on board a crowded refugee ship.) Despair yields to hope, resignation becomes determination. This process occurs, on-screen, in the space of only a few days. Although the horrors of the immediate past are not forgotten, the movie graphically proves how creating the state and reclaiming the Jewish homeland is the Jews' answer to Hitler.

Ari Ben Canaan (Paul Newman) and Taha (John Derek) in Jerusalem.

In a crucial scene overlooking Mt. Tabor, Preminger casts Israel's significance as the Jewish homeland in terms of a symbolic Jewish-American ethnicity. At the heart of the scene is an emphatic statement by the hero that "people are different." He delivers this banal but revealing declaration as something of a manifesto that must be accepted eventually by the heroine (despite her initial rejection of it). Hardly a complex idea, the notion that "people are different" carried significant ideological freight, especially for American Jews in 1960.

Preminger departs from this chapter in Uris's novel in several ways. In the novel, the hike up Mt. Tabor involves a group of Palmach veterans; Kitty and Ari are not alone. (The lovemaking occurs late at night between Ari's sister and her lover, David.) As Kitty looks at Ari Ben Canaan and the other fighters, the "electrifying revelation" that "this was no army of mortals" hits her. "These were the ancient Hebrews," Kitty realizes, "the army of Israel, and no force on earth could stop them for the power of God was within them!"[22] Contrast this with the movie's use of Mt. Tabor as a site for Kitty's education. (See sidebar, page 214.)

This scene occurs midway through the movie when Ari, the handsome blue-eyed hero (Paul Newman), pulls off the road in a typical *sabra* gesture to show Kitty, the pretty blond American Christian nurse (Eva Marie Saint), the Valley of Jezreel and Mt. Tabor. The movie has already shown him to be a laconic soldier and fighter, a clever underground organizer and audacious leader of men. Now he appears as a *moreh derekh*, an interpreter of the land and of the *Tanakh* (Hebrew Scriptures) to the American outsider. Eschewing a subtlety inappropriate to movies and Hollywood, Ari spells out his Zionist history lesson for Kitty (and all Americans): "I just wanted you to know

I'm a Jew. This is *my* country." Ari's defiant statement to the American nurse echoes Sabra's similar response to the British in *Sword in the Desert*.

Kitty replies that she understands; after all, she is a smart American woman. She then goes on to express the universalist American creed of equality. Her rejoinder sounds like an Anti-Defamation League educational pamphlet prepared for Brotherhood Week, a popular observance in Eisenhower's America that Jews strongly supported. Ari answers as the new Jew, the post-Holocaust Jew, the Jew who lives in his own land, who fights for his freedom, the Jew so secure in his Jewishness and sense of purpose, a hero of such integrity, that he can be friends with all who respect him. As a Jew rooted in Israel, the land of his birth, he deals equally with Arab and Englishman, even with feuding father and uncle, personifications of Haganah and Irgun. "Don't ever believe it," he tells Kitty. "People are different. They have a right to be different."

Ari Ben Canaan (Paul Newman) and Major Caldwell (Peter Lawford) at checkpoint.

Ari's forthright defense of "the right to be different" mimics theories of cultural pluralism articulated fifty years earlier by the American philosopher Horace Kallen. An Israeli hero, Ari eschews any pandering for Gentile approval. Although *Exodus* projects intermarriage as the future of Kitty and Ari's relationship, it also assures the audience that Ari will not lose his ethnic distinctiveness. Nor, by the way, will Kitty. Ari will remain a Jew; there can be no doubt in any viewer's mind. When Kitty will come to love and accept him, she will love and accept him as a Jew. Her eventual acceptance of Ari signifies approbation of Israel by Americans; her embrace of the new Jew suggests the possibility of welcoming those Jews who identify with Israel. These Gentiles like Israelis because they don't need Gentile support.

In an interview conducted during the movie's shooting, Saint admitted that she identified with Kitty. "I know the type of person she is because I was like her myself once," the actress explained. "Ten years ago I had many misunderstandings about people and certain unconscious prejudices. When I heard people voice these things I rebelled inside but said nothing and did nothing although I felt I should." She understood the "passive anti-Jewish point of view." Making the movie, Saint discovered that she felt "like I'm part of history—a history I had nothing to do with but I have a compassion for." She hoped that "if I can involve the audience, perhaps change someone's prejudice to understanding, it will all be to the good." When the reporter responded that Kitty never existed but is merely a prototype, Saint answered, "Women like her did. She's real to me."[23] This sense of reality radiated from the screen.

Kitty mirrors the engagement in the movie's drama for American viewers. Like most Americans watching the movie, she starts as a tourist. But she becomes a committed participant. "I'm an American," she announces at the beginning. As such, she indicates no

# EXODUS: "PEOPLE ARE DIFFERENT"

*En route from Jerusalem to his home up north, Ari Ben Canaan pulls the car carrying him and Kitty Fremont to the side of the road.*

ARI: Every time I come home I stop here and just look for a minute. Do you want to look with me?

KITTY: Sure.

*They get out of the car, climb to the top of the hill, pass in front of three cypress trees, and then descend to a ledge overlooking a stunning panorama.*

ARI: The Valley of Jezreel. If you dug straight down, far enough, then you'd find the ruins of Megiddo. You'd find the very same paving stones that Joshua walked on when he conquered it. [pointing] That's Abu Yesha. It's an Arab village. To the left is Gan Dafna. [sweep of scenery] Do you know your Bible?

KITTY: In a Presbyterian sort of way.

ARI [sitting down]: That's Mt. Tabor.

KITTY: I remember. When Deborah gathered her armies.

ARI: That's where she stood when she watched Barak march out to fight the Canaanites. "So Barak went down from Mt. Tabor and 10,000 men with him." It's in the Book of Judges. [pause] The Canaanites had nine hundred iron chariots. But Barak had men. Thirty-two hundred years ago. That's when the Jews first came to this valley. It wasn't just yesterday or the day before.

KITTY: Isn't your father's name Barak?

ARI: In Russia he was Ya'akov Rabinsky. But when he came here he took the name of Deborah's general. He called himself Barak Ben Canaan, Barak the son of Canaan. And this valley became a Jewish land once again. He can give you the date that every clump of trees was planted down there, to the month.

KITTY: Don't get excited. We're not debating now. I'll grant anything you say.

ARI: No. I just wanted you to know I'm a Jew. This is *my* country.

KITTY: I do know. I understand.

ARI: Sometimes it's not that easy.

KITTY: It's the easiest thing in the world, Ari. All these differences between people are made up. People are the same no matter what they're called.

ARI: Don't ever believe it. People are different. They have a right to be different. They *like* to be different. It's no good pretending that differences don't exist. They do. They have to be recognized and respected.

KITTY: I recognize them. I respect them. [sigh] Don't you understand that . . . that you make me feel like a Presbyterian when you can't just for a minute or two forget that you're a Jew? [Ari looks at her.] You're wrong, Ari. There are no differences. [Kitty moves toward him for an embrace.]

particular interest in Jews or their struggles. Kitty pulls viewers into the drama to explore anti-Semitism in an intelligent person of good faith. She feels strange among Jews, yet she is drawn to Karen (Jill Haworth), a beautiful, blond teenage survivor whom she meets in the Cyprus internment camp. When she offers Karen a life without risk as an American, Kitty demonstrates her condescending lack of understanding and her anti-Semitism. Shocked by Karen's refusal, she comes to understand and accept Jews as they are—that is, "different." Her path through the movie resembles the film's own approach to the historical reality it dramatizes. At first superficial and curious in the scenes set on Cyprus, the movie draws closer to the historical conflict as Kitty boards the ship to travel with Karen to Palestine. Soon Kitty and the film are swept into the struggle for a Jewish state. They become essential to the story and integral to the action, as witnessed in the dramatic prison escape. *Exodus* eventually becomes so convincing that viewers are hard put to contest its authenticity.[24]

In subordinating the conflicts of Jews with Arabs and British, *Exodus* emphasizes instead the theme of brothers at war in a common land. Ari's most difficult task is to reunite the warring factions of his own family. But he cannot overcome the implacable anger between the two brothers, his uncle, Akiva (David Opatoshu), head of the Irgun, and his father, Barak (Lee J. Cobb), a Hagannah leader. Each adheres passionately to his Zionist ideology. Ari seeks an alliance of Irgun and Hagannah to fight the British, their common enemy. Akiva opposes the alliance; he is unwilling to renounce terrorism. Violence is the midwife of nations, he explains to Ari. Barak will neither countenance terrorism nor forgive his brother for being a terrorist. By portraying both brothers as good men, *Exodus* suggests that both ideologies, political parties, and military organizations—Labor Zionism and Revisionism, Mapai and Herut, Hagannah and Irgun—are ultimately reconcilable because both are right. This is a very American solution, championing consensus rather than factionalism.

Preminger noted with approval that he angered representatives of the Labor Government and their Herut opponents. "You do not want to rewrite the script," he told the former, "you want to rewrite history!"[25] In his autobiography Preminger recalls telling Golda Meir, David Ben Gurion, and Moshe Dayan that Israel would not "have emerged as a nation without the terrorists. I don't like violence but that is unfortunately the truth. The British would never have given in without the high pressure from the radical element."[26] Menachem Begin, however, objected that the movie didn't give his Irgun enough credit.

The cinematic Israel addressed postwar dilemmas confronting American Jews, but refocused them for the silver screen. It gave Jewish- and Gentile-Americans a hero to root for and to identify with, if only in a darkened movie theater. The plucky little Jewish state fighting for its freedom became a Hollywood legend. And possibly because Gentile-Americans momentarily identified with the Israel of the screen, American Jews considered going even further: they welcomed a Jewish movie image of romance and heroism. Willing to blur the distinction between imagination and reality, American Jews accepted *Exodus*'s version of Zionist history.

*Exodus*'s compelling power drew American Jews to visit the scene of its historic events. Accessible, heroic, uplifting, Israel on screen promised redemption, a way to be Jewish in America with pride. The movie's logo featured flames licking at raised, clenched fists, one of which held a gun. The image suggested an updated version of the biblical burning bush that is not consumed. Ernest Gold's theme music was given lyrics and became a popular song. "This land is mine, God gave this land to me!" crooned

Kelly Fremont (Eva Marie Saint) and Ari Ben Canaan (Paul Newman).

Pat Boone. Those who knew Israel well—Israelis and American Zionists—disliked the distortion, but few challenged Israel's new popularity through alternative images. Instead, El Al, Israel's national airline, sponsored a tour of Israel in 1961 that followed in Preminger's footsteps, stopping at places he had made famous on film. Tour guides found that American visitors "keep asking them where is this or that village" portrayed in the movie or novel.[27] Israel's Ministry of Tourism recorded significant increases in tourism, with figures more than doubling between 1958 and 1961.[28]

The reverential embrace of Israel sparked by the creation of a screen legend did not reach one significant segment of American Jews: its intellectuals. A 1961 symposium published in *Commentary* magazine produced remarkably ambivalent comments about Israel and no expressions of pro-Israel piety despite a specific question asking about "any special connection with the State of Israel." Although a few writers admitted that "at the time of the Sinai campaign I felt a distinct physical elan: a sense of victory," they immediately concluded, "even Israel, however, cannot save us."[29] Distanced from American popular culture—usually defined as mass culture—intellectuals were largely removed, as well, from Israel. Midge Decter, in a piece aptly titled "Popular Jews," first confessed that for two years she adamantly refused to read *Exodus*, and then admitted that when she did finally pick it up, she couldn't put it down.[30] Neither Hollywood's progressivism, which contributed to the creation of *Exodus*, nor its principled socialist Zionism engaged these mostly New York intellectuals. Their Jewish world was an unredeemable diaspora.

Barak Ben Canaan (Lee J. Cobb) and his son, Ari (Paul Newman).

However, the story of Israel's creation lodged in the fantasies of most American Jews. In its cinematic form, Israel became their homeland and Israelis their heroic alter egos. Indeed, it could be argued that many American Jews responded so quickly to the crisis of May–June 1967 because, as they saw it, Israelis followed the Hollywood script without faltering. First came three weeks of increasingly unendurable tension, until, by the beginning of June, Israel stood completely alone—as a Hollywood hero should stand—against the massed might of the entire Arab world. Then, in six brilliant, tension-filled days, Israel not only single-handedly fought off the Arab armies of Egypt, Syria, and Jordan but the Israeli military reunited Jerusalem, recaptured the Sinai, and doubled the territory of the state. In the Six Day War, Israel miraculously lived up to its legend. Image and reality fused; Israel redeemed its promise, and frontier visions became living history.

When Otto Preminger cast blue-eyed, ruddy-cheeked, handsome Paul Newman for the title role in the film version of *Exodus*, he represented Ari Ben Canaan as the prototypical Israeli, the new Jew for a generation of Americans who would watch the Six Day

War unfold. The novel and movie provided Americans with a popular representation of Israelis as well as a potential script with which to read events in the Middle East.

*Life* magazine made the connection between the fictional and real explicit. Next to a photograph of Yitzhak Rabin, "commander of Israel's land, sea and air forces," ran the caption: "General Rabin, a master of sabotage technique and a military planner respected for his cunning, was the man on whom Leon Uris based his fictional character Ari Ben Canaan in *Exodus*." The portrait shows Rabin in military dress, his shirt unbuttoned at the neck, his head raised as he looks up at Jerusalem's Western Wall pictured behind him. *Life*'s references to cunning and sabotage technique notwithstanding, the image presents

Ari Ben Canaan (Paul Newman) in a contemplative moment.

a genuine hero, whose armies overran large swatches of blue territory shown in the black-and-white map above Rabin's head. The "extraordinary elan of Rabin's army" praised by the magazine also registers in the casualty rate, which includes a high percentage of officers; the fact is portrayed graphically in a photo of rows of fresh graves in a cemetery outside Tel Aviv.[31]

*Exodus*'s power to influence visual imagery around the Six Day War appears as well in the second issue of *Life* magazine devoted to the battles. Its first coverage, on June 16, 1967, offers types of photos we might expect: scenes of the wounded, of Israeli tanks riding through Jerusalem, of fighting in the desert, of handsome young soldiers standing in awe looking up at the Western Wall, and of surrender. The cover features a photo of Israeli soldiers, fully clad in battle gear, standing at a distance and looking at the raised hands of captured Egyptians who are lying face down. The Egyptians are in civilian dress and the faces of the Israelis are not prominent. Contrast this with the shot on the cover of the following week's issue: an Israeli soldier emerges from the Suez Canal exultant; smiling, gun in hand. Ralph Cameron's photo suggests a generic blue-eyed hero, his muscular body visible beneath a wet suit, surrounded by the brilliant blue water that obliterates any horizon line or point of reference. Without the caption, "Israeli soldier cools in the Suez Canal," there would be no way of knowing that this man is an Israeli soldier. Even the weapon he holds is not an uzi but a Russian kalishnikov, a captured trophy of the Six Day War (close inspection reveals some Arabic on the gun).[32] *Life*'s cover presented Americans with a compelling portrait of a man with a gun, a handsome grinning hero who, the magazine tells us, is Israeli.[33]

Here is the new Jew reborn after his baptism of fire, emerging out of the waters of the Suez. Why choose this shot for the cover? Where might Americans have seen such an image before? Those who remembered the movie *Exodus* would recall that the first time they saw Paul Newman, he was coming out of the sea onto the shores of Cyprus. Newman is bare-chested in the scene, wearing only a prominent Star of David around his

Ari Ben Canaan (Paul
Newman) emerging from
the Mediterranean.

neck to identify him. It is night, not day, and he carries no weapon. But the palpable
physicality of the hero's rise from the water suggests why *Life*'s editors might have
selected the photo for the cover, instead of a shot taken in Jerusalem.

*Life* was not alone in connecting the movie version of Israel and its heroic Jews
with the real-life version seen through other cameras. A *New York Times* profile, titled
"Hero of the Israelis," shows a youthful Rabin in a three-quarter shot. The caption
reads, "Prototype of fictional hero." The text itself begins with Rabin's words that conjure up courage and single-handed triumph: "The bulk of the Egyptian forces are fleeing
in disorder and we have occupied most of Sinai. We have fought with our own forces,
and nobody has aided us." After establishing Rabin's bravery in the 1948 fighting, the
*Times* describes him at forty-five as "still boyish looking." This "blue-eyed, sandy-
haired, and rugged" hero "inspired many of the episodes in which Leon Uris cast the
fictional Ari Ben Canaan in *Exodus*." Like Ben Canaan, once the Nazis are defeated,
Rabin is ready to fight for the Jews. As the *Times* reports, "when the Nazi threat passed,

the young fighter used his training to combat the British blockade of Jewish immigration. . . . The raid against a British detention camp in Athlith, south of Haifa, to liberate more than 200 'illegal' Jewish immigrants, described in *Exodus*, was actually led by young Rabin."[34] History and fiction merge seamlessly into a compelling narrative: Rabin "actually led" the raid that Ben Canaan conducted in the novel. A figure of the silver screen commands Israeli armies across the Sinai desert.

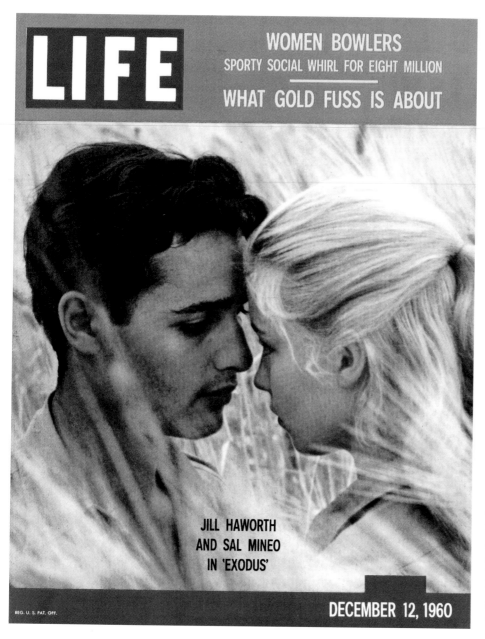

LIFE

WOMEN BOWLERS
SPORTY SOCIAL WHIRL FOR EIGHT MILLION
—————————————
WHAT GOLD FUSS IS ABOUT

JILL HAWORTH
AND SAL MINEO
IN 'EXODUS'

REG. U. S. PAT. OFF.

DECEMBER 12, 1960

Cover of *Life* magazine featuring *Exodus*, December 12, 1960.

Israel on-screen transmuted Zionist political rhetoric into the rallying cries of heroes. The Jews who produced the movies adopted without reservations the Zionist message of statehood as salvation for survivors. Here was their answer to Hitler's murder of European Jews: the creation of a screen Israel larger than life. Roth saw this and found it disturbing. "One week *Life* magazine presents on its cover a picture of Adolf Eichmann; weeks later, a picture of Sal Mineo as a Jewish freedom fighter," he wrote. The conjunction of the Eichmann trial in Jerusalem with *Exodus* in movie theaters produced this bizarre juxtaposition. "A crime to which there is no adequate human response, no grief, no compassion, no vengeance that is sufficient seems, in part then, to have been avenged."[35]

With the film *Exodus*, Israel entered the popular Jewish-American imagination as a romantic screen legend. As Hollywood had done with countless other stars, so it did with Israel. The "dream factories" took the mundane reality of a small, poor state struggling to absorb hundreds of thousands of destitute immigrants and remade it into a living romance. By securing Israel and Israelis as proverbial "good guy" heroes, *Exodus* also expanded possibilities for Jews who were "different" and their stories to appear on stage and screen. In the movie's wake came an array of films and musicals that did not camouflage Jewish difference. Despite a barrage of critics bemoaning "the vanishing American Jew," Jewish visibility in American culture increased.[36] *Exodus* gave Jews a proud self-consciousness and a new way of imagining Jewishness. It encouraged those who performed Jewish identities in public to renegotiate what it meant to be Jewish by integrating Israel into the imagination of American Jews.

# FLAUNTING IT: THE RISE AND FALL OF HOLLYWOOD'S "NICE" JEWISH (BAD) BOYS

J. HOBERMAN

Dustin Hoffman and Anne
Bancroft in *The Graduate*
(1967).

*Turn to any TV variety show, await the stand-up comic, and chances are good that he'll come on with accents and gestures and usages whose origins are directly traceable to the Borscht Belt by way of the East European shtetl and the corner grocery store. . . . The Jewish style, with its heavy reliance upon Yiddish and Yiddishisms, has emerged not only as a comic style, but as the prevailing comic style.*
—Wallace Markfield, "The Yiddishization of American Humor," *Esquire* (October 1965)

*Walk into any New York bookstore today and probably the first beckoning display you encounter will be the Jewish fun books. Stacked in revolving metal racks are the James Bond spoofs,* Oy Oy Seven, Loxfinger, Matzoball; *the "How-to" books,* How to Be a Jewish Mother, A Jewish President, A Jewish Madam; *and many other shrugged-shoulder versions of standard entertainment genres. . . . Just a little less prominently displayed are the latest works of the American Jewish comic novelists. These range in style from the Pop art of Wallace Markfield's* To an Early Grave *to the show-biz fantasy of Bruce Jay Friedman's* A Mother's Kisses; *from the Aristophanic farce of Saul Bellow's* The Last Analysis *to the subtle social comedy of Philip Roth's* Letting Go.
—Albert Goldman, "Boy-Man Schlemiel: The Jewish Element in American Humor," *Explorations* (1967)

Duck into any cinema. For a time, there were movies too—crazy comedies, most set in New York, many directed by or featuring stand-up comics. Among other self-consciously broken show-biz commandments governing permissible jokes and acceptable sexual (or filial) behavior, these films featured a hitherto unspeakable degree of Jewish content.

In particular, such Jewish comedies were predicated on the spectacle of nice boys acting out, fooling around, and even going berserk. Were these urban, middle-class professionals, the "Jewish bad guys" who the comedian Lenny Bruce maintained were never shown on screen? Anticipating the so-called blaxploitation and Italian-American films of the 1970s, the movies of this kind thrived on the sort of ethnic stereotyping that had largely disappeared from Hollywood films thirty years before. The image, however, was something new.

Hollywood's Jewish "new wave" (a subset of the larger new wave that refreshed Hollywood content and personnel in the late sixties) had its moment between 1967 and 1973, roughly between Israel's Six Day and Yom Kippur wars or Barbra Streisand's appearances in *Funny Girl* (Columbia, 1968) and *The Way We Were* (Columbia, 1973). These seven years not only brought Streisand's apotheosis as an openly ethnic, unreconstructed Jewish diva, but also saw the appearance of several male counterparts—including Dustin Hoffman, Elliott Gould, George Segal, and Richard Benjamin—as well as the emergence of the comic auteurs Woody Allen and Mel Brooks.[1]

During this period, Jewish humor reigned confidently supreme. The paperback

Barbra Streisand as Fanny
Brice in *Funny Girl* (1968).

# You don't have to be Jewish

## to love Levy's
### real Jewish Rye

Advertisement for Levy's rye
bread.

original *How to Be a Jewish Mother* went through fifteen editions and sold three million copies. Stand-up comedian Bruce, repeatedly busted for his vulgar language and sexually explicit routines, was canonized as a counterculture martyr (and was eventually the subject of a Hollywood bio-pic starring Hoffman); Jewish comics were ubiquitous on late-night TV. Even television ads had jokingly appropriated a measure of Jewish ethnicity, most famously in the campaign that used Asian- and African-American models to demonstrate that, "You don't have to be Jewish to love Levy's real Jewish Rye." As suggested by the "mad rushin' to *mama-lushen* [mother tongue]" noted among American humorists by Wallace Markfield in 1965, Yiddish, as the funkiest manifestation of Jewishness, was understood to be hip. Indeed, in his 1966 review of a novel by Jewish-American writer Irvin Faust, Stanley Kauffmann identified a "Lenny Bruce syndrome" based on the assumption that "anyone who doesn't understand Yiddish references is not just Gentile but square."[2]

This presupposition of a new Jewish-American cultural visibility informs the dozen or so movies—all characterized by their insolent black humor and social satire—that featured (mainly) young, (sometimes) neurotic, and (by and large) not altogether admirable Jewish male protagonists cut off from their roots but disdainful of white-bread America. Self-hatred merged with self-absorption, narcissism seemed indistinguishable from personal liberation, and alienation was a function of identity. Released to increasing critical displeasure among both Jews and Gentiles, these films were considered offensive in their representation of Jewish (and sometimes non-Jewish) ethnicity as well as Jewish (and Gentile) women.

221

# "HOW THE JEW GOT INTO SHOW BUSINESS"

Performing for a mixed audience of Jews and Gentiles, stand-up comedian Lenny Bruce, born Leonard Schneider (1925–1966), created an act with an unprecedented degree of explicitly Jewish content, as well as Yiddish slang. Moreover, Bruce used such material to project the image of a taboo-breaking, show-biz hipster. In one of his most famous routines, Bruce laid out his definition of Jewishness: "Dig: I'm Jewish. Count Basie's Jewish. Ray Charles is Jewish. Eddie Cantor's goyish. B'nai Brith is goyish; Hadassah, Jewish. Marine corps—heavy goyim, dangerous. All Drake's Cakes are goyish. Pumpernickel is Jewish. . . . Trailer parks are so goyish that Jews won't go near them."

As noted by his future biographer Albert Goldman, Bruce's obsession with his Jewishness proved to be prophetic. It was also constructed. Goldman pointed out that the comedian was not "a product of the New York urban ghetto [but] grew up in an Andy Hardy town on Long Island and never spoke a Yiddish word until he was twenty-five."[1]

Bruce's "How the Jew Got into Show Business" is a riff that evokes the Book of Exodus, as well as the myth of Jewish Hollywood, to satirize both Jewish and Gentile perceptions. This transcription is taken from *The Essential Lenny Bruce*, a posthumous anthology compiled and edited by John Cohen. Although Cohen does not give a specific source, Bruce recorded a similar version of the routine during his performance at the Berkeley Community Theater on December 12, 1965.
—J.H.

Lenny Bruce, early 1960s.

From *The Essential Lenny Bruce,* ed. John Cohen (New York: Ballantine Books, 1974), 50–51.

The Jew had a hip boss, the Egyptian, oh yeah. Couldn't bullshit the Egyptian, you know. No, he was pretty slick. But the Jew kept working at it, working at being charming.

EGYPTIAN: Never mind the horseshit, thank you. We got the pyramids to build, and that's where it's at. Gonna get it up, takes your generation, next generation, do a nice workman-like job here.

JEW: Oh thank you, thank you.

EGYPTIAN: Get outta here with that horseshit! Now stop it now.

But the Jew kept working at it, working at being charming. And he got so slick at it—he never carried it off—but he honed his arguments so good, he got so good at it, that that was his expertise:

EGYPTIAN: These Jews got bullshit that don't quit! I mean, it's an *art* with them. C'mon. Let's go watch a Jew be charming. Hey! Jew! Do that charming bit for us, there. We know you're bullshitting, but you do it so good we get a kick out of it. Do it for us, will ya please?

See? That was it, and he was on his way,

Now dig the switch-around. Now the Jew gets into show business. And, he writes motion pictures, he's making the images—he has the film industry knocked up—he controls it! And the Jew naturally writes what he thinks is pretty, what he thinks is ugly—and it's *amazing*, but you never see one Jewish bad guy in the movies. Not even a Jewish villain, man. Gregory Peck, Paul Muni—haha! It's wonderful! Who's the bad guy? *The goyim!* The Irish!

And you see a lot of pictures about Christ—a ton of religious pictures, in the most respectful position. And the reason that is, I'm sure, it's the way the Jew's saying, "I'm sorry." That's where it's at.

The movies of the Jewish new wave, many adapted from recent novels, could never have been made in the old Hollywood and, indeed, a significant minority were produced by non-major studios, usually Joseph E. Levine's Embassy Pictures and Avco Embassy Pictures. In the beginning was *The Graduate* (Embassy), which opened a few days before Christmas 1967 and went on to become the sensation of the season and, ultimately, the decade's second highest grossing Hollywood release. Directed by onetime improvisational

Dustin Hoffman and Katharine Ross in *The Graduate*.

stand-up Mike Nichols, *The Graduate* seemed—like Arthur Penn's nearly contemporaneous *Bonnie and Clyde* (Warner Bros., 1967)—to be the harbinger of a Hollywood new wave. This was in part due to Nichols's showy filmmaking, which was replete with references to and cribs from fashionable European directors Federico Fellini, Michelangelo Antonioni, and François Truffaut, and in part because of his (mildly) rebellious antihero. Recent college graduate Benjamin Braddock (Hoffman) is seduced into an affair with one of his parents' friends, Mrs. Robinson (Anne Bancroft), before eloping with her daughter—his true love—the Berkeley student Elaine (Katharine Ross), whom he rescues from the church where she has just married a medical student.

Was young Benjamin of Beverly Hills a Jew or was this vaguely critical, comically maladroit youth just a little Jewish? Certainly, there was no mistaking Hoffman's ethnicity. In any case, *The Graduate* was cited as an example of an ascendant Jewishness. Pointing out that the movie's hero "bore an uncanny resemblance to a ubiquitous character in Jewish folk and literary imagination— the schlemiel," Esther Romeyn and Jack Kugelmass maintain that the movie "signaled the return of the anti-hero, and with it, representations of Jews suddenly burst upon the screen."[3]

If the schlemiel was a new American everyman, so the Jewish condition was understood to be universal. The prime ideologue of this sentimental myth was literary critic Leslie Fiedler. In an appreciation of Saul Bellow, written in 1957, a few years after the publication of *The Adventures of Augie March* (1953), Fiedler made the arrogant declaration that current American literature was now, at all levels, a Jewish province: "What Saul Bellow is for highbrow literature, [J. D.] Salinger is for upper middlebrow, Irwin Shaw for middle middlebrow and Herman Wouk for lower middlebrow. . . . The acceptance of Bellow as the leading novelist of his generation must be paired off with the appearance of Marjorie Morningstar on the front cover of *Time*. On all levels, the Jew is in the process of being mythologized into the representative American."[4]

Hollywood had long denied it, but Albert Goldman expanded on Fiedler's idea by declaring that the American Jew was now the representative modern man. By the mid-sixties, Goldman stated: "The Jew was raised from his traditional role of underdog or invisible man to the glory of being the most fascinating authority in America. Benefiting from universal guilt over the murders by the Nazis, stiffening with fresh pride over the achievements of the State of Israel, reaping the harvest in America of generations of hard work and sacrifice for the sake of the 'children,' the Jews burst suddenly into prominence in a dozen different areas of national life." The more "Jewish" Jews appeared, the more universal they became. Or so Goldman decreed in this essay, "Boy-Man Schlemiel: The Jewish Element in American Humor," an analysis of Jewish novelists and those mainly Jewish "sick" comedians—Mort Sahl, Shelly Berman, Mike Nichols and Elaine May, Tom Lehrer, and especially Lenny Bruce—who made much of psychoanalytic jargon in treating such apparently unfunny subjects as mental illness, racial prejudice, religion, sexual pathology, and nuclear fallout.[5]

This development was read both as evidence of Jewish-American cultural confidence and as proof of Jewish-American insecurity. Some made a specific connection to Israel's victory in the June 1967 Six Day War. In her monograph *The Schlemiel as Modern Hero*, Ruth R. Wisse noted that "alongside chest-thumping accounts" of the war, New York bookstores stocked *"Irving of Arabia: An Unorthodox Interpretation of the Israeli-Arab War*, which shows a soldier going off to battle with his mother in the background, pleading 'Marvin, please. Take your galoshes'" and a "poster of a shrunken Hasid emerging from a telephone booth in a familiar cape bearing the inscription 'Super-Jew.'" For Wisse, the "tenacious hold of the schlemiel on the American Jewish consciousness" was less a Jewish prefiguration of a universal type than a reflexive self-protective instinct that had gripped certain elements of the Jewish-American public in the war's aftermath. Perhaps American Jews deemed it safer to identify with the "schlemiel-loser" than the victorious Israeli soldier, or perhaps Israel's martial proficiency served to reinforce the American Jew's negative self-perception.[6]

Others more committed to the transformation of Jewish life in America saw writers such as Philip Roth and performers like Bruce, Mel Brooks, and the team of Nichols and May as anything but afraid. For Goldman, these artists seemed fearlessly honest in articulating "feelings shared by tens of thousands of young American Jews." The "anger and self-pity" expressed in this "potent new humor" was a factor of newfound security. "No longer persecuted, [Jews] were progressing triumphantly toward their goals of social and cultural achievement." Israel's victory contributed to this new confidence, but so did the tolerant atmosphere of postwar America: "The traditionally conformist tendencies of American Jewry changed. The old feeling of shame was transformed into one of pride and, in some cases, of arrogance." Among other things, Jewish comedians openly riffed on the Jewish role in American show business.[7]

Jack Warden, Sorrell Brooke, Joseph Wiseman, Godfrey Cambridge (as a Yiddish-speaking cab driver), and George Segal in *Bye Bye Braverman* (1968).

## A POST-*GRADUATE* CINEMA

Benjamin Braddock, a nice boy who acted badly in his bumbling sexual transgression and defiance of parental authority, was a crypto-Jew. There was, however, no mistaking the protagonists of *Bye Bye Braverman* (Warner Bros.) and *The Producers* (Avco Embassy), two comedies that opened in New York during the winter of 1968. *Bye Bye Braverman* was adapted by Herbert Sargent from Wallace Markfield's 1964 novel *To an Early Grave*, a roman à clef that imagined the response of various New York intellectuals to the untimely death of the *Partisan Review* writer Isaac Rosenfeld. Sidney Lumet, the son of Yiddish actor Baruch Lumet and himself a child performer in the Yiddish theater, directed *Braverman* as the follow-up to his adaptation of a far more somber Jewish novel, *The Pawnbroker*, the most notable and controversial Hollywood treatment of the Holocaust between *The Diary of Anne Frank* (Twentieth Century Fox, 1959) and *Schindler's List* (Universal, 1994).

The mode of *Bye Bye Braverman* is bleakly humorous. Having learned of Leslie Braverman's fatal heart attack (news delivered as a laugh line), a quartet of laboriously wisecracking intellectuals—George Segal, Jack Warden, Sorrell Brooke, and Joseph Wiseman—set off in a red Volkswagen on a journey across Brooklyn in search of their friend's funeral. *Bye Bye Braverman* is set in the totally Jewish world of a 1930s Yiddish talking picture, complete with Jewish black man. (Even the various couples are Jewish.) The credits evoke the principals' Lower East Side or Brooklyn childhoods and their formative experiences—catching an Italian neorealist film at a Greenwich Village movie house, attending a rally on the Columbia campus for Socialist presidential candidate Norman Thomas—before introducing them in the contexts of their current Manhattan neighborhoods.

This neo-shtetl geography is scarcely *Braverman*'s lone parochial element. The cast's heavy New York accents and Jewish inflections are close to kabuki. The dialogue is peppered with Yiddishisms, some of which—as when Wiseman's dour, sarcastic character refers to his son as a *kocker* (shit)—would have pushed the boundaries of then-acceptable English vulgarity. There are also numerous impossibly obscure references, at least for a Hollywood movie—not just to Franz Kafka and Søren Kierkegaard, but to (the pre-*Portnoy's Complaint*) Philip Roth, the collectivization of Soviet agriculture, and the "Tsadek [holy sage] of Lublin"—as well as an arcane debate on the morality of a Jew owning a German automobile.

Wiseman, the group's self-appointed conscience, complains directly to God, while the bleak ending has the hapless Segal addressing a row of gravestones. These characters were something previously unseen on the screen. Confronted with a novel expression of ethnic identity, critics fell back on earlier models. *Newsweek* reviewer Paul Zimmerman bizarrely described Braverman's sexy, voluble widow (Jessica Walter) as "an imitation of Molly Goldberg," while, in the *Village Voice*, Andrew Sarris imagined that Segal's guilty intellectual might once have been a role for tough kid John Garfield.[8]

A *New York Times* production story describes Lumet directing Wiseman in Yiddish before taking his cast out for "a nice dairy lunch." Lumet informed the *Times* that his film was a new sort of Jewish comedy: "It's not the Molly Goldberg kind of humor. . . . It's the irreverent but wholly universal humor of the bookish, Jewish intellectual." Critics, however, found the movie to be both unduly insular and overly broad. Several reviews paraphrased the current Levy's rye bread ad campaign. The Catholic weekly *Commonweal* asserted that "you *do* have to be Jewish to appreciate *Bye Bye Braverman*." The *Nation* modified this position: "You don't have to be Jewish to love [*Bye Bye Braverman*] but it helps a lot to be a New Yorker." Indeed, *Newsday* wondered whether "anyone west of the Hudson" could even understand the movie.[9]

Filled with the attention-grabbing bits that Jewish comedians called "shtick," *Bye Bye Braverman* stops in its tracks for solos by two stand-up comics, Godfrey Cambridge as a black Jewish cab driver, and Alan King as a rabbi delivering a funeral oration. (As Sig Altman notes, King's performance was "an instance of the comedian-turned-rabbi-turned-comedian.") From their pews, the boys irreverently comment on or kibbitz King's routine—a virtual Borscht Belt shpritz of one-liners—only to discover that they have wandered into the wrong funeral. *Variety* was put off by the "tasteless jokes, all at the expense of Jewish people," and speculated that *Bye Bye Braverman* would "offend the sensibilities of many, and merely titillate the prejudices of others." Others deemed the stereotypes to be accurate. Robert Hatch wrote in the *Nation* that he was "not going to let the Anti-Defamation League con me out of saying that modern urban

Jewry has developed a gallery of personality styles that can be defined by fraternal caricature."[10]

Reviewing the movie in the *New Republic*, Kauffmann cited his previous review of Markfield's novel: "These educated Jews slip into their exaggerated music-hall turns with an air of 'Who's kidding whom? Culture-shmulture, this is what we *are*.' . . . Whether Markfield mocks these men because they are still too Jewish or are not Jewish enough is not clear." The movie, however, made this point moot. The protagonists are recognizably Jewish and so are their attitudes. These characters "could hardly pass for intellectuals," Pauline Kael wrote in the *New Yorker*, "but they have become even *more* 'Jewish' . . . they're Jewish comics." In her dislike for the film, Kael recognized that *Bye Bye Braverman* had less to do with Jewish-American life than Jewish-American show business—or, rather, that the tropes of Jewish-American show business had come to signify Jewish-American life.[11]

This was even more true of *The Producers*, the first feature written and directed by Mel Brooks. The film's well-known premise has a seedy Broadway impresario, Max Bialystock (Zero Mostel), who finances his shows by romancing and bilking elderly widows, and a timorous, if ultimately crooked, accountant named Leo Bloom (Gene Wilder), hatch a scheme to defraud their investors by overselling shares in a show so offensive to the Broadway audience that it is certain to close after one performance. To this end, the partners select *Springtime for Hitler*, a musical by an unreconstructed Nazi, Franz Liebkind. Bialystock and Bloom further guarantee their show's failure by hiring a dimwitted cross-dressing director Roger De Bris and bestowing the role of Hitler on a mind-blown method-acting hippie known as LSD. As ultimate insurance, Bialystock insults the drama critic from the *New York Times* by proffering him an opening night bribe. But, as terrible as *Springtime for Hitler* is, the audience takes it for a comedy—even a satire. The show is a hit and the swindlers wind up in jail.

"Springtime for Hitler," *The Producers*' initial title until the distributor, Joseph H. Levine, prevailed upon the filmmaker to change it, was a gag that Brooks had nurtured for years—an ultimate *Show of Shows* skit, complete with a dialect role perfect for Sid Caesar, the TV star for whom Brooks had created countless comic German characters. Brooks—who himself played several comic Nazis in the comedy albums he recorded with Carl Reiner—promoted his idea in a *Playboy* interview published two months before the musical *Cabaret* opened on Broadway in late 1966.[12]

Unstinting in its comic aggression, *The Producers* gave the sense—not altogether uncommon in the 1960s—of putting something on the screen for the first time. Mostel's Bialystock is a sort of frenzied Groucho Marx (complete with asides to the audience) inflated to Falstaffian proportions—a fount of libidinal energy and rampant orality who not only chews the scenery and devours the camera lens but kisses everything in range. Staring out his office window, Bialystock spies another show-biz type exit a limousine with a statuesque blonde and is moved to scream, "Flaunt it, baby! Flaunt it."[13]

Although far less flashy in its technique than *The Graduate*, *The Producers* was, in its way, one more example of a Hollywood (as well as a Jewish) new wave. Brooks flaunted his own historical references by evoking the movies of the 1930s, predicating gags on knowledge of such *Partisan Review* heroes as James Joyce, Kafka, and Fyodor Dostoyevsky—as well as incorporating the sort of Yiddishisms that had been a leitmotif on *Your Show of Shows*. (Roger De Bris might be the name for an aristocratic *mohel*.) In its confrontational "bad boy" attitude, *The Producers* was also a manifestation of the "sick." That financing was arranged by Sidney Glazier, Oscar-winning producer of a

movie as dignified as *The Eleanor Roosevelt Story* (Allied Artists, 1965), seems like one of Brooks's bad-taste jokes.

The words "Jew" and "Jewish" are never used in *The Producers*. Indeed, one of the best gags is the Nazi playwright's strategic obliviousness to the evident Jewishness of his producers. Not only are their names, professions, and demeanors stereotypically Jewish, their interpreters were as well. Having created the role of Tevye in *Fiddler on the Roof* four seasons earlier, Mostel was a Jewish icon. In 1969, after Wilder was nominated for an Oscar for best supporting actor, *Hollywood Reporter* declared that he was now in "dueling contention" with Hoffman for the title role in a movie version of Roth's just-published *Portnoy's Complaint*.

Not surprisingly, some found *The Producers* not only coarse, but also overly ethnic. The movie, Kael wrote in the *New Yorker*, "revels in the kind of show business Jewish humor that used to be considered too specialized for movies." Kael attributed this new, brazen sensibility to the rise of Jewish stand-up comics and their appearance on TV. "Screenwriters used to take the Jewish out but, now that television comedians exploit themselves as stereotypes, screenwriters are putting the Jewish in, pushing it for laughs—and getting them." (Interestingly, Kael had cited a similar phenomenon—the popularization of a hitherto in-group attitude—to explain why some people felt threatened by the seemingly nihilistic violence of the year's surprise hit, *Bonnie and Clyde*.)[14]

Far from self-deprecating in its Jewish humor, *The Producers* conveys considerable cultural confidence—loud and proud, it is a rebellion against invisibility, the equivalent of dancing on the Führer's grave, a sort of twentieth-century Purim play with Hitler invoked as the absurd Haman. When the movie was reincarnated a third of a century later, in 2001, as a wildly successful Broadway musical, Brooks's entire "Springtime for Hitler" concept became a self-fulfilling prophesy.[15]

Dick Shawn as LSD playing Hitler, and Renée Taylor as the actress playing Eva Braun, in "Springtime for Hitler," *The Producers*.

The original *Producers* was scarcely so popular. Embassy chose to first release the movie outside New York, premiering it in Washington and Philadelphia over Thanksgiving 1967. Turnout was sparse and laughter nonexistent. When *The Producers* opened several months later at a midtown Manhattan art house, it was greeted with mainly negative notices—including pans from New York's leading critics. The movie did, however, have a full-page endorsement from Peter Sellers, himself a Jew. "Those of us who have seen this film and understand it have experienced a phenomenon which occurs only once in a lifetime," Sellers wrote. In fact, Sellers had some responsibility for getting *The Producers* released. He first saw the then-shelved movie in January 1968 as part of "the outrageous, hash-infused psychedelic-era screenings" held during the filming of his own new-wave Jewish comedy, *I Love You, Alice B. Toklas!*, and was so impressed that he phoned Levine at 2:00 A.M. Three days later, Sellers took out an ad in *Daily Variety* in support of the movie (later repeated in the *New York Times*).[16]

Directed by TV refugee Hy Averback from an original screenplay by Paul Mazursky and Larry Tucker, two writers for *The Danny Kaye Show*, *I Love You, Alice B. Toklas!* (Warner Bros.) was released in late 1968. Sellers plays repressed Los Angeles lawyer Harold Fine, the neurotic scion of a nouveau riche Jewish family, former owners of a Brooklyn candy store. Annoying, accented, and obtrusive, Fine's mother (Jo Van Fleet) is the movie's most intense and stereotyped character. Perhaps concerned that he is marrying a version of his mother, Fine leaves his Jewish fiancée Joyce (Joyce Van Patten) flanked by

the Twin Cantors under the *huppah* (wedding canopy), and subsequently takes up with a presumably Gentile flower child (Leigh Taylor-Young). Under her influence and that of her hashish brownies, the lawyer drops out and transforms his house into a hippie crash pad. "In my *gantse lebn* [whole life] I never saw such a mess," mom exclaims before she and dad sample some brownies themselves.

Like *Bye Bye Braverman*, *Alice B. Toklas* employs vulgar Yiddishisms. (It also features a comic funeral to which Fine's brother arrives dressed as a Hopi Indian.) According to Mazursky, Warner Bros. initially feared the movie was "too Jewish" and hence a commercial risk. What seems equally striking is its tolerance for drugs and the counterculture. Released without a rating, but with the proviso "for mature audiences," *I Love You, Alice B. Toklas!* was compared (usually unfavorably) to *The Graduate*, not the least in the ending in which, having abandoned Joyce for the second time under the *huppah*, Harold runs out into the streets of Los Angeles, still expressing his own alienation with the hope that "there's got to be something beautiful out there."[17]

## ROTH'S COMPLAINTS

*Going wild in public is the last thing in the world that a Jew is expected to do—by himself, by his family, by his fellow Jews, and by the larger community of Christians whose tolerance for him is often tenuous to begin with.*
—Philip Roth, "Imagining Jews" (*New York Review of Books*, September 29, 1974)

As Sanford Pinsker has pointed out, Lenny Bruce's "need to shock the Jews, to 'go public' with their secrets; the need to *shpritz* the *goyim*, to exorcize all their 'Southern-dummy-cheapo-drecko-dumbbell shit,' all their white bread Protestantism, raised comedy-as-hostility and comedy-as-tragic catharsis to new levels, and to new expectations." The same could be said of Bruce's literary analogue, Philip Roth.[18]

*Goodbye, Columbus* (Paramount) was directed by Larry Peerce and based on Arnold Schulman's adaptation of the novella for which the twenty-seven-year-old Roth won the National Book Award for fiction a decade before (and for which he had been attacked as a self-hating Jew). The film opened in March 1969, scarcely a month after the publication of the scandalous *Portnoy's Complaint*—an outrageously profane psychoanalytical monologue by a compulsively onanist, shikse-obsessed protagonist—established Roth as literature's ultimate "nice" Jewish bad boy.

Just as Roth's protagonist Alexander Portnoy was torn between his socially responsible, parent-pleasing public role as a New York commissioner of human services and his excitingly shameful sexual escapades, so the author himself used his serious fiction to break tribal taboos and express what some considered self-hatred and others misogyny. In *Goodbye, Columbus*, Roth provided the definitive portrait of the "Jewish-American princess"; in *Portnoy's Complaint*, he attacked the Jewish mother.[19]

ABOVE, TOP
Repressed lawyer Harold Fine (Peter Sellers) meets free-spirited flower child (Leigh Taylor-Young) in *I Love You, Alice B. Toklas!* (1968).

ABOVE, BOTTOM
Harold Fine (Peter Sellers) with his guru (Louis Gottlieb) in *I Love You, Alice B. Toklas!*

Writing in *Life* magazine, Goldman hailed *Portnoy* as "the final perfection of an art, the comic art of this Jewish decade. . . . Purging the Jewish joke and comic novel of their lingering parochialism, Roth has explored the Jewish family myth more profoundly than any of his predecessors, shining his light into all its corners and realizing its ultimate potentiality as an archetype of contemporary life."[20]

Less sweeping than *Portnoy* in focusing on class (as well as sexual) relations in an entirely Jewish context, *Goodbye, Columbus* concerns a summer romance between a well-off Radcliffe junior, Brenda Patimkin (Ali McGraw), and a lower-middle-class librarian, Neil Klugman (Richard Benjamin). Working out her own family romance, Brenda orchestrates their relationship for maximum parental involvement. She not only brings Neil home so that they might make love in her bedroom, but ends their affair by unconsciously leaving her diaphragm where her mother will find it. This imperious, suburban daddy's girl was the first of her kind to appear in a Hollywood movie since *Marjorie Morningstar*. The *New York Times* readily identified Brenda as "a Jewish princess." The sarcastic and, for many, smarmy Neil was a more exotic leading man. Both *Time*'s anonymous reviewer and *Village Voice* critic Andrew Sarris compared

Benjamin unfavorably to Hoffman, although Sarris wondered if "his creepiness may turn out to make his fortune in this anti-heroic period." (In fact, he became one of the most critically reviled actors of the era.)[21]

Albeit based on a novella published a decade before, *Goodbye, Columbus* was widely considered as derivative of *The Graduate*—a point that the film's publicists reinforced in the print ads. Like *The Graduate*, *Goodbye, Columbus* was self-consciously new wave in its breezy stylistics, including a soft-rock title song written and performed by the Association: "It's a lucky day. Hello life, goodbye Columbus!" *Variety* deemed the film successfully contemporary, noting that it "fits patly into today's youth market which demands a hip approach to sex." Indeed, as Sarris pointed out, the movie had made the novel's sex more explicit—as well as breaking new cinematic ground with a frank on-screen discussion of contraception.[22]

Richard Benjamin and Ali MacGraw in *Goodbye, Columbus* (1969).

Richard Benjamin and a library patron in *Goodbye, Columbus*.

The insider material in *Goodbye, Columbus* goes well beyond kitchen Yiddish. Brenda's recent nose job occasions a long discussion that serves as the prelude to the first kiss she and Neil exchange. The characters are openly insular and engage in particular stereotypes. Learning that Neil's parents have relocated to Arizona, Brenda remarks, "I didn't think there were people in Arizona, I mean Jewish people." Perceiving that Neil has insinuated himself into a country club above his class, his cousin calls him "pushy." Brenda's nouveau riche parents are broadly drawn. Her brother's lavish wedding is a heavily satiric set piece in which gluttony vies with ostentatious display, both in terms of food and cleavage.

Like Roth's novella, the movie created a stir—as some considered its intent. In the *New Republic*, Kauffmann tweaked the filmmakers for "feeling so courageous at making a non-complimentary picture about Jews. . . . No choice in the casting of the peripheral roles, no reading of a line, no framing of an action fails to proclaim that the Jewish producer and director and screenwriter are pulling no punches." The wedding scene, in particular, was criticized as tasteless and even anti-Semitic. Vincent Canby concluded his otherwise highly favorable *New York Times* review by stating, "I somehow resent the really vulgar manners that Mr. Peerce allows his middle-class Jews."[23]

Canby was not the only Gentile offended on behalf of Jews. Altman transcribed the following exchange on *The Tonight Show* among the host Johnny Carson, his sidekick Ed McMahon, and guest Jan Peerce, the well-known cantor and the father of the director of *Goodbye, Columbus*.

**JOHNNY CARSON TO JAN PEERCE:** I've heard some people thought *Goodbye, Columbus* offensive to Jewish people.

**ED MCMAHON:** *I thought it was.*

**JAN PEERCE:** Let me say first, I am a Jew, I am a practicing Jew and I follow as far as I can the laws of our Bible and our teachings. . . . I don't want that our people, or any people, should be offended. . . . This movie is not bad for the Jews. It is not only about Jews; it could be about Italians or Irishmen or anybody. That's how people behave. My son respects his people, his parents, his background, and I'm sure he wouldn't want to offend them either.[24]

Others praised *Goodbye, Columbus* for its verisimilitude. Paraphrasing the well-known Levy's rye bread ad and dropping a bit of Yinglish, Judith Crist assured the readers of *New York* magazine: "You don't have to be Jewish to catch the haimishness of the Bronx household where Neil lives with a bustling rhetorical question-ridden aunt and cipherish [*sic*] uncle, the zestful vulgarity of Brenda's affluent Westchester background or the ritualistic and calorific excesses of her brother Ronald's super-elegant wedding—but if you are you will know the precision of detail that the Arnold Schulman screenplay and a knowing cast has provided under Larry Peerce's direction."[25]

Promotional event for
*Goodbye, Columbus*, 1969.

Indeed, the movie was defended, with a somewhat questionable jocularity, by Rex Reed in *Women's Wear Daily*, a trade paper with a large Jewish readership:

There's a lot of absurd talk going around about *Goodbye, Columbus* being an anti-Semitic movie. I'm not surprised. They've been accusing Philip Roth of being an anti-Semitic writer for years. Trouble is, Roth knows his own people—knows and cares about them—better than most Jews know themselves. He is the most Jewish Jew in captivity today, and *Goodbye, Columbus* is the best thing he ever wrote. I think he wrote it before he learned how to masturbate.

There is the wildest Jewish wedding in the history of movies, blazing with a huge collage of carousel impressions—cigars and chopped chicken livers and two uncles in the carpet business named Manny and Max pacing the dance floor measuring their carpets, little girls dancing with each other and eating the bells off the cake, people who look like leftovers from a Grossinger's Passover party dancing to Havah Nagilah . . . of course it's vulgar. But it is also endearing and spirited and true.[26]

Wedding reception in
*Goodbye, Columbus.*

*Nation* critic Hatch took *Goodbye, Columbus* as evidence that "anti-Semitism is at last behind us." Five years ago, he imagined, "it would have sent B'nai B'rith marching through the streets—now there seems no poison in it." And, writing in *Life* magazine, Richard Schickel reiterated the Fiedler theory of Jewish universality: "We are all beginning to recapitulate the Jewish experience in this country. That is, all of us, regardless of race, creed or color, are now experiencing alienation from our traditional values. . . . We are becoming guilty, ironic moralists recording our anguish not in sermons, but in one-line gags. Brenda's house in Westchester seems to me no longer—except for purposes of literary coloration—a specifically Jewish home. We all live there."[27]

Although *Goodbye, Columbus* represents the critical high-water mark of the Jewish new wave, the nice Jewish bad boy was becoming a familiar movie trope. Woody Allen cast himself as an inept criminal in *Take the Money and Run* (Cinerama, 1969) while, in a somewhat more unusual permutation, Harry Belafonte played the title character, a celestial former mugger, Jewish as well as African-American, in *Angel Levine* (United Artists, 1970), which was directed by Jan Kadar from the Bernard Malamud story. Michael Roemer's independent *The Plot against Harry* (shot in 1968 but unreleased for twenty years) depicts the nice Jewish bad boy in reverse, a numbers racketeer who is inadvertently reintegrated into middle-class respectability.[28]

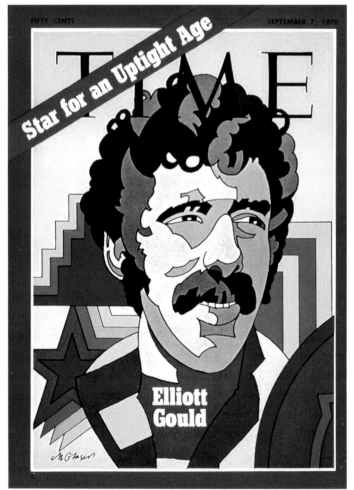

Two bad-boy novels, both set on the West Side of Manhattan, had already sold to the movies before publication. *Move* (Twentieth Century Fox, 1970) was directed by Stuart Rosenberg from Joel Lieber's adaptation of his 1968 book. Published ten months before the movie's July premiere, the paperback edition suggested a grand synthesis in comparing its hero to Benjamin Braddock ("It's *The Graduate*—Five Years Out!") as well as Roth's bad boy ("If You Think Alex Portnoy's Got Cause for Complaint, Meet Hiram Jaffe"). Gould, then at the zenith of his career as a movie icon, riding three successive hits in *Bob and Carol and Ted and Alice* (Columbia, 1969), *M\*A\*S\*H* (Twentieth Century Fox, 1970), and *Getting Straight* (Columbia, 1970), was cast as Jaffe, a wacky pornographer who picks up extra money by walking his neighbors' dogs.

George Segal in gorilla costume attempts to scare his mother (Ruth Gordon) to death in *Where's Poppa?* (1970).

Mother and son in *Where's Poppa?*

Gould's "torrid reputation" and resplendent "Jewish Afro" (*Newsweek*) notwithstanding, *Variety* was less than enthusiastic about his performance as an "oddball New Yorker, repeatedly confounded in his attempt to move to a new apartment with wife Paula Prentice." Interspersed with Hiram's fantasies and memories—including one of his wedding where he is unable to break the glass and winds up stomping on it—*Move* "walks the tightrope of zany comedy-fantasy, and doesn't make it across." (More literary, *Time* called the movie "a very low mutation of Kafka.") At one point, the antihero whines, "My whole existence is scatological." At another, he strips and bellows "Hatikvah." Like Portnoy or Groucho Marx, Gould addresses his audience directly. If the *Motion Picture Herald* mistakenly assumed that Gould's presence would make *Move* a hit, critics were divided as to his status as a male sex star. The *New York Times* speculated that Gould's "curly-haired back may now be the secret symbol of the sexy, Jewish subculture hero," while the *Village Voice* considered "his sex appeal, at its best [was] that of a circumcised Droopy Dog."[29]

November brought Carl Reiner's genuinely outrageous *Where's Poppa?* (United Artists)—"an insane movie," per *Variety*—which twenty-seven-year-old Robert Klane adapted from his self-proclaimed "tasteless novel." George Segal plays Gordon Hocheiser, a nice, not quite young Manhattan lawyer burdened with a nightmarish, senile mother (Ruth Gordon, who would play a concentration camp survivor in her next comedy, *Harold and Maude* [Paramount, 1972]). In the first scene, the childish protagonist dresses in a gorilla suit and wakes his sleeping parent, hoping to induce a fatal heart attack. He fails, of course, and merely precipitates the first of his mother's many inquiries as to the whereabouts of her long-deceased husband.

A series of extended slapstick riffs in which each dreamlike scene heads straight into psychosexual hyperbole, *Where's Poppa?* has passages that seem Hollywood's equivalent of the Kafkaesque. In thrall to his mother, Gordon establishes an instant if doomed rapport with an innocent, extremely Gentile nurse, Louise (Trish Van Devere). Mother repeatedly scares off Louise, most spectacularly when she pulls down her son's pants to nuzzle his adorable posterior. Meanwhile, Gordon's equally neurotic brother, Sidney, runs back and forth across Central Park, regularly accosted by the same gang of muggers (who at one point coerce him to partake in the rape of what turns out to be a male police officer).[30]

Use of Yiddish in *Where's Poppa?* is minimal, although *Variety* felt obligated to explain that *tush* was a "familiar Jewish word for derriere." Still, critics had no difficulty in locating the movie's comic nexus. *New York*'s Crist noted that Segal was "again the poor-shnook type (Elliott Gould missed this one somehow)," while Canby described the movie as concerning "a nice, decent, *trapped* 35-year-old Jewish boy and his ancient, ter-

Topol as Tevye in *Fiddler on the Roof* (1971).

rible, senile mother." The most extreme example of Portnoyism to date, *Where's Poppa?* ends with Gordon's failure to escape and his surrender to his mother's delusions. In the last shot, he dives into bed with his mother: "Poppa's home!" This denouement was evidently changed twice during industry and press screenings, then reinstated for a subsequent re-release. (As 1970 ended, Brooks, Segal, *How to Be a Jewish Mother* author Dan Greenburg, and stand-up comedian David Steinberg were convened for an emergency session of *The David Susskind Show* on the subject "How to Be a Jewish Son.")[31]

Although the most important Jewish movie of 1971 was surely *Fiddler on the Roof* (United Artists), the summer was bracketed by nice bad-boy vehicles for

Hoffman and Benjamin, both with heroes suffering from premature midlife crises. In *Who Is Harry Kellerman and Why Is He Saying Those Terrible Things About Me?* (National General), directed by Ulu Grosbard from a Herb Gardner script widely perceived as autobiographical, Hoffman plays George Soloway, a successful, emotionally disconnected Brooklyn-born folk rocker. For all George's problems with his lower-middle-class Jewish parents, assorted women, and shape-shifting psychoanalyist (Jack Warden), his story is less comedy than fantasy, at least as close to Federico Fellini as Philip Roth. The film was a failure; critical response was significant for articulating an unmistakable weariness with the character and milieu. Writing in New York's *Daily News*, Reed attacked *Harry Kellerman* for its provincialism: "[This is] the kind of movie that goes nowhere but gets laughs from New Yorkers who spent their childhoods living on bagels, getting Jewish girls from Brooklyn pregnant and riding the subway to Rockaway Beach, to whom growing up meant graduating to a one-room apartment on Bleecker Street. I doubt if it will mean anything at all in any of 3,999,999 other locations on the face of the globe."[32]

Benjamin played alienated college professor Harold Weiss in *The Steagle* (Avco Embassy, 1971), which was written and directed by television veteran Paul Sylbert from

Irvin Faust's well-received 1966 book—"yet again, a novel about a perplexed contemporary urban American Jew," as Kauffmann put it in his *New Republic* review. The title refers to the hero's nostalgia for the 1940s and total recall of wartime trivia; like the protagonists of *To an Early Grave*, the intellectual here is obsessed with American pop culture. Weiss suffers a sort of breakdown during the 1962 Cuban Missile Crisis and goes on the road—traveling from Long Island to Chicago to Las Vegas and finally Hollywood, where *The Steagle* ends with a movie-set war suggesting the climax of the Marx Brothers' *Duck Soup*. Benjamin seems too young to be a World War II vet; his unsympathetic character is beset by whining women throughout. Adding to its abrasive quality, the movie affects a *cinéma vérité* immediacy and is cut with jazzy insouciance.

*Cue* found *The Steagle* over-familiar, as did *Variety*, which saw Benjamin as "another variation of the character he has played in previous films." Similarly, Reed characterized Benjamin's disaffected professor as one more of the "creeps he's making a career out of playing these days in rotten movies—repulsively." Nor did Reed mince words in characterizing the director: "Sylbert manages to be almost anti-everything. He takes care of Protestants with a minister who is a slobbering, drunk-gambler-letch. He takes care of Middle America with a war-mongering Texas bigot. And he hatchets the Catholics to death by showing a prostitute's crib in which the floosie [*sic*] says her rosary during a grisly assignation under a crucifix and a photo of the Virgin Mary. How about one for the rabbis, Mr. Sylbert? I didn't notice you giving it to the Jews."[33] Clearly Reed missed the Hasid, strategically placed on a commuter train in the movie's opening scene—most likely for laughs. Nor did he seem to realize that Benjamin himself had become a negative Jewish image.

The year ended with Kael's *New Yorker* critique of Hollywood's young leading men, "Notes on New Actors, New Movies." Most were associated with the Jewish new wave. Kael began with an analysis of Benjamin, "a gifted light romantic comedian" who is "physically well-suited to the urban Jewish heroes who dominated American fiction for over a decade and have now moved onto the screen. . . . Benjamin is good at miming frustration and wild fantasies, and he's giggly and boyishly apologetic in a way that probably pleases men, because it reminds them of their adolescent silliness, but he doesn't quite appeal to women. What's missing seems to be that little bit of male fascism that makes an actor like Robert Redford or Jack Nicholson dangerous and hence attractive. Benjamin needs some sexual menace, some threat; without that there's no romantic charge to his presence." Kael (whose forthright taste for Gentile actors and provocative reference to fascism is suggestive of a Jewish bad girl) goes on to wonder if Benjamin could get by if he *did* develop sex appeal, suggesting that he's in demand as an actor "just *because* he can project lack of confidence and suggest sexual inadequacy," thus fulfilling "the new movie stereotype of the American male as perennial adolescent."[34]

ABOVE
Dustin Hoffman in *Who Is Harry Kellerman and Why Is He Saying Those Terrible Things About Me?* (1971).

RIGHT
Richard Benjamin strikes a pose on the paperback edition of Irvin Faust's 1966 novel *The Steagle*.

AVON / N357 / 95¢

IRVIN FAUST'S celebrated novel of a man breaking out....

the Steagle

NOW A SENSATIONAL MOTION PICTURE

Clearly the perceived insularity and diminishing shock value of the Jewish bad-boy film had begun to grate on critics. The much-maligned Benjamin (and indeed, the entire tendency) hit bottom nine months later with the debacle of *Portnoy's Complaint* (Warner Bros., 1972), which Ernest Lehman wrote and directed. Originally scheduled for Twentieth Century Fox, the project had moved to Warners after Fox's disastrous adaptation of *Myra Breckinridge* (1968), another sensational, but unfilmable bestseller.

*Portnoy's Complaint* opens with thirty-three-year-old Alexander Portnoy, a New York City human rights commissioner, leering at a miniskirted supplicant. As she lists

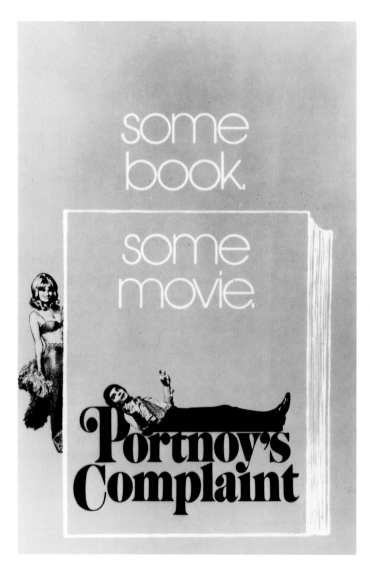

Poster for *Portnoy's Complaint* (1972).

her complaints against her landlord, he imagines her in her underwear—a conceit that might have been lifted from such late fifties "nudie-cuties" as *The Immoral Mr. Teas* (Pad-Ram Enterprises, 1959). The smarmy mood is sustained as Portnoy ogles his way through midtown streets filled with equally shortskirted "birds," en route to his psychoanalyst's, where he introduces himself as "the bad little good little Jewish boy." Trying to entertain the silent shrink, Portnoy proclaims his credo: "To be bad and enjoy it, that's the real struggle." His monologue is illustrated by flashbacks to his bickering Jewish family—his overprotective mother and constipated father with their constant insistence on the distinction between Jews and goyim, as well as an account of his sexual relationship with his shikse girlfriend (Karen Black).

Benjamin is "so ideally cast as Philip Roth that it is almost frightening to think of his ever playing anything else," Sarris wrote in his review of *Goodbye, Columbus*. Be that as it may, Benjamin couldn't handle Portnoy's stand-up dialogue, reciting it as though it were beat poetry rather than a manic *shpritz*. Nor is his credibility enhanced by scenes in which he is compelled to play a whining teenager. "It is one thing to read about the adolescent Alex's marathon of masturbation," wrote Robert Alter, "It is quite another actually to see the adult Richard Benjamin—incredibly got up as a fifteen-year-old—with his face buried in purloined female underpants, supposedly trembling in onanistic ecstasy, though photographed 'tastefully,' of course, from the shoulders up."[35]

Although *Variety* considered *Portnoy* to be an "effective," "honest," "strong," and "appropriately bawdy study in ruinous self-indulgence," as well as "something of a milestone in cinematic treatment of sensitive subject matter," most reviewers were openly

Alexander Portnoy (Richard Benjamin) regales his psychoanalyst in *Portnoy's Complaint*.

Flashback to adolescence: Sophie Portnoy (Lee Grant) admonishes her son in *Portnoy's Complaint*.

Portnoy and girlfriend (Karen Black) in *Portnoy's Complaint*.

appalled, many by the specifically Jewish content. By this time, Reed had had more than enough, pronouncing "this insult to the world" to be "screenwriter-producer-nincompoop director Ernest Lehman's revenge against God for making him Jewish." Reed found *Portnoy* "so anti-Semitic it seems like Fascist propaganda . . . even in the silliest and most exaggerated clichés of Yiddish theater, you are supposed to laugh, not go away secretly thinking Hitler was right." Crist agreed— "Somebody up there (if not down here) must be laughing—and we suspect it's Joseph Goebbels"—as did Penelope Gilliatt, who compared aspects of the movie to the portrayal of Jews in the Nazi periodical *Der Sturmer*.[36]

Six weeks after *Portnoy's Complaint* opened in New York in late June 1972, the *Daily News* reported a number of recent synagogue sermons "bitterly castigating" the film. Dore Schary, onetime head of MGM and then-current chairman of the Anti-Defamation League, declared that *Portnoy* was "outrageous and goes far beyond the good taste of a Jewish joke." In an attack published on the front page of the *New York Times* "Arts and Leisure" section, Fred M. Hechinger bluntly termed *Portnoy's Complaint* "a truly anti-Semitic film." In effect, Hechinger turned Albert Goldman's defense of Lenny Bruce on its head. The filmmakers "appear to have been convinced that Jews today feel so secure in American society that nothing could possibly offend them. . . . The taboos are gone. The bathroom is no longer unmentionable. Racial and religious themes are no longer off-limits." In this permissive climate, Hechinger maintained, "the Jews are the easy target because their greater political sophistication and tolerance make them less likely to strike back than other ethnic power groups." Jewish security had opened the door to anti-Semitism.[37]

In vain, writer-director Lehman attempted to defend himself: "I'm Jewish myself, and it certainly wasn't my intent to put Jews in a bad light. . . . I feel I toned down the book. How in the world could anyone do the movie less ethnically than I did?" Perhaps this is why, as Alter noted, the words kosher and *treyf* (nonkosher) are never used while the less theologically loaded *khazeray* (literally, "swinishness"; metaphorically, "filth" or "obscenity") was employed, albeit mispronounced.[38]

The horrified response to Lehman's inept adaptation of *Portnoy's Complaint* signaled the end of the Jewish new wave. But, as sometimes happens, the masterpiece of the cycle would be among the last examples to appear. The year 1972 ended with *The Heartbreak Kid* (Twentieth Century Fox), directed by Elaine May from Neil Simon's elaboration on a laconic Bruce Jay Friedman story first published in the mid-sixties.[39]

"You're in my spot."
Lenny meets Kelly (Cybill Shepherd) on the beach in *The Heartbreak Kid*.

New York sporting goods salesman Lenny Cantrow (Charles Grodin) meets and marries Lila Kolodny (Elaine May's daughter, Jeannie Berlin), but deserts her on their Florida honeymoon to follow a golden shikse Kelly Corcoran (Cybill Shepherd) back to her Minnesota home. Lenny's pursuit of Kelly defies all logic and he ultimately marries her, over the objections of her ferociously protective father (Eddie Albert). The last scene shows Lenny at his second wedding, having gotten what he wanted and seeming even more discombobulated than when the movie began. "This time," noted *Commonweal*, "the nice Jewish boy . . . is out of his mind."[40]

*The Heartbreak Kid* was widely seen as an answer to *The Graduate*, directed as it was by Mike Nichols's former stand-up partner. Praising the movie in the *New York Times*, Stephen Farber wrote that May's movie had "none of the sentimentality that ruined *The Graduate*." Where Nichols "pandered to the young audience, treating the two earnest, anguished, goody-goody lovers as the heroes of a corrupt world," May's kids "are hard, selfish, stupid, just like the adults. . . . *The Heartbreak Kid* is [Elaine May's] hard-edged *Graduate* and I think it's everything *The Graduate* should have been—not a soft caramel optimistic comedy but a comprehensive, fully-achieved, dark satiric vision." Indeed, *The Heartbreak Kid* is the only Jewish new-wave film (and one of the few Hollywood movies of any sort) to suggest the hollowness of the American Dream.

Unlike its precursors, *The Heartbreak Kid* was praised for its nuances. "Mr. Corcoran's anti-Semitism is subtly established without being belabored; and we can imagine a whole Portnoy-like history for Lenny on the basis of his compulsive pursuit of Kelly, his shikse golden girl," Farber wrote. Stuart Byron pointed out that, as Lenny and Lila drive from New York to Florida, the landscape grows increasingly American. *The Heartbreak Kid* is about "how a minority culture has had to exist within a majority culture, about strangers in a strange land."[41]

Writing in the *Saturday Review*, Thomas Meehan called *The Heartbreak Kid* "a triumph of New York Jewish humor, which has become the dominant humor in all of the best of America's most recent comic films. . . . I have an idea that the American film comedy may be entering a new golden age as a result of the rise of the semi-surreal comedy of mishap, pain, insult, and desperation that is perhaps the only sort of comedy we're able genuinely to laugh at anymore." In fact, *The Heartbreak Kid* marked the twilight of this golden age.[42]

Ethnic Jewish characters lost their prominence, although ethnic characterizations did not. Among other things, the Jewish new wave might be seen as an example of premature identity politics—the tendency crested before reviewers and audiences were accustomed to addressing issues of ethnicity in popular entertainment. The period of blaxploitation films ushered in by the phenomenal success of the independent *Sweet Sweetback's Baadasssss Song* and MGM's *Shaft* (both released in 1971) continued into the mid-1970s. Meanwhile, as presaged by the extraordinary popularity of *The Godfather* (Paramount) in 1972, Italian-Americans supplanted Jews as Hollywood's white ethnic group of choice. *MAD* magazine suggested as much when its parody of *The Heartbreak Kid* ended with Jewish "Benny" ditching Protestant "Kooly" to marry into *The Godfather* family.[43]

ABOVE, TOP
Lenny (Charles Grodin) comforts his bride Lila (Jeannie Berlin) during their honeymoon in *The Heartbreak Kid* (1972).

ABOVE, BOTTOM
Lenny pursues Kelly to her Minnesota campus in *The Heartbreak Kid*.

With the end of the Jewish new wave, the urban neurotic antihero disappeared as well. Or, rather, this figure was subsumed into the persona of Woody Allen—at least until he resurfaced, a less abrasive wise guy, in the TV sitcoms of the 1990s.

# AT HOME ON THE SMALL SCREEN: TELEVISION'S NEW YORK JEWS

JEFFREY SHANDLER

*"In the old days," crack docudrama writer Ernest Kinoy remembers, "in the days of live television, you'd come into* Studio One, *or NBC, and* Philco, *and you'd tell them this long story about this marvelous Italian family. And they would say, 'It's too Jewish.' Because they knew very well that it wasn't an Italian, it was a Jewish family. Paddy Chayefsky did it a number of times. The* Catered Affair *is about an Irish family: In a pig's eye it's about an Irish family!* Marty, *the Italian butcher. . . . It was because a number of the Jewish writers would come in with material, and the networks would say, 'It's too Jewish. The rest of America won't understand.'"*
—Todd Gitlin, *Inside Prime Time* (1983)[1]

One Friend Tells Another

"Jewish Television gives more joy to Jewish people."

TUNE IN • ENJOY THESE

**FAMOUS JEWISH TV SHOWS**
**ALL ON WATV - CHANNEL 13**

Tuesday 3:15 P.M.
**CLUB TEL-AVIV**
*featuring stars of Israel*
PABST BREWING CO.

Tuesday 3:30 P.M.
**FREHLACH TIME**
*with Mickey Freeman*
MAXWELL HOUSE COFFEE    INSTANT MAXWELL HOUSE COFFEE

Tuesday 3:45 P.M.
**JAN BART SHOW**
WHITEHALL PHARMACAL CO.

Wednesday 3:15 P.M.
**JEWISH MATINEE TIME**
*with Miriam Kressyn*
*and Seymour Rechtzeit*
THE COCA-COLA BOTTLING COMPANY OF NEW YORK, INC.

Wednesday 3:30 P.M.
**JEWISH TALENT UNLIMITED**
*with Abe Ellstein*
BORDEN'S CREAM CHEESE

Wednesday 3:45 P.M.
**OUR JEWISH HERITAGE**
DIAMOND CRYSTAL SALT CO.

Thursday 3:15 P.M.
**IRVING FIELDS SHOW**
SUNSWEET PRUNE JUICE
MOTT'S APPLE JUICE    CLAPP'S BABY FOODS

Thursday 3:30 P.M.
**JEWISH HOME SHOW**
*with Ruth Jacobs*
BIRDS EYE FROZEN FOODS         MAXWELL HOUSE COFFEE
POST CEREALS         INSTANT MAXWELL HOUSE COFFEE

Promotional card for Jewish broadcasts on New York channel WATV, c. 1950. The existence of such local programming in television's early days testifies to the size of the Jewish audience in the New York area at the time.

American Jews have forged special attachments to television since its early years as a national broadcast medium. To a certain extent, perhaps, this was originally a matter of demographics. As had been the case during the nickelodeon era, the advent of a new entertainment medium coincided with the concentration of Jewish settlement in the United States. During the late 1940s and early 1950s, when most TV sets were found in middle-class homes in major urban centers, Jews made up a sizable part of the television audience.[2] Jews were also prominent among the first talents working in the medium, both before and behind the camera. They often came to television from careers in radio, the Broadway stage, or other forms of live entertainment performed in and around New York City, where television production was centered.

As Ernest Kinoy's reminiscence suggests, some American Jews have sought ways to employ television as a venue for self-exploration since the industry's early days. They may have been motivated to do so by signal changes in Jews' sense of "at-homeness" in America during the decades following World War II, a period when many of the nation's Jews shared in the postwar economic boom and were able to take advantage of unprecedented social, educational, and professional opportunities. Some of the Jews who worked in early American television were inspired by the notion that the medium's small scale and intimacy of viewing made it particularly suited to introspective, psychological drama. Paddy Chayefsky, who was one of the first scenarists to gain fame initially by writing for the small screen, saw television drama as particularly appropriate to the self-reflexive spirit of the modern age. In the 1950s, he observed: "These are strange and fretful times and the huge inevitable currents of history are too broad now to provide individual people with any meaning to their lives. People are beginning to turn into themselves. . . . The jargon of introspection has become everyday conversation, . . . and the drama of introspection is the drama that the people want to see. . . . [Television] may well be the basic theater of our century."[3]

However, as Kinoy's recollection also indicates, the efforts of Jewish television artists to use the medium during its early days as a vehicle for self-portraiture frequently met with resistance—and it often came from other Jews. Writing on the television industry several decades later, sociologist Todd Gitlin attributed this to Jewish network executives' "sense of marketplace predilections, compounded perhaps by self-protectiveness against any real or conceivable anti-Semitic charge that Jews are too powerful in the media."[4] The problem had been similarly diagnosed at the time, notably in "The Vanishing Jew of Our Popular Culture," an essay that appeared in *Commentary* in 1952 by the young critic Henry Popkin, who decried "what may be called [the] 'de-Semitization' [that] is by now a commonplace in the popular arts in America."[5] Popkin characterized the phenomenon as originating "in a misguided benevolence, or fear—its name is 'sha-sha' [Yiddish for 'hush, hush']."[6] Significantly, Popkin invoked Yiddish as a double-edged sign, marking the silencing of Jewishness as a Jewish act in itself.[7]

The complex and sometimes contentious relationship between the small screen and American Jewry is more than a passing curiosity. Rather, it is key to understanding the Jewish community's place in national culture during the second half of the twentieth century and into the next millennium. In a sense, it is a continuation and elaboration of the "Jewish Question" that coalesced around the Hollywood studios during the first half of the 1900s. Today television plays a leading role in shaping most Americans' public awareness of Jews and Jewishness. Not only does this medium present portraits of numerous Jewish politicians, journalists, and other public figures, but the most widely recognized images of Jewish-American life are those of fictional characters, especially those who have made weekly appearances, sometimes for years, in nationally broadcast entertainment series. At the same time, television has provided American Jews with shared texts that they can scrutinize, dissect, dispute, revile, or adore. Indeed, these telecasts may be more widely familiar than any other form of modern Jewish cultural expression, and so their scrutiny by American Jews enables discussions of Jewishness on an unrivaled scale.

Within the inventory of television's Jewish characters, those situated in New York City are of special interest. Again, the reason is, in part, demographic—New York is the home of the world's largest Jewish community and of almost one-third of the Jews in the United States. Moreover, the public image of the city has, in this century, become bound up with its Jewish residents, who constitute one of its most distinctively recognizable communities. (In their landmark study *Beyond the Melting Pot*, Nathan Glazer and Daniel Patrick Moynihan wrote, "The euphemistic use of the term 'New Yorker' to refer to 'Jew,' which is not uncommon in the United States, is . . . based on some reality.")[8]

Conversely, the Jewish-American mythos lays claim to New York as its defining, central locus for Jews' complicated, sprawling diaspora within the United States. The arrival of twenty-four Jews in 1654 in what was then Nieuw Amsterdam roots Jewry in American history during the colonial era (and was celebrated as such, including on American radio and television, during the 1954 tercentenary year). Ellis Island and Manhattan's Lower East Side are hailed as the immigrant generations' official point of entry into America, together with millions of other immigrants at the turn of the previous century, most from Southern and Eastern Europe. Several generations later, many American Jews, regardless of where they live, still identify New York, especially its densely Jewish residential neighborhoods, as the proving ground for their own distinctive ethnic culture. Television's stories of New York Jews, then, constitute some of the most broadly familiar and widely discussed images of Jewish life in America in the post–World War II era. The dynamics of popular series featuring New York Jewish characters provides a key to tracking changes not only in Jewish representation, but also in the protocols of this entertainment medium as a venue for ethnic self-portraiture.

Only one Jewish family figured among the virtual pioneers of television's early postwar years: the title characters of the show *The Goldbergs*, which was among the first situation comedies to make a successful transition from radio to television. *The Goldbergs* was one of a spate of situation comedies about the domestic life of ethnic Americans: *Amos 'n' Andy*, *Hey Jeannie*, *I Remember Mama*, *The Life of Riley*, *Life with Luigi*— all of which vanished from the airwaves by the end of the 1950s.[9] When *The Goldbergs* went off the air in 1956—a year after the eponymous family left their home in the Bronx for the suburbs of Long Island—Jews, along with other ethnics, no longer appeared to be "at home" in the virtual geography of television entertainment. Thereafter, until the mid-1970s, explicitly Jewish characters were seen in prime-time series—even those set in New York City—only as comic foils or as occasional guests. The liminal status for ethnics generally and Jews in particular on American television during this period was perhaps most evident in guest appearances made at the time by a plethora of Jewish stand-up comedians on television talk shows, where, the sociologist Sig Altman argued, "of all [religious or ethnic] groups the Jews are given by far the most comic presentation, and . . . this humor is based on an automatic assumption that Jewishness is funny."[10]

At the same time that television networks avoided presenting regular characters that might be considered "too Jewish" (similar, it should be noted, to its approach to the portrayal of particular ethnic, religious, and racial groups generally), the medium offered more oblique representations of Jews. The protagonists of two of the most popular situation comedies of the 1960s and 1970s, for example, were actually crypto-Jews. Both Robert Petrie of *The Dick Van Dyke Show* (CBS, 1960–66) and Archie Bunker of *All in the Family* (CBS, 1971–83) were innovative exercises in self-portraiture (Carl Reiner based Petrie on his own experiences writing for Sid Caesar's television variety series in the 1950s) and portraiture (Bunker was modeled on producer Norman Lear's father), stripped of their Jewishness.[11] (The fact that, over the years, this information has shifted from industry insider talk to being frequently reported in television histories and recounted in interviews is itself a revealing indicator of changes in the protocols of Jewish visibility in American public culture and of a more general self-consciousness about ethnic portraiture in mass media.)

In the mid-1970s, the New York Jew made a virtual "return home" on television when Rhoda Morgenstern, a popular character from the *Mary Tyler Moore Show* (CBS, 1970–77) during its first four seasons, became the central figure of the "spin-off" situation comedy *Rhoda* (CBS, 1974–78). Rhoda's return from Minneapolis to New York was, in a sense, a reverse of the journey out of New York made by the Goldbergs a generation earlier. Rhoda's "repatriation" was also a move from playing a comic foil to occupying the central role of a series, as it was a shift from being a comic outsider (a New York Jew in self-imposed exile to the Midwest) to being forthrightly at home in her "native" environment.

# RHODA'S RETURN

During the first seasons of *Rhoda*, Valerie Harper recited the following monologue off camera while the opening title sequence rolled:

*My name is Rhoda Morgenstern. I was born in the Bronx, New York, in December 1941. I always felt responsible for World War II. The first thing I remember liking that liked me back was food. I had a bad puberty—it lasted seventeen years. I'm a high school graduate. I went to art school. My entrance exam was on a book of matches. I decided to move out of the house when I was twenty-four. My mother still refers to this as the time I ran away from home. Eventually I ran to Minneapolis, where it's cold, and I figured I'd keep longer. Now I'm back in Manhattan. New York—this is your last chance!*

The Morgenstern women— Ida (Nancy Walker), Rhoda (Valerie Harper), and Brenda (Julie Kavner)—in their Bronx apartment in the sitcom *Rhoda*, 1974.

In returning to New York, Rhoda was also at the vanguard of a spate of characters explicitly identified as Jews among the casts on various television entertainment series, as prime time featured ever more overtly diverse ensembles during the late 1970s and into the 1980s. While some of these characters appeared in series set in Los Angeles (*LA Law*; NBC, 1986–94), Philadelphia (*thirtysomething*; ABC, 1987–91), Boston (*St. Elsewhere*; NBC, 1982–88), Washington (*Murphy Brown*; CBS, 1988–98), or an anonymous city (*Hill Street Blues*; NBC, 1981–87), most of television's Jewish characters could be found in New York. By the mid-1990s, New York Jewish characters were a staple of prime-time television entertainment series. During the 1997–98 television season, no fewer than twenty series were set in the city (though most were produced and taped, along with the majority of prime-time network programming, in Los Angeles). "These [characters] are New York stereotypes," critic Caryn James noted in the *New York Times*, "yet they have been hauled out with a distinct air of rediscovery lately, along with a few fresher images."[12] Jewish New Yorkers were particularly prominent in the casts of these situation comedies, which have come to portray the city as the comic inverse of the rest of America—where the most at-home figures, perhaps, are Jews.

Cast members of the TV series *Brooklyn Bridge*: Matthew Siegel, Danny Gerard, and Marion Ross. Gary David Goldberger's tribute to growing up Jewish in 1950s Brooklyn was telecast from 1991 to 1993.

The first entirely Jewish family to take up residence on prime-time television since *The Goldbergs* left the air appeared on the situation comedy *Brooklyn Bridge* (CBS, 1991–93). Indeed, this deliberately anachronistic series seemed to pick up more or less where the Goldbergs had left off in the mid-1950s, chronicling the comic adventures of young Alan Silver, the first-born son in a multigenerational, middle-class Jewish family living in Flatbush. By linking mid-century Brooklyn with the naiveté of childhood (series creator Gary David Goldberger was a native of the borough), *Brooklyn Bridge* also evoked a longing for the more innocent television programming of yore. The series was touted as a healthy alternative to other situation comedies of the early 1990s, such as *Married . . . with Children* (Fox, 1987–97) and *Roseanne* (ABC, 1988–97), which showed the American nuclear family in meltdown. But *Brooklyn Bridge*'s nostalgic look back at ostensibly simpler, more wholesome times was actually a hyper-real vision of the borough in its "golden age." In fact, *Brooklyn Bridge* celebrated the kind of outer-borough high-rise ethnic enclave that the Goldbergs were portrayed as striving to leave behind. It was an incarnation of family cohesiveness and American prosperity, enriched by moral values that are conceptualized as inherent in immigrant ethnic heritage.

The season after *Brooklyn Bridge* folded witnessed the debut of another series in which outer-borough Jews took center stage. But on *The Nanny* (CBS, 1993–99), the portrait of this ethnic group shifted from respectful sentimentality to playful assertiveness. Though set in the present, *The Nanny* is also an exercise in televisual myth-making. The series' title sequence, like that of *Rhoda* during its first seasons, offers a capsule narrative of the title character's life history. Whereas Rhoda's is a story of return to urban roots, Nanny Fran Fine's saga is more of an urban fairy-tale, in which her move from Queens to Manhattan becomes a mythic journey both from the lower-middle class to the upper class and from romantic failure to success. At the same time, it is a tale of gender, class, religious, and ethnic revolution, in which the "flashy girl from Flushing" subverts the social order at every turn. Indeed, Fine's Jewishness is only one element at play in a complex negotiation of television audience sensibilities. The Nanny's employer is an Englishman, producer Robert Sternin explained early in the series' run, "to make the free-wheeling Fran a better surrogate for the audience." He says, "Because the family is British, to the audience Fran becomes an American. If the family was WASP, she'd be Jewish."[13]

In contrast to *Rhoda*'s self-mocking humor, *The Nanny* celebrates its heroine's chutzpah, which brings much-needed life force into the otherwise constrained lives of a family of elite Britons. Fran Fine may be, in a sense, a virtual descendant of Rhoda in her original incarnation as the comic ethnic foil—earthy, edgy, appetitive—to the excessive superego of WASP Mary Richards.

But the Nanny is not a humorous fish out of water—that is, a Jew out of New York, as was her virtual contemporary, Dr. Joel Fleischman, on *Northern Exposure* (CBS, 1990–95). Exiled to the remote town of Cicely, Alaska, New York native Fleishman was the comic voice of reason (by default) in an imaginary American frontier town in which each inhabitant has reinvented himself or herself, flouting all conventional expectations.

# THE NANNY

"The Nanny Named Fran" by Ann Hampton Callaway

*She was working in a bridal shop in Flushing Queens,*
*'Til her boyfriend kicked her out in one of those crushing scenes.*
*What was she to do? Where was she to go?*
*She was out on her fanny.*

*So over the bridge from Flushing to the Sheffields' door,*
*She was there to sell makeup but the father saw more,*
*She had style, she had flair—she was there*
*That's how she became the Nanny.*

*Who would have guessed that the girl we described*
*Was just exactly what the doctor prescribed?*
*Now the father finds her beguiling (Watch out, C.C.!)*
*The kids are actually smiling (Such joie de vivre!)*
*She's the lady in red when everybody else is wearing tan.*
*The flashy girl from Flushing, the Nanny named Fran.*

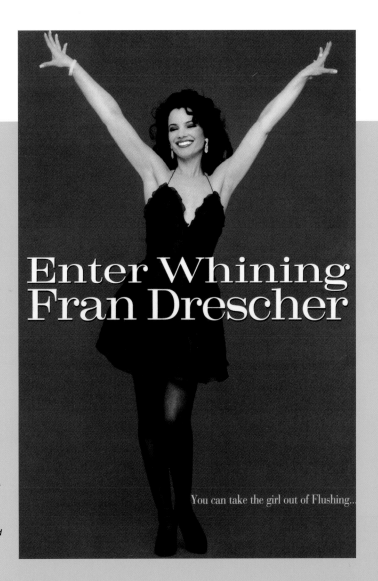

You can take the girl out of Flushing...

"You can take the girl out of Flushing . . . but you can't take Flushing out of the girl." Cover of Fran Drescher's memoir *Enter Whining* (1996). Like Gertrude Berg's Molly Goldberg, Drescher's Fran Fine became more of a public persona than a semi-eponymous character—reincarnated in a campaign for hosiery and in the feature film *The Beautician and the Beast* (1997).

Instead, the Nanny is the centerpiece of a series that uses the broad strokes of a situation comedy verging on farce to validate what anthropologist Jack Kugelmass characterizes as "ethnicity's infectious salubrity and its resilience."[14] The Nanny's ethnic exuberance did not please all viewers; some Jewish women, in particular, took umbrage at this representation. In the Jewish feminist magazine *Lilith*, Nora Lee Mandel complained that "the Jewish woman on TV today with the highest ratings is a caricature: *The Nanny*. Executive producer and star Fran Drescher is a whiny, manipulative clotheshorse hunting rich (non-Jewish) men by projecting a nonthreatening ditziness. A hit for CBS, the Nanny has the whole world laughing at her. The first thing my Australian e-mail pal asked me when she found out I was a Jewish woman from Queens was, 'Do you talk like The Nanny?'"[15] (Not all Jewish women agree; the *Forward*'s Robin Cembalest counters that Drescher "is not merely rehashing stereotypes, but questioning them. She subverts conventional assumptions.")[16]

While *The Nanny* provoked considerable stir about the value of its portrait of Jews, the most extensively discussed entertainment series of the 1990s was doubtless another one centered around a New York Jewish character. Like *Roseanne*—as well as *Cosby* (NBC, 1984–92) and, to take another New York Jewish example, *Mad about You* (NBC, 1992–99)—*Seinfeld* (NBC, 1990–98) was, as media scholar David Marc has noted, "part of a revival of an old sitcom technique" that can be traced back to George Burns's and Jack Benny's 1950s television series: fabricating a comic world "derived from the persona that a star-comedian had developed on the stand-up stage."[17] *Seinfeld* not only proved to be enormously popular with viewers; when it went off the air, it was considered the financial anchor of the NBC schedule.

The series has also provided a greater volume and wider range of public conversation than any television comedy has in years. Discussions of the series go well beyond analyzing its provocative disquisitions on the stuff of everyday life to address the uncompromising sharpness of its humor, its tweaking of the conventions of television comedy (in contrast to *The Nanny*, which regularly pays knowing homage to the sitcom genre), and its convoluted self-reflexivity. "Where it might once have been asked if *Seinfeld* was a commentary on society," wrote Geoffrey O'Brien in the *New York Review of Books*, "the question now should probably be asked whether society has not been reconfigured as a milieu for commenting on *Seinfeld*."[18]

Complicating this discourse is *Seinfeld*'s forthrightly paradoxical claim that, unlike explicitly issue-oriented situation comedies that follow the trend set by *All in the Family* two decades earlier, this one was "about nothing." One of the many issues in which *Seinfeld* did (or did not) engage was the sensibility of a certain kind of New York Jew: the single, neurotic, irreverent, middle-class, thirty-something denizen of the Upper West Side epitomized by the series' title character, who is (and is not) the same as stand-up comedian Jerry Seinfeld. At the height of its popularity, the series became a cultural touchstone, an oft-cited "Sein of the times."[19]

Indeed, sometimes *Seinfeld*'s trademark obfuscation of the boundary between the virtual and the actual had telling consequences in the public sphere. When its stars demanded salaries of one million dollars per episode in 1997, the series—rather than the performers—was denounced by Leon Wieseltier, literary editor of the *New Republic*, as "the worst, last gasp of Reaganite, grasping, materialistic, narcissistic, banal self-absorbtion." *New York Times* columnist Maureen Dowd declared it "our Dorian Gray portrait, a reflection of the what's-in-it-for-me times that allowed Dick Morris and Bill Clinton to triumph."[20] Since the series ended, *Seinfeld*'s thematic irony has been transmuted into a sign of the moral limits of meaninglessness. Author Jedediah Purdy cited *Seinfeld* as epitomizing the deleterious presence of irony in modern American life. And, in the wake of the destruction of the World Trade Center on September 11, 2001, a *Washington Post* staff writer invoked the series' "meaningless angst" as an example of a sensibility that "cultural pulse-takers" had since declared "unseemly."[21]

As with every other aspect of the series, *Seinfeld*'s presentation of Jewishness is never straightforward. Unlike the anxiously obscured, "sha-sha" Jewishness offered on American television in earlier decades, this series does not treat the subject gingerly. Yet in contrast to *The Nanny*'s forthright, if attitudinous, celebration of ethnicity, on *Seinfeld* Jewishness is self-consciously double-edged and contradictory—beginning with the Jewish identity of its protagonists.[22]

Although of the four principals only Jerry Seinfeld is identified as a Jew, all the characters have been understood—at least by many Jewish viewers—as televisual crypto-Jews who were deliberately, playfully, and transparently disguised as something else. Thus, critic Walter Goodman wrote that "Seinfeld and his pals, even those operating under different ethnic disguises, kvetched in television's copyright New York Jewish manner."[23] David Marc identifies Jerry's friend George Constanza as "a *nebbish*," and argues that Jerry "keeps George around to remind him of this Jewishness, which, despite the problems it presents, is after all the engine of his professional success. . . . Despite his curious surname, George Constanza personifies the Jewish side of Jerry's personality."[24]

# TV'S NEW YORK JEWS

The following Jewish characters (identified in some instances explictly, in others arguably) appeared in television series set in New York that were broadcast during the 1980s and 1990s:

Grace Adler (Debra Messing), *Will and Grace* (NBC, 1998–present)

Neil Barash (Corey Parker), *Flying Blind* (Fox, 1992–93)

Marshall Brightman (Joshua Rifkind), *The Marshall Chronicles* (ABC, 1990)

Paul Buchman (Paul Reiser), *Mad about You* (NBC, 1992–99)

Sylvia Fine (Renée Taylor), *The Nanny* (CBS, 1993–99)

Jackie Fischer (Jackie Mason), *Chicken Soup* (ABC, 1989)

Rachel Green (Jennifer Aniston), *Friends* (NBC, 1994–present)

Selma Hacker (Selma Diamond), *Night Court* (NBC, 1984–92)

Melissa Kirshner (Fran Drescher), *Princesses* (CBS, 1991)

Murray Klein (Martin Balsam), *Archie Bunker's Place* (CBS, 1979–83)

Barney Miller (Hal Linden), *Barney Miller* (ABC, 1975–82)

Dr. Steven Mitchell (Richard Lewis), *Daddy Dearest* (Fox, 1993)

Alex Rieger (Judd Hirsch), *Taxi* (ABC/NBC, 1978–83)

Burt Samuels (Al Waxman), *Cagney and Lacey* (CBS, 1982–88)

Adam Schiff (Steven Hill), *Law and Order* (NBC, 1990–2000)

Jerry Seinfeld (Jerry Seinfeld), *Seinfeld* (NBC, 1990–98)

Nina Shapiro (Maureen Anderman), *The Days and Nights of Molly Dodd* (NBC/Lifetime, 1987–91)

Jay Sherman (voice of Jon Lovitz), *The Critic* (ABC/Fox, 1994–95)

Benjamin Shorofsky (Albert Hague), *Fame* (NBC/syndication, 1982–87)

Sidney Shorr (Tony Randall), *Love, Sidney* (NBC, 1981–83)

Alan Silver (Danny Gerard), *Brooklyn Bridge* (CBS, 1991–93)

Nathan Singer (Harold Gould), *Singer and Sons* (NBC, 1990)

Jack Stein (Jay Thomas), *Love and War* (CBS, 1992–95)

D.A. Jesse Steinberg (Hector Elizondo), *Foley Square* (CBS, 1985–86)

Dr. Josef Wallach (Jan Rubes), *Kay O'Brien* (CBS, 1986)

Jewishness is often signaled—and deconstructed—on *Seinfeld* through other, quirkier tactics, such as elevating New York Jewish bakery staples (chocolate babka, black-and-white cookies, marble rye bread) to the status of social icons and debating such moral questions as the appropriateness of necking during a screening of *Schindler's List* or the right of a recent convert to Judaism to tell Jewish jokes.

The series' edgy, playful representation of identity extends to its setting, described by critic J. Hoberman as "an imaginary Upper West Side" where, "as in Kafka, the J-word is never mentioned."[25] "Ironically," a feature on the series in *New York* magazine reports, NBC turned down *Seinfeld* at first "because it had a very New York feel. People would say, 'They won't laugh at it; it's too New York.'"[26] Other sources report that NBC executive Brandon Tartikoff pronounced *Seinfeld* to be "too Jewish" when the network first considered the series.[27]

"Cashing in his chips." This caricature by Thomas L. Fluharty of the *Seinfeld* cast appeared in *Time* magazine in 1998 when Jerry Seinfeld announced the end of the series.

Like most situation comedies set in New York, *Seinfeld* relies on establishing shots of building exteriors filmed on location to situate the various homes, workplaces, and gathering spots of its characters, while the series was actually filmed in studios in Los Angeles. The falseness of Seinfeld's virtual New York was tweaked further by the re-creation of typical commercial blocks of the Upper West Side on a Los Angeles back lot, sometimes featuring simulations of actual locations (such as H & H Bagels) shining surreally in the bright southern California sun. Astute New Yorkers also picked up on the occasional faux pas in the depiction of their hometown. One careful observer noted that the characters read the national edition of the *New York Times*, not the local editions that appear on city newsstands.[28]

This warping of the boundary between the fictional and the actual in *Seinfeld* has extended beyond the series itself. Visitors to New York can take "Kramer's Reality Tour," led by Kenny Kramer, "the across the hall neighbor of Seinfeld Executive Producer and Co-Creator Larry David," who is "the inspiration behind Seinfeld's Kramer character." This "theatrical multi-media bus and video tour of New York City" includes stops at locations where the characters supposedly lived and worked. ("Of course, I'm the real Kramer!" the tour guide proclaims on his brochure. "Who else could have thought up a scheme like this?")[29]

On the occasion of the show's final broadcast on May 14, 1998, a special issue of *TV Guide* featured a detailed map of New York identifying the series' various settings,

# SEINFELD (AND OTHERS) ON *SEINFELD*

"New York is like a pie in the face every day. . . . Walking down the streets of New York is like being in a pie fight. And that's good for your sense of humor. . . . To me it's like a huge cocktail party, with all these interesting people and unusual things that are just an arm's length away. Even if you're not talking with exactly who you want to be talking with, you can see them right across the room. And you're just glad that you're in the room, you know. That's what a good party's about. It's nice to be in the room."

—Jerry Seinfeld on "What's So Funny about NewYork City?" *New York* (1995)[1]

"I would compare writing *Seinfeld* to writing the Talmud—a dark Talmud. You have a lot of brilliant minds examining a thought or ethical question from every possible angle."

—Seinfeld writer Larry Charles[2]

"[Jerry Seinfeld and Larry David] made a show that drew from Jack Benny (Jerry's direct, affable manner with his audience), Abbot and Costello (the repartee), Philip Roth (the mixture of the fantastic and the everyday, not to mention masturbation and a Hitler obsession), *MAD* magazine (Kramer is like a Don Martin drawing sprung to life), Mel Brooks (the scatological stuff, a devil-may-care treatment of ethnic differences, Hitler) and its most closely related progenitor, [Barry Levinson's 1982 movie] *Diner*, with its boys clubhouse sensibility and endless banter over small topics that mean everything in the world to its characters."

—Ron Rosenbaum, *New York Observer* (1998)[3]

"I fell in love with *Seinfeld* because it combines the two things that Yeshiva students identify with most, talmudic casuistry and frustrations with females."

—Chaim Saiman, "Seidman, Seinfeld and Formalist Frustrations," *G-Cubed* (1999)[4]

"A friend brought up the question: How do I know Elaine's Jewish?

'Of course she's Jewish. It's her name. Bennis [*sic*]. She's short. And she has ethnic hair,' says Sheryl.

'*Seinfeld*'s a Jewish show,' adds Lisa.

'She's Jewish by association,' continues Sheryl. 'She hangs around with Jews.'

'But George isn't Jewish,' says Richard. 'Constanza is an Italian name.'

'George is Jewish! His parents are so Jewish!' says Lisa.

'Elaine's Jewish. All her mannerisms are Jewish. She has a Jewish style,' says Leslie.

Elaine has to be Jewish. What else could she be?"

—Karen Bender, "Why We Watch 'Seinfeld' and Cry: 'I Want to Be Elaine,'" *Forward* (1994)[5]

Cast of *Seinfeld* (Michael Richards, Jason Alexander, Jerry Seinfeld, and Julia Louis-Dreyfus), 1990s.

**THE WORLD ACCORDING TO**
*SEINFELD*: **A HANDY MASTER**
**GUIDE TO THE DOMAIN**
**OF FOUR NEUROTIC NEW**
**YORKERS**

Like Saul Steinberg's
famous *New Yorker* cover
of 1975, *View of the World*
*from 9th Avenue*, this illustration by Yan Nascimbene
suggests that Manhattan
is a world unto itself. It
appeared with the following
key in a special issue of
*TV Guide* that marked the
broadcast of the final
episode of *Seinfeld* in May
1998.

**1.** Site of the Maestro's vacation house, the envy of Jerry
and his friends (episode 107)
**2.** Jerry's parents live here
until his dad is impeached as
condo president (118)
**3.** George tries to convince
his parents to retire here
(119)
**4.** Point of purchase for
Jerry's pricey suede jacket (8)
**5.** Where Jerry courts his
date Miss Rhode Island while
she prepares for the Miss
America pageant (83)
**6.** Store where Kramer and
Newman try to sell an old
record collection (56)
**7.** After buying an unflatter-
ing dress, Elaine accuses the
department store of using
distorted mirrors (91)
**8.** George boasts he can drive
here in less than 25 minutes
(45)
**9.** Site of the Thanksgiving
Day Parade, during which
Mr. Pitt holds the ropes for
Woody Woodpecker (90)
**10.** Jerry and George are mistaken for white supremacists
en route to a Knicks game
here (35)
**11.** Tired of warming the
crowd for rival comic Bania,
Jerry takes a dive at this club
(149)
**12.** Where Kramer tries to
make it big, only to be mistaken for the Smog Strangler
(40, 41)
**13.** After picking up a woman
on the subway, George is
brought here and mugged
(30)
**14.** Kramer is serenaded by
Mel Tormé at a benefit performance at this hotel (99)
**15.** Where Jerry returns a
library book that's 20 years
overdue (22)

**16.** Jerry accidentally borrows
a jacket from this club, jeop-
ardizing his chances of
becoming a member (121)
**17.** Kramer and Jerry drop a
Junior Mint into the body of
"Triangle Boy" Roy here (58)
**18.** Place where Jerry bombs
after being heckled (80)
**19.** Site of the fab four's
search for their parking space
(38)
**20.** Babu's once and future
home (53)
**21.** Restaurant where Jerry
takes Bania for a "meal" to
thank him for an Armani suit
(89)
**22.** 16 West 75th St., Apt.
2G, where Elaine lives
**23.** Home of the Soup Nazi
(110)
**24.** Site of "the pitch" for a
sitcom "about nothing" (42)
**25.** Where Jerry's family runs
up a huge bill at Elaine's
expense (100)
**26.** Elaine's onetime place of
business. She worked as a
manuscript reader, then as an
editor (11)
**27.** Where Kramer accuses
designer Calvin Klein of steal-
ing his idea and is then hired
as an underwear model (51)
**28.** Where Kramer tries to sell
Jerry's cigar-store Indian (71)
**29.** Site of Kramer and
Mickey's soap-opera stand-in
work (77)
**30.** Regular performance
place of Pavarotti, who Elaine
and Jerry see in "I Pagliacci"
(47)
**31.** Where Jerry befriends
Mets star Keith Hernandez
(34)
**32.** Site of Jerry and his girlfriend's scam to get discount
dry cleaning by pretending to
be married (78)
**33.** The blinking red lights
from this fast-food restaurant
keep Kramer up at night
(134)
**34.** 129 West 81st St., where
Jerry, Kramer, and Newman
live
**35.** Kramer takes a stand here
and tries to return aging fruit
(62)
**36.** Where George injures
Bette Midler during a softball
game and Kramer drives a
hansom cab (104, 115)
**37.** Jerry, Kramer, and
Newman stakeout their suspicious accountant at this landmark (65)

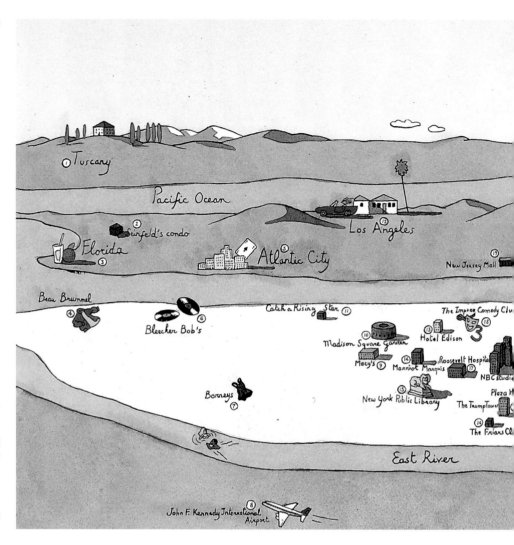

and the event was marked with celebrations throughout the city. Efforts to stage mass
broadcasts of the final episode on giant screens in Times Square and Bryant Park, rejected
by municipal officials as unfeasible, would have symbolically transformed the heart of
the city into an oversized communal living room in which New Yorkers might "bid
adieu to their alter egos" on "the quintessentially New York sitcom."[30]

For many American viewers, the series' appeal is its offer of a virtual visit to this
"island off the coast of America" that is both alien and familiar, tantalizing and daunting. In a place as remote and different from New York as, say, Boise, Idaho, *Seinfeld*'s
ratings were often higher than the national average. *New York Times* reporter Bruce
Weber has likened exporting its distinctive comic sensibility of "Manhattan kvetching"
to the dissemination of bagels to the hinterlands. Yet Boiseans (and others) forge readings of *Seinfeld* that suit their own sensibilities. For example, one regular viewer from
Boise explained his admiration for this avowedly unsentimental show because it portrays "people who are friends and who stay friends no matter what."[31]

New York viewers, of course, have evolved their own special attachments to the
series, especially when its reruns are aired every weekday on a local channel at eleven
o'clock at night. Many New Yorkers watch *Seinfeld* reruns instead of local late-night
newscasts, journalist Jim Windolf suggests, because the situation comedy "delivers the
real news for a city marked by cutthroat ambition and the accompanying fear of suc-

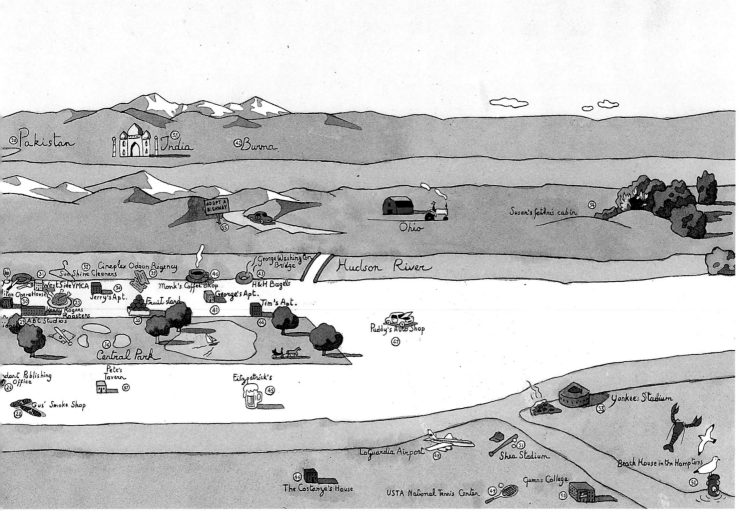

cess. . . . *Seinfeld* gives the city the same nightly dose of clarity and community that an ideal newscast would provide."[32]

Likewise, many Jewish viewers find that *Seinfeld* has had special implications as a Jewish phenomenon. Their often highly charged discussions of the series offer a telling measure of the power of a work of fiction to drive a community's internal discourse on its own identity. Thus, "it's not surprising," Lisa Lipkin reported in the *Forward* in 1996, that in a recent survey asking some New York Jewish children to name their Jewish heroes, "God placed fourth, behind Jerry Seinfeld, Adam Sandler and Howard Stern."[33]

Throughout the 1990s, *Seinfeld* surfaced repeatedly as a reference point in public discussions of issues far removed from the realm of television comedy, such as Zionism and the Holocaust, that loom large in Jewish-American culture. Despite its popularity with Jewish viewers—or precisely for this reason—these invocations of the series were rarely positive. The Anti-Defamation League's national director, Abraham Foxman, decried the use of the epithet "Soup Nazi" on one *Seinfeld* episode as a trivialization of the Holocaust. (At the same time, this notoriety has made the actual Manhattan soup merchant who inspired the episode into an urban hero, and it has spawned the creation of a chain of soup stores called Soup Nutsy).[34] Pondering the future of support for the State of Israel in the wake of American Jews' current "identity crisis," the *Wall Street Journal* wondered, "What unites them now?" and answered, "'Seinfeld.'" A Hillel rabbi in the Midwest interviewed for the *Wall Street Journal* reported that "when he first began working with college students in 1972, they were passionate about Israel. . . . Now he tries to entice students by sponsoring an evening watching the television sitcom."[35] Indeed, *Seinfeld* has come to serve as a shorthand term, epitomizing what some Jewish community activists fear as their eventual demise. Thus, *New York* magazine's 1997 cover story on the "vanishing" American Jew, termed the religious and cultural estrangement of growing numbers of American Jews the "*Seinfeld* effect"—a phenomenon the author and editors felt required no explanation.[36]

It is, most likely, an unforeseen extension of *Seinfeld*'s double-edged sensibility that some American Jews identify the series as a Jewish cultural touchstone, while others see it as a signpost of Jewish demise. What these contradictory impulses have in common is their testimony to the power of Jewish television-watching as a communal (pre)occupation. This practice evolved over the course of the second half of the twentieth century from the task of decoding Jewish encryptions of earlier decades (spoofed in a TV quiz show parody, "Jew/Not a Jew," on *Saturday Night Live* in 1988) into more extensive and elaborate discussions of the Jewish presence on American television. These take place in private conversations, in the press, in films, and even on the small screen itself. Jewish television-watching is no mere idle endeavor. This largely domestic activity replicates the larger search that Jews make outside their homes for the telltale signs of Jewishness in others, as they make their way through the complex challenges of modern life.

A final irony of these imaginary portraits of New York Jewish life is their peculiar endurance. Long after some of the neighborhoods they purportedly represent have yielded to demographic change and the vagaries of urban development, these broadcasts—preserved on videotape, housed in television museums and archives, and re-aired on cable channels (such as the appropriately named "TV Land")—enable repeat visits to the medium's virtual world of Jewish New York. Some day, perhaps, American Jews may feel they are more at home culturally when they "visit" these imagined urban places than those locations where American Jews actually live.

Card promoting Kenny Kramer's *Seinfeld* tour of Manhattan. Kramer's "three-hour multi-media, fun-filled tour" promises "a romp through what's factual and fantasy in the world of *Seinfeld*."

## FOR SEINFELD FANS

### Kramer's Reality Tour

### All about The Tour & KENNY KRAMER

IT HAS BEEN WRITTEN ABOUT in the *New York Times, People Magazine,* and in newspapers and magazines throughout the world You've seen it on *Extra, Hard Copy, Inside Edition, CNN, Entertainment Tonight.* **Mayor Giuliani** said, *"Kramer's Reality Tour is a valuable entertainment and cultural venture."*

**WHAT IS IT:** There really is a Seinfeld show. Everybody knows that, and, most people know that there is a real soup shop and a restaurant where the gang meets.

But there's also a **REAL KRAMER**. It's true. **KENNY KRAMER**, the across the hall neighbor of Seinfeld Executive Producer and Co-Creator Larry David, is the inspiration behind Seinfeld's Kramer character.

**NOW** the Real Kramer, Kenny Kramer, invites you to join him on a theatrical multi-media bus and video tour of New York City to sights made famous on America's #1 sitcom. Of course there will be a stop for photos at the real Monk's Restaurant where every week the plot thickens. Along the way, Kenny Kramer will answer your questions, share backstage information on how the show was created, and tell you how many story lines and characters' names came right from real life.
**AND THERE'S MORE...** Exclusive rare video footage, surprise guests and even some Real Kramer's Original Famous Pizza served with a beverage and dessert.
*Kramer's Reality Tour is a great time for Seinfeld fans.*

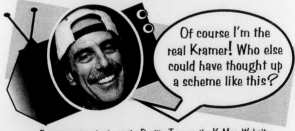

Of course I'm the real Kramer! Who else could have thought up a scheme like this?

For more info: check out the Reality Tour on the K-Man Website:
**http://www.kennykramer.com**

# MEDIATING JEWS AND THE MEDIA

The ultimate expression of American Jews' "at-homeness" with television may be found in works in another medium—feature films that claim television's early days in New York as a landmark of American Jewish culture. The earliest of these, *The Front* (Columbia, 1976), dramatizes anti-Communist blacklisting in the television industry during the 1950s, focusing on its consequences for a group of New York writers and actors, most of them Jews. Created by men who had themselves suffered the persecution of blacklisting—including Hershel Bernardi, Walter Bernstein, Jack Gilford, and Zero Mostel—*The Front* is a performance of public vindication, reclaiming these artists' roles before and behind the camera as they reenact efforts to deny them and their fellow artists the right to work.

In the plot of *The Front*, an ethnic, secular Jewishness figures both as a base of solidarity among most of the film's protagonists and as an implicit moral force. Jewishness works similarly in *Quiz Show* (Hollywood Pictures), a 1994 feature that revisits the television quiz-show scandal of the late 1950s. Here Jewishness figures as a moral signifier juxtaposed against hypocrisy among an American WASP elite. In *Quiz Show*, television's early troubled history is also linked with social and political anxieties among New York Jews in the early post–World War II years, which are epitomized by the plight of contestant Herbert Stempel, whom executives of the quiz show *Twenty-One* coerced into losing to Charles Van Doren.

Other films celebrate Jewish life in mid-twentieth-century New York as a touchstone of the medium's early successes in providing entertainment, especially comedy, to a national audience. *My Favorite Year* (MGM, 1982), the coming-of-age story of a young Jewish comedy writer, is one of several works inspired by the backstage world of *Your Show of Shows* (NBC, 1948–54). *Mr. Saturday Night* (Columbia, 1992), presents the biography of Buddy Cole, a fictitious veteran television comedian, perhaps modeled in part on Milton Berle (who was widely known as "Mr.

Television" in the early 1950s, when his comedy-variety show dominated prime time on Tuesday nights). Both films suggest that the birth of American television comedy took place not so much on Manhattan soundstages as in these New York Jews' own outer-borough, middle-class living rooms.

All these films are, in turn, part of a larger inventory of features that self-consciously examine various entertainment media and their connections to American Jews. These include Milos Forman's *Ragtime* (Paramount, 1981), which includes a portrait of a turn-of-the-century immigrant Jewish entrepreneur's early foray into silent movies; Woody Allen's *Radio Days* (Orion, 1987), a paean to Depression-era radio programs, recalled as part of one Queens Jewish family's life; Barry Levinson's *Avalon* (TriStar, 1990), the saga of an extended, multigenerational Jewish family in Baltimore, in which the TV set serves as a running symbol of economic success at the expense of family cohesiveness; and Joel and Ethan Coen's *Barton Fink* (Twentieth Century Fox, 1991), a Jewish screenwriter's Kafkaesque journey through Hollywood in the heyday of the studio system.

Through these and other features, Jews' reflections on the "Jewishness" of American mass media—once the stuff of private, internal discussions—have come to be offered in a highly public, popular forum. This change evinces a larger desire among American Jews

to situate themselves *as Jews* in the nation's cultural landscape—and to do so prominently, in the eyes of all fellow Americans. These films strive to provide American Jews with a sense of indigenousness not only along the dimensions of time and place, but also, most significantly, in terms of popular entertainment media. Among earlier generations of American Jews, these media epitomized for many the desire to leave the restrictions of being Jewish behind and to integrate oneself into the American mainstream. By the final decades of the twentieth century, film, television, and radio have come to be seen by many American Jews—those in the audience as well as those in entertainment industries—as distinctly Jewish landmarks in the national landscape.
—J.S.

# AMERICAN MEDIA AND THE HOLOCAUST

JEFFREY SHANDLER

ROD STEIGER in
THE PAWNBROKER

directed by Sidney Lumet

THE MOST TALKED ABOUT PICTURE!

co-starring Brock Peters
with Jaime Sanchez and Geraldine Fitzgerald

© Art Theatre Guild 1965

Cover of promotional leaflet
for *The Pawnbroker*.

Over the course of the second half of the twentieth century, the Holocaust became a prominent fixture of American public culture. This is a remarkable phenomenon, given that most Americans have no direct connection to the Nazi extermination of European Jewry. Indeed, no other event of modern history looms so large in our nation's moral landscape that did not either take place in this country or involve large numbers of Americans abroad. For most Americans—unlike Europeans or Israelis—the Holocaust has been encountered only through some kind of representation: news reports, memoirs, monuments, public ceremonies, exhibitions, educational programs, works of art, music, and theater. Films and radio and television broadcasts have not only presented the Holocaust to the largest number of Americans, but have played leading roles in shaping the nation's relationship to this forbidding subject.[1]

In order to understand how so many Americans have come to feel that they are "at home" with the Holocaust, we must turn to the nation's media, including many examples drawn from the field of entertainment. The discomfort that this very idea engenders should not be overlooked; indeed, it speaks to the heart of the value of these works as touchpoints for larger concerns about the relationship of history and public memory, of the popular and the unspeakable.

Radio introduced American audiences to the details of Nazi atrocities while the war was still in progress. On the eve of Yom Kippur in 1943, NBC radio first aired Morton Wishengrad's docudrama, *The Battle of the Warsaw Ghetto*, less than six months after this landmark of Jewish resistance against Nazi persecution took place. Many Americans first learned of the conditions inside Nazi concentration camps from radio journalists, particularly Edward R. Murrow's April 15, 1945, report for CBS news about Buchenwald, which began: "Permit me to tell you what you would have seen, and heard, had you been with me on Thursday. It will not be pleasant listening." Shortly thereafter, the nation's cinemas presented footage of this and other recently liberated camps to audiences in newsreel reports. Viewers were not only shown graphic footage of persecution the likes of which had never previously been shown in public. Audiences were also told that viewing these images was a morally galvanizing, transformative experience: "Grim and ugly . . . GI's at the front *had* to face it. We at home *must* see it to believe and understand."[2] This notion has continued to inform hundreds of documentary films, news reports, and, more recently, displays in Holocaust museums that present these images to the public.

During the two decades after the war, a number of film and television dramas integrated the Holocaust into American narratives. Original dramas broadcast live on television in the 1950s on such series as *Philco Television Playhouse*, *Playhouse 90*, and *Studio One* portrayed the experiences of Americans encountering Nazi anti-Semitism in Europe or of Holocaust survivors struggling to build new lives in the United States. The

258

feature film *The Pawnbroker* (Allied Artists, 1965), based on Edward Lewis Wallant's novel, offered Americans a powerful image of a Holocaust survivor living in New York, haunted by the torments of his wartime experiences.

Some American dramatic films and telecasts dealing with the Holocaust have

William Shatner and Leonard Nimoy disguised as Nazis in "Patterns of Force," a 1968 episode of the original series *Star Trek*.

become among the most widely seen and influential works on this subject: George Stevens's film *The Diary of Anne Frank* (Twentieth Century Fox, 1959), based on the stage play by Frances Goodrich and Albert Hackett; *Judgment at Nuremberg* (United Artists, 1961), the film version of Abby Mann's original teleplay, which was aired on *Playhouse 90* in 1959; the miniseries *Holocaust: The Story of the Family Weiss* (NBC, 1978), scripted by Gerald Green; Steven Spielberg's film of Thomas Kenneally's historical novel *Schindler's List* (Universal, 1993). In reaching vast international audiences, these works have imported distinctively American visions of the Holocaust and its significance to other countries, including those where it took place. At the same time, the appearance of the Holocaust as a "guest" subject on episodes of a wide array of American television series— including *The Defenders*, *Star Trek*, *The FBI*, *All in the Family*, *Seventh Heaven*, *ER*, *The X-Files*—has made the subject a familiar element of the nation's repertoire of moral issues.

Burt Lancaster (left) as one of the defendants in the film version of *Judgment at Nuremberg* (1961).

Throughout the past half-century, these films and broadcasts have engendered a contentious debate on representing the Holocaust in America's popular media, becoming one of the most extensive discussions of the media's ability to facilitate public memory in American culture. The discussion dates back to the early postwar years. For example, when CBS blanked out references to poison gas during *Playhouse 90*'s live telecast of *Judgment at Nuremberg*—at the behest of the American Gas Company, one of its sponsors—it created a sensation in the broadcasting industry. The incident has since become an epitomizing example of what some consider to be the inherently flawed nature of the "Hollywood version of the Holocaust."[3] With the premier telecast of the *Holocaust* miniseries on NBC in April 1978, the debate on representing the Holocaust became something of a national concern. At that time, many observers were of the opinion that

America's popular media were inherently incapable of dealing with a subject increasingly understood as testing the very limits of representation. Most famously, Elie Wiesel
asserted in the *New York Times* that the miniseries had turned "an ontological event
into soap-opera. . . . Art and Theresienstadt were perhaps compatible in Theresienstadt,
but not . . . in a television studio."[4]

Such sentiments did not discourage American broadcasters and filmmakers from
portraying the Holocaust. On the contrary, since the late 1970s, films and television
programs on the subject have burgeoned. Even Wiesel seems to have had a change of
heart about the medium he once disparaged, stating in a 1988 interview in *TV Guide*
that had there been television during the Nazi era, "I think it would have exposed Hitler
. . . and millions of lives might have been saved. In that way, it is a wonderful tool. The
camera cannot lie—not when it is always there."[5] And in December 1994, Wiesel put
the medium—and himself—to the test, making a highly publicized visit to war-torn
Bosnia, using his moral force as a witness to the Holocaust to attempt to bring another
genocide to a halt.[6]

Despite, or precisely because of, their ubiquity, films and telecasts dealing with
the Holocaust now regularly provoke discussions of appropriateness. Sometimes the

surrounding debates overwhelm the reception of the media works themselves. Such was the case in the contentious response to casting anti-Zionist activist Vanessa Redgrave as Auschwitz inmate Fania Fénelon in Arthur Miller's television drama *Playing for Time* (1980). Similarly, the documentary *Liberators: Fighting on Two Fronts in World War II* (1992), which chronicled the experiences of African-Americans facing prejudice both at home and on the battlefield during the war, became the subject of a protracted controversy when questions arose about the accuracy of statements made in the film concerning the participation of all-black units of the U.S. Army in liberating major concentration camps in Germany.

A spate of Holocaust comedies of the late 1990s—*Life Is Beautiful* (Miramax, 1997), *The Train of Life* (Paramount, 1998), and the American remake of *Jakob the Liar* (TriStar, 1999)—prompted questions on the appropriateness of humor as a mode of engagement with this forbidding subject. Abraham Foxman, national director of the Anti-Defamation League, opined in the *New York Times* in 1998 that, despite his preliminary misgivings about *Life Is Beautiful* and other recent Holocaust films, he believes that "the mass media are the vehicle for teaching new generations about the Holocaust" and has discovered that "the tools to convey the Holocaust message can be unexpected. And they can change over time."[7]

Brochure for *Schindler's List* tour, a popular tourist attraction in Cracow since the mid-1990s. The tour visits actual historical sites as well as places where the film was made. The brochure cover depicts a simulation of tombstones from a desecrated Jewish cemetery that was re-created especially for the film (during World War II, German forces ordered Jewish gravestones be used to pave roadways in occupied Poland). These fake tombstones were left in place after filming was completed in the environs of Cracow and became a fixture of the *Schindler's List* tour, until they were eventually removed.

FRANCISZEK PALOWSKI

Śladami "Listy Schindlera"
Retracing "Schindler's List"
Auf den Spuren von "Schindlers Liste"

GUIDE            REISEFÜHRER

PRZEWODNIK

Perhaps no other American work of media on the Holocaust has generated such extensive epiphenomena as has *Schindler's List*. Though critical reception varied, the overwhelming public response fulfilled Spielberg's claims for its vast impact: "[It's] about human suffering. About the Jews, yes, because they were the ones Hitler wanted to annihilate. But it's [also] about AIDS, the Armenians, the Bosnians. It's a part of all of us."[8] The film's American premiere was widely publicized, prompting *ABC News Nightline* to proclaim 1993 "the year of the Holocaust."[9] The debut of *Schindler's List* abroad also received exceptional attention, especially in Israel, Poland, and Germany, and it created controversy when efforts were made to ban the film in Islamic nations.[10]

American reactions to the film also became newsworthy. For example at a screening in Oakland, California, on Martin Luther King, Jr.'s birthday, a group of African-American high school students laughed during a scene in which a German officer shot a Jewish prisoner; they were then asked to leave the theater. The incident quickly became the subject of extensive comment: "The national reaction was pure Rorschach," reflected Amy Schwartz in an op-ed piece for the *Washington Post*; she saw in it "a morality tale on the dangers of the current hair-trigger mind-set toward anything that might qualify as cultural insensitivity."[11]

The awe with which so many Americans approached viewing *Schindler's List* was spoofed in the April 28, 1994, episode of the situation comedy *Seinfeld*, in which the title character and his current girlfriend are caught necking at a screening of the film; this episode also features a guest character who parodies Oskar Schindler's obsession with saving Jews by becoming excessively devoted to Seinfeld's parents. The premier American network telecast of *Schindler's List* by NBC on February 23, 1997, engendered controversy over the presentation of its graphic violence to general audiences. After questioning the appropriatenesss of the film's telecast, Oklahoma congressman Tom Coburn was obliged to issue a public apology. Even the sponsorship of the broadcast by Ford Motor Company became a subject of public discussion.[12]

Shimon Attie's *Walk of Fame*, an installation displayed in Cracow in 1996. Attie placed stars in the pavement of a Cracow street that were reminiscent of Hollywood Boulevard's Walk of Fame. In Attie's version, the stars were adorned with the names of Jews who were on Oskar Schindler's list. This installation suggests how these Holocaust survivors were transformed into film celebrities by the popularity of *Schindler's List*.

Arguably the film's most enduring impact has been the transformation of its director's public image. Not only did many critics consider *Schindler's List* a turning point in Spielberg's career, evidence of a new maturity from a director whose greatest successes had been films possessed of a juvenile exuberance (*Raiders of the Lost Ark* [Paramount, 1981], *E.T. the Extra-Terrestrial* [Universal, 1982]). Spielberg also altered his public image through his own discussion of the film, frequently speaking about what making *Schindler's List* meant to him as a Jew and as a father: "I wanted to give my kids something that I could say I was proud of, that would give my parents pride in me. . . . I wanted something that would confirm my Judaism to my family and myself, and to a history that was being forgotten."[13]

Since the film's release, Spielberg has extended his commitment to using media to further Holocaust remembrance with the creation of the Shoah Visual History Foundation. Underwritten in part by profits from *Schindler's List*, the foundation has compiled filmed testimony from thousands of Holocaust survivors internationally, which can be searched by means of an elaborate computerized database. As a result, Spielberg has now equaled, if not surpassed, Wiesel as America's most widely recognized living figure associated with the Holocaust. This is a telling development, evincing a larger shift in Holocaust remembrance from its focus on survivors and other eyewitnesses to the event to a new center of attention: the creators of Holocaust representations. Indeed, in his review of *Schindler's List* for the *New Yorker*, Terrence Rafferty declared that Spielberg's accomplishment was less inspiring than Schindler's "only because art is less important than life."[14]

# OSCARS FOR HOLOCAUST FILMS

"'Be a Part of History and the Most Successful Foreign Film of All Time'— Advertisement for 'Life Is Beautiful!'" Art Spiegelman's drawing appeared in the *New Yorker* in 1999, shortly after Roberto Benigni's 1997 film *Life Is Beautiful* was awarded an Oscar for best foreign language film.

1959: *The Diary of Anne Frank* (Twentieth Century Fox)
• Supporting Actress: Shelley Winters

1961: *Judgment at Nuremberg* (United Artists)
• Actor: Maximilian Schell
• Adapted Screenplay

1965: *The Shop on Main Street* (Filmové Studio Barrandov)
• Foreign Language Film

1971: *The Garden of the Finzi-Continis* (Documento Films)
• Foreign Language Film

1972: *Cabaret* (ABC Circle Films)
• Actress: Liza Minnelli
• Supporting Actor: Joel Grey
• Director: Bob Fosse
• Cinematography
• Art Direction
• Sound; Score

1981: *Genocide* (Simon Wiesenthal Center)
• Documentary Feature

1982: *Sophie's Choice* (Universal)
• Actress: Meryl Streep

1989: *Hotel Terminus* (Samuel Goldwyn Company)
• Documentary Feature

1993: *Schindler's List* (Universal)
• Picture
• Actor: Liam Neeson
• Supporting Actor: Ralph Fiennes
• Director: Steven Spielberg
• Adapted Screenplay
• Cinematography
• Editing
• Art Direction
• Score

1995: *Anne Frank Remembered* (Sony Classics)
• Documentary Feature

1997: *The Long Way Home* (Moriah Films)
• Documentary Feature

1998: *Life Is Beautiful* (Miramax)
• Actor: Roberto Benigni
• Foreign Language Film

1998: *The Last Days* (James Moll and Ken Lipper)
• Documentary Feature

2000: *Into the Arms of Strangers: Stories of the Kindertransport* (U.S. Holocaust Memorial Museum)
• Documentary Feature

# THE VIRTUAL REBBE

JEFFREY SHANDLER

The most extensive use of mass media by any organized Jewish religious community in recent years—and, perhaps, the most extraordinary—has been that of the Lubavitcher hasidim. Television and video have assumed a vital role in establishing Lubavitch's high public profile and maintaining connections among the movement's widely dispersed international following. Although Rabbi Menachem Mendel Schneerson (1902–1994), the last Lubavitcher Rebbe, never left New York City during his forty-three years as the community's leader, he was seen via satellite broadcast or videotape by followers around the world.

Under the late Rebbe's leadership, the full range of electronic communications media became integral to the culture of Lubavitch (also known as Chabad); they are as much a part of the community's extensive public presence as its "mitzvah tanks," "Chabad houses" (mobile and fixed stations, respectively, where Lubavitcher hasidim appeal to fellow Jews to become more observant of Jewish religious traditions), and the kindling of giant outdoor Hanukkah menorahs in cities around the world. Public discourses delivered by the late Rebbe were recorded on audiotape beginning in the 1950s and then on videotape in the 1970s; they have been broadcast on both radio and television. In addition to inspirational and devotional videos and telecasts, Lubavitcher hasidim have produced children's programming, talk shows, telethons, and other works that realize Chabad's spiritual agenda within the conventions of American entertainment. During the last years of Rabbi Schneerson's life, Lubavitcher hasidim used telephone

Advertisement for Chabad's annual Hanukkah telethon in New York, 1994.

TUNE IN TO
**CHANUKAH**
THE CHABAD
**TELETHON**
SATURDAY 10PM-4AM
**DECEMBER 3**

1 800 CHABAD 9

TV55
WLIG

CABLEVISION OF WOODBURY
CABLEVISION OF HAUPPAUGE
BROOKHAVEN CABLE
CABLEVISION OF RIVERHEAD
CABLEVISION OF ISLIP
CABLEVISION OF EAST HAMPTON
CABLEVISION OF GREAT NECK
CABLEVISION OF LYNBROOK
BROOKLYN-QUEENS CABLE
TIME WARNER CABLE MANHATTAN
PARAGON CABLE MANHATTAN
CABLEVISION OF BROOKLYN/BRONX
TCI OF CABLE OF WESTCHESTER
CABLEVISION OF YONKERS
CABLEVISION OF S. CONNECTICUT
CABLEVISION OF CONNECTICUT
STATEN ISLAND CABLE
SUBURBAN CABLE OF NEW JERSEY
SIMMONS CABLE

pagers to summon the community to their central headquarters in Crown Heights, Brooklyn, whenever the Rebbe made a public appearance, and, toward the end of his life, an extensive telephone network kept Chabad communities around the world informed of their ailing leader's condition. Since his death, the Rebbe's followers have used faxes to deliver *kvitlekh* (personal petitions) to his grave; affiliates of Chabad continue to produce a range of sound recordings, telecasts, and videotapes; and Jews around the world can request information about Chabad via the Internet.

Among the array of Lubavitch cultural activities involving electronic media, their use of television and video is especially noteworthy—not the least because most hasidim shun the medium (at least officially).[1] Chabad, however, has openly and officially embraced video and broadcast television, albeit on its own terms. Rabbi Schneerson conceptualized technological advances not as inherently corrupting distractions, but rather as having the potential to be integrated into Jewry's spiritual mission: "Developments such as television [are] . . . instances of tapping and understanding G-dly forces that are manifested in nature. Man has been charged with tapping these resources to refine and civilize the world, to transform our material surroundings into a proper home for spirituality and G-dliness."[2]

This attitude is, in part, exemplary of how Lubavitch has distinguished itself ideologically from other hasidic communities, especially in its singular stands on outreach to potential *baley tshuve* (non-observant Jews who "return" to traditional religious practice) and, more recently, on messianism. Indeed, some attributes of these media are especially well suited to realizing Chabad's distinctive approach to hasidism. Television and video figure strategically in two core elements of Lubavitch culture in particular. First, they facilitate the movement's high degree of interface with others, both Jews and non-Jews. Second, they play an important role in shaping the spiritual relationship of Lubavitcher hasidim with their Rebbe, an issue of special interest since his death.

Chabad's most elaborate and extensive use of television as a vehicle for outreach takes place in its annual telethons. The brainchild of Rabbi Boruch Shlomo Kunin, director of the West Coast Chabad in Los Angeles, the first Lubavitch telethon was aired in 1981. To a considerable extent, these broadcasts are typical of the American charity telethon genre, interlarding musical performances and celebrity appearances with appeals for funds. Donations support Chabad's own community institutions as well as programs the hasidim offer to the general Los Angeles community, such as treatment for substance abusers and aid for the homeless. Over the course of these marathon telecasts Jews mingle with non-Jews, ultra-Orthodox Jews with those less (or not at all) traditionally observant. Modern social problems are juxtaposed against traditional religious values, while spiritual devotion merges with popular entertainment. Hasidim dance joyously with Hollywood stars (most notably Jon Voigt, a longtime supporter of Chabad) as the sums of money raised are announced. Heartfelt testimonials by drug addicts helped by Lubavitch follow spirited musical performances by Mordecai Ben David and the Miami Boys Choir, performers popular among Brooklyn-based, ultra-Orthodox American Jews. One year, Argentinian native Yehudah Glanz sang "La Bamba" in Yiddish.

At the same time, Chabad exercises careful control over the propriety of public appearances made in its name during the telethon. Notably, women never sing on the broadcasts, in keeping with the traditional prohibition against Jewish men listening to a woman's singing voice, lest they be seduced. Female celebrities' dresses feature long sleeves, low hemlines, and high collars, as befits traditional Jewish notions of public modesty. The telethon invokes the Rebbe through repeated references to his teachings, as well as still and moving images of him. At once quintessentially American and distinctively Lubavitch in character, these broadcasts celebrate the movement's sense of the compatibility of its spiritual mission with the modern world.

Since Rabbi Schneerson's death, television and video have come to play a powerful new role among Lubavitcher hasidim. During the final years of his life, some of the Rebbe's followers claimed that he was the Jews' long-awaited messiah. Rabbi Schneerson himself had claimed that the messianic age was imminent and his responses to the suggestion that he might be the messiah were equivocal. The Rebbe died without designating a successor and left both the question of the messiah's arrival and the future of his hasidim very much unresolved. (Traditionally, hasidic communities follow a leader who either inherits the title of *rebbe* or is appointed by his predecessor.)

Because many of the Rebbe's public appearances since the mid-1970s had been filmed, part of his legacy is an enormous video inventory. This, in turn, has enabled new possibilities for recalling the Rebbe's teachings and invoking his presence. For example, a 1995 report described visitors to the Rebbe's grave in Queens going afterwards to a house nearby to pray, wash their hands, have some refreshment, and watch videos of the Rebbe, which played there continuously.[3] Those who had gone to see the Rebbe in Brooklyn on one of the many Sundays when he gave each of hundreds of visitors a dollar bill—which was later meant to be donated to charity by the recipient—can relive their brief encounter with the Rebbe by purchasing a copy of the videotape record of their own visit.

התוועדות עם הרבי מליובאוויטש – יו״ד שבט ה׳תשל״ב

ב״ה

פארברענגען
FARBRENGEN

*An Evening with the Lubavitcher Rebbe – Yud Shevat 5732*

Cover of a videotape of a *farbrengen* (hasidic gathering) with the Lubavitcher Rebbe, originally recorded in 1972. The four-and-a-half-hour video was issued in 1997.

Footage of the Rebbe is also used to invoke his presence in dozens of telecasts and videos made since his death. A number of videos released since 1994 offer compilations of footage of the Rebbe recorded during various public events, which depict him speaking before groups, at prayer, performing rituals associated with various holidays, or simply walking down the street in Crown Heights. Most provocative among these are videos and telecasts created by followers who believe that the Rebbe is the messiah and anxiously await his reappearance. They are among the most striking expressions of Lubavitch messianism, which was especially intense during the first years following the Rebbe's death. Consider, for example, the "International Demonstration of Unity to

Greet Moshiach [the Messiah]," a live, worldwide broadcast aired on January 31, 1996 (the anniversary of the date when Rabbi Schneerson assumed the leadership of Lubavitch in 1951). The broadcast—organized by the International Campaign to Bring Moshiach, a staunch messianist faction of Chabad—linked Lubavitch communities in Russia, France, Australia, South Africa, and Israel with Crown Heights "to declare the Rebbe as King Moshiach and to pray for his immediate revelation." During the hour-long telecast, live images of a *farbrengen* (hasidic gathering) in Chabad's central headquarters in Crown Heights were intercut with videotape footage of the late Rebbe in the same building, simulating his presence before those assembled around the world on the occasion of the live telecast. At the program's culmination, multiple images on a split screen presented this international array of Chabad communities joining in the simultaneous chanting of the messianists' proclamation: "Yechi Adoneinu Moreinu V'Rabbenu Melech Hamoshiach L'olom Vo'ed [Long live Our Lord, Our Teacher, and Our Master, King Messiah Forever and Ever]!" In the words of Rabbi Shmuel Butman, chairman of the International Campaign to Welcome Moshiach, "Moshiach has become a major media event."

This and similar public statements provoked much controversy—not only among other orthodox Jews, who have rejected Chabad's messianism, but also within the Lubavitch community, where such sentiments are not uniformly shared and are the source of considerable internal strife. Indeed, the future of the Chabad movement is unclear; it is very rare for a hasidic community to function without the leadership of a *rebbe*. And yet Chabad's extensive infrastructure, including its various mass communications efforts, appears to play a key role in sustaining the community.

Indeed, Chabad's future may serve as a test of the limits of virtual reality as a vehicle for Jewish, or indeed any other, communal spirituality. Television and video now serve Lubavitcher hasidim as strategic resources for maintaining a sense of cohesiveness as a diasporic spiritual community, providing them with virtual access to their late leader. The Rebbe's virtual legacy is not only reckoned in the hundreds of hours of audio and video recordings of his public appearances over more than four decades; it is also a consequence of his ideological commitment to the use of electronic mass media as a vital component of Chabad's spiritual mission. With no human successor to continue the leadership of Chabad, this virtual legacy has become—if, perhaps, only by default—the Lubavitcher Rebbe's heir. While Chabad's future now appears very open-ended, its uses of these media promise to continue to shape the course for maintaining contact with his presence and perpetuating his spiritual mission.

# BILL CLINTON, HOLLYWOOD PRESIDENT: A CHRONOLOGY

### J. HOBERMAN

Bill Clinton was not the first American president to enjoy personal ties to the American motion picture industry. But no other president, not even Ronald Reagan, has been as closely associated with Hollywood's liberal social values or moved with such enthusiastic ease among movie stars and industry leaders, particularly those most publicly identified with their Jewishness. The president's celebrated friendships with Barbra Streisand and Steven Spielberg, in particular, gave Hollywood the sense of being America's official culture. The film industry provided a major source of funds for Clinton's presidential race, as well as for the Democratic Party during the 1990s. Not surprisingly, Hollywood itself reemerged as a political issue during those years, particularly during the 1996 election, when criticism of the movie industry provided a means for Republicans to attack the president.

Hollywood's relationship with Clinton was complicated by the cycle of movies portraying fictional contemporary presidents or presidential candidates—including *The American President* (Columbia, 1995), *Primary Colors* (Universal, 1998), and *The Contender* (DreamWorks, 2000)—some clearly modeled on the nation's current leader. Emerging late in Clinton's second term, *The West Wing* (NBC, 1999– ) was a popular television series that, in effect, continued an idealized Clinton presidency by other means, providing a virtual alternative to the Republicans' return to the White House in 2001.

President Bill Clinton talking with Steven Spielberg at a Democratic Party fundraiser in Los Angeles in May 1999.

**September 16, 1992**
Barbra Streisand headlines a $1.5 million Beverly Hills fundraiser for Democratic presidential candidate Bill Clinton; it is broadcast by satellite to New York City, Washington, D.C., Atlantic City, and San Francisco.

**January 19, 1993**
Streisand appears as the closing act in Clinton's inaugural gala.

**December 1, 1993**
After attending the Washington premiere of *Schindler's List* (Universal), President Clinton makes a televised endorsement: "I implore every one of you to go see it."

**March 10, 1994**
"Reel Appeal" (*The Hollywood Reporter*)
President Clinton joins in celebrating Steven Spielberg: "From *Jaws* to *ET* to *Schindler's List*, his prolific work has made us laugh, cry and believe in all the wonders of our imaginations. I join in honoring him for his unparalleled creativity and vision."[1]

**March 23, 1994**
"Clinton Arts Dinner Whetted Appetites Still Unsatisfied: When the White House Thinks of Art, Its Thoughts Run to Hollywood" (*New York Times*)

268

Early hopes notwithstanding, movie stars and Hollywood executives have been more conspicuous at the White House than "practioners of high culture."

**May 10, 1994**
President and Mrs. Clinton attend opening of Streisand's American tour.

**September 28–29, 1994**
Steven Spielberg, David Geffen, and Jeffrey Katzenbach, overnight guests at the White House following a state dinner for Russian President Boris Yeltsin, decide to create a new studio, DreamWorks.

David Geffen, Steven Spielberg, and Jeffrey Katzenberg, founders of DreamWorks, 1995.

**June 1, 1995**
"Dole Lashes Out at Hollywood as Undermining Social Values"
(*New York Times*)
Campaigning for the Republican nomination for the presidency, Senator Bob Dole tells a Los Angeles audience that "we have reached the point where our popular culture threatens to undermine our character as a nation" and denounces the movie industry—Time Warner, in particular—for producing "nightmares of depravity."

**June 2, 1995**
"Filmmakers Discount Criticism by Dole"
(*New York Times*)
Responding to Senator Dole's attack, Hollywood executives note that he has avoided criticism of movies featuring action stars Arnold Schwarzenegger, Bruce Willis, and Sylvester Stallone, all of whom have supported Republican candidates. Oliver Stone, whose feature *Natural Born Killers* (Warner Bros., 1994) Dole specifically cited, compared Dole's comments to the anti-Communist crusade of the early 1950s, adding "it's the height of hypocrisy for Senator Dole, who wants to repeal the assault weapons ban, to blame Hollywood for the violence in our society."

**June 4, 1995**
"Reviews by Weekend Moviegoers Are In: Dole Gets Thumbs Down"
(*New York Times*)
"Most patrons interviewed at a Pittsburgh multiplex movie theater disagree with Senator Dole blaming Hollywood for the decline of American morality."

**June 12, 1995**
"There's Big Presidential Box-Office in Bashing Hollywood" (*Washington Post National Weekly Edition*)
Ralph Reed, executive director of the Christian Coalition, calls Dole's Hollywood speech a "defining moment for his candidacy."

Rob Reiner (right) directs
Michael Douglas in *The
American President* (1995).

November 1995

Columbia Pictures releases *The American President*, directed by Rob Reiner, in which
a U.S. president (Michael Douglas), who is a widower with a young daughter, and a
lobbyist (Annette Bening) fall in love.

September 8, 1996

"Top Contributors of 'Soft Money' " (*New York Times*)

The four leading contributors to the Democratic Party committees from January 1,
1995, through June 30, 1996, are Joseph E. Seagram and Sons/MCA, Inc. (corporate
parent of Universal Studios); MacAndrews and Forbes Holdings/Revlon; Walt Disney
Co.; and DreamWorks.

September 1996

"Stars and Money: A Tale of Two Babylons" (*CounterPunch*)

During the first six months of 1996, the entertainment and communication industries
have contributed $7 million to the Democratic National Committee, including three
fund-raisers organized by David Geffen and Steven Spielberg.

November 11, 1996

"Motherlode ZIP Code: Pols Mine 90210 for Cash" (*Variety*)

Beverly Hills contributions to Democrats top those to Republicans by more than two
to one.

Hanukkah dreidel sporting
Mickey and Minnie Mouse.

**January 29, 1998**

"Aspiring Movie Mogul Bill Urged Flee DC Job Now" (*New York Post*)
As the story of President Clinton's relationship with White House intern Monica
Lewinsky breaks, syndicated columnist Cindy Adams reports that the president has
been advised by "Hollywood players" to resign now if he wants to fulfill his ambition
to run a movie studio.

**February 18, 1998**

"Clinton's Travolta Fever" (*New York Times*)
Frank Rich notes that the published guest list for the recent state dinner in honor of
British Prime Minister Tony Blair was "full of moguls and movie stars and Disney
employees" and wonders if the White House will "lend its imprimatur to the hype for
DreamWorks's potentially make-or-break new animated film, *The Prince of Egypt*."

**March 1998**

Universal Pictures releases *Primary Colors*, directed by Mike Nichols and based on the
novel by Joe Klein. John Travolta plays a southern governor running for the Democratic
nomination for president of the United States.

**August 2, 1998**

"In the Hamptons, High-Profile Parties for Clinton" (*New York Times*)
Movie stars Alec Baldwin and Kim Basinger co-host an East Hampton party that is
expected to raise $2 million for the Democratic National Committee. President and
Mrs. Clinton are the guests of Steven Spielberg at his Georgica Pond estate.

**August 24–30, 1998**

"'The Clinton Show': 2,406 days running" (*Variety*)
"With 57 channels on 24 hours a day, Clinton has become a real-life version of *The
Truman Show* . . . . TV networks spent more time covering the Monica Lewinsky case
than the other major stories combined."

A scene from the animated
film *The Prince of Egypt*,
released by DreamWorks
Pictures in 1998.

**September 18, 1998**

"Oy Vey! Monica Is Mocked as a
'Princess' as Community Rallies for the
President" (*Forward*)
While one Jewish woman "betrayed"
President Clinton before a grand jury, the
rest of the nation's Jewish community is
reported to be "standing by their man."

**September 29, 1998**

"Among Hollywood Democrats,
President Is Supported as One of Their
Own" (*New York Times*)
There has never been an American
president who has "worked the powerful
and rich Democratic establishment in
Hollywood" as well as Bill Clinton. ("'He

outdoes J.F.K.,' said Lew R. Wasserman, the eighty-five-year-old former chairman of MCA, Inc., and the dominant Democratic mogul and fundraiser here since the days of Harry S. Truman.") Reporter Bernard Weinraub notes that the president's "taste and style seem to mirror . . . the tastes and style of many of those executives and stars, like Ms. Streisand, Tom Hanks, Steven Spielberg, Jeffrey Katzenberg, Rob Reiner and others, who support him."

John Travolta as Jack Stanton, the progressive governor of a small Southern state, in *Primary Colors* (1998).

October 5, 1998
"Hollywood Beats Harvard" (*Weekly Standard*)
David Brooks notes, "Hollywood donors didn't just send money the Clintons way. Some of them sent their children and their friends' children to work as interns, including one Monica Lewinsky."

May 15, 1999
"First Lady Pays Visit to a Camp" (*New York Times*)
Visiting a refugee camp in Skopje, Macedonia, Hillary Clinton says that the plight of the expelled Kosovars reminded her of the situation depicted in the movie *Schindler's List*.

May 16, 1999
"Spielberg Consults on Clinton Museum Project" (*Drudge Report*)
President Clinton tells Hollywood audience that he and Spielberg have discussed the possibility of "some virtual reality effects in my [presidential] library."

May 28, 1999
"Clinton's Delicate Dance with Hollywood: How Far Will President Go in Blaming Industry for School Shootings" (*Forward*)
Convening a White House summit on the problem of youth violence, President Clinton invokes the 1998 documentary *Hollywoodism*: "Not very long ago there was a fascinating story on the birth of Hollywood, the virtual creation of Hollywood by immigrants, on one of our cable channels. And the story really graphically demonstrated how these immigrants—who came to the United States, faced initial discrimination, went to California to make a new life—created an image of American life in the movies that they made that had a very positive impact on the culture of America for decades."

June 8, 1999
"Power Soup for the Soul: Jews and the President" (*New York Observer*)
A recent poll shows that Jewish approval for Bill Clinton has ranged from 76 to 83 percent, far above the average.

September 29, 1999

The Warner Bros. series *The West Wing* has its television premiere on NBC. The show is produced by Aaron Sorkin, who wrote the screenplay for *The American President*. In the first episode, an infatuated White House staffer ignores the warnings of his colleagues and publicly pursues a high-priced call girl.

April 24, 2000

"Bowing Out of the Fund-Raiser Role: Citing Donor Fatigue, Hollywood Moguls End Their Big-Money Support for the Democrats" (*Washington Post National Weekly Edition*)

Having raised "millions of dollars at a time" for the Democratic National Committee, Geffen, Katzenberg, and Spielberg signal that they will be retiring from political fundraising following the November 2000 election.

August 8, 2000

"Gore's Veep Leap: Running Mate Lieberman Fierce H'wood Critic" (*Variety*)

The movie industry notes that Senator Joseph Lieberman, Al Gore's choice of a running mate, has "a shrill record of Hollywood-bashing."

August 11, 2000

"Moguls Rattled by Gore's Choice of Critic of Entertainment Industry" (*New York Times*)

With "moguls" like Wasserman and Geffen, as well as stars like Streisand, preparing to "open their gated compounds for Democratic fundraisers," few Hollywood Democrats are willing to publicly express their reservations about vice-presidential candidate Lieberman.

August 13, 2000

"Democrats Backed by Star-Studded Cast" (*Washington Post*)

As Democrats gather for their first Los Angeles convention since 1960, the party is reported "making maximum use of all the Hollywood glitz it can get to attract donors, stroke them, and hit them up for more." DreamWorks estimates that it has helped raise $15 million for the Democrats during Bill Clinton's term.

September 18, 2000

"Hollywood Insiders Give Thumbs-Down to Critics" (*New York Times*)

Many from "the Hollywood trenches" have begun to resent political criticism of the movie industry, particularly that Democratic candidates Gore and Lieberman are "helping to lead the charge."

May 3, 2002

"Bill: TV or Not TV" (*New York Daily News*)

Former President Bill Clinton rejects NBC's offer of a syndicated daytime television show, "the latest in $100 million worth of TV deals dangled in front of Clinton from the big broadcast networks since he left office."

# NOT THE
# LAST WORD:
# A CONVERSATION

J. HOBERMAN AND JEFFREY SHANDLER

J.S.: *Entertaining America* comes at a strategic moment in the history of its subject. Today, there are very few Americans who can remember life without movies and broadcasting. What are the implications of having ready access to entertainment media on a daily basis? What satisfactions and challenges does this provide, what impact has this had on people's behavior and sense of identity? The case of American Jews and their relationships with these media, now a century old, is especially revealing.

J.H.: I think it's fair to say that popular culture plays a leading role in defining what being Jewish is for many American Jews—just as Eastern European cuisine and "kitchen" Yiddish did, a generation or two earlier. Some twenty-five years ago, the sociologist Norman L. Friedman published an article on "media Jewishness," in which he discussed the importance of bestsellers like *Exodus* and *Portnoy's Complaint* to the creation of a new, leisure-based Jewish community. This community, which he saw as predicated on "sociability" and steeped in nostalgia, was an alternative to the organization of Jewish life around religion or political ideology. [1]

J.S.: The idea of "media Jewishness," or what is now often referred to as being a "cultural Jew," has a considerable history. In the 1950s there were American Jewish scholars—Abraham Duker, Joshua Fishman—calling for the study of American Jewish popular culture. Rabbi Mordecai Kaplan, the founder of Reconstructionism, had raised the issue earlier in his notion of "Judaism as a civilization." There are even antecedents in the work of early-twentieth-century writers and artists in Eastern Europe—Y. L. Peretz, Marc Chagall, S. Ansky—who envisioned creating a new, modern, secular Jewish culture centered on literature, art, music, performance. What's distinctive about most of the material we're dealing with in *Entertaining America*, though, is that it hasn't been created primarily for Jews—it's intended for large national, even international, audiences.

J.H.: As Jews become more American, America becomes more Jewish. But the Jewish audience is still important here, even in the case of works created for mainstream mass media. This is a communitarian activity—witness, for example, the extraordinary proliferation of Jewish film festivals in the past dozen years. They don't only provide a chance to see films of special interest to Jews that aren't otherwise widely available; they provide a place to see them and discuss them as a community.

J.S.: Yes, it's the discussion—the act of getting together and talking about these films and broadcasts—that defines this as a Jewish phenomenon. It's the Jewish reading of these media, and of the individuals and industries that create them, that is key.

J.H.: Of course, there are competing notions of what makes this topic "Jewish."

J.S.: Including ones that we question in this book and in the exhibition—especially the insistence, for good or for ill, that there's something essentially Jewish about Hollywood, about Tin Pan Alley, or even all of American popular culture.

J.H.: Let's consider the appeal of this insistence. In nineteenth- and twentieth-century Europe, Jews were associated, often in a negative way, with modernity and, specifically, with the new mass culture of movies and jazz. This is one reason why a Gentile like Charlie Chaplin could be perceived as Jewish. He's the poster boy for a revolution in popular entertainment. Another way to look at it, of course, would be that Jewish cosmopolitanism and visibility are themselves factors of modernization.

J.S.: Still, we need to be wary of essentialist arguments.

J.H.: Of course. Had there been no great immigration out of the Russian empire, there still would have been an American movie industry and, with the crippling of the French movie industry during World War I, it would have become the world's primary producer. But this is not to say that Thomas Edison and D. W. Griffith had the same sensibility as Adolph Zukor or Ernst Lubitsch. Without immigrant businessmen and émigré artists, Hollywood might not have had the same universal appeal. To my mind, both the moguls' drive to assimilate and their success at building an audience are rooted in a minority's acute awareness of the conventions that govern the majority culture. There's no question that Hollywood would have been more provincial without the presence of Jewish immigrants and other "foreigners." But, it's equally true that Jews contributed to the creation of Hollywood's overall Americanist (rather than, say, Christian) ideology—with particular political results.

J.S.: There are important generational differences at work in how this notion of the Jewishness of Hollywood gets discussed. Anti-Communist blacklisting of Jewish performers during the early years of the Cold War, for example, continues to resonate with older generations on both sides of the political divide, but for young adults—such as the undergraduates we teach, who were youngsters when the Berlin Wall came down and the Soviet Union was dissolved—that issue can seem incomprehensibly remote. They don't understand what the fuss was about.

J.H.: It also may not be immediately apparent why the blacklist is a Jewish issue—which is, in part, because the anti-Communist rhetoric of the period, as well as the attack on the entertainment industry, so closely echoed the anti-immigrant and anti-Semitic rhetoric of the 1920s and 1930s. People need to be reminded that American popular culture has often been a contested terrain and, as prominent figures in that culture, American Jews have played a political role. It goes with the territory. Neil Simon naturally imported fear of the blacklist into his nostalgic recollection of the now quintessentially "Jewish" entertainment, *Your Show of Shows*, in his play *Laughter on the Twenty-Third Floor*. Even so patriotic and popular a figure as Gertrude Berg couldn't avoid being tarred by the blacklist.

J.S.: It's striking how some issues—such as the question of Jews "controlling" American media, or the notion that Jews need to use popular culture as a forum to "prove" their Americanness—persist over the decades, albeit with important shifts in who makes these claims, responding to changing agendas and with varying consequences. Or, to take a very different kind of phenomenon, consider the remarkable endurance of *The Jazz Singer*. Thanks to the various remakes, adaptations, and critical discussions, it has been a near constant public presence for several generations. And yet the discussions of the film that have prevailed in the past decade, centered on the issue of its racial imagery, would doubtless seem very strange, if not untenable, to a critic writing about the film in the 1950s or 1960s, let alone to its original audience.

J.H.: Jolson's desire to do whatever it took as an entertainer to succeed, to become American, was a crucial aspect of his adopting blackface. By the time Jolson began blacking up, blackface was one of the oldest conventions in American show business. It's striking, though, that virtually the only blackface performers who are remembered now are first-generation Jewish performers of 1920s: Jolson and Eddie Cantor and, possibly, Sophie Tucker. Perhaps this is because, as argued by Michael Rogin, blackface had the secondary consequence of rendering Jews—who were still considered a distinct, Asian race—effectively "white."[2] As the vulgar, brashly self-described "King of All Media," Howard Stern might be a contemporary analogue to Jolson. Certainly Stern's success combines a deep understanding of American mores and a willingness to say anything. In some respects he's the quintessential Stand-Up Jew— or at least the most notorious.

J.S.: I'm not sure I agree that Howard Stern is an avatar of Al Jolson—after all, Jolson was intent on ingratiating himself with his audience, whereas Stern is hell-bent on shocking them. But the notion does raise an important point about Jewish celebrity in America as a distinctively modern, secular phenomenon. It has nothing to do with traditional Jewish notions of what attributes one looks for in a prominent, memorable figure; indeed, some of these personalities—Lenny Bruce, Roseanne, Adam Sandler—would seem to fly in the face of any convention of Jewish respectability. This reflects a radically different notion of defining Jewishness, and I think the discomforting mix of pride and obstinacy that it entails is telling.

J.H.: But don't forget that both Jolson and Tucker were associated with cantors; they were self-consciously linked to a "high" Jewish tradition. They represented a community. And even comedians—Groucho Marx, Lenny Bruce, and Jerry Seinfeld, to name a few—are used to support the idea that Jewish entertainers are truth tellers. Of course, for much of America, Jews and comedy are nearly synonymous—something that, *pace* Henry Popkin, has been true at least since the 1960s, but has nothing to do with Judaism. I once moderated a discussion with a Jewish audience following a screening of the documentary *Hollywoodism*, and more than a few people questioned whether these secular, assimilationist movie moguls could be considered Jews in any meaningful sense. Of course, there were other people who criticized the documentary for not mentioning this or that Jewish actor.

J.S.: And the same thing has happened with *Entertaining America*. Every time I've discussed this project with friends or colleagues, they invariably ask, "Are you including so-and-so? Are you going to deal with this movie, that TV program? Are you going to address such and such issue?" More often than not, it's something that we decided not to include; sometimes it's something we didn't even consider. And of course, they want to know why. At first these exchanges felt very frustrating—we clearly weren't capable of making everyone happy—but now I'm convinced that such conversations are a positive sign. They demonstrate how immediately the subject engages people, how they draw on their own considerable command of the material.

J.H.: I think you can see this sensibility materialized in very elaborate ways in the star-based projects we asked the individual artists—Ben Katchor, Aline Kominsky-Crumb, Rhonda Leiberman, and Mark Rappaport—to create for the exhibition. One point that Norman L. Friedman makes about "media Jewishness" is that it is fundamentally idiosyncratic—people pick and chose, and everyone can be his or her own expert. There is no higher authority.

"Let's All Sing Together," a booklet of Jewish songs, 1936. Horowitz-Margareten, manufacturers of Jewish foods, distributed this small booklet to mark the inaugural broadcast of its weekly radio program, *Lomir Alle Zingen* (Sing-along Hour), on the New York station WMCA. The sponsors invite listeners "not alone to listen, but to participate as well" by singing along with the broadcast: "Some of us will be doing it at the studio and others alongside their radios at their own firesides."

J.S.: Indeed, fandom can engender remarkable creativity. Contrary to the widely accepted notion that mass media foster cultural homogeneity and passivity, we discover in much of the material that we've collected for this project examples of how they can promote active, innovative, and highly personal forms of engagement. American Yiddish radio, for instance, following the precedent of the immigrant Yiddish press, developed as an interactive medium, with person-in-the-street interviews, local talent programs, and sing-along musical broadcasts.

Sheet music for the 1916 song "Since Sarah Saw Theda Bara." Written by Alex Gerber to music by the prominent African-American ragtime composer Harry Jentes, the song was published at the height of the Theda Bara craze, during a year in which she made nine features. The lyrics describe the star's impact on one ghetto girl:

*Ev'ry night Sarah Cohn would go to a moving picture show / And there she saw up on the screen, Miss Theda Bara, the "Vampire Queen." / She saw men fall for her dev'lish smile. They loved her but she fooled them all the while. / Then Sarah said, "It's an easy game. I think I can do just the same." / Since Sarah saw Theda Bara, she became a holy terror. / Oi, how she rolls her eyes. Oi, she can hypnotize. / With a wink she'll fascinate, and she wiggles like a snake. / She'll take you and try to break you. Then like a Vampire she'll "vamp" away. / The fellers all fall at her feet, and her smile is as false as her teeth. / Since Sarah saw Theda Bara, she's a wera wera dangerous girl.*

J.H.: We can trace this phenomenon back to the beginning of the twentieth century. The song "Since Sarah Saw Theda Bara" both celebrates and mocks the young immigrant Jewish woman who, inspired by the silent movie star's screen persona, apes her femme fatale performance in real life. The irony, of course, is that this is a case of double-edged ethnic travesty: Theda Bara masked (albeit, some people might argue, even as she exaggerated) her own East European Jewish origins by becoming an exotic "vamp"; Sarah Cohn's appropriation of this persona is presented as a comical "ghetto girl" act. But Sarah is not only becoming more American—like Theda, the then-modern movie star—she is perhaps assimilating Theda's strategy for becoming American.

J.S.: Sarah's mimicking what she sees on-screen shouldn't be understood simply as frivolous; it reveals the desire she has in common with many people who, since the early twentieth century, have longed to enter the worlds they see and hear in films and broadcasts. There's a telling link between Sarah Cohn in 1916 and, say, the contemporary artist Mark Bennett, whose obsessively detailed floor plans of sitcom family homes grow out of his wish to inhabit these virtual environments.

J.H.: In the case of Jewish fandom, people are invested in identifying personalities, works, or institutions as intrinsically Jewish not just as a matter of individual taste but also to connect their own consumption of popular culture with a collective Jewish experience.

J.S.: This is what I find most intriguing about the Jewish practice of inventorying Jews—not only in the entertainment media, where it's most extensive, but also in the arts, politics, academia, etc. Grandparents, parents, and children may have different names in their inventories and collect them in different ways (grandparents in private conversations, their grandchildren on Web sites), but all express a common desire to map Jewish presence and Jewish continuity, two constantly contested issues in the modern age, in terms of celebrity.

J.H.: The context, though, is always in flux. Even when a film or television program gets revisited, it takes on new meaning—we see this with *The Jazz Singer, Your Show of Shows* . . .

J.S.: Or *The Producers*! That's a truly remarkable transformation. Mel Brooks's film wasn't especially popular when it first appeared in early 1968. It received its share of

Mark Bennett's drawings of the imaginary Bronx and Haverville homes occupied by the Goldbergs, commissioned in 2002 for the exhibition *Entertaining America*.

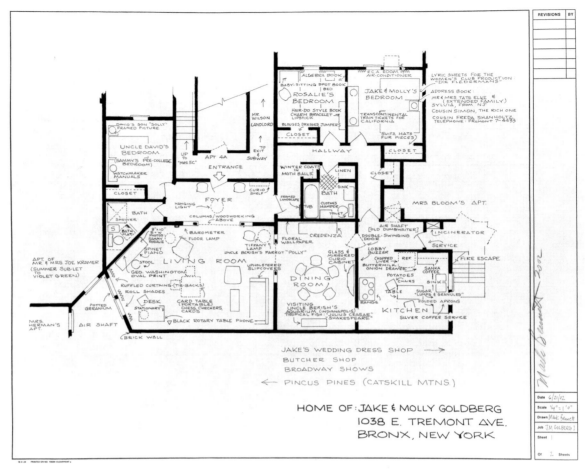

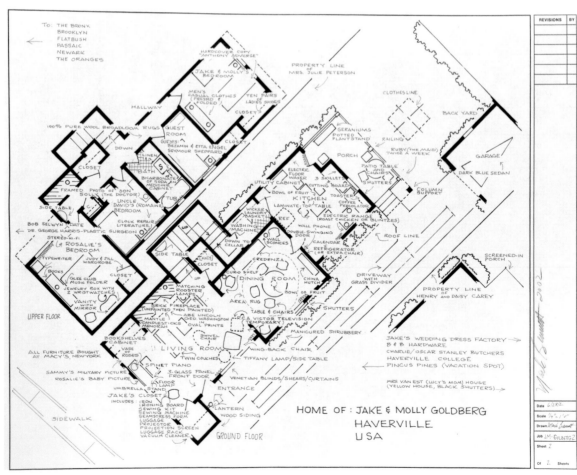

attention as cultural provocation and then receded from public attention—though it developed a considerable cult following over the years.

J.H.: I think it was a touchstone. No one who saw "Springtime for Hitler" ever forgot it.

J.S.: True. And now, it's proved to be such a huge hit as a musical—still the hottest ticket in town as we speak. *The Producers*' apotheosis on Broadway makes it something both new and not new in interesting ways. The musical's initial popularity rested, in large part, on the film's devoted audience. There were people who'd seen it over and over again on videotape who then came to the theater waiting to see their favorite moments (re)enacted live. As a friend of mine who saw the musical reported, it's like *The Rocky Horror Picture Show* for Jews.

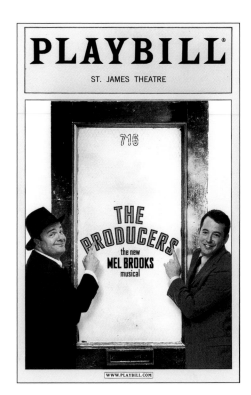

Playbill for the Broadway musical *The Producers* (2001), starring Nathan Lane and Matthew Broderick, based on the 1968 film written and directed by Mel Brooks.

J.H.: It's still a cult object! *The Producers* is really a *purim-shpil*. Brooks is tap-dancing on Hitler's grave.

J.S.: Yes, I doubt Brooks was aware of it, but in Europe's Displaced Persons camps, Purim was celebrated as early as 1946 with people dressing up as Hitler, making fun of Nazis . . .

J.H.: But I don't think that American audiences had that consciousness when they saw the film. *The Producers* was genuinely shocking then, it articulated something new. The Broadway version is something else. It's no longer any sort of scandal.

J.S.: In that regard *The Producers* traces an interesting dynamic in American Holocaust remembrance. The shock value of a Broadway musical about Hitler was key to the original film (which predated musicals that do deal with assassination, serial killing, or even the Holocaust). Now shock has given way to a kind of nostalgia for the aesthetic innocence that the movie assumed.

J.H.: The stage version of *The Producers* also reaffirms a Jewish claim to the Broadway musical, this time with triumphantly Jewish subject matter. The movie turns out to have been prophetic—of itself.

J.S.: As this catalogue goes to press, I'm most curious about how both it and the exhibition it accompanies will become part of what we have been collecting and analyzing. We've envisioned *Entertaining America* both as the latest in a series of artifacts documenting the discussion of Jews and American entertainment media and as a catalyst for further discussion.

J.H.: I think that it will serve as a source of pride and inspire a measure of nostalgia. Hopefully, it will provoke people to reconsider their notions of ethnic identity as well as offer some new perspectives on the history of entertainment.

J.S.: And thanks to the newest of the "new media" of the twentieth century—the Internet—we'll be able to see how the discussion unfolds on www.thejewishmuseum.org.

# NOTES

## NICKELODEON NATION

J. HOBERMAN AND JEFFREY SHANDLER
**Introduction**

1. See George C. Pratt, *Spellbound in the Darkness: A History of the Silent Film* (Greenwich, Conn.: New York Graphic Society, 1966), 39–54.

2. Joseph Medill Patterson, "The Nickelodeons, The Poor Man's Elementary Course in the Drama," *Saturday Evening Post*, Nov. 23, 1907, 10. See also Lewis Jacobs, *The Rise of the American Film: A Critical History* (1939; reprint, New York: Teachers College Press, 1968), 62–63.

3. Abraham Cahan, *Jewish Daily Forward*, May 24, 1908; quoted in Irving Howe, *World of Our Fathers: The Journey of the East European Jews to America and the Life They Found and Made* (New York: Harcourt Brace Jovanovich, 1976), 213.

4. Robert Sklar's highly influential *Movie-Made America: How the Movies Changed American Life* (New York: Random House, 1975) is the historical narrative that most cogently shifted emphasis to Hollywood's ghetto origin, articulating a sense of early movies as a manifestation of excluded social forces and cultural energies that, fueled by immigrants and the urban poor, erupted from below, in opposition to more official American culture.

5. Miriam Hansen, *Babel and Babylon: Spectatorship in American Silent Film* (Cambridge, Mass.: Harvard University Press, 1991), 61.

6. The phrase comes from testimony given by the chaplain of City Prison. See Tom Gunning, *D. W. Griffith and the Origins of American Narrative Film: The Early Years at Biograph* (Urbana: University of Illinois Press, 1991), 151–53. Lary L. May provides another account in *Screening Out the Past: The Birth of Mass Culture and the Motion Picture Industry* (New York: Oxford University Press, 1980), 43–45.

7. Terry Ramsaye, *A Million and One Nights: A History of the Motion Picture through 1925* (New York: Simon and Schuster, 1926), 478.

8. See Gunning, *D. W. Griffith and the Origins of American Narrative Film*, 152–53. For greater historical perspective, see Daniel Czitrom, "The Politics of Performance: From Theater Licensing to Movie Censorship in Turn-of-the-Century New York," *American Quarterly* 44, no. 4 (Dec. 1992): 525–53.

# TIMELINE

**1895**

Captain Alfred Dreyfus, found guilty of treason against France at a court martial, exiled to Devil's Island

Guglielmo Marconi first sends a wireless message

Lumiére brothers' *cinematographe* inaugurates the motion picture age

**1896**

U.S. Supreme Court accepts doctrine of "separate but equal" segregation

Theodor Herzl publishes *The Jewish State*

Lumiére brothers produce *Jerusalem Railroad Station*, first movie made in Palestine

**1897**

First World Zionist Congress meets in Basel

*Jewish Daily Forward* begins publication in New York

The Bund, a Jewish socialist workers' party, founded in Vilna

9. The Motion Picture Patents Company comprised seven American firms—Biograph, Edison, Essanay, Kalem, Lubin, Selig, and Vitagraph—along with two French firms, Pathé Frères and Méliès. While Chicago-based Essanay was cofounded by the Jewish actor Gilbert "Bronco Billy" Anderson, the lone Jewish immigrant businessman to belong to the trust was the German-born, Philadelphia-based former gold prospector and eyeglass peddler Sigmund "Pop" Lubin.

10. See Richard Abel, *The Red Rooster Scare: Making Cinema American, 1900–1910* (Berkeley and Los Angeles: University of California Press, 1999).

11. Carrie Balaban, *Continuous Performance: The Story of A. J. Balaban as Told to His Wife* (New York: G. P. Putnam's Sons, 1942), 33; and Ramsaye, *A Million and One Nights,* 828.

12. See May, *Screening Out the Past,* 152–53, 284 n. 10. Some years later, William Fox wrote of the particular appeal that early movies held for the foreign-born. See "Reminiscences and Observations," in Joseph Kennedy, *The Story of the Films* (Chicago: A. W. Shaw, 1927), 302. Characterizing entrepreneurs such as Laemmle and Fox as "immigrants with bourgeois values," Lary May considers them the "ideal middle men"

for realizing cultural fusion and suggests that, more than American-born filmmakers, the largely immigrant exhibitors understood how to "sanction group mingling" by appealing to the "consumption desires [of both] middle and working class audiences." See May, *Screening Out the Past,* 175. When they entered film production, these exhibitors extrapolated the attraction of luxury theaters to the motion picture screen by creating studios to manufacture movies worthy of their most elaborate architectural extravaganzas.

13. Ramsaye, *A Million and One Nights,* 674; quoted in Steven J. Ross, *Working-Class Hollywood: Silent Film and the Shaping of Class in America* (Princeton: Princeton University Press, 1998), 190.

JUDITH THISSEN
## Charles Steiner and the Houston Hippodrome

1. "Vu zaynen ahingekumen di yidishe myuzik-hols?" *Jewish Daily Forward,* May 24, 1908. See also "Di muving piktshur geleris," *Jewish Daily Forward,* Mar. 4, 1908.

2. *Jewish Daily Forward,* May 24, 1908.

3. Morton Minsky, *Burlesque* (New York: Arbor House, 1986), 17–18.

4. For more on the history of the Houston Hippodrome, see Judith Thissen, "Charlie Steiner's Houston Hippodrodrome: A Jewish Moviegoing Experience on New York's Lower East Side (1909–1913)," in *American Silent Film: Discovering Marginalized Voices,* ed. Gregg Bachman and Thomas J. Slater (Carbondale: Southern Illinois University Press, 2002). For an overview of moviegoing among immigrant Jews, see Thissen, "Jewish Immigrant Audiences in New York City (1905–1914)," in *American Movie Audiences: From the Turn of the Century to the Early Sound Era,* ed. Melvyn Stokes and Richard Maltby (London: BFI, 1999), 15–28.

5. Three films were made about the Mendel Beilis case: *The Black 107* (Ruby, 1913), *Terrors of Russia* (Italian American Film Co., 1913), and *The Mystery of Mendel Beilis/Der Beilis Prozess* (A. Mintus, 1914).

J. HOBERMAN
## The First "Jewish" Superstar: Charlie Chaplin

1. Sholem Aleichem, *Adventures of Mottel the Cantor's Son,* trans. Tamara Khana (New York: Collier Books, 1961), 216. Some forty years after Motl discovered Chaplin, another fictional Jewish go-getter had a similarly protective response.

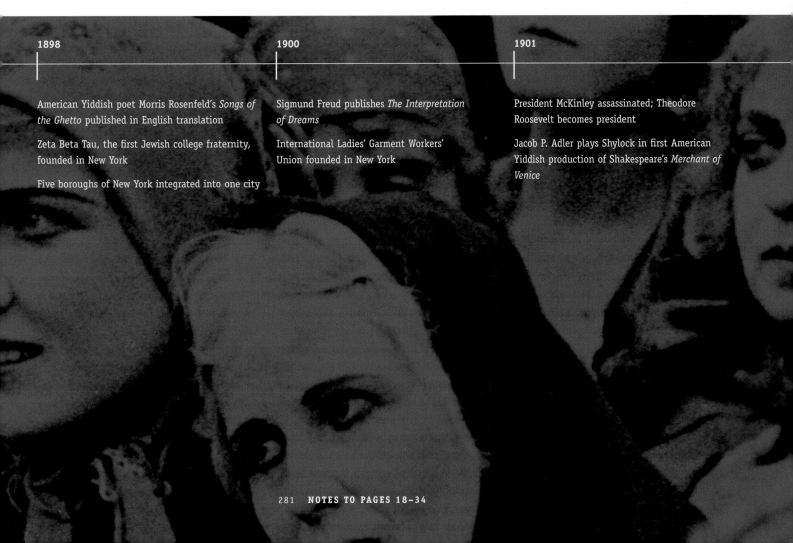

**1898**

American Yiddish poet Morris Rosenfeld's *Songs of the Ghetto* published in English translation

Zeta Beta Tau, the first Jewish college fraternity, founded in New York

Five boroughs of New York integrated into one city

**1900**

Sigmund Freud publishes *The Interpretation of Dreams*

International Ladies' Garment Workers' Union founded in New York

**1901**

President McKinley assassinated; Theodore Roosevelt becomes president

Jacob P. Adler plays Shylock in first American Yiddish production of Shakespeare's *Merchant of Venice*

Informed by a Gentile friend that some of the world's greatest men—Julius Caesar, Jesus Christ, Fyodor Dostoyevsky, and Charlie Chaplin—were epileptics, Duddy Kravitz quickly claims Chaplin as a Jew. See Mordecai Richler, *The Apprenticeship of Duddy Kravitz* (1959; reprint, New York: Ballantine Books, 1974), 185. This exchange was included in the novel's 1974 film version.

2. Jewish performers rarely played Jewish characters. Although a few Yiddish stage veterans, notably Vera Gordon, Rosa Rosanova, and Rudolph Schildkraut, appear as Jewish parents during the silent era, their children are almost invariably played by Gentiles. Two exceptions were Carmel Myers (1900–1980), the daughter of a San Francisco rabbi, who appeared as the immigrant heroine of *Cheated Love* (Universal, 1921), a remake of the Irene Wallace vehicle *Heart of a Jewess* (Universal, 1913), and Ricardo Cortez (1899–1977), born Jacob Kranz in Vienna, who played an assimilationist Jewish son in Frank Capra's *The Younger Generation* (Columbia, 1929). As Myers would be more often cast as an exotic temptress, so Cortez typically appeared as a Latin lover.

3. Chaplin's contemporaries do include specifically "Jewish" comedians who were themselves Jewish.

The Berlin-born Max Davidson (1875–1950) began playing a succession of bearded, shrugging Jewish tailors, junk dealers, and pawnbrokers in 1912 and even had his own series of comedy shorts at the Hal Roach Studios in the late 1920s. Vaudeville performer George Sidney (1878–1945) also played a series of comic Jews, most famously Jacob Cohen in the multifilm series based on *The Cohens and the Kellys*. (These stereotypes ultimately proved offensive to some Jews; Davidson, in particular, has largely been written out of history.) See Patricia Erens, *The Jew in American Cinema* (Bloomington: Indiana University Press, 1984), 89–96. Other Jewish comedians Erens identifies are Leo Carey, Sammy Cohen, and George Jessel. Ernst Lubitsch (1892–1947) broke into German movies in 1913, playing Jewish characters in two-reel comedies. At least one of these was imported to the United States.

4. Charles Musser, "Work, Ideology, and Chaplin's Tramp," in *Resisting Images: Essays on Cinema and History*, ed. Robert Sklar and Charles Musser (Philadelphia: Temple University Press, 1990), 53–54.

5. Mark Winokur, *American Laughter: Immigrants, Ethnicity, and 1930s Hollywood Film Comedy* (New York: St. Martin's Press,

1996), 76; and Reginald R. Chaplin, "Charlie Chaplin's Ancestors," *Historical Journal of Film, Radio, and Television* 5, no. 2 (1985): 209–11. See also Joyce Milton, *Tramp: The Life of Charlie Chaplin* (New York: Da Capo Press, 1998), 115–16. On his father's side, Chaplin descended from many generations of English farmers. Milton speculates that his mother, Hannah, was at least part Romany. In 1925, Chaplin announced his Gypsy ancestry in an "authorized" interview published by *Collier's* magazine; see Milton, *Tramp*, 215.

6. Terry Ramsaye, *A Million and One Nights: A History of the Motion Picture through 1925* (New York: Simon and Schuster, 1926), 645–46; and Milton, *Tramp*, 115.

7. David Robinson, *Chaplin: His Life and Art* (New York: McGraw-Hill, 1985), 154; Winokur, *American Laughter*, 277; and Searchlight, "Profiles: Funny Legs," *New Yorker* May 23, 1925, 10.

8. Milton, *Tramp*, 116; and Samuel Rosenblatt, *Yossele Rosenblatt: The Story of His Life as Told by His Son* (New York: Farrar, Straus and Young, 1954), 291.

9. *Jewish Tribune* Apr. 6, 1928, 38; cited in Michael Alexander, *Jazz Age Jews* (Princeton: Princeton University Press, 2001), 146–47.

**1902**

Hutchins Hapgood publishes *The Spirit of the Ghetto*, detailing Jewish life on the Lower East Side

Theodor Herzl publishes Zionist novel *Altneuland* (Old New Land)

**1903**

Wilbur and Orville Wright make the first powered flight at Kitty Hawk, N.C.

Three-day pogrom in Kishinev, Russia, kills forty-five Jews

Edwin S. Porter directs *The Great Train Robbery*

Oscar Straus appointed U.S. Secretary of Labor and Commerce, the first Jew to hold a Cabinet post

*The Protocols of the Elders of Zion* published in Russia

**1904**

Theodor Herzl dies in Vienna at age forty-four

First major subway line opens in New York

The Jewish Museum founded in New York when Judge Mayer Sulzberger donates twenty-six objects to the Jewish Theological Seminary of America

Alexander notes that even to themselves, Jews seemed most comic in their "essential victimization, defeat, and sadness," adding that "because the Little Tramp shared these characteristics, and because Chaplin was in fact a Jew [sic], his act became Jewish."

10. David Matis, *Di velt fun Tsharli Tshaplin* (The World of Charlie Chaplin) (New York: Yidisher Kultur Farband, 1959), 67; and Luc Sante, "Goodbye Charlie," *New York Review of Books*, Dec. 19, 1985, 14. Chaplin told Foster that he opposed the new regulations that had been established by the movie industry: "We are against any kind of censorship, and particularly against Presbyterian censorship." See R. M. Whitney, *Reds in America* (New York: Beckwith Press, 1924), 151. According to informant A. A. Hopkins, Chaplin then showed the Communist leader the sign "Welcome Will Hays" affixed to a toilet door. The bureau forwarded this report to Hays. See Milton, *Tramp*, 202.

11. Hannah Arendt, "The Jew as Pariah: A Hidden Tradition," *Jewish Social Studies* 6, no. 2 (Apr. 1944): 111, 112–13.

12. Sig Altman, *The Comic Image of the Jew: Explorations of a Pop Culture Phenomenon* (Rutherford, N.J.: Fairleigh Dickinson University Press, 1971), 187–88. Many have linked Chaplin to the most beloved of Yiddish writers, Sholem Aleichem, who died in 1916, soon after "Chaplinitis" swept the United States and Britain. Psychoanalyst and Yiddish literature scholar A. A. Roback attributed this association to Chaplin's "underdog" status. Like Aleichem's characters, Chaplin's Tramp "banks on the immediate future and therefore leaves out of account the probable, if not absolutely certain, consequences, attributing the results to tough luck, a quip of fate, or the will of God." See Roback, "The Humor of Aleichem," in *Sholom Aleichem Panorama*, ed. Melech Grafstein, (London, Ontario: *Jewish Observer*, 1948), 22. The Soviet Yiddish poet Peretz Markish made the same point in a 1939 essay, suggesting that Sholem Aleichem and Chaplin employ similar comic strategies: "Sholem Aleichem's little man, just like Charlie, takes the road of his misfortunes." See postings by L. Fridhandler and Ester Vaisman on the Yiddish discussion list www.shakti.trincoll.edu/~mendele/ (June 16, 1999).

13. Sabine Hake, "Chaplin Reception in Weimar Germany," *New German Critique* 51 (fall 1990): 103; Thomas Doherty, *Pre-Code Hollywood: Sex, Immorality, and Insurrection in American Cinema, 1930–1934* (New York: Columbia University Press, 1999), 97; David Robinson, *Chaplin: The Mirror of Opinion* (London: Secker and Warburg, 1984), 119; and Beeke Sell Tower, *Envisioning America: Prints, Drawings, and Photographs by George Grosz and His Contemporaries, 1915–1933*, exh. cat. (Cambridge, Mass.: Harvard University Art Museums, 1990), 105 n. 37.

With World War II, the Nazis' racial antipathy spread. In Vichy, France, Robert Brasillach and Maurice Bardéche changed the Chaplin entry in their pioneering film encyclopedia, *Histoire du cinéma*, by substituting the word "Hebraic" for "human": "Volumes could be written about a certain toughness in Charlie and the suppressed resentment which often lends a strangely Hebraic note to his misfortune; he is less resigned than we sometimes imagine." (Bardéche later recalled that German censors objected to including even a photograph of Chaplin on the grounds that he was a Jewish filmmaker.) See Alice Yaeger Kaplan, *Reproductions of Banality: Fascism, Literature, and French Intellectual Life* (Minneapolis: University of Minnesota Press, 1986), 146, 171.

The six-foot-high photograph of Chaplin that presided over the Munich exhibition was captioned "An Englishman? No, a Jew." See Wolfgang Gersch, *Chaplin im Berlin: Illustrierte Miniatur*

**1905**

Russo-Japanese War ends

Seventh Zionist Congress rejects East-Africa scheme

Albert Einstein publishes *The Special Theory of Relativity*

First nickelodeon opens in Pittsburgh

Tsar Nikolai II issues the October Manifesto in response to public demonstrations, promising to establish the Duma; later, the government suppresses a workers' uprising in Moscow

**1906**

Major earthquake destroys much of San Francisco

Construction begins on the Panama Canal

Word "television" used in *Scientific American*

First extended broadcast of the human voice transmitted over the airwaves from Brant Rock, Mass., by Reginald Fessenden

American Jewish Committee founded to safeguard Jewish rights

*Variety* reports the proliferation of five-cent storefront theaters

**1907**

Physicist Albert A. Michelson is first American Jew to win Nobel Prize

More than one million immigrants arrive at Ellis Island in the peak year of immigration

Galveston Project initiated to divert Jewish immigration from large cities on the East Coast

Irving Berlin publishes his first song, "Marie from Sunny Italy"

The four Warner brothers establish a film distribution company

*nach Berliner Zeitungen von 1931* (Berlin: Parthas Verlag, 1999), 100–101.

14. Charles J. Maland, *Chaplin and American Culture: The Evolution of a Star Image* (Princeton: Princeton University Press, 1989), 171. Chaplin's performance in *The Great Dictator* had the power to render Jews "Chaplinesque." Reflecting on "The Jews and I" in *National Review Online* (posted Apr. 19, 2001), British conservative John Derbyshire confessed that "There are aspects of distinctively Jewish ways of thinking that I dislike very much. The world-perfecting idealism, for example, that is rooted in the most fundamental premises of Judaism, has, it seems to me, done great harm in the modern world. That dreadful speech Charlie Chaplin gives at the end of *The Great Dictator* made me gag instinctively, even before I understood why."

15. Matis, *Di velt fun Tsharli Tshaplin*, 66. Here again Chaplin personifies the most subversive, anti-Christian, alien aspects of the movie industry. In the course of his notorious July 18, 1945, address on the relationship between Communism and Christianity, Mississippi Congressman John Rankin listed Chaplin first among Hollywood subversives ("notorious for his forcible seduction of white girls") and suggested that "this perverted subject of Great Britain" be deported. See *Congressional Record* 91, pt. 6 (July 2, 1945–Sept. 10, 1945), 7737.

Although Chaplin was subpoenaed by the House Committee on Un-American Activities, his appearance was postponed three times and he was never called to testify. Nevertheless, he was frequently attacked as a Communist or fellow traveler. In 1948, Chaplin planned to travel to Britain to make a film in London. When he applied for an American reentry permit, he was questioned for four hours by the FBI. According to David Robinson, the "unexpected inquisition" began with "personal questions about Chaplin's racial origins and sex life." The actor canceled his trip. See Robinson, *Chaplin: His Life and Art*, 548.

16. Spencer Golub, "Charlie Chaplin, Soviet Icon," in *The Performance of Power: Theatrical Discourse and Politics*, ed. Sue-Ellen Case and Janelle Reinelt (Iowa City: University of Iowa Press, 1991), 215; and Timothy J. Lyons, "The United States v. Charlie Chaplin," *American Film* (Sept. 1984): 34.

17. Matis, *Di velt fun Tsharli Tshaplin*, 66. In 1991, Israel's National Lottery initiated an extensive campaign associating itself with Chaplin's Little Tramp, whose image—as a seller of lottery tickets—was plastered on billboards and bus kiosks throughout the country. Chaplin's family sued for copyright infringement and finally won the case in February 2000. See "Little Tramp Beats Israel's Lottery," *International Herald Tribune*, Feb. 18, 2000.

18. Altman, *The Comic Image of the Jew*, 186; and Albert Goldman, "Laughtermakers," in *Next Year in Jerusalem: Portraits of Jews in the Twentieth Century*, ed. Douglas Villiers (New York: Viking Press, 1976), 221.

19. Altman, *The Comic Image of the Jew*, 221. Some are content to claim Chaplin as an honorary Jew, as in Morris Dickstein's 1985 essay on urban comedy and modernity: Chaplin's fundamental insecurity connects him to "the whole tradition of Jewish humor, from the defensive saintliness and ineptitude of the classic schlemiel, to the nihilistic antics of the Marx Brothers, to the neurotic intellectuality of Woody Allen." For Dickstein, "Chaplin's early life was so painful he didn't have to be Jewish." See Dickstein, "Urban Comedy and Modernity: From Chaplin to Woody Allen," *Partisan Review* 52, no. 3 (1985): 277.

20. David Desser and Lester D. Friedman, *American-Jewish Filmmakers: Traditions and Trends* (Urbana: University of Illinois Press,

**1908**

Henry Ford begins manufacturing the Model "T"

D. W. Griffith joins Biograph studio as an actor and directs his first films

National Board of Censorship formed to establish uniform guidelines for state and local censors

*The Melting Pot*, Israel Zangwill's play about Jewish life in New York, opens in Washington, D.C., with President Theodore Roosevelt in attendance

**1909**

National Association for the Advancement of Colored People (NAACP) founded

Motion Picture Patents Company pools patents on motion picture equipment in attempt to freeze out competitors

Col. William N. Selig, a rival of inventor Thomas Edison, opens the first Hollywood motion picture studio

*New York Times* publishes the first movie review, reporting on D. W. Griffith's *Pippa Passes*

Al Jolson applies blackface in a San Francisco vaudeville show

**1910**

First secular Yiddish school system in America established by the Labor Zionist movement

American-born Fanny Brice has a hit, singing Berlin's "Sadie Salome, Go Home" with a Yiddish accent

1993), 11. The association seems eternal. A recent French exhibition exploring the cultural history of the Wandering Jew concluded with a film loop fashioned from the final frames of *The Tramp* (Essany, 1915): in the exhibition's ultimate image, Chaplin walks off alone down the road, twirling his cane, a twentieth-century manifestation of a medieval legend. *Le Juif errant: Un témoin du temps* (The Wandering Jew: A Witness of Time), Musée d'art et d'histoire du Judaïsme, Paris, Oct. 22, 2001–Feb. 24, 2002.

J. HOBERMAN AND JEFFREY SHANDLER
**Virtually Jewish**

1. Vanessa Ochs, "Why We Watched Rhoda Religiously: The Artistic Construction of a Jewish Woman," lecture, The Jewish Museum, New York, Nov. 13, 2001. See also Elizabeth Gold's memoir of her Rhoda obsession, "Headwraps and All, Rhoda Morgenstern Is a Misfit Girl's Dream," *Forward*, Feb. 4, 2000, 18.

J. HOBERMAN
**John Turturro**

1. Rebecca Ascher-Walsh, "Does Hollywood Have a Jewish Problem?" *Entertainment Weekly*, Aug. 18, 1995, 28–31.

## MOGULDOM

J. HOBERMAN AND JEFFREY SHANDLER
**Introduction**

1. Steven Alan Carr, *Hollywood and Anti-Semitism: A Cultural History up to World War II* (Cambridge, U.K.: Cambridge University Press, 2001), 28, 91. Carr's study provides a detailed analysis of what he terms "the Hollywood Question" through 1941.

2. "Budd Schulberg: The Screen Playwright as Author," in *The Cineaste Interviews*, ed. Dan Georgakas and Lenny Rubenstein (Chicago: Lake View Press, 1983), 367.

J. HOBERMAN AND JEFFREY SHANDLER
**Hollywood's Jewish Question**

1. Although Robert Sklar's influential *Movie-Made America: How the Movies Changed American Life* (New York: Random House, 1975) asserts that the term "movie moguls" was current as early as 1915, it is remarkably absent from the discourse of the 1920s. For all the colorful biblical and orientalizing metaphors that Terry Ramsaye employs in *A Million and One Nights: A History of the Motion Picture through 1925* (New York: Simon and Schuster, 1926), "mogul" is not among

them. *Time*, which has been credited with the coinage of "cinemogul," makes no mention of Hollywood producers in any context through 1928, while the *New Yorker* consistently employed the more dignified "movie magnates." The same term is used in the two standard histories of the 1930s, Benjamin B. Hampton's *A History of the Movies* (New York: Covici, Friede, 1931; republished as *History of the American Film Industry* [New York: Dover Publications, 1970]), and Lewis Jacobs's *The Rise of the American Film: A Critical History* (1939; reprint, New York: Teacher's College Press, 1968), as well as in Leo C. Rosten's *Hollywood: The Movie Colony and the Movie Makers* (New York: Harcourt, Brace and Company, 1941). None of these three books refers to "movie moguls," although Rosten does employ the playful term "cellulord."

2. "Profiles: The Celluloid Prince," *New Yorker*, Apr. 25, 1925, 13.

3. Ramsaye, *A Million and One Nights*, 823.

4. Hampton, *History of the American Film Industry*, 26.

5. For example, Henry Fairfield Osborn, president of the American Museum of Natural History, wrote, "The entire control of the 'movie' industry

**1911**

Triangle Shirtwaist Factory fire, in New York, leaves 146 dead, most of them young Jewish and Italian immigrant women

Mendel Beilis accused of the ritual murder of a young Christian boy in Kiev

Yossele Rosenblatt emigrates from Russia to New York to serve as cantor for Congregation Oheb Tzedek

Tel Aviv exhibitor Ya'acov Davidson tours western Russia with a documentary film on Jewish life in Palestine

**1912**

Woodrow Wilson is elected president

*Titanic* sinks after hitting an iceberg on her maiden voyage

Henrietta Szold founds Women's Zionist Organization, Hadassah, in New York

New law requires broadcast licenses

*Photoplay* debuts as the first magazine for movie fans

**1913**

B'nai B'rith establishes Anti-Defamation League, designed to combat anti-Semitism in the U.S.

The Armory Show shocks New York audiences with modernist art from Europe

Samuel Goldwyn, Jesse Lasky, and Cecil B. DeMille produce the first feature-length American movie, *The Squaw Man*

Sidney M. Goldin makes five films on Jewish themes for Universal, most starring Irene Wallace

[is] now in the hands of people of near or remote Oriental origin." See Osborn, "Shall We Maintain Washington's Ideal of Americanism," in *The Alien in Our Midst, or "Selling Our Birthright for a Mess of Pottage": The Written Views of a Number of Americans (Present and Former) on Immigration and Its Results*, ed. Madison Grant and Charles Stewart Davison (New York: Galton, 1930). Noting the post–World War I association of Jews with "Tartars and other Asiatic nomad elements . . . races impregnated with radicalism, Bolshevism and Semitic anarchy," historian Neil Baldwin cites Osborn, among others, in stating that "the 'gospel of racism' permeated American academia, making such views commonplace and respectable to the culture at large." See Baldwin, *Henry Ford and the Jews: The Mass Production of Hate* (New York: Public Affairs, 2001), 170–71.

6. See Holly Edwards, *Noble Dreams, Wicked Pleasures: Orientalism in America, 1880–1930* (Princeton: Princeton University Press, 2000), 45.

7. The first complete edition of *The Protocols of the Elders of Zion* published in the U.S. appeared in Boston in 1920. On the *Protocols* in the United States, see Norman Cohn, *Warrant for Genocide: The Myth of the Jewish World-Conspiracy and the Protocols of the Elders of Zion*, Brown Judaic Studies 23 (Chico, Calif.: Scholars Press, 1981), 156–64. The 1920 edition of the *Protocols* includes an appendix listing the *noms de guerre* of Bolshevik leaders alongside, in many cases, their original Jewish names. This established a precedent for similar inventories of "hidden" Jewishness in the names of suspected subversives in the post–World War II anti-Communist crusade.

8. Ford later recanted his attacks on a Jewish conspiracy, but his initial accusation that "as soon as the Jew gained control of the 'movies' we had a movie problem" has had a lingering impact on the discussion of Jews and Hollywood.

9. Frank Walsh, *Sin and Censorship: The Catholic Church and the Motion Picture Industry* (New Haven, Conn.: Yale University Press, 1996), 19.

10. "Profiles: Doctor of Movies," *New Yorker*, May 8, 1926, 21–22.

11. Cited in Steven Alan Carr, *Hollywood and Anti-Semitism: A Cultural History up to World War II* (Cambridge, U.K.: Cambridge University Press, 2001), 66. See William Sheafe Chase, *Catechism on Motion Pictures in Inter-State Commerce*, 3rd ed. (Albany: New York Civic League, 1922), 115–19.

12. Francis G. Couvares, "Hollywood, Main Street, and the Church," in *Movie Censorship and American Culture*, ed. Francis G. Couvares (Washington, D.C.: Smithsonian Institution Press, 1996), 152.

13. Thomas Doherty, *Pre-Code Hollywood: Sex, Immorality, and Insurrection in American Cinema, 1930–1934* (New York: Columbia University Press, 1999), 98.

14. On the latter point, see for example the public relations campaign waged against Soviet filmmaker Sergei Eisenstein when he visited Hollywood in 1930, as described in Doherty, *Pre-Code Hollywood*, 98.

15. See Michael E. Birdwell, *Celluloid Soldiers: Warner Bros.'s Campaign against Nazism* (New York: New York University Press, 2001), 13–20; and Doherty, *Pre-Code Hollywood*, 93–96.

16. Walsh, *Sin and Censorship*, 85. Rev. Cantwell published his own manifesto a few years later, blaming the "vileness" of Hollywood movies on the influx of Broadway playwrights who arrived with the coming of the talkies: "*Seventy-five per cent of these authors are pagans. . . . Most of them are living lives of infidelity and worse, wherein there is to be found not a suggestion of respect for*

**1914**

World War I begins following assassination of Austrian Archduke Ferdinand

Panama Canal opens

The American Jewish Joint Distribution Committee is organized to provide relief for Jewish victims of the war in Europe

Charlie Chaplin arrives in the U.S. from England

New York's first "movie palace," the Strand, opens on Broadway

**1915**

German U-boat sinks British luxury liner *Lusitania*, killing 1,198 passengers

Leo Frank lynched in Marietta, Ga.

D. W. Griffith releases *The Birth of a Nation*, the most expensive and controversial American movie to date

The Folksbiene, amateur Yiddish theater company, organized in New York

Charlie Chaplin becomes world's highest paid entertainer

William Fox introduces movie vamp Theda Bara in *A Fool There Was*

**1916**

Louis Brandeis, first Jewish justice, appointed to the U.S. Supreme Court

Over 100,000 mourners attend New York funeral of Yiddish writer Sholem Aleichem

D. W. Griffiths's epic film *Intolerance* released

religion or for spiritual values." See Cantwell, "The Motion Picture Industry," in *The Movies on Trial*, ed. William J. Perlman (New York: Macmillan, 1936), 21.

17. Doherty, *Pre-Code Hollywood*, 102. For similar reasons, perhaps, MGM abandoned plans to film Sinclair Lewis's antifascist novel *It Can't Happen Here* (1935), after paying $200,000 for the screen rights.

18. HANL was founded by Otto Katz—a.k.a. Rudolf Breda, a.k.a. André Simon—a Czech Communist (and future victim of the Slansky trial) with a background in Weimar workers' theater, who arrived in Hollywood in early 1936 accompanied by the Catholic anti-Nazi aristocrat Prince Hubertus zu Lowenstein. Both men made a great show of wooing the Los Angeles dioceses. Breen's disapproval was not immediate; his presence was noted, along with that of luminaries Jack Warner, Walter Wanger, and Mervyn Leroy, at the star-studded gala celebrating HANL's first anniversary in February 1937. See Saverio Giovacchini, *Hollywood Modernism* (Philadelphia: Temple University Press, 2001), 83–84; and Paul Buhle and Dave Wagner, *Radical Hollywood* (New York: New Press, 2002), 78.

Neal Gabler describes the more cautious antifascist activities of the Los Angeles Community Relations Council (CRC), which was supported by Louis B. Mayer, Irving Thalberg, and Harry Cohn, among other moguls; see Gabler, *An Empire of Their Own: How the Jews Invented Hollywood* (New York: Crown, 1988), 341. Between 1933 and 1946, the Los Angeles CRC infiltrated a number of pro-Nazi and anti-Semitic organizations active in the Los Angeles area, disseminating information through its own News Research Service. The CRC also prepared a report on fascist activities in southern California, which was presented to the House Committee on Un-American Activities in September 1938; this report was amended a year later and twice in 1940.

19. Walsh, *Sin and Censorship*, 157; and Larry Ceplair and Steven Englund, *The Inquisition in Hollywood: Politics in the Film Community, 1930–1960* (Garden City, N.Y.: Doubleday, 1980), 109.

20. Carr, *Hollywood and Anti-Semitism*, 166. According to John Howard Lawson, the attacks on *Blockade* and many exhibitors' subsequent cancellations of its screening were "related to the anti-trust suit against the major motion picture companies instituted on July 20, 1938. The Department of Justice charged that the major companies, through their control of exhibition, prevented film theaters from reflecting 'the taste of their communities.'" See Lawson, "Comments on Blacklisting and Blockade," *Film Culture* 50–51 (summer–fall 1970): 28.

21. Clayton R. Koppes and Gregory D. Black, *Hollywood Goes to War: How Politics, Profits, and Propaganda Shaped World War II Movies* (New York: Free Press, 1987), 26–27.

22. Giovacchini, *Hollywood Modernism*, 94–95; Bosley Crowther, "Little Caesar Waits His Chance," *New York Times*, Jan. 22, 1939; and Thomas Doherty, *Projections of War: Hollywood, American Culture, and World War II* (New York: Columbia University Press, 1993), 40. Nevertheless, the movie made no mention of German anti-Semitism, as noted in *Variety*'s unusually long and serious, as well as favorable, review (May 3, 1939). *Variety* considered this omission "inevitable." Jack Warner had, after all, personally ordered that all references to Alfred Dreyfus's Jewishness be eliminated from the script of Warners' 1937 bio-pic *Zola* (1937). See Giovacchini, *Hollywood Modernism*, 92.

23. Birdwell, *Celluloid Soldiers*, 58; Koppes and Black, *Hollywood Goes to War*, 27–29; Carr,

**1917**

Russian Revolution; Russia withdraws from World War I

United States enters World War I

Balfour Declaration favors the establishment of a Jewish state in Palestine

Charlie Chaplin makes *The Immigrant*

Abraham Cahan's novel of immigrant life, *The Rise of David Levinsky*, published

**1918**

World War I ends in the eleventh hour of the eleventh day of the eleventh month

Congress rebuffs Navy's bid for permanent control of radio in U.S. and urges private monopoly

American Jewish Congress founded

Maurice Schwartz launches Yiddish Art Theater in New York

**1919**

Benito Mussolini founds fascist party in Italy

Russian civil war; Simon Petliura's Ukrainian nationalists massacre thousands of Jewish civilians

Weimar Republic established in Germany

Attorney General A. Mitchell Palmer raids "Bolshevik headquarters" in eleven American cities

Anarchists Emma Goldman and Alexander Berkman deported to Soviet Union

Eighteenth Amendment to U.S. Constitution bans sale of alcohol

Charlie Chaplin, D. W. Griffith, Douglas Fairbanks, and Mary Pickford establish United Artists in an attempt to control their own work

Charles Davenport's *Khavah* is the first film adapted from Sholem Aleichem's Tevye stories

*The Cabinet of Dr. Caligari* premieres in Berlin

*Hollywood and Anti-Semitism*, 170; and Birdwell, *Celluloid Soldiers*, 76. Although the movie did poorly outside of northeastern cities (and was even censored in Great Britain), Warner Bros. was reported to be "mulling the possibility of sequel" as late as August 1939. See *Variety*, Aug. 16, 1939, 22.

24. Giovacchini, *Hollywood Modernism*, 113. Giovacchini points out that refugees served as the "new aliens" in attacks on Hollywood (114–15).

25. Gabler, *An Empire of Their Own*, 345. Lindbergh was reinforced in his views by his friend (and sometime employer) Henry Ford. Indeed, Ford remarked in the course of a July 1940 interview that "when Charles [Lindbergh] comes out here, we only talk about the Jews." See Baldwin, *Henry Ford and the Jews*, 288.

26. Gerald Nye, "War Propaganda: Our Madness Increases as Our Emergency Shrinks," *Vital Speeches of the Day*, Sept. 15, 1941, 721.

27. Thomas Doherty, *Projections of War*, 40. See also Thomas Schatz, *Boom and Bust: American Cinema in the 1940s* (Berkeley and Los Angeles: University of California Press, 1999), 39. The movies Nye singled out as interventionist and/or anti-Nazi propaganda included *Confessions of a Nazi Spy*, Charlie Chaplin's enormously popular

*The Great Dictator*, the Twentieth Century Fox thriller *The Man I Married* (1940; originally known as *I Married a Nazi* and one of the few Hollywood features to use the word "Jew"), MGM's family melodrama *The Mortal Storm* (released the week the Germans entered Paris), and two other features from Twentieth Century Fox—a remake of the John Ford antiwar silent *Four Sons* (1940; updated by John Howard Lawson to reflect the Nazi occupation of Czechoslovakia) and *Man Hunt* (1941; the story of a fictional attempt to assassinate Hitler, directed by German émigré Fritz Lang). The most popular was Warners' World War I drama *Sergeant York* (1941), directed by Howard Hawks and starring Gary Cooper. Released during the summer of 1941 and building in popularity through the Senate hearings, this story of a Tennessee pacifist who goes to war against Germany would be the year's top grossing movie.

28. Schatz, *Boom and Bust*, 40.

29. Gabler, *An Empire of Their Own*, 338.

30. Carr, *Hollywood and Anti-Semitism*, 197. Birdwell maintains that Harry and Jack Warner were the only studio heads to support the Hollywood Anti-Nazi League; see Birdwell, *Celluloid Soldiers*, 26.

31. Walter Wells calls *What Makes Sammy Run?* a novel about "the death of the American Dream," with Sammy the personification of "the Dream's breakdown." See his *Tycoons and Locusts: A Regional Look at Hollywood Fiction of the 1930s* (Carbondale: Southern Illinois University Press, 1973), 92. Carr similarly characterizes *The Last Tycoon* as "about the death of the American Dream." See Carr, *Hollywood and Anti-Semitism*, 223.

32. Budd Schulberg, *What Makes Sammy Run?* (1941; reprint, New York: Penguin Books, 1978), 228. Schulberg, a Communist when he conceived his novel, was concerned with universalizing his protagonist. He not only portrays Glick's character flaws as the result of his miserable childhood in the slums of the Lower East Side, but more than once equates Glick's capacity for amoral manipulation with that of fascist demagogues. Schulberg broke with the Communist Party over its critique of the novel; see Victor S. Navasky, *Naming Names* (New York: Penguin, 1991), 239–40.

33. F. Scott Fitzgerald, *The Last Tycoon* (New York: Charles Scribner's Sons, 1941), 147.

34. Leo C. Rosten, *Hollywood: The Movie Colony, the Movie Makers* (New York: Harcourt, Brace and Company, 1941), 5–6. Anthropologist

## 1920

Nineteenth Amendment to U.S. Constitution grants American women the right to vote

League of Nations holds first meeting

Pittsburgh's KDKA transmits results of the presidential race in the first U.S. commercial radio broadcast

S. Ansky's play *The Dybbuk* performed for the first time, in Warsaw

Henry Ford publishes *The International Jew*, a collection of essays denouncing Jewish "control" of American politics, finance, and culture, including the film industry

## 1921

Vladimir I. Lenin introduces New Economic Policy (NEP)

Charlie Chaplin directs his first feature-length film, *The Kid*

American Yiddish actress Molly Picon tours Europe and returns home a star

State Yiddish Theater in Moscow premieres *A Sholem Aleichem Evening*, with sets by Marc Chagall

Fatty Arbuckle tried for manslaughter in the death of Virginia Rapp

Rudolph Valentino stars in *The Sheik*

## 1922

Mordecai M. Kaplan founds Society for the Advancement of Judaism, leading to Reconstructionist movement

AT&T introduces "toll" broadcasting (i.e., commercials) at $100 for ten minutes

British Broadcasting Company (BBC) founded in London

Approximately three million households in the U.S. have radios

James Joyce publishes *Ulysses*

Hollywood studio heads hire Will Hays as head of the new Motion Picture Producers and Distributors of America

Samuel Goldwyn produces movie version of Anzia Yezierska's Lower East Side stories *Hungry Hearts*

Cecil B. DeMille releases *The Ten Commandments*

*Abie's Irish Rose* debuts on Broadway

Hortense Powdermaker seems to have taken this methodology to heart in *Hollywood, the Dream Factory: An Anthropologist Looks at the Movies* (Boston: Little, Brown, 1950), in which she applies skills honed by her previous study of a Polynesian village to make sense of the movie colony. Powdermaker makes no comment on the ethnic origins of studio heads or other personnel. Instead, her suggestion that the film industry is fundamentally undemocratic resonates with Cold War rhetoric: "Hollywood represents totalitarianism. . . . The concept of man as a passive creature to be manipulated extends to those who work for the studios, to personal and social relationships, to the audience in the theaters and to the characters in the movies" (327).

35. Rosten, *Hollywood*, 178. He further explains that "Mr. Zanuck is of Czech descent and comes from Wahoo, Nebraska; Mr. Freeman is a Methodist from Atlanta; the Messrs. Kent, Le Baron, Roach, and DeMille are Protestants from Lincoln (Neb.), Elgin (Ill.), Elmira (N.Y.), and Ashfield (Mass.) respectively; the Messrs. Schaefer, Mannix, and Breen are Catholics from Brooklyn, Philadelphia, and Fort Lee (N.J.)."

36. Ibid., 67.

37. Alvah Bessie, *Inquisition in Eden* (New York: Macmillan, 1965), 128.

38. Gabler, *An Empire of Their Own*, 357.

39. Navasky, *Naming Names*, 109.

40. See Gordon Kahn, *Hollywood on Trial: The Story of the Ten Who Were Indicted* (New York: Boni and Gaer, 1948), 105.

41. Myron C. Fagan, *Documentation of the Red Stars in Hollywood* (Hollywood, Calif.: Cinema Education Guild, 1950), 56. See also Bernard F. Dick, *Radical Innocence: A Critical Study of the Hollywood Ten* (Lexington: University Press of Kentucky, 1988), 129–32.

42. Navasky, *Naming Names*, 112–13.

43. Pauline Kael, *Deeper into Movies* (Boston: Atlantic–Little, Brown, 1973), 327. In this essay, originally published in the *New Yorker* (Nov. 13, 1971), Kael uses Dorothy Parker's anecdote as a means to discuss *Fiddler on the Roof* (United Artists, 1971), which she praises as "probably the only successful attempt to use [the movie musical] as the subject of its own sources—that is, of the heritage that the Jewish immigrants brought to this country," a "joyously square" celebration of "American Jewish show business."

44. Lary L. May and Elaine Tyler May, "Why Jewish Movie Moguls: An Exploration in American Culture," *American Jewish History* 72, no. 1 (Sept. 1982): 9–10.

45. Diana Altman argues that *Hollywood Rajah*, published three years after Mayer's death, set the tone for subsequent exaggerations of the studio executives' power, opportunism, and lasciviousness. See her "The Movie Moguls as Anti-Semitic Cartoons," *Midstream* 49 (Feb.–Mar. 1993): 25.

46. Norman L. Friedman, "Hollywood, the Jewish Experience, and Popular Culture," *Judaism* 19 (fall 1970): 484.

47. Ibid., 487. Scarcely a year after the publication of the French and Zierold books, John Updike offered a similar, if more ethnically specific, thesis in *Bech: A Book* (New York: Alfred A. Knopf, 1970), attributing the argument to the Jewish writer who is the novel's protagonist: "The artistic triumph of American Jewry lay, [Bech] thought, not in the novels of the fifties but in the movies of the thirties, those gargantuan, crass conceptions whereby Jewish brains projected Gentile stars upon a Gentile nation and out of their own immigrant joy gave a formless land dreams and even a kind of conscience" (5).

**1923**

Adolf Hitler arrested and Nazi Party banned after unsuccessful coup d'etat in Munich

Vladimir Zworykin invents iconoscope, a precursor to the cathode ray (picture) tube

Inventor Lee de Forest exhibits early sound-on-film movies using Phonofilm process in New York

New York police shut down English-language production of Sholem Asch's play *God of Vengeance*, in a landmark obscenity case

**1924**

Lenin dies, leading to a power struggle between Joseph Stalin and Leon Trotsky

U.S. Congress enacts restrictive quotas on immigration

Nathan Leopold and Richard Loeb sentenced to life in prison for murder of Robert Franks in Chicago

Metro-Goldwyn-Mayer film studios formed by merger of Metro Pictures, Goldwyn Pictures, and Louis B. Mayer Company

RCA transmits first pictures by wireless telegraph, from London to New York

George Gershwin premieres *Rhapsody in Blue*

**1925**

Scopes "Monkey" trial pits William Jennings Bryan against Clarence Darrow in debate on teaching evolution in public schools

Hitler publishes *Mein Kampf*

YIVO Institute for Jewish Research founded in Vilna

F. Scott Fitzgerald publishes *The Great Gatsby*

Edna Ferber is first American Jew to win Pulitzer Prize in fiction

First public demonstration of a television system, developed by Charles Francis Jenkins

Sergei Eisenstein releases *Battleship Potemkin*

Members of Moscow State Yiddish Theater appear in *Jewish Luck*, a motion picture adapted by Isaac Babel from the stories of Sholem Aleichem

48. Joseph P. Eckhardt and Linda Kowall, *Peddler of Dreams: Siegmund Lubin and the Creation of the Motion Picture Industry, 1896–1916*, exh. cat. (Philadelphia: National Museum of American Jewish History, 1984), 1, 17.

49. E. L. Doctorow, *Ragtime* (1975; reprint, New York: Penguin, 1996), 215–18 passim.

50. May and May, "Why Jewish Movie Moguls," 6–25 passim.

51. Gabler, *An Empire of Their Own*, 6–7.

52. Carr notes the same contradiction in Gabler's thesis. According to Gabler, he writes, Jews acted as Jews in "inventing" Hollywood but, in excluding Afro-Americans from participation in the empire, Jews were acting as Americans—that is, no differently than other white Gentiles. See *Hollywood and Anti-Semitism*, 3.

53. In a notorious two-hour lecture, delivered on July 20, 1991, at the Empire State Black Arts and Cultural Festival in Albany and subsequently broadcast, Jeffries (then chairman of the Department of African-American Studies at City College of New York) declared that "there was a conspiracy planned and plotted and programmed out of Hollywood, with people named Greenberg

and Weisberg and Trigliani. Russian Jewry had a particular control over the movies and their financial partners, the Mafia, put together a financial system for the destruction of black people." Paired with Norman Lear on a May 1995 edition of the ABC News program *Nightline*, Buchanan informed the liberal television producer that "you people in Hollywood" are undermining "America's Christian values." Brando's comments were made during the April 5, 1996, broadcast of the CNN program *Larry King Live*.

54. William Cashman, "Kings of the Deal," *Spectator*, Oct. 29, 1994, 14–16. Cashman addressed his critics both in the *Spectator* (Nov. 6, 1994) and in a letter to the *New York Times* (Nov. 18, 1994). Gabler responded in the *Los Angeles Times* (Nov. 13, 1994).

55. More recently, Gerald Horne has argued that a post–World War II upsurge in anti-Semitic agitation—as well as the murder of Jewish mobster Bugsy Siegel—intimidated the leaders of the movie industry, causing them to demonstrate their "American-ness" by breaking the progressive Conference of Studio Unions (CSU) and purging the industry of Jewish radicals: "When the moguls 'did the right thing' and smashed

CSU, they showed they could set aside presumed ethno-religious interests and that they were qualified to advance further within the ruling elite." See Horne, *Class Struggle in Hollywood, 1930–1950: Moguls, Mobsters, Stars, Reds, and Trade Unionists* (Austin: University of Texas Press, 2001), xi–xii.

56. Michael Medved, *Hollywood vs. America: Popular Culture and the War on Traditional Values* (New York: Harper Collins, 1992), 1, 10, 90, 202.

57. Paul Buhle, "The Hollywood Blacklist and the Jews: An Exploration of Popular Culture," *Tikkun* 10, no. 5 (Sept.–Oct. 1995). These ideas are elaborated in Paul Buhle and Dave Wagner, *Radical Hollywood* (New York: New Press, 2002), 57–59 passim.

JEFFREY SHANDLER
**Henry Ford**

1. The first edition of *The International Jew* appeared in late 1920; three similar anthologies were published over the next year and a half. It has been estimated that Ford had at least two hundred thousand and perhaps as many as half a million copies printed in the U.S., many of which were

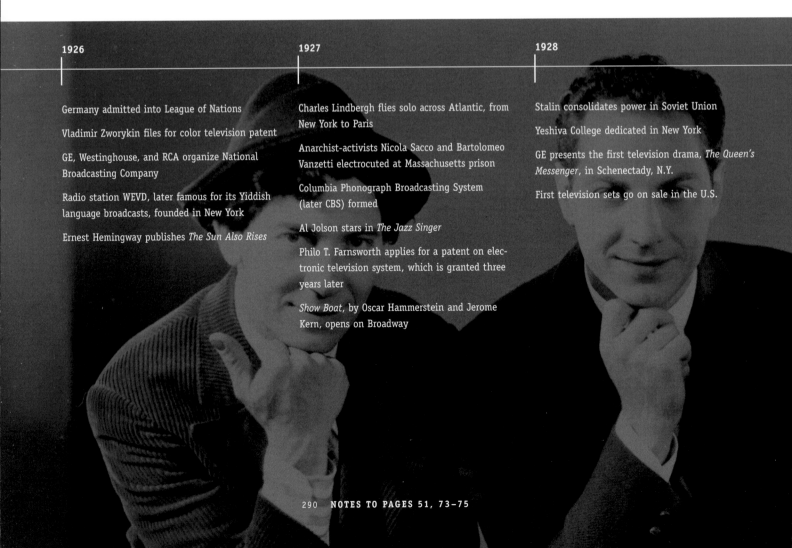

**1926**

Germany admitted into League of Nations

Vladimir Zworykin files for color television patent

GE, Westinghouse, and RCA organize National Broadcasting Company

Radio station WEVD, later famous for its Yiddish language broadcasts, founded in New York

Ernest Hemingway publishes *The Sun Also Rises*

**1927**

Charles Lindbergh flies solo across Atlantic, from New York to Paris

Anarchist-activists Nicola Sacco and Bartolomeo Vanzetti electrocuted at Massachusetts prison

Columbia Phonograph Broadcasting System (later CBS) formed

Al Jolson stars in *The Jazz Singer*

Philo T. Farnsworth applies for a patent on electronic television system, which is granted three years later

*Show Boat*, by Oscar Hammerstein and Jerome Kern, opens on Broadway

**1928**

Stalin consolidates power in Soviet Union

Yeshiva College dedicated in New York

GE presents the first television drama, *The Queen's Messenger*, in Schenectady, N.Y.

First television sets go on sale in the U.S.

distributed free to community leaders. The book was translated into sixteen languages; six German editions were published between 1920 and 1922. Ten years before Adolf Hitler became Germany's chancellor, he kept a large portrait of Henry Ford in his office and multiple copies of *The International Jew* in his outside waiting room. See Neil Baldwin, *Henry Ford and the Jews: The Mass Production of Hate* (New York: Public Affairs, 2001), 144–45, 172–73.

WILLIAM SHEAFE CHASE
**Catechism on Motion Pictures**

1. The continuation of Chase's answer includes citations from *The Protocols of the Elders of Zion* and Henry Ford's *The International Jew*.

J. HOBERMAN
**The EPIC Campaign**

1. Nancy Lynn Schwartz, *The Hollywood Writers' Wars* (New York: Alfred A. Knopf, 1982), 36, 37; and Budd Schulberg, *What Makes Sammy Run?* (1941; reprint, New York: Penguin Books, 1978), 84–88.

2. *New York Times*, Nov. 4, 1934.

3. Greg Mitchell, *The Campaign of the Century:*

*Upton Sinclair's Race for Governor of California and the Birth of Media Politics* (New York: Random House, 1992), 510–11.

4. Steven Alan Carr, *Hollywood and Anti-Semitism: A Cultural History up to World War II* (Cambridge, U.K.: Cambridge University Press, 2001), 160–61.

5. Max Knepper, *Sodom and Gomorrah: The Story of Hollywood* (Los Angeles: End Poverty League, 1935), 178, 236.

J. HOBERMAN
**Crossfire**

1. James Agee, *Agee on Film* (Boston: Beacon Press, 1958), 270.

2. One of several novels on anti-Semitism that appeared in the years directly following World War II, *Gentleman's Agreement* was not the only one to concern a faux Jew. The protagonist of Arthur Miller's *Focus* (1945) is a casual anti-Semite who loses his job and is identified by his neighbors as Jewish when he begins wearing glasses.

3. Frank Miller, *Censored Hollywood: Sex, Sin, and Violence on Screen* (Atlanta.: Turner Publishing, 1994), 144.

4. Elliot E. Cohen, "Letter to the Moviemakers: The Film Drama as a Social Force," *Commentary* (Aug. 1947): 116. Dore Schary replied in defense of *Crossfire* in *Commentary*'s October 1947 issue.

5. Nora Sayre, *Running Time: Films of the Cold War* (New York: Dial Press, 1982), 40.

J. HOBERMAN
**The Last Temptation of Christ**

1. See Mary Pat Kelly, *Martin Scorsese: A Journey* (New York: Thunder's Mouth Press, 1991), 161–80.

2. Charles Lyons, *The New Censors: Movies and the Culture Wars* (Philadelphia: Temple University Press, 1997), 163; and John Dart, "Church Likely to Condemn 'Temptation,' Mahoney Says," *Los Angeles Times*, July 20, 1988, pt. 2, p. 3.

3. Aljean Harmetz, "Film on Christ Brings out Pickets, and Archbishop Predicts Censure," *New York Times*, July 21, 1988, C19; Harmetz, "7,500 Picket Universal over Movie about Jesus," *New York Times*, Aug. 12, 1988, C4; Peter Steinfels, "Robertson Draws a Rebuke on Film," *New York Times*, Aug. 24, 1988; Lyons, *The New Censors*, 168. Defending the crusade against *The Last*

**1929**

The stock market crashes, precipitating the Great Depression

William Faulkner publishes *The Sound and the Fury*

First Academy of Motion Picture Arts and Sciences awards (Academy Awards) ceremony is held

Comedy series *Amos 'n' Andy* and *The Rise of the Goldbergs* debut on NBC radio

**1930**

Marx Brothers appear in *Animal Crackers*

Edward G. Robinson plays Italian gangster in *Little Caesar*

Sidney Goldin directs *East Side Sadie*, first Yiddish-language partial talkie

**1931**

Japan invades Manchuria

Empire State Building, world's tallest structure, opens

Charlie Chaplin releases the silent picture *City Lights*

*Temptation of Christ*, Michael Medved pointed out that, hardly a lunatic fringe, the campaign included "The National Council of Catholic Bishops, the National Catholic Conference, the Southern Baptist Convention (with 14 million members), the Eastern Orthodox Church of America, the Archbishop of Canterbury (head of the worldwide Anglican Church), the archbishop of Paris, twenty members of the U.S. House of Representatives (who cosponsored a bipartisan resolution condemning the film), the Christian Democratic Party of Italy (that nation's largest political party), and Mother Teresa of Calcutta." Devoting a chapter to the incident in his book-length critique of Hollywood, Medved says nothing about the characterization of *The Last Temptation* as Jewish, although he uses similar logic when he jokes that fear of "enraging the Islamic faithful" deterred Universal from filming Salman Rushdie's *The Satanic Verses* (1988) or wonders if Hollywood would support a movie showing Anne Frank as "an out-of-control teenage nymphomaniac." See Medved, *Hollywood vs. America: Popular Culture and the War on Traditional Values* (New York: Harper Collins, 1992), 37–49.

4. John Dart, "Church Declares 'Last Temptation' Morally Offensive," *Los Angeles Times*, Aug. 10, 1988, pt. 2, p. 3; and *New York Times*, Aug. 12, 1988.

5. Lyons, *The New Censors*, 174; and Laura Sessions Stepp, "Long Lines For 'Last Temptation,'" *Washington Post*, Aug. 13, 1988, C4.

6. Clyde Haberman, "Scorsese's 'Last Temptation' Creates a Furor at Venice Festival," *New York Times*, Sept. 8, 1988. The most violent response to the movie was in France, where isolated showings in Paris, Lyons, Nice, and Grenoble inspired public disturbances and acts of arson in late September and early October 1988.

J. HOBERMAN
**On *The Jazz Singer***

1. In *A Right to Sing the Blues: African Americans, Jews, and American Popular Song* (Cambridge, Mass.: Harvard University Press, 1999), Jeffrey Melnick suggests that the persistent link between popular entertainers and traditional *khazonim* (cantors) was a form of public relations: "Given that the 1910s and 1920s gave rise to some broad rhetorical attacks on secular urban Jews—as factory managers, white slavers, Reds, World Series fixers, bootleggers, and so on—it was quite savvy for Jews and their friends to construct a public narrative which decontaminated American Jews by making them over in the (invented) image of their Old World ancestors" (176).

Thus, much was made of the fact that the fathers of popular songwriters Irving Berlin and Harold Arlen were cantors. Indeed, the archetypal Yiddish stage performer is often a cantor's son or daughter. Actor Esther-Rokhl Kaminska was the child of a cantor, as is the actress-heroine of Sholem Aleichem's *Wandering Stars*. Boris Thomashefsky, Sigmund Mogulesko, Seymour Rechtzeit, composer Sholom Secunda, and poet Peretz Markish were all either cantors' sons or child cantors, or both.

Melnick's omission of Jewish movie magnates and entertainers from his gallery of negative "secular urban Jews" is striking. Downplaying the nativist and religious campaigns waged against "Jewish" movies and popular music, he maintained that "the generally conservative Jews of the entertainment business offered an antidote to the image of Jews as bomb-throwing radicals which became especially popular in the wake of the Red Summer of 1919" (103).

2. If Jolson seemed to the pioneering pop culture critic Gilbert Seldes to possess a "daemonic" vitality, to his disciple George Jessel he was something else. "In 1910," eulogized Jessel at Jolson's West Coast funeral (there were East Coast rites as well),

**1932**

Franklin Delano Roosevelt elected president

Benjamin Cardozo appointed to the U.S. Supreme Court

Paul Muni plays Italian gangster in *Scarface*

Kodak introduces the first 8mm home movie camera

**1933**

First hundred days of the New Deal

Prohibition repealed

Hitler becomes chancellor of Germany; SS establishes the first concentration camp at Dachau, near Munich

Independent Yiddish-language feature *The Wandering Jew* is the first American film to attack Nazi regime

Screen Actors Guild (SAG) established

**1934**

Communications Act passed, establishing the Federal Communications Commission (FCC)

Hollywood studios begin to enforce industry-wide Production Code of moral standards

Birobidjan, located on the Soviet-Manchurian border, established as a Jewish autonomous region

Henry Roth publishes *Call It Sleep*

Detroit Tigers first baseman Hank Greenberg refuses to play on Yom Kippur

Darryl F. Zanuck produces *House of Rothschild*

Group Theater stages Clifford Odets's *Waiting for Lefty* in New York

The Jewish people who emigrated from Europe to come here were a sad lot. Their humor came out of their troubles. Men of thirty-five seemed to take on the attitudes of their fathers and grandfathers, they walked with stooped shoulders. When they sang, they sang with lament in their hearts. . . . And then there came on the scene a young man, vibrantly pulsating with life and courage, who marched on the stage, head held high like a Roman Emperor, with a gaiety that was militant, uninhibited and unafraid. . . . Jolson is the happiest portrait that can ever be painted about an American of the Jewish faith.

Perhaps that happiness was itself a form of minstrelsy. In that case, the Jazz Singer is a kind of Jewish Faust and *The Jazz Singer* a movie about the psychic cost of being American. Michael Rogin's reading of the movie in *Blackface, White Noise* gives it a tragic dimension. The price of American success is not only the jettisoning of one's own unhappy traditions, but assuming responsibility for the unfortunate traditions of others. See Rogin, *Blackface, White Noise: Jewish Immigrants in the Hollywood Melting Pot* (Berkeley and Los Angeles: University of California Press, 1996).

3. That the term *jazz* then encompassed many forms of popular music—including ragtime, show tunes, and Tin Pan Alley—may account for the absurdly sweeping claim Raphaelson makes in his preface to the published version of his play: "Jazz is Irving Berlin, Al Jolson, George Gershwin, Sophie Tucker. Jews are determining the nature and scope of jazz more than any other race—more than the Negroes, from whom they have stolen jazz and given it a new color and meaning." See Raphaelson, *The Jazz Singer* (New York: Brentano's, 1925), 9. It is important to note also that Jolson's tremendous success on the legitimate stage in the years just before and after World War I coincides with a de facto banning of African-American performers on Broadway.

4. Robert L. Carringer cites contemporary reports in the trade press attributing *The Jazz Singer*'s stage popularity to a "massive promotional campaign aimed mainly at the Jewish community" and estimating that the audience was 90 percent composed of Jews. See the introduction of Carringer, ed., *The Jazz Singer* (Madison: University of Wisconsin Press, 1979), 13–14.

5. "It appeals to those who themselves have no deep feeling for the dogmatism of their fathers but who somehow feel that by seeing this play and weeping over it and cheering the boy's decision to come home and sing in *shul* they will in some mysterious way vicariously be cleansed." The Playgoer, "Cantors and Jazz-Singers in This Broadway Play," *Jewish Daily Forward*, Sept. 27, 1925, 3.

The following month, having gone to see Jolson in his current vehicle *Big Boy*, the same reviewer commented on the "relationship between suffering and song," noting various "points of resemblance between Negroes and Jews," and citing Jolson's affinity for Negro spirituals: "The son of a line of Rabbis well knows how to sing the songs of the most cruelly wronged people in the world's history." See The Playgoer, "A Brace of Comic Operas Has Captured New York," *Jewish Daily Forward*, Oct. 16, 1925, 3.

6. As the Warners had not intended to make "talking" pictures so much as automate the music that accompanied silent ones, this short spoken interlude has been credited with destroying the silent cinema. In fact, research done by Donald Crafton and others suggests that it was the tremendous success of Jolson's second partial-talkie, *The Singing Fool* a year later, that confirmed the viability of sound pictures.

7. Sander Gilman, *The Jew's Body* (New York: Routledge, 1991), 238.

**1935**

Nuremberg Laws restrict the civil rights of German Jews

Italy attacks Ethiopia

Isaac Bashevis Singer emigrates from Poland to the U.S.

Audimeter appears as research tool, becomes basis of Nielsen ratings

George and Ira Gershwin's *Porgy and Bess* has world premiere in Boston

Rouben Mamoulian directs first full Technicolor feature, *Becky Sharp*

**1936**

Stalin launches mass terror, arresting and executing millions in the U.S.S.R.

Civil War begins in Spain

Fanny Brice introduces her character "Baby Snooks" to radio listeners

Charlie Chaplin releases *Modern Times*

Joseph Green's *Yidl mitnfidl* opens in Warsaw, first Yiddish talkie to enjoy international success

CBS Columbia Workshop begins broadcasting radio dramas, including works by Norman Corwin and Archibald MacLeish

**1937**

German airship *Hindenburg* bursts into flames while landing in New Jersey

Film version of *The Dybbuk* opens in Warsaw

Broadcast performers' union AFTRA inaugurated

Paul Muni stars in the Warner Bros. film, *The Life of Emile Zola*

J. HOBERMAN
**The Jazz Singer: A Chronology**

1. Frances planned for years to write a novel about Hollywood that would open with the premier of *The Jazz Singer*. See A. Scott Berg, *Goldwyn: A Biography* (New York: Alfred A. Knopf, 1989), 175.

2. *The Jazz Singer* was released in Poland under the title *Kol Nidre*.

3. Jolson appeared in some form or other in six subsequent Warner Bros. cartoons: *Cleaner Pastures* (1937); *Porky's Preview* (1941); the government-produced *Any Bonds Today* (1941), in which Bugs Bunny blacks up to impersonate Jolson; *Swooner Crooner* (1944); *Curtain Razor* (1948); and the Bugs Bunny bio-pic *What's Up, Doc?* (1950).

4. Brustein dates this production to summer 1952, but other information in his account, including his reference to Jolson's recent death, suggest that it was likely staged the previous summer. See Robert Brustein, "Boris and the Second Avenue Muse: A Memoir," *The Third Theater* (New York: Alfred A. Knopf, 1969), 262–76.

5. Krin Gabard speculates that complaints about this scene account for the absence of blackface in *The Jazz Singer* remake that would also be directed by Michael Curtiz and would feature Danny Thomas. See Gabard, *Jammin' at the Margins: Jazz and the American Cinema* (Chicago: University of Chicago Press, 1996), 299.

6. As Gabard observes, the cantor is not only thoroughly assimilated into American society, but he "also appears to be comfortable with popular culture, at one point singing every word of a rapid-fire soap commercial that his son has recorded for radio. The father's demand that his son follow in a family tradition of several generations of cantors takes on the marks of a neurotic symptom, a familiar convention during Hollywood's romance with psychoanalysis in the 1950s" (47). However, the romantic interest, played by Peggy Lee is coded as Gentile but designated Jewish. Invited to the cantor's house for Passover, she remarks that she hasn't attended a seder since she left home.

7. As late as 2000, the sixty-six-year-old Baldwin was touring the U.S., Great Britain, and Australia with his nostalgic blackfaced Jolson impersonation. See Joe Hagan, "An Incorrect Artifact with Aging Fans," *New York Times*, Oct. 22, 2000, sec. 2, p. 34.

8. "There is only one person who can bridge the cultural gap that stretches between Jews of the MTV generation and Jews of the Benny Goodman era. That person is the Jewish Elvis, the Jazz Singer, the true king of pop. That person is Neil Diamond. At a recent concert of his in Ft. Lauderdale, I sat with men and women using walkers and hearing aids. They assumed I knew Yiddish simply because I was there." So begins Seth Mnookin's celebration of Diamond, "The 'Jewish Elvis' Rocks On after 30 Years, Linking the MTV Generation to Its Elders," *Forward*, Dec. 17, 1999, 11. Although Mnookin brackets Diamond with Jewish singer-songwriter contemporaries Bob Dylan and Carole King, he neglects Barbra Streisand, with whom Diamond attended high school in Brooklyn and many years later recorded the 1979 chart-topping duet, "You Don't Bring Me Flowers."

9. Michael Rogin, *Blackface, White Noise: Jewish Immigrants in the Hollywood Melting Pot* (Berkeley and Los Angeles: University of California Press, 1996), 89.

MARK SLOBIN
**Putting Blackface in Its Place**

1. Michael Rogin, *Blackface, White Noise: Jewish Immigrants in the Hollywood Melting*

**1938**

Germany annexes Austria and parts of Czechoslovakia

Nazis attack Jews and destroy their property throughout Germany during Kristallnacht

Orson Welles's radio adaptation of H. G. Wells's *War of the Worlds* creates widespread panic in the U.S.

Jazz clarinetist Benny Goodman and his orchestra play at Carnegie Hall

Superman debuts as comic book character

**1939**

Hitler warns that war in Europe will result in the "annihilation of the Jewish race"

Germany invades Poland, starting World War II

The *St. Louis*, carrying several hundred Jewish refugees, is not allowed to land in a U.S. port

John Steinbeck publishes *The Grapes of Wrath*

RCA television demonstrated at New York World's Fair

*Tevye*, the most lavish Yiddish talkie produced in the U.S., opens in New York

MGM releases *Gone with the Wind*

**1940**

Paris falls to the Germans

Trotsky assassinated in Mexico

F. Scott Fitzgerald dies, leaving *The Last Tycoon* unfinished

*The Great Dictator*, directed by Charlie Chaplin, satirizes Hitler and Mussolini

Hank Greenberg has career-high .340 batting average

Budd Schulberg publishes *What Makes Sammy Run?*

Pot (Berkeley and Los Angeles: University of California Press, 1996). For an extended account of the interaction between African- and Jewish-Americans in the arena of popular song, see Jeffrey Melnick, *A Right to Sing the Blues* (Cambridge, Mass.: Harvard University Press, 1999).

2. Stuart Hall, "What Is This 'Black' in Black Popular Culture?" in *Representing Blackness: Issues in Film and Video*, ed. Valerie Smith (New Brunswick, N.J.: Rutgers University Press, 1997), 123–34.

3. Dale Cockrell, *Demons of Disorder: Early Blackface Minstrels and Their World* (Cambridge, U.K.: Cambridge University Press, 1997); Eric Lott, *Love and Theft: Blackface Minstrelsy and the American Working Class* (New York: Oxford University Press, 1993); and William J. Mahar, *Behind the Burnt Cork Mask: Early Blackface Minstrelsy and Antebellum American Popular Culture* (Urbana: University of Illinois Press, 1998), are just three books marking an upsurge of interest in the topic of minstrelsy.

4. Charles Hamm, *Yesterday: Popular Song in America* (New York: Norton, 1979), 184.

5. Edward B. Marks, *They All Sang: From Tony Pastor to Rudy Vallee* (New York: Viking Press,

1934). Quotations are from pp. 50 and 84.

6. Hamm, *Yesterday*, 182.

7. Marks, *They All Sang*, 174.

8. Robert L. Carringer has obligingly included a complete listing of the soundtrack music in a modern edition of the script he edited, *The Jazz Singer* (Madison: University of Wisconsin Press, 1979).

9. Hamm, *Yesterday*, 339.

10. Susan Gubar, *Racechanges: White Skin, Black Face in American Culture* (New York: Oxford University Press, 1997), 75.

11. Rogin, *Blackface, White Noise*, 219.

12. Elmer Bernstein, "The Man with the Golden Arm," *Film Music* (1956): 3–13.

13. Leith Stevens, "The Wild One," *Film Music* (1954): 3–5.

14. Patricia Williams, "Racial Ventriloquism," *Nation*, July 5, 1999, 9.

15. Paul Gilroy, *Against Race: Imagining Political Culture beyond the Color Line* (Cambridge, Mass.: Harvard University Press, 2000).

## AN AMERICAN AT HOME, A JEW ON THE AIR

J. HOBERMAN AND JEFFREY SHANDLER

**Introduction**

1. Erik Barnouw, *The Golden Web: A History of Broadcasting in the United States, 1933–1953* (New York: Oxford University Press, 1968), 6.

2. Gerald Nachman, *Raised on Radio* (New York: Pantheon, 1998), 4.

3. Susan J. Douglas, *Listening In: Radio and the American Imagination* (New York: Times Books, 1999), 123.

4. See Henry Sapoznik, "Broadcast Ghetto: The Image of Jews on Mainstream American Radio," *Jewish Folklore and Ethnology Review* 16, no. 1 (1994): 37–39; and Melvin Patric Ely, *The Adventures of Amos 'n' Andy: A Social History of an American Phenomenon* (New York: Free Press, 1991).

5. See, for example, Alfred McClung Lee and Elizabeth Briant Lee, eds., *The Fine Art of Propaganda: A Study of Father Coughlin's Speeches* (New York: Harcourt, Brace, 1939); and *Father Coughlin: His "Facts" and Arguments* (New York and Washington, D.C.: General Jewish Council, 1939).

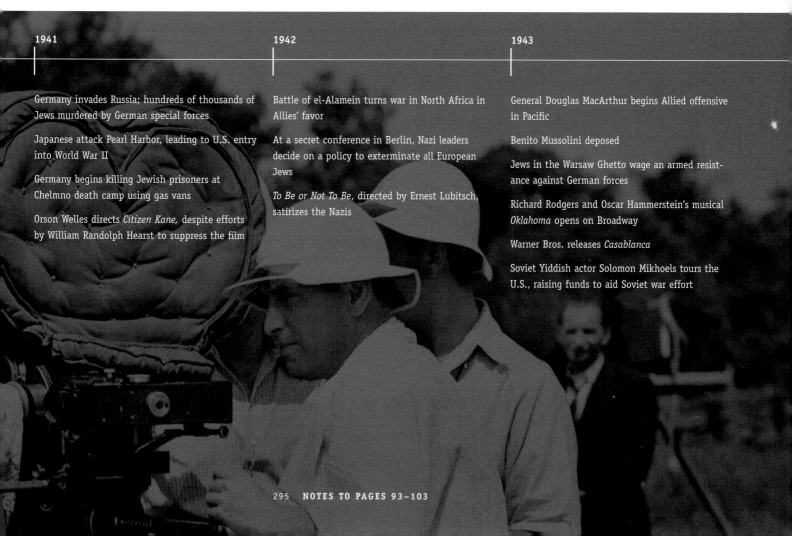

**1941**

Germany invades Russia; hundreds of thousands of Jews murdered by German special forces

Japanese attack Pearl Harbor, leading to U.S. entry into World War II

Germany begins killing Jewish prisoners at Chelmno death camp using gas vans

Orson Welles directs *Citizen Kane*, despite efforts by William Randolph Hearst to suppress the film

**1942**

Battle of el-Alamein turns war in North Africa in Allies' favor

At a secret conference in Berlin, Nazi leaders decide on a policy to exterminate all European Jews

*To Be or Not To Be*, directed by Ernest Lubitsch, satirizes the Nazis

**1943**

General Douglas MacArthur begins Allied offensive in Pacific

Benito Mussolini deposed

Jews in the Warsaw Ghetto wage an armed resistance against German forces

Richard Rodgers and Oscar Hammerstein's musical *Oklahoma* opens on Broadway

Warner Bros. releases *Casablanca*

Soviet Yiddish actor Solomon Mikhoels tours the U.S., raising funds to aid Soviet war effort

J. HOBERMAN AND JEFFREY SHANDLER

**The Media That "Speak Your Language":
American Yiddish Radio and Film**

1. On the history of Yiddish film, see J. Hoberman, *Bridge of Light: Yiddish Film between Two Worlds* (New York: Museum of Modern Art and Schocken, 1991).

2. Henry Sapoznick, *Klezmer! Jewish Music from Old World to Our World* (New York: Schirmer Books, 1999), 130.

3. See the Yiddish Radio Project website: www.yiddishradioproject.org.

4. Sapoznik, *Klezmer!*, 144.

5. See Henry Sapoznik, "Broadcast Ghetto: The Image of Jews on Mainstream American Radio," *Jewish Folklore and Ethnology Review* 16, no. 1 (1994): 37–39.

6. Joshua A. Fishman, *Yiddish in America: Sociolinguistic Description and Analysis* (Bloomington: Indiana University Press, 1965).

7. For a case study of the American Yiddish radio audience at the end of the twentieth century, see Shulamis Dion, "The Simkha that Speaks Your Language! (But Is It Art?)," *Jewish Folklore and Ethnology Review* 16, no. 1 (1994): 6–8.

DONALD WEBER

**Goldberg Variations: The Achievements of Gertrude Berg**

1. Gilbert Seldes, "The Great Gertrude," *Saturday Review*, June 2, 1956, 26. For an overview of Berg's career, see Cary O'Dell, "Gertrude Berg Calls the Shots," *Television Quarterly* 28, no. 3 (1996): 50–56; and O'Dell, *Women Pioneers in Television: Biographies of Fifteen Industry Leaders* (Jefferson, N.C.: McFarland, 1997), 41–51 (includes a good chronology of Berg's career, 49–50). According to Rick Mitz's *The Great TV Sitcom Book* (New York: Perigee, 1983), 14, Berg may have written as many as ten thousand radio and television scripts. In a 1949 *Life* magazine profile, Berg is pictured surrounded by a literal mountain of scripts. See "The Goldbergs March On," *Life*, Apr. 25, 1949, 59.

    In preparing this essay I have drawn on the following essays: "Memory and Repression in Early Ethnic Television: The Example of Gertrude Berg and *The Goldbergs*," in *The Other Fifties: Interrogating Midcentury American Icons*, ed. Joel Foreman (Urbana: University of Illinois Press, 1997), 144–167; "The Jewish-American World of Gertrude Berg: *The Goldbergs* on Radio and Television, 1930–1950," in *Talking Back: Images of Jewish Women in American Popular Culture*,

ed. Joyce Antler (Hanover: University Press of New England, 1998), 85–99, 262–65; and "Taking Jewish American Popular Culture Seriously: The Yinglish Worlds of Gertrude Berg, Milton Berle, and Mickey Katz," *Jewish Social Studies* 5 (1999): 124–53.

2. Letters in Notebooks, 1931–32, Berg Papers, Syracuse University Library, Syracuse, N.Y.

3. See, for example, these early profiles: Hilda Kassell, "An Off-Stage View of Molly Goldberg," *American Hebrew and Jewish Tribune*, Oct. 21, 1932, 419; Lorraine Thomas, "The Rise of Molly Goldberg," *Radio Guide*, Nov. 17, 1939, 13, 43; and Mel Heimer, "'Pushcarts' Keep Her on Park Avenue," *Pictorial Review*, Sept. 13, 1953, 4–5. All these articles are in the Scrapbook, according to year, Berg Papers, Syracuse University Library.

4. For the origins of *The Goldbergs*, see Gertrude Berg, "The Goldbergs Are Born," in *Molly and Me* (New York: McGraw-Hill, 1961), 174–94.

5. Gertrude Berg, "Why I Hate the Term 'Soap Opera,'" *Everywoman's Magazine* (Feb. 1945), 28.

6. Notebook, 1931–32, Berg Papers.

7. For this characterization of 1930s America, see Warren I. Susman, "The Culture of the Thirties,"

**1944**

D-Day invasion of Normandy, France

Camp for Jewish war refugees opened at Oswego, N.Y.

Jewish Theological Seminary and NBC initiate *The Eternal Light* radio broadcasts

Columbia releases *None Shall Escape*, first Hollywood movie to acknowledge German genocide of Europe's Jews

**1945**

President Roosevelt dies; Harry S. Truman becomes president

Germany surrenders to Allied forces after Hitler commits suicide

America drops two atomic bombs on Japanese cities; war ends in the Pacific

The American Jewish Committee inaugurates *Commentary* magazine

Bess Myerson is first Jewish woman to win the Miss America Pageant

**1946**

United Nations General Assembly holds first meeting

International war crimes tribunals commence in Nuremberg

Production and sale of television sets resume in the U.S.

Frank Capra directs *It's a Wonderful Life*

in *Culture as History: The Transformation of American Society in the Twentieth Century* (New York: Pantheon, 1984), 150–83.

8. Berg, *Molly and Me*, 179. Berg appeared on *Person to Person* on June 4, 1954. Murrow began the interview by asking Berg to lean outside a window of her Park Avenue duplex apartment and voice her famous "Yoo-hoo, is anybody?" phrase. Tape 269, National Jewish Archive of Broadcasting, The Jewish Museum, New York.

9. Radio and TV Scripts, 1930, Berg Papers. A year later, Berg transcribed this exchange in the published short-story version of the episode. See Gertrude Berg, *The Rise of the Goldbergs* (New York: Barse and Co., 1931), 219–20.

10. I use the term *sediment* in the sense employed by George Lipsitz in his important analysis of the meaning of early ethnic television. Popular culture, Lipsitz argues, often contains layers of historical memory "sedimented" in the very forms themselves. At times, audiences respond to these "textured layers of immigrant experience" and use them to resist the authorizing ideas of the contemporary moment. George Lipsitz, "The Meaning of Memory: Family, Class, and Ethnicity in Early Network Television," in *Times Passages: Collective Memory and American Popular Culture*

(Minneapolis: University of Minnesota Press, 1990), 71, 48.

11. Notebooks, 1935, 1943, 1949, Berg Papers.

12. Notebooks, Berg Papers.

13. General Scrapbooks 1934, Berg Papers.

14. Notebooks. Berg Papers.

15. Comic Strip Scrapbook 1944, Berg Papers.

16. Brooks Atkinson, review of *Me and Molly*, *New York Times*, Mar. 7, 1948. For the record, in the winter of 1948 these were among the plays on Broadway: Ethel Merman in *Annie Get Your Gun*; Judy Holliday in *Born Yesterday*; Eva Le Gallienne in *Hedda Gabler*; Judith Anderson in *Medea*; Henry Fonda in *Mister Roberts*; John Garfield in *Skipper Next to God*; Helen Hayes in *Happy Birthday*; and *A Streetcar Named Desire*.

17. See "The Goldbergs March On," *Life*, Apr. 25, 1949, 59–62.

18. According to Lynn Spigel, Milton Berle wanted *The Goldbergs* to become a regular sketch in order to revitalize his floundering *Texaco Star Theater* variety show. Berg made a few guest appearances on *Texaco*, notably in 1952 and 1953. In one case, the plot turns on Milton's

misunderstanding that he's agreed to perform for Molly's Bronx social club. On the relation between Berg and Berle, see Spigel, *Make Room for TV: Television and the Family Ideal in Postwar America* (Chicago: University of Chicago Press, 1992), esp. 149.

19. This episode, which aired on Sept. 5, 1949, may be screened at the Museum of Television and Radio, New York (videotape T7650).

20. On the Loeb affair and TV blacklisting in general, see Merle Miller, *The Judges and the Judged* (New York: Doubleday, 1952); and Stefan Kanfer, *A Journal of the Plague Years* (New York: Athenaeum, 1973). For contemporary journalism on Loeb, see "Loeb and Red Channels," *New Republic*, Jan. 1, 1952, 8; and "Red Channels Rides Again," *New Republic*, Feb. 18, 1952, 22. For an evaluation of his life, see the moving column by Murray Kempton, "The Victim," *New York Post*, Sept. 13, 1955. See also Lipsitz, "The Meaning of Memory," 62–63.

The Philip Loeb Papers at the New York Public Library hold precious little information about the Loeb case. There are, however, letters of encouragement from such figures as Harold Clurman and Elia Kazan, and copies of letters protesting Loeb's firing from outraged fans of *The*

---

## 1947

U.S. Congress adopts Marshall Plan for reconstruction of Europe

House Committee on Un-American Activities investigates alleged Communist influence in Hollywood

John Garfield stars in *Body and Soul*

Movies *Crossfire* and *Gentleman's Agreement* address subject of anti-Semitism

Jackie Robinson joins Brooklyn Dodgers, integrating major league baseball

## 1948

United Nations votes to partition Palestine; Israel declares its independence

Soviets blockade Berlin

NATO established

Truman outlaws segregation in the U.S. military

Yugoslavian leader Marshal Tito expelled from Comintern

Communist coup in Czechoslovakia

Yiddish actor Solomon Mikhoels murdered by Soviet secret police

Milton Berle and Ed Sullivan launch variety programs on television

## 1949

Communists take control of Chinese mainland

Russians explode their first atomic bomb

Arthur Miller wins Pulitzer Prize for *Death of a Salesman*

U.S. Supreme Court compels Hollywood studios to sell their movie theaters

George Orwell publishes *1984*

*The Goldbergs* makes television debut

National Academy of Television Arts and Sciences presents the first Emmy Awards

*Goldbergs.* The most interesting material on Loeb is gathered in the Berg Papers, which contain a scrapbook filled with clippings from the New York press about the case. From my reading, important local journalists like Victor Reisel and Ed Sullivan (before he became a TV show variety host) were staunchly in favor of Loeb's dismissal. In the end, under pressure from the Internal Revenue Service and mounting medical bills for his institutionalized son, Loeb, who had been living at Zero Mostel's apartment on West Eighty-Sixth Street, tragically gave up the fight for his political and professional integrity and committed suicide. Mostel eventually honored the memory of his friend's tragic life by playing a version of Loeb ("Hecky Green") in *The Front* (Columbia, 1976), Martin Ritt's attack on the sordid era of blacklisting in early television.

21. Morris Freedman, "The Real Molly Goldberg," *Commentary* 21 (Apr. 1956): 359–60. Interestingly, the Loeb case is not discussed in this piece. A year earlier, in the *Person to Person* interview, Murrow does not ask Berg about the Loeb matter either.

22. Nan Robertson, "Molly in Japan," *New York Times,* Feb. 15, 1959, 1.

23. Seldes, "The Great Gertrude," 26.

### Religion, Democracy, and Radio Waves: *The Eternal Light*

1. For a more detailed history of *The Eternal Light,* see Jeffrey Shandler and Elihu Katz, "Broadcasting American Judaism: The Radio and Television Department of the Jewish Theological Seminary," in *Tradition Renewed: A History of the Jewish Theological Seminary,* ed. Jack Wertheimer (New York: Jewish Theological Seminary, 1997), 363–401.

2. Philip Roth, *The Ghost Writer* (1979; reprint, New York: Ballantine, 1983), 106–7.

3. "The Eternal Light: Tenth Anniversary Year, brochure" (New York: 1954), 7; see Jewish Theological Seminary Archives, RG 11C, box 30, folder 33.

J. HOBERMAN AND JEFFREY SHANDLER

### "The Vanishing Jew"

1. N. L. Rothman blames the rise of Jewish comedians on Jewish motion picture producers: "Where else, in the history of civilization, can such a spectacle be seen or imagined—a race in self-ridicule, selling its pride for a mess of

money!" See Rothman, "The Jew on Screen," *Jewish Forum* 11, no. 10 (Oct. 1928): 528.

2. Goldman goes on to cite the changed names, elevated diction, tasteful clothes, and presumed corrective surgery of Jewish comedians such as Jack Benny and Danny Kaye. According to Goldman, it was Sid Caesar and his writers who introduced Jewishness into American popular culture, followed by Lenny Bruce and other stand-up comedians. Like Popkin's essay, Goldman's piece is a valedictory, claiming that the "golden age" of Jewish comedy was over, as indicated by the disappearance of nightclubs and TV variety shows giving way to situation comedy. Albert Goldman, "Laughtermakers," in *Next Year in Jerusalem: Portraits of Jews in the Twentieth Century* (New York: Viking Press, 1976), 220–32.

J. HOBERMAN AND JEFFREY SHANDLER

### Our *Show of Shows*

1. Wallace Markfield, "The Yiddishization of American Humor," *Esquire,* Oct. 1965, 114.

2. Irving Howe, *World of Our Fathers: The Journey of the East European Jews to America and the Life They Found and Made* (New York: Harcourt Brace Jovanovich, 1976), 569.

---

**1950**

Korean War begins

Senator Joseph McCarthy declares that the U.S. State Department has been infiltrated by Communists

*Red Channels* lists broadcast artists suspected of supporting Communism

Richard Nixon defeats Helen Gahagan Douglas in California senate race

Billy Wilder directs *Sunset Boulevard*

*Your Show of Shows* premieres on NBC

**1951**

Anti-Communist blacklisting institutionalized at broadcasting networks and talent agencies

Jewish-American author and journalist Abraham Cahan dies at age ninety-one

J. D. Salinger publishes *The Catcher in the Rye*

*I Love Lucy* premieres on CBS

Movie attendance drops sharply in cities with television

Louis B. Mayer retires from MGM

**1952**

Dwight Eisenhower elected president in first campaign to use TV ads; Republicans return to the White House for the first time in twenty years

U.S. successfully tests hydrogen bomb

*The Diary of a Young Girl* by Anne Frank appears in English translation

*Life Is with People: The Jewish Little-Town of Eastern Europe,* a landmark ethnography of Jewish life before the Holocaust, is published

Ralph Ellison publishes *Invisible Man*

298 **NOTES TO PAGES 122–44**

3. Ted Sennett, *Your Show of Shows* (New York: Collier, 1977), 22.

4. Interview with Carl Reiner in the documentary film *Next Time, Dear God, Please Choose Someone Else: The Legend of Jewish Humor* (1990); directed by Rex Bloomstein.

5. See David Marc, *Comic Visions* (Boston: Unwin Hyman, 1989), 91–120 passim. See also Vince Waldron, *The Official Dick Van Dyke Show Book: The Definitive History and Ultimate Viewer's Guide to Television's Most Enduring Comedy* (New York: Hyperion, 1994), 21–34 passim.

## STAR GALLERY

J. HOBERMAN AND JEFFREY SHANDLER
### Introduction

1. Richard Dyer, *Stars* (London: British Film Institute, 1979), 6ff, 22, 30.

J. HOBERMAN
### Theda Bara

1. Accounts of Theda Bara's initial launch may be found in Terry Ramsaye's *A Million and One Nights: A History of the Motion Picture through 1925* (New York: Simon and Schuster, 1926), 702–4; and *Upton Sinclair Presents William Fox* (Los Angeles: Upton Sinclair, 1933), 56–57. See also the witty recollection of *A Fool There Was*, "Cloudland-Revisited: The Wickedest Woman in Larchmont," anthologized in *The Most of S. J. Perelman* (New York: Simon and Schuster, 1963), 618–23.

2. Theda Bara, "How I Became a Film Vampire," *Forum* 61 (June 1919), 83; and Ronald Genini, *Theda Bara: A Biography of the Silent Screen Vamp, with a Filmography* (Jefferson, N.C.: McFarland and Company, 1996), 7.

3. Genini, *Theda Bara*, 81. In 1919, Bara tried to change her image by playing an innocent peasant girl in *Kathleen Mavoureen* (Fox), which was advertised as "The Sweetest Irish Love Story Ever Told." According to Ronald Genini, "Hibernian societies caused chaos at many theaters because an Irish heroine was being played by a Jewish actress." Genini cites a riot at a San Francisco theater in which, "inflamed by two Catholic priests," a mob "rioted and caused $3,000 damage to the theater and its projection equipment." Released from her Fox contract, Bara made a disastrous return to the stage and soon after retired.

4. Ramsaye, *A Million and One Nights*, 704; and Bram Dijkstra, *Evil Sisters: The Threat of Female Sexuality and the Cult of Manhood* (New York: Alfred A. Knopf, 1996), 261. Dijkstra links Bara to those "sexual terrorists, socialists, [and] subversive agents" whom certain early-twentieth-century American white supremacists imagined pouring out of Asia—"Bolshevism with Semitic leadership and Chinese executioners"—to overwhelm the Nordic race.

5. Genini, *Theda Bara*, 19.

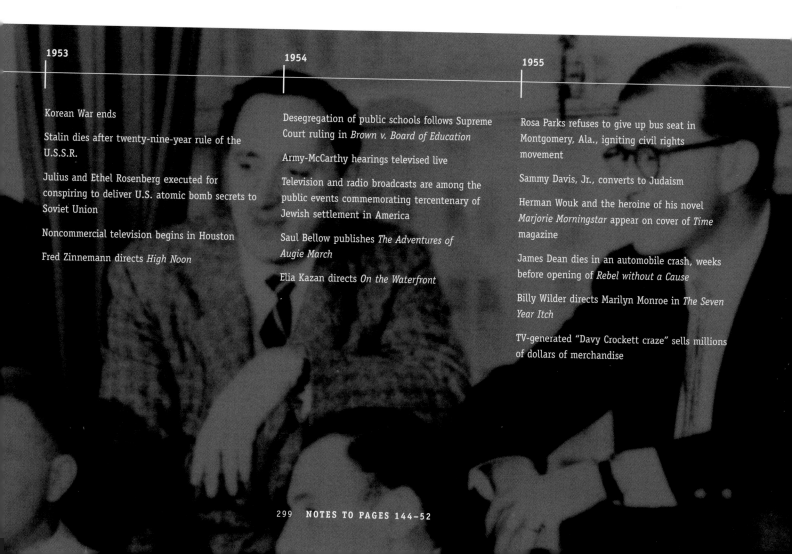

**1953**

Korean War ends

Stalin dies after twenty-nine-year rule of the U.S.S.R.

Julius and Ethel Rosenberg executed for conspiring to deliver U.S. atomic bomb secrets to Soviet Union

Noncommercial television begins in Houston

Fred Zinnemann directs *High Noon*

**1954**

Desegregation of public schools follows Supreme Court ruling in *Brown v. Board of Education*

Army-McCarthy hearings televised live

Television and radio broadcasts are among the public events commemorating tercentenary of Jewish settlement in America

Saul Bellow publishes *The Adventures of Augie March*

Elia Kazan directs *On the Waterfront*

**1955**

Rosa Parks refuses to give up bus seat in Montgomery, Ala., igniting civil rights movement

Sammy Davis, Jr., converts to Judaism

Herman Wouk and the heroine of his novel *Marjorie Morningstar* appear on cover of *Time* magazine

James Dean dies in an automobile crash, weeks before opening of *Rebel without a Cause*

Billy Wilder directs Marilyn Monroe in *The Seven Year Itch*

TV-generated "Davy Crockett craze" sells millions of dollars of merchandise

## J. HOBERMAN
### Bronco Billy Anderson

1. Ezra Goodman, *The Fifty-Year Decline and Fall of Hollywood* (New York: Simon and Schuster, 1961), 341.

2. Harry Golden, "Bronco Billy: Straight Shooter," *Philadelphia Evening Bulletin*, Feb. 15, 1971.

## J. HOBERMAN AND JEFFREY SHANDLER
### Fanny Brice

1. Eve Bernstein, "Fanny Brice Tells Her Story," *Jewish Tribune*, Dec. 28, 1928.

2. Herbert G. Goldman, *Fanny Brice: The Original Funny Girl* (New York: Oxford University Press, 1992), 112, 136.

3. Abel., *Variety*, Sept. 25, 1968. *Funny Girl* (Columbia, 1968) was followed in 1975 by the less successful sequel, *Funny Lady* (Columbia).

4. Camille Paglia, "Brooklyn Nefertiti: Barbra Streisand," in *Vamps and Tramps* (New York: Vintage Books, 1994), 141–45.

5. Sander L. Gilman, *Making the Body Beautiful: A Cultural History of Aesthetic Surgery* (Princeton: Princeton University Press, 1999), 204–5.

## J. HOBERMAN
### Eddie Cantor

1. Herbert G. Goldman, *Banjo Eyes: Eddie Cantor and the Birth of Modern Stardom* (New York: Oxford University Press, 1997), 57, 100.

2. *Among the Indians or The Country Peddler*, a Yiddish vaudeville routine about two Jewish salesmen out West, was first performed in 1895 at the Windsor Theater on the Lower East Side. The Indians spoke broken Yiddish. See Mark Slobin's translation, "From Vilna to Vaudeville: Minikes and among the Indians," *Drama Review* 24, no. 3 (Sept. 1980). Fannie Brice also had a Yiddish-inflected Indian number, "Look on Me, I'm an Indian." Nathanael West included a Yiddish-accented movie Indian, Chief Kiss-My-Towkus, in his 1939 Hollywood novel *Day of the Locust* (1939). In the most recent example of this venerable joke, Mel Brooks cast himself as a Yiddish-speaking Indian chief in *Blazing Saddles* (Warner Bros., 1974).

3. Ernest Rogers, *Variety*, Nov. 6, 1929. See the chapter "'Shall We Make It for New York or for Distribution?' Eddie Cantor, Whoopee, and Regional Resistance to the Talkies" in Henry Jenkins, *What Made Pistachio Nuts? Early Sound Comedy and the Vaudeville Aesthetic* (New York: Columbia University Press, 1992). Jenkins writes that "the de-Semitization of Eddie Cantor was simply one aspect of a complex process by which stage stars were repackaged in order to appeal to a broader national audience. Depression era America was still polarized around regional and ethnic differences and still distrustful of the increasingly important place of the city within its culture" (182).

The studio biography prepared for *Palmy Days* (United Artists, 1931) cited Cantor's "Russian background," while, according to Jenkins, Cantor told the audience at the film's New York premiere that, while he hoped they enjoyed the picture, it wasn't made for them: "It was made for the masses." (At the same time, Jenkins notes, United Artists took care to direct press releases specifically to the Yiddish press.) In *A Right to Sing the Blues: African Americans, Jews, and American Popular Song* (Cambridge, Mass.: Harvard University Press, 1999), Jeffrey Melnick suggests that Cantor's escape from blackface "seems to dovetail with a move away from his self-identification as a Jewish performer" (113). In fact, the opposite is true. Cantor began to minimize his use of blackface as soon as he became a Ziegfeld star, even as he incorporated Jewish jokes

**1956**

Backed by Great Britain and France, Israel attacks Egypt

Soviets suppress anti-Communist revolt in Hungary

Drama anthology series *Playhouse 90* begins broadcasting

Elvis Presley appears three times on *The Ed Sullivan Show*

Marilyn Monroe marries Arthur Miller and converts to Judaism

Cecil B. DeMille releases remake of *The Ten Commandments*

First use of videotape by American television broadcasters

**1957**

U.S. Army occupies Little Rock, Ark., to enforce integration of public schools

U.S.S.R. launches Sputnik I

Dodgers and Giants depart New York for California

*West Side Story*, a collaboration of Arthur Laurents, Leonard Bernstein, and Stephen Sondheim, debuts on Broadway

Jack Kerouac publishes *On the Road*

**1958**

Charles de Gaulle becomes Premier of France

Eisenhower sends U.S. troops to Lebanon

Leon Uris publishes *Exodus*

Vladimir Nabokov's *Lolita* is published in the U.S.

Sidney Poitier and Tony Curtis star in *The Defiant Ones*

and bits of Yiddish into his act. Indeed, Cantor only returned to blackface with *Palmy Days*, subsequently applying burnt cork in *Roman Scandals* (United Artists, 1933) and *Kid Millions* (United Artists, 1934).

4. Goldman, *Banjo Eyes*, xiii; and Gerald Nachman, *Raised on Radio* (New York: Pantheon, 1998), 45.

5. Goldman, *Banjo Eyes*, 4.

6. Ibid., 277–78.

### J. HOBERMAN AND JEFFREY SHANDLER
### The Marx Brothers

1. "Horse Feathers," *Time*, Aug. 13, 1932. In an unfinished memoir, S. J. Perelman describes a timorous visit he paid, along with fellow writer Arthur Sheekman, to Herman Mankiewicz, supervising producer of *Horse Feathers*:

> "What the devil do you want?" Mankiewicz barked. "Get the marbles out of your mouth."
>
> "Well, it's like this," I squeaked, moistening my lips. "In this sequence we're working on we're kind of perplexed about the identity of the Marx Brothers—the psychology of the characters they're supposed to represent, so to speak. I mean, who are they? We—we wondered if you could analyze or define them for us."
>
> "Oh you did, did you?" he grated. "O.K., I'll tell you in a word. One of them is a guinea, another a mute who picks up spit, and the third an old Hebe with a cigar."

See Perelman, *The Last Laugh* (New York: Simon and Schuster, 1981), 159–60.

2. Groucho Marx, *The Groucho Phile: An Illustrated Life* (Indianapolis: Bobbs-Merrill, 1976), 18. The joke is quoted in Neal Gabler, *An Empire of Their Own: How the Jews Invented Hollywood* (New York: Crown, 1988), 276. Woody Allen invokes this joke as a kind of quintessential Jewish prooftext (crediting it to Groucho and misattributing its origins to Freud's *Wit and Its Relation to the Unconscious*) during his opening monologue in *Annie Hall* (United Artists, 1977). Richard Raskin devotes a chapter of his study of "classic Jewish jokes" to this joke. See Raskin, *Life Is Like a Glass of Tea* (Aarhus, Denmark: Aarhus University Press, 1992), 121–30. Raskin notes that, according to Arthur Marx's *Life with Groucho* (New York: Simon and Schuster, 1954), the club in question was the Friar's Club. In his own memoir *Groucho and Me* (New York: Bernard Geis, 1959), Groucho names it the Delaney Club, a fictitious name.

3. Lester D. Friedman, *Hollywood's Image of the Jew* (New York: Ungar, 1982), 66. These references can be extratextual. In his biography of Groucho, Hector Arce compares the Marx Brothers' maternal grandfather, the itinerant fairground performer Lafe Schoenberg, to Isaac Bashevis Singer's Magician of Lublin. See Arce, *Groucho* (New York: Putnam, 1979). Commenting on a photograph of the "bar mitzvah–aged" Julius Marx standing with his older brother on a New York City apartment house stoop, the Anglo-Israeli writer Simon Louvish imagines that the young Groucho not only has "a face that can only be described as typically European Jewish," but that "he looks oddly like the child in the famous Holocaust photograph who is being hustled away by German soldiers, with his hands up." See Simon Louvish, *Monkey Business: The Lives and Legends of the Marx Brothers* (London: Faber and Faber, 1999), 37.

4. Friedman, *Hollywood's Image of the Jew*, 65.

5. Long after their retirement and even posthumously, the Marx Brothers have endured as

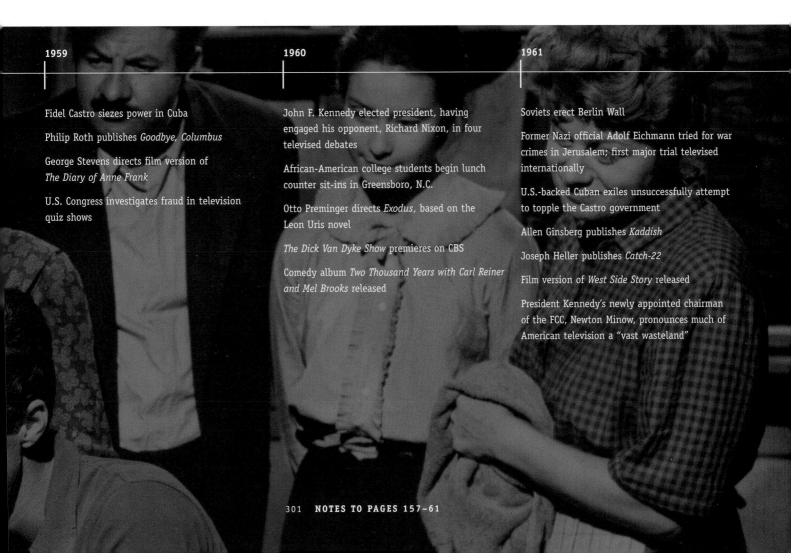

**1959**

Fidel Castro siezes power in Cuba

Philip Roth publishes *Goodbye, Columbus*

George Stevens directs film version of *The Diary of Anne Frank*

U.S. Congress investigates fraud in television quiz shows

**1960**

John F. Kennedy elected president, having engaged his opponent, Richard Nixon, in four televised debates

African-American college students begin lunch counter sit-ins in Greensboro, N.C.

Otto Preminger directs *Exodus*, based on the Leon Uris novel

*The Dick Van Dyke Show* premieres on CBS

Comedy album *Two Thousand Years with Carl Reiner and Mel Brooks* released

**1961**

Soviets erect Berlin Wall

Former Nazi official Adolf Eichmann tried for war crimes in Jerusalem; first major trial televised internationally

U.S.-backed Cuban exiles unsuccessfully attempt to topple the Castro government

Allen Ginsberg publishes *Kaddish*

Joseph Heller publishes *Catch-22*

Film version of *West Side Story* released

President Kennedy's newly appointed chairman of the FCC, Newton Minow, pronounces much of American television a "vast wasteland"

show-business icons, with particular talismanic significance for Jewish performers. The brothers' youthful vaudeville exploits—as filtered through their on-screen personae—provided the basis for the Broadway musical *Minnie's Boys*, (1970), co-written by Groucho's son, Arthur Marx, and starring Shelley Winters as stage mother Minnie Marx. A decade later, the musical "double feature" *A Day in Hollywood/A Night in the Ukraine* featured a trio of Marx Brothers imitators—as well as a faux Margaret Dumont—disrupting a version of Anton Chekhov's one-act play *The Bear*.

Barbra Streisand attends a costume party in *The Way We Were* (Columbia, 1973) dressed as Harpo, while the Marx Brothers references characteristic of Woody Allen's movies begin with the Groucho masks worn by his character's parents in *Take the Money and Run* (Cinerama, 1969) and culminate with the costume party that ends *Everyone Says I Love You* (Miramax, 1996), in which the guests all appear as Groucho. This film also takes its title from a song Groucho sings in *Horse Feathers*. At the end of *Hannah and Her Sisters* (Orion, 1986), Allen's character receives an almost religious degree of comfort and inspiration from a viewing of the Marx Brothers in *Duck Soup*. Philip Roth conflates high and low Jewish modernism when he imagines a movie adapted from Franz Kafka's *The Castle* that would star Groucho as the land surveyor K., with Chico and Harpo playing his two assistants. See Roth, "On *Portnoy's Complaint*," in *Reading Myself and Others* (New York: Bantam Books, 1977), 19.

6. Sig Altman, *The Comic Image of the Jew: Explorations of a Pop Culture Phenomenon* (Rutherford, N.J.: Fairleigh Dickinson University Press, 1971), 188–89.

7. Patricia Erens, *The Jew in American Cinema* (Bloomington: Indiana University Press, 1984), 133.

8. James Yaffe, *The American Jews* (New York: Random House, 1968), 36–37.

9. Joel Rosenberg, "Jewish Experience on Film—An American Overview," *American Jewish Year Book 1996*, ed. David Singer (New York: American Jewish Committee, 1996), 17.

10. Ruth Perlmutter, "The Melting Plot and the Humoring of America: Hollywood and the Jew," *Film Reader 5* (Evanston, Ill.: Northwestern University Press, 1982), 253.

11. Charles Musser, "Role-playing and Film Comedy," in *Unspeakable Images: Ethnicity and the American Cinema*, ed. Lester D. Friedman (Urbana: University of Illinois Press, 1991), 63.

12. Esther Romeyn and Jack Kugelmass, *Let There Be Laughter! Jewish Humor in America* (Chicago: Spertas Press, 1997), 48.

13. Albert Goldman, "Laughtermakers," in *Jewish Wry: Essays on Jewish Humor*, ed. Sarah Blacher Cohen (Bloomington: Indiana University Press, 1987), 82

14. Mark Winokur, *American Laughter: Immigrants, Ethnicity and 1930s Hollywood Film Comedy* (New York: St. Martin's Press, 1996), 127.

15. Irving Howe, *World of Our Fathers: The Journey of the East European Jews to America and the Life They Found and Made* (New York: Harcourt Brace Jovanovich, 1976), 567.

16. Louvish, *Monkey Business*, 279.

AMELIA S. HOLBERG
**Betty Boop**

1. This article is adapted from the author's more extensive paper "Betty Boop: Yiddish Film Star," in *American Jewish History* 87, no. 4 (Dec. 1999): 291–312.

**1962**

Cuban Missile Crisis

First communications satellite launched into space

Violence erupts as James Meredith registers as the first African-American student at the University of Mississippi

John Glenn is first astronaut to orbit earth

*I Can Get It for You Wholesale*, a musical featuring Barbra Streisand, opens on Broadway

David Lean's *Lawrence of Arabia* opens

Jack Smith shoots *Flaming Creatures*

**1963**

President Kennedy assassinated; television networks air four days of news coverage

Atomic test-ban treaty signed with the U.S.S.R.

Martin Luther King delivers "I have a dream" speech at National March on Washington, D.C.

Betty Friedan publishes *The Feminine Mystique*

Los Angeles Dodgers pitcher Sandy Koufax wins Most Valuable Player award

Peter, Paul, and Mary record Bob Dylan's "Blowin' in the Wind"

Television networks expand nightly national news reports from fifteen minutes to a half hour

**1964**

Gulf of Tonkin resolution begins escalation of war in Vietnam

Three civil rights workers are murdered in Mississippi

President Lyndon Johnson signs Civil Rights Act

Johnson defeats Barry Goldwater in a landslide election

Palestinian Liberation Organization formed

The Beatles make their first appearance on *The Ed Sullivan Show*

Stand-up comedian Lenny Bruce tried for obscenity in New York

*Fiddler on the Roof*, starring Zero Mostel, opens on Broadway

Barbra Streisand stars in TV special, *Color Me Barbra*

2. The Hebrew characters representing *kosher* are almost a leitmotif in the Fleischer cartoons, and are sometimes used to make a joke that has a secondary meaning to audiences familiar with Jewish tradition. In Betty's screen debut, *Dizzy Dishes* (1930), hungry customers badger an enraged restaurateur. One yells, "I want ham!" The restaurateur hits him with a ham that is labeled "בשׂר"—a gag in and of itself, since ham could never be kosher. In *I'll Be Glad When You're Dead You Rascal You* (1932), Koko the Clown is literally "burning up the road," as he is chased around the world. Suddenly, his jacket begins to bulge and a thermometer pops out. At first the numbers rise as expected, but then the gauge reads "?," and then "!," and finally "בשׂר" The kosher sign is funny not only because of the unexpected Hebrew characters, but also because the way to *kasher* (make kosher) a dish is to hold it over an open flame of a certain temperature. Koko had run so fast, that he was now Kosher Koko. Unlike the ethnic humor of vaudeville, which poked fun through broad stereotypes, the Fleischers' references to the laws of kashruth required actual knowledge of Yiddish culture to get the entire joke, which indicates their insider status.

3. Betty's creator, Max Fleischer, was born in Vienna in 1889 and brought as a child by his immigrant Jewish parents to New York. A cartoonist and mechanical illustrator for *Popular Science Monthly*, he worked with his younger brother Dave, a film-cutter for Pathé, to invent the rotoscope, a device that in permitting the frame-by-frame tracing of live-action footage created the basis for the Fleischers' first star, Koko the Clown. (Their most successful and long-lived character would be Popeye the Sailor, whose popularity topped that of Mickey Mouse by the late 1930s.) The Fleischer Brothers were the last New York–based moguls; nearly the entire family was involved in some capacity with their studio before it relocated to Miami in 1938. Fleischer cartoons were originally released through Paramount. Although their characters would enjoy a long life on TV, they ceased production with the full-color, noirish Superman cartoons made in 1941 and 1942.

4. Mae Questel (1908–1998), the Bronx-born vaudevillian who provided Betty Boop's distinctive voice from 1931 through the character's retirement in 1939, subsequently played a number of specifically Jewish roles on stage and screen, including the skeptical Mrs. Strakosh in *Funny Girl* (Columbia, 1968). She is best known for her part as the great Jewish mother in the sky in Woody Allen's segment of the anthology film *New York Stories* (Touchstone, 1989).

J. HOBERMAN
**Superman**

1. Jules Feiffer, "Jerry Siegel: The Minsk Theory of Krypton," *New York Times Magazine*, Dec. 29, 1996, 14–15.

2. Jeff Salamon, "Up, Up, and Oy Vay!: The Further Adventures of Supermensch," *Village Voice*, Aug. 4, 1992, 86–88.

3. Batman and the Spirit, to name only two other masked superheroes of the 1940s, were also created by Jewish artists: Bob Kane and Will Eisner. In the course of his wide-ranging article (see n. 2), Salamon notes that the two men most instrumental in developing the Marvel Comics formula of the 1960s, Stan Lee and Jack Kirby, were Jews as well.

J. HOBERMAN AND JEFFREY SHANDLER
**Bess Myerson**

1. Edward S. Shapiro, *A Time for Healing: American Jewry since World War II* (Baltimore: Johns Hopkins University Press, 1992), 9.

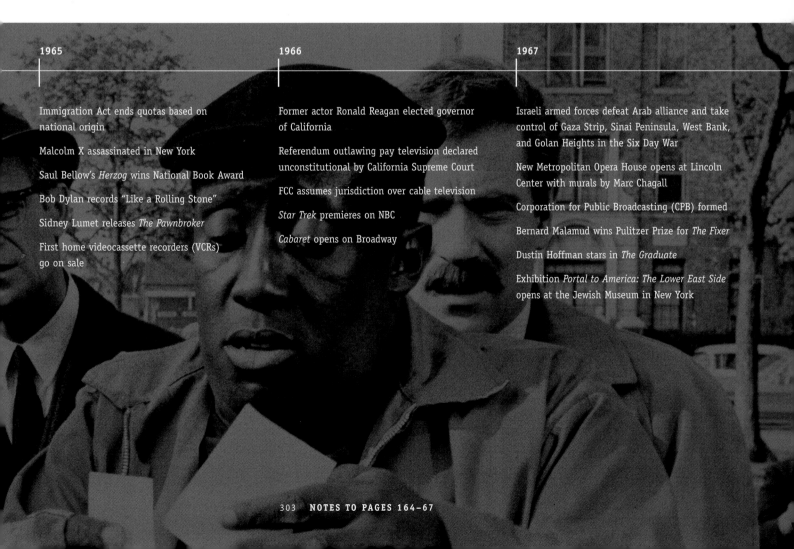

**1965**

Immigration Act ends quotas based on national origin

Malcolm X assassinated in New York

Saul Bellow's *Herzog* wins National Book Award

Bob Dylan records "Like a Rolling Stone"

Sidney Lumet releases *The Pawnbroker*

First home videocassette recorders (VCRs) go on sale

**1966**

Former actor Ronald Reagan elected governor of California

Referendum outlawing pay television declared unconstitutional by California Supreme Court

FCC assumes jurisdiction over cable television

*Star Trek* premieres on NBC

*Cabaret* opens on Broadway

**1967**

Israeli armed forces defeat Arab alliance and take control of Gaza Strip, Sinai Peninsula, West Bank, and Golan Heights in the Six Day War

New Metropolitan Opera House opens at Lincoln Center with murals by Marc Chagall

Corporation for Public Broadcasting (CPB) formed

Bernard Malamud wins Pulitzer Prize for *The Fixer*

Dustin Hoffman stars in *The Graduate*

Exhibition *Portal to America: The Lower East Side* opens at the Jewish Museum in New York

2. Shana Alexander, *When She Was Bad: The Story of Bess, Hortense, Sukhreet and Nancy* (New York: Random House, 1990), 28.

3. Ibid., 33–34.

4. Ibid., 41–42.

5. Bernard Weinraub, "At the Movies," *New York Times*, Mar. 26, 1999, E15.

J. HOBERMAN
**Judy Holliday**

1. Brog., "Born Yesterday," *Variety*, Nov. 22, 1950.

2. Will Holtzman, *Judy Holliday* (New York: Putnam, 1982), 3.

SAMUEL J. ROSENTHAL
**John Garfield**

1. This policy was, in fact, debated and memorialized during the preproduction stage of *Humoresque*. See Glazer to Wald, memorandum (undated), *Humoresque*, Warner Bros. Archives.

2. Mark Winokur, "Improbably Ethnic Hero: William Powell and the Transformation of Ethnic Hollywood," *Cinema Journal* 27, no. 1 (1987): 7.

3. *Philadelphia Jewish Times*, Nov. 11, 1938, 14; and *Los Angeles B'nai B'rith Messenger*, Jan. 27, 1939, 15.

4. Helen Zigmund, "Hollywood Chatter," *Boston Jewish Advocate*, Dec. 9, 1938, 12; Leon Gutterman, "Our Film Folk," *Philadelphia Jewish Exponent*, Mar. 31, 1950, 4; Zigmund, "Our Film Folk," *Philadelphia Jewish Times*, Oct. 17, 1941, 19; and *Philadelphia Jewish Exponent*, May 2, 1947, 17.

5. Dick Chase, "Hollywood Merry-Go-Round," *Los Angeles B'nai B'rith Messenger*, June 21, 1938, 7; "Our Film Folk," *Philadelphia Jewish Times*, Aug. 6, 1943; and Dick Chase, "Hollywood Merry-Go-Round," *Los Angeles B'nai B'rith Messenger*, June 21, 1938.

6. Phineas Baron, "Strictly Confidential," *Philadelphia Jewish Exponent*, 8; see also Tyle Brooke, "Movie Score," *Boston Jewish Advocate*, Apr. 3, 1947, 18.

7. Patricia Erens, *The Jew in American Cinema* (Bloomington: Indiana University Press, 1984), 181–82.

8. Nathan Norman Weiss, "Bostonian on Broadway," *Boston Jewish Advocate*, Nov. 20, 1947, 16.

9. Ben Feingold, "Broadway Tales," *Boston Jewish Advocate*, June 12, 1952, 11.

J. HOBERMAN
**Shelley Winters**

1. Winters has changed the date of her birth to Aug. 18, 1920, the day American women got the vote.

2. The *New York Post* reported that Winters planned to title her autobiography *The Myth of the Mensch*. Her publisher objected and the book appeared in 1980 as *Shelley: Also Known as Shirley*.

J. HOBERMAN
**Dustin Hoffman**

1. Renata Adler, *A Year in the Dark* (New York: Random House, 1969), 63.

2. Susan Applebaum and Ellen Bendow, "Is He Jewish?" Movie Mailbag, *New York Times*, Feb. 25, 1968. Mrs. Robinson (Anne Bancroft), the older woman with whom Benjamin has an affair, also seemed to possess some Jewish traits. Adler noted the Yiddish construction and inflection of her line "Now if you won't do me a simple favor I don't know what" and suggested

**1968**

Warsaw Pact nations invade Czechoslovakia, squelching Prague Spring

Martin Luther King and Senator Robert Kennedy assassinated

Antiwar protests at the Democratic National Convention

Johnson declines to run for reelection; Nixon elected president

Student protesters occupy buildings at Columbia University

New York teachers strike

New motion picture rating system introduced, using classifications G, PG, R, and X

Barbra Streisand stars in *Funny Girl*

Comedy-variety series *Rowan and Martin's Laugh-In* debuts on NBC

**1969**

Apollo 11 lands on moon

Stonewall Riots in Greenwich Village galvanize gay liberation movement

Golda Meir elected Prime Minister of Israel

Woodstock music festival attracts 300,000 enthusiasts

Philip Roth publishes *Portnoy's Complaint*

Public Broadcasting System (PBS) established; *Sesame Street* debuts

**1970**

President Gamal Abdul Nasser of Egypt dies, replaced by Anwar Sadat

Four students killed by National Guard during antiwar demonstration at Kent State University in Ohio

Chicago Seven convicted for inciting riots at 1968 Democratic National Convention

John Updike publishes *Bech: A Book*

Vittorio De Sica directs *The Garden of the Finzi-Continis* about plight of Italian Jews during World War II

that she, too, was "sharing in the film's ethnic schizophrenia."

3. Bruce Vilanch, "A 'Mensh,'" Movie Mailbag, *New York Times*, Feb. 25, 1968; and T. B., "'Grad' All Over," *Entertainment Weekly*, Oct. 23, 1992, 68. Charles Grodin was originally cast as the lead in *The Graduate*. When he dropped out, Hoffman left the cast of *The Producers* (1968), another Avco Embassy production in which he was to play Franz Liebkind, to take Grodin's place. After Gene Wilder received an Academy Award nomination for his role in *The Producers*, *The Hollywood Reporter* opined that "Wilder's Oscar nomination moves him into dueling contention with Dustin Hoffman for the title role in *Portnoy's Complaint*." That role ultimately went to Richard Benjamin, star of *Goodbye, Columbus* (Paramount, 1969), a movie that was frequently compared to *The Graduate*.

4. It seems appropriate that when Hoffman made his first (and only) western, *Little Big Man* (National General Pictures, 1971), he played a Native American, and it was prescient that his first television role was in a 1961 episode of *The Naked City* entitled "Sweet Prince of Delancey Street."

MEL GORDON
**Howard Stern**

1. *Pintele yid* means literally "the little dot Jew," but what it means figuratively is the essential core of Jewishness, usually in a person. The expression plays on the double meaning of *yid*, which means Jew, and *yid/yud* (dialectical variant), which is the tenth letter of the Jewish alphabet, the vocal equivalent of I or Y in Yiddish and Hebrew. The shape of the letter *yud*, which is like a small dot, can be found in all the other letters of the Jewish alphabet, implying a pervasive presence of Jewishness (yiddishkeit, which, like *yid*, begins with the letter *yud*).

J. HOBERMAN
**Adam Sandler**

1. Although born in Brooklyn, Sandler was reared in suburban Manchester, New Hampshire, where his father was employed as an electrical engineer. Three years after graduating from New York University, Sandler joined the cast of *Saturday Night Live*, where he remained for four seasons. *SNL* served as the launching pad for his persona, as well as for "The Chanukah Song," which eventually went platinum.

2. Philip Roth, *The Counterlife* (New York: Farrar, Straus and Giroux, 1986), 324.

3. Lisa Lipkin, "Long Live American Heroes: God Places Fourth Behind Seinfeld, Sandler, and Howard Stern," *Forward*, Nov. 22, 1996, 13.

4. Ariel Levy, "The Chosen: Jewish Girls Go Gaga for Adam Sandler," *New York*, July 19, 1999, 15; and Benjamin Dreyfus, "How to Read Adam Sandler's 'Goat Song' as an Allegory for Jewish History," *New Voices* (Nov. 1999), 20–24.

As presented in movies like *Billy Madison* (Universal, 1995) and *Happy Gilmore* (Universal, 1996), Sandler's persona is that of the violent or vengeful klutz who, however socially maladroit, is nevertheless a good boy at heart. Sandler has never appeared as an explicitly Jewish character, although the contemporary *klezmer* musician he played in his crossover hit *The Wedding Singer* (New Line, 1997) seems implicitly Jewish—at one point singing in a fake Hebrew-Yiddish patois—and *Big Daddy* (Columbia, 1999) is a contemporary gloss on Charlie Chaplin's *The Kid* (First National, 1921). *Little Nicky* (New Line, 2000), Sandler's big-budget flop in which the star cast himself as Satan's youngest son, has its share of free-floating Hebrew school tropes. The relationship between Sandler's little *mazik* (devil) and his

**1971**

Indira Ghandi elected leader of India

People's Republic of China admitted into the United Nations

U.S.-backed military coup topples Allende government in Chile

John F. Kennedy Center for the Performing Arts opens in Washington, D.C., with the premiere of Leonard Bernstein's *Mass*

*All in the Family* debuts on CBS

Clint Eastwood stars in *Dirty Harry*

**1972**

Nixon visits China

Palestinian extremists kill eleven Israeli athletes at the Munich Olympic village

Reform movement ordains Sally Priesand as its first woman rabbi

*Bridget Loves Bernie*, situation comedy about Jewish-Catholic intermarriage, debuts on CBS-TV and is canceled after one season

Liza Minnelli stars in the movie version of *Cabaret*

Francis Ford Coppola directs *The Godfather*

**1973**

U.S. signs cease-fire agreement with North Vietnam, allowing American troops to withdraw

Yom Kippur War in the Middle East

David Ben-Gurion, first prime minister of Israel, dies at age seventy-nine

U.S. Congress begins investigating Watergate break-in of the previous year

Abraham D. Beame elected first Jewish mayor of New York

*Ten from Your Show of Shows*, a compilation of the variety series' comic sketches, released as a feature film

older siblings echoes Joseph and his brothers; his climactic confrontation with the evil Adrian is staged to suggest Moses appearing before Pharaoh.

Essentially tolerant, *Little Nicky* follows Jewish mysticism in positing a cosmic design wherein demons and angels are opposing, necessary opposites. Nor do hellfire and damnation have nearly the gravitas with which the Christian imagination can imbue them. Unafraid to show Jews with horns, Sandler presents hell as the equivalent of a family-run Borscht Belt hotel (existing mainly to torture Adolf Hitler) that was founded by Sandler's boyhood idol Rodney Dangerfield and is currently administered by friendly dad Harvey Keitel (who is outed as a Jew in Sandler's second "Chanukah Song").

# STAND-UP JEWS

DEBORAH DASH MOORE
## *Exodus*: Real to Reel to Real

1. The other three were Gen. Dori, Ze'ev Shind, and Minna Ben-Zvi. Reuven Dafni, Oral History Interview, Mar. 16, 1979, 1, Oral History of the UJA, Oral History Archives, Institute for Contemporary Jewry, Hebrew University.

2. Minutes of Annual Meeting of Jewish Community Council of the Bay Cities, Jan. 21, 1948, Jewish Community Council of the Bay Cities, Histories File, Archives, Jewish Community Library, Jewish Federation Council of Los Angeles.

3. Bosley Crowther, "On Taking Sides," *New York Times*, Aug. 28, 1949, sec. 2, p. 1; Bosley Crowther, review of *Sword in the Desert, New York Times*, Aug. 25, 1949.

4. The phrase is the writer Michael Blankfort's; he is quoted in Patricia Erens, *The Jew in American Cinema* (Bloomington: Indiana University Press, 1984), 217.

5. Ibid., 219.

6. On the film's budget, see Otto Preminger, *Preminger: An Autobiography* (Garden City,

N.Y.: Doubleday, 1977), 166; on its gross earnings, see Willi Frischauer, *Behind the Scenes of Otto Preminger* (London: Michael Joseph, 1973), 195.

7. Preminger, *An Autobiography*, 165–66.

8. Philip Roth, "Some New Jewish Stereotypes," in *Reading Myself and Others* (New York: Farrar, Straus and Giroux, 1975), 138.

9. Frank Cantor, "A Second Look at *Exodus*," *Jewish Currents* (Nov. 1959): 20–21, emphasis in the original.

10. David Boroff, "Jewish Readers and Jewish Writers," *Congress Bi-Weekly*, Dec. 19, 1960, 4.

11. As reported by Milton Friedman in *Rochester Jewish Ledger*, July 17, 1959; quoted in Cantor, "A Second Look at *Exodus*," 40.

12. Philip Roth, "Some New Jewish Stereotypes," 145–46.

13. Gerald Pratley, *The Cinema of Otto Preminger*, International Film Guide Series (New York: A. S. Barnes, 1971), 133–34.

14. Bosley Crowther, review of *Exodus, New York Times*, Dec. 16, 1960, 44.

15. *Time*, Dec. 19, 1960, 69.

**1974**

Nixon resigns; Gerald Ford assumes the presidency

*Daily News* headline: "Ford to New York: Drop Dead"

Ordination of first Reconstructionist woman rabbi

Rhoda Morgenstern weds Joe Gerard in special one-hour episode of situation comedy *Rhoda*

Richard Dreyfuss stars in *The Apprenticeship of Duddy Kravitz*, based on a novel by Mordecai Richler

Mel Brooks releases *Blazing Saddles*, the highest-grossing western ever made

Dustin Hoffman stars in *Lenny*, based on the life of Lenny Bruce

**1975**

All of Vietnam comes under Communist control; Vietnam War ends

Visiting Russian dissident Aleksandr Solzhenitsyn not invited to White House

E. L. Doctorow publishes *Ragtime*

Joan Micklin Silver directs *Hester Street*, based on Abraham Cahan's 1894 novella *Yekl*

Steven Spielberg's *Jaws* replaces *The Godfather* as highest-grossing Hollywood movie

Comedy-variety series *Saturday Night Live* debuts on NBC

Home Box Office (HBO) begins operating

**1976**

Jimmy Carter elected president

Saul Bellow wins Nobel Prize for Literature

Woody Allen stars in *The Front*, Martin Ritt's film about victims of television's anti-Communist blacklists of the 1950s

Martin Scorsese releases *Taxi Driver*, starring Robert De Niro

*Roots* miniseries broadcast on ABC

Library of Congress establishes its American Television and Radio Archives

16. *New York Times*, Jan. 20, 1960, 1.

17. *New York Times*, Feb. 10, 1960, 42; and Dec. 22, 1960, 16.

18. *New York Times*, May 11, 1960.

19. Pratley, *The Cinema of Otto Preminger*, 133–35.

20. Nick Martin and Marsha Porter, *Video Movie Guide 1989* (New York: Ballantine Books, 1988), 535.

21. Lester D. Friedman, *Hollywood's Image of the Jew* (New York: Ungar, 1982), 192.

22. Leon Uris, *Exodus* (Garden City, N.Y.: Doubleday, 1958), 371.

23. Joe Hyams, "Miss Saint Happy in *Exodus* Role," clipping, June 14, 1960, in *Exodus* file, David Matis Collection, Steven Spielberg Jewish Film Archives, Hebrew University, Jerusalem.

24. Jacques Lourcelles, *Otto Preminger, Cinéma d'Aujourd'hui* (Paris: Éditions Seghers, 1965), 68–71.

25. Frischauer, *Behind the Scenes*, 195.

26. Preminger, *An Autobiography*, 169.

27. *Jewish Daily Forward*, Apr. 16, 1961, 7, carried a full-page El Al ad filled with pictures from the movie for a sixteen-day *Exodus* tour of Israel. Tour guides quoted in "*Exodus* and Israel," *New York Times*, Oct. 4, 1959, sec. 2, part 2, pp. 1, 8.

28. The number of tourists who visited Israel in 1958 was 75,518; in 1959, it rose to 91,860; in 1960, to 117,661; and in 1961, it reached 159,600. See "Tourist Trade to Israel," in *The Israel Year Book* (1962), 123.

29. "A Symposium: Jewishness and the Younger Intellectuals," *Commentary* (Apr. 1961): 306, questions on 311. For examples of ambivalence, see Irving Feldman, 321; Enoch Gordis, 324; Andrew Hacker, 327; John Hollander, 331; Michael Maccoby, 341. There were also a few expressions of straightforward commitment, for example, Elihu Katz, 335; Herbert Gold, 323; and Robert Lifton, 340.

30. Midge Decter, "Popular Jews," *Commentary* (Oct. 1961): 358.

31. *Life*, June 23, 1967, 24B.

32. Ibid., cover.

33. Israelis, on the other hand, immediately iden-tified the man: Yossi Ben Hanan, who built a career in the army and subsequently became a general.

34. "Hero of the Israelis: Itzhak Rabin," *New York Times*, June 8, 1967, 16.

35. Roth, "Some New Jewish Stereotypes," 146.

36. Thomas B. Morgan, "The Vanishing American Jew," *Look*, May 5, 1964.

J. HOBERMAN

### Flaunting It: The Rise and Fall of Hollywood's "Nice" Jewish (Bad) Boys

1. Parallel developments include the nostalgic Jewish Museum show *Portal to America: The Lower East Side* (1966), the publication of Leo Rosten's bestselling *The Joys of Yiddish* (1968), Philip Roth's scandalous bestseller *Portnoy's Complaint* (1969), and the hegemony of Neil Simon as the most successful playwright on Broadway, which, throughout the sixties, had seen a number of successful Jewish-themed musical comedies, several of which were also made into films—most spectacularly *Fiddler on the Roof* (United Artists, 1971). It was in the late sixties as well that the tabloid term "movie mogul" was rehabilitated as a fond, historical construct.

**1977**

Egyptian President Sadat visits Israel

U.S. unemployment rises to 7 percent

Elvis Presley dies of a drug overdose

*Star Wars* becomes highest-grossing Hollywood movie

Woody Allen's *Annie Hall* released; later wins Academy Award for Best Picture

*East Side Wedding*, first recording by the Klezmorim, initiates klezmer "revival"

**1978**

OPEC raises price of oil 50 percent

Yiddish writer Isaac Bashevis Singer wins Nobel Prize for Literature

Miniseries *Holocaust* airs on NBC; one-half of all Americans watch at least part of the four-day telecast

Meryl Streep and Robert De Niro star in *The Deer Hunter*

**1979**

Camp David accords result in peace treaty between Israel and Egypt

Sadat and Israeli Prime Minister Menachem Begin share Nobel Peace Prize

Muslim fundamentalists overthrow monarchy in Iran

Soviet troops invade Afghanistan

Francis Ford Coppola releases *Apocalypse Now*

Holocaust Survivors Film Project, one of the first efforts to videotape testimony of Holocaust survivors, inaugurated in Connecticut

National Jewish Archive of Broadcasting established at The Jewish Museum in New York

2. Robert Alter, for one, was notably unimpressed by the use of Yiddish. He observed in his essay "Sentimentalizing the Jews" (1965) that Yiddish words were "waved like a magic wand" just as "the idea of the Jew is invoked and the naked invocation is expected to conjure up all sorts of images, from epiphany to pogrom, of a unique history and a unique moral heritage." See Alter, *After the Tradition: Essays on Modern Jewish Writing* (New York: E. P. Dutton, 1971), 74.

3. Esther Romeyn and Jack Kugelmass, *Let There Be Laughter! Jewish Humor in America* (Chicago: Spertus Press, 1997), 67. In addition to the Jewish antiheroes discussed in this survey, a significant number of Hollywood comedies during this period were thought to be characterized by a New York Jewish sensibility, despite the absence of overt Jewish characters: these include the romantic comedies *The Owl and the Pussycat* (Columbia, 1970; starring Barbra Streisand and George Segal) and *Lovers and Other Strangers* (ABC Pictures, 1970; a movie about Italians and Irish), Mike Nichols's *Catch-22* (Paramount, 1970; from the Joseph Heller novel), and *Carnal Knowledge* (Avco Embassy, 1971; written by Jules Feiffer), *Little Murders* (Twentieth Century Fox, 1971; also written by Feiffer), Elaine May's *A New Leaf* (Paramount, 1971), and the various films based on the plays of Neil Simon.

4. Leslie Fiedler, "Saul Bellow," *To the Gentiles* (New York: Stein and Day, 1972), 58. Although he ignored the avant-garde Allen Ginsberg, Fiedler expanded this universality into popular culture, writing in 1966 on the musical version of *Golden Boy*, Clifford Odets's "soupy play about Jews updated to get the box office that only Negro drama gets these days; and in the midst of it all Sammy Davis, trying to live the part he acted, a Negro turned Jew being the John Garfield of the sixties. And remembering, of course, Marilyn Monroe and Elizabeth Taylor, I found myself slipping away into a daydream in which Frank Sinatra (second only unto Jehovah in Sammy Davis' pantheon) would end up playing Frankie Alpine in the movie made of Bernard Malamud's *The Assistant*, and insisting upon being really circumcised in the last scene where that character becomes a Jew. And then there would be no goyim left at all in the world of pop culture, not a single one" (138–39).

By the mid-sixties, some thought this epoch was already over. For Robert Alter, "the peculiar cultural phenomenon which some choose to call an American Jewish literary renaissance [was] showing signs of having overstayed its critical welcome." Indeed, Alter had begun to wonder if "too much [had] been made of what may not have been such a significant or valid development in the first place." He considered the younger Jewish writers who appeared in the wake of Bellow, Malamud, and Roth as only nominally Jewish, their "typical involvement in Jewish culture consists of an acquaintance with gefilte fish and crass bar-mitzvahs, a degree of familiarity with overstuffed Jewish matriarchs, and a mastery of several pungent Yiddish synonyms for the male organ." With few exceptions, these writers were "culturally American in all important respects and only peripherally or vestigially Jewish. . . . The role of the Jew—and especially the intellectual Jew—as an outsider in American life has generally dwindled into an affectation or a stance of pious self-delusion." (See Alter, *After the Tradition*, 71, 73.)

5. Albert Goldman, "Boy-Man Schlemiel: The Jewish Element in American Humor," in *Freakshow: The Rocksoulbluesjazzsickjewblackhumorsexpoppsych Gig and Other Scenes from the Counter-Culture* (New York: Atheneum, 1971), 169–86. Associated since the late fifties with stand-up comedians, the term "sick humor" may have been popularized by *Village Voice*

**1980**

Ronald Reagan elected president

Iranian militants occupy U.S. embassy in Teheran

Sadat assassinated

Iraq invades Iran

John Lennon assassinated

Cable News Network (CNN) initiates twenty-four-hour telecasts

San Francisco holds first Jewish film festival in the U.S.

Arthur Miller's original television drama *Playing for Time* airs on CBS; casting of pro-Palestinian activist Vanessa Redgrave as Holocaust survivor causes great controversy

**1981**

Reagan administration advocates "supply-side" economics and higher military spending

Martial law in Poland outlaws Solidarity and imprisons its leader, Lech Walesa

Sandra Day O'Connor named first female Supreme Court Justice

First cases of the illness that would come to be known as AIDS are reported

Wedding of Prince Charles and Lady Diana Spencer televised internationally

**1982**

Israeli invasion of Lebanon forces out Yasir Arafat's Palestinian Liberation Organization terrorists

Meryl Streep stars in *Sophie's Choice*, based on a novel by William Styron

Music Television (MTV) broadcasts for the first time

*E.T.* replaces *Star Wars* as highest-grossing movie in history

cartoonist Jules Feiffer, who called his first collection of work *Sick, Sick, Sick*.

6. Ruth R. Wisse, *The Schlemiel as Modern Hero* (Chicago: University of Chicago Press, 1971), 72–73.

7. Goldman, *Freakshow*, 171.

8. Paul D. Zimmerman, "To Brooklyn with Tears," *Newsweek*, Mar. 11, 1968; and Andrew Sarris, "Films," *Village Voice*, Mar. 21, 1968.

9. A. H. Weiler, "A Funeral Grows in Brooklyn," *New York Times*, Dec. 20, 1967, sec. 2, pp. 15, 20; Philip Hartung, "The Screen," *Commonweal*, Mar. 8, 1968, 76; Robert Hatch, *Nation*, Mar. 11, 1968, 357; and Joseph Gelmis, "On Movies: 'Braverman' a Voyage of Discovery about Life," *Newsday*, Feb. 22, 1968.

10. Sig Altman, *The Comic Image of the Jew: Explorations of a Pop Culture Phenomenon* (Rutherford, N.J.: Fairleigh Dickinson University Press, 1971), 20; Murf., "Bye Bye Braverman," *Variety*, Feb. 7, 1968; and Robert Hatch, *Nation*, Mar. 11, 1968, 358.

11. Stanley Kauffmann, "On Film," *New Republic*, Mar. 9, 1968; and Pauline Kael, "That Clean Old Peasant Again," *New Yorker*, Mar. 2, 1968. The year 1968 ended with two nostalgic evocations of Jewish show biz on a reconstructed Lower East Side, William Wyler's *Funny Girl* and William Friedkin's *The Night They Raided Minsky's*, featuring Barbra Streisand's husband Elliot Gould as Billy Minsky.

12. "Playboy Interview: Mel Brooks," *Playboy*, Oct. 1966, 80. Although *The Producers* anticipates the flood of Nazi kitsch that would soon appear, *Cabaret* was an established hit and the POW sitcom *Hogan's Heroes* (CBS, 1965–71) was among the most popular shows on TV by the time the movie opened.

13. Zero Mostel could be considered the forerunner of the Jewish stand-up comedians, having worked as a stand-up in 1942 and 1943 at Café Society with an act that included impressions—Hitler among them. See Jared Brown, *Zero Mostel: A Biography* (New York: Atheneum, 1989), 25.

14. Pauline Kael, "O Pioneer!," *New Yorker*, Mar. 28, 1968. Although Kael mentions no names, the greatest exponent of this humor was Lenny Bruce, who had died of a drug overdose eighteen months earlier. Bruce's routines included several that riffed on the relationship between Jews, Nazis, and show business—including one routine known as "Hitler and the MCA," in which two talent agents, desperate to find a German dictator, discover and recruit a handy housepainter.

15. "Never in my long theatergoing life have I been part of such an ecstatic audience," critic Robert Brustein wrote in the *New Republic*'s cover story on *The Producers*. "I do not mean people desperate, at $100 a throw, to applaud their expenditure. I mean a really happy audience—wreathed in smiles before, during, and after the performance." See Brustein, "The Jew Who Buried Hitler," *New Republic*, May 28, 2001, 27.

16. Cliff Rothman, "Sellers' Choice: A Party for the 'Alice B. Toklas' Gang Led to Peter Sellers's Championing of 'The Producers,'" *Los Angeles Times Calendar*, May 30, 2001, www.calendarlive.com. Four years later, Sellers announced his own never-realized version of *The Producers*. In this untitled movie, the comic-strip hero, known as the Phantom, pursues the ninety-year-old Hitler, to be played by Sellers, from the South American jungle to the stage of the Royal Albert Hall. See "Springtime for Hitler," *Time*, Aug. 28, 1972, 38.

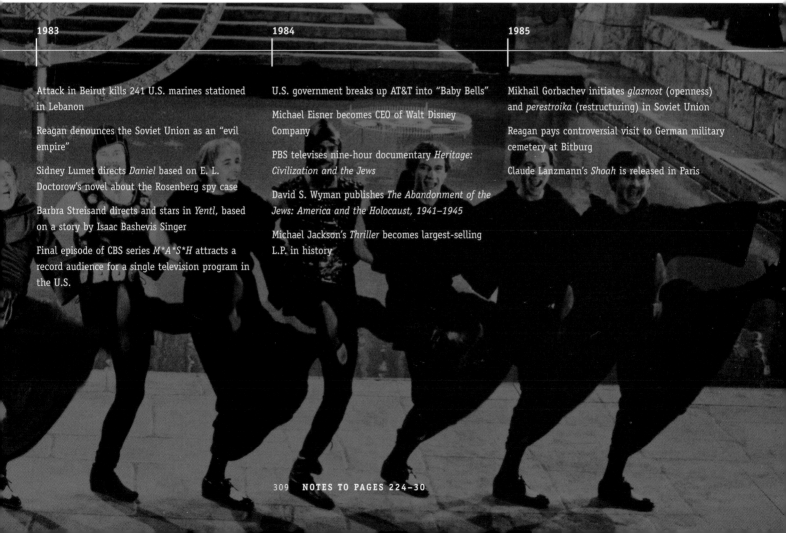

**1983**

Attack in Beirut kills 241 U.S. marines stationed in Lebanon

Reagan denounces the Soviet Union as an "evil empire"

Sidney Lumet directs *Daniel* based on E. L. Doctorow's novel about the Rosenberg spy case

Barbra Streisand directs and stars in *Yentl*, based on a story by Isaac Bashevis Singer

Final episode of CBS series *M*A*S*H* attracts a record audience for a single television program in the U.S.

**1984**

U.S. government breaks up AT&T into "Baby Bells"

Michael Eisner becomes CEO of Walt Disney Company

PBS televises nine-hour documentary *Heritage: Civilization and the Jews*

David S. Wyman publishes *The Abandonment of the Jews: America and the Holocaust, 1941–1945*

Michael Jackson's *Thriller* becomes largest-selling L.P. in history

**1985**

Mikhail Gorbachev initiates *glasnost* (openness) and *perestroika* (restructuring) in Soviet Union

Reagan pays controversial visit to German military cemetery at Bitburg

Claude Lanzmann's *Shoah* is released in Paris

17. David Desser and D. Lester Friedman, *American-Jewish Filmmakers: Traditions and Trends* (Urbana: University of Illinois Press, 1993), 231.

18. Sanford Pinsker, "Lenny Bruce: Shpritzing the Goyim, Shocking the Jews," in *Jewish Wry: Essays on Jewish Humor*, ed. Sarah Blacher Cohen (Bloomington: Indiana University Press, 1987), 103.

19. Pearl K. Bell calls *Portnoy's Complaint* the novel that, in effect, drove a stake through the heart of Molly Goldberg: It dared to say "the Jewish mother's goodness was a sentimental myth." See Bell, "Philip Roth: Sonny Boy or Lenny Bruce?" *Commentary* 64, no. 5 (Nov. 1977): 61.

20. Albert Goldman, "Shaking Hands with Philip Roth," *Freakshow*, 232.

21. Vincent Canby, "Screen: A Vivid 'Goodbye Columbus,'" *New York Times*, Apr. 4, 1969; "Klugman's Complaint," *Time*, Apr. 11, 1969, 104; and Andrew Sarris, "Films: Waxing Roth," *Village Voice*, Apr. 3, 1969, 51.

22. Whit., "Goodbye Columbus," *Variety*, Mar. 19, 1969; and Sarris, "Films: Waxing Roth," 51. *Mad* magazine's parody, "Hoo Hah Columbus,"

included Dustin Hoffman as a guest in the wedding scene—as well as "Philip Raw." See Mort Drucker and Arnie Kogen, "Hoo-Boy, Columbus," *Mad*, no. 131, Dec. 1969.

23. Stanley Kauffmann, "On Films," *New Republic*, Apr. 5, 1969, 33; and Canby, "Screen: A Vivid 'Goodbye Columbus.'"

24. Altman, *The Comic Image of the Jew*, 93–94.

25. Judith Crist, *New York*, Apr. 7, 1969, 53.

26. Rex Reed, "Movies," *Women's Wear Daily*, Apr. 4, 1969.

27. Robert Hatch, "Goodbye, Columbus," *Nation*, Apr. 29, 1969, 550; and Richard Schickel, "An Early Portnoy in Suburbia," *Life*, Apr. 25, 1969.

28. Robert Altman, who effectively transformed Raymond Chandler's private detective Philip Marlowe into a schlemiel for *The Long Goodbye* (United Artists, 1973) by casting Elliott Gould in the role, added a further Jewish element to his noir travesty in the person of the Jewish gangster, played by fellow director Mark Rydell. Another, more political variant would be Abraham Polonsky's *Romance of a Horse Thief* (Allied Artists, 1971), which, based on a novella by

Yiddish writer Joseph Opatoshu, concerns Jewish criminals and revolutionaries in pre-Revolutionary Russia.

29. Raymond A. Sokolov, "Cheat," *Newsweek*, Aug. 10, 1970; Mark Goodman, "Granny Knot," *Time*, Aug. 24, 1970; "Move," *Motion Picture Herald*, Aug. 12, 1970; Roger Greenspun, "Rosenberg Comedy at Baronet and Criterion," *New York Times*, Aug. 1, 1970, 12; and Richard Corliss, "Film: Move," *Village Voice*, Aug. 13, 1970.

30. Interestingly, Archer Winsten saw *Where's Poppa?* as less a Jewish than an underground comedy, which "proves that the influence of uncensored avant-garde films has unleashed the people who make the big, glossy Hollywood-type pictures." Winsten, *New York Post*, Nov. 11, 1970.

31. Rich., "Where's Poppa?" *Daily Variety*, Nov. 10, 1970; Judith Crist, "Wherever Poppa Is, He's Better Off," *New York*, Nov. 30, 1970; and Vincent Canby, "Poppa Laughs Best," *New York Times*, Dec. 6, 1970, sec. 2, p. 5.

In "How to Be a Jewish Son," *The David Susskind Show* (Nov. 29, 1970, WNEW-TV), Susskind several times tries attempts to engage Segal on the subject of *Where's Poppa?* Asked if he

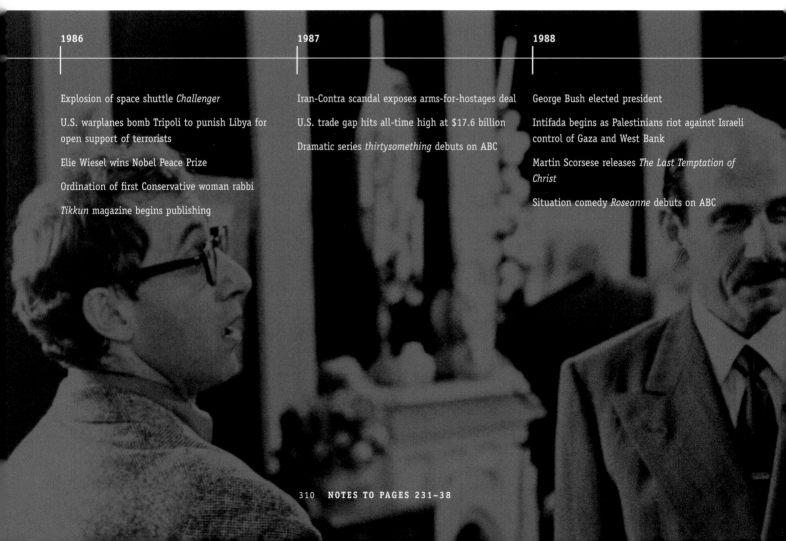

**1986**

Explosion of space shuttle *Challenger*

U.S. warplanes bomb Tripoli to punish Libya for open support of terrorists

Elie Wiesel wins Nobel Peace Prize

Ordination of first Conservative woman rabbi

*Tikkun* magazine begins publishing

**1987**

Iran-Contra scandal exposes arms-for-hostages deal

U.S. trade gap hits all-time high at $17.6 billion

Dramatic series *thirtysomething* debuts on ABC

**1988**

George Bush elected president

Intifada begins as Palestinians riot against Israeli control of Gaza and West Bank

Martin Scorsese releases *The Last Temptation of Christ*

Situation comedy *Roseanne* debuts on ABC

identifies with the character of the movie's Jewish son, Segal replies, "Totally." Later, Susskind appears shocked when informed that the movie's original ending had the Segal character going to bed with his elderly mother. All subsequent discussions of *Where's Poppa?* are, however, derailed by Brooks, who dominates this chaotic and often hilarious show. "How to Be a Jewish Son" is also notable for enlarging its critique on Jewish mothers into an attack by Steinberg and, especially, Brooks on the "Jewish princess." Their exchange was reprinted in Julie Baumgold's influential article, "The Persistence of the Jewish American Princess," *New York*, Mar. 22, 1971, 25.

32. Rex Reed, "Who Is Harry, Etc., and Why Is It So Dreary?" *Daily News*, June 18, 1971.

33. "The Steagle," *Variety*, Sept. 15, 1971; and Rex Reed, "Benjamin a Creep Again in Another Rotten Film," *Daily News*, Sept. 7, 1971, 70.

34. Pauline Kael, "Notes on New Actors, New Movies," *New Yorker*, Dec. 4, 1971. Although enormously supportive of Streisand, Kael had little sympathy for her male counterparts. She scorned Gould's "loutish" performance in Ingmar Bergman's *The Touch* (ABC Pictures, 1971): "Most of the women I know felt Gould's touching Bibi Andersson as a physical affront to her and recoiled in the same kinesthetic, empathetic way that I did." Hoffman was too clever and lacking in actorly intuition: "When his role isn't funny, he's usually helplessly tense; you can see him wishing he had something to *play*." Clearly, neither of these Jewish men had the requisite "male fascism." Kael damned Segal with faint praise as "probably the best light comedian in American movies," noting that "he gets better all the time."

35. Sarris, "Films: Waxing Roth," 51; and Robert Alter, "Defaming the Jews," *Commentary* 55, no. 1 (June 1973): 78.

36. Murf., "Portnoy's Complaint," *Variety*, June 21, 1972; Rex Reed, "'Portnoy'—Sick, Sick, Sick," *Daily News*, June 23, 1972, 66; Judith Crist, "Grounds For Complaint," *New York*, July 3, 1972, 52; and Penelope Gilliatt, "You May See a Stranger, Across a Crowded Bed," *New Yorker*, Sept. 1, 1972. Going back to the book, Sarris was puzzled by the accusations of anti-Semitism. "It is not entirely clear why so many Jewish readers have been offended, nor why Portnoy's various complaints are considered exclusively Jewish. Besides, how can you interpret a personal confession as an ethnic defamation?" Finding his own universality in the material, Sarris seemed oblivi-ous to the particular sexual logic of Portnoy's case—an ethnically determined variation on the Madonna-whore complex characterized by fearful contempt of Jewish women and contemptuous attraction to shikses. For Sarris, "What Roth is describing . . . is not so much the maladjustment of any particular ethnic group as the intense psychological strain of climbing socially and intellectually out of the provincial cellar of one's despised family and ethnicity. . . . The essential truths of *Portnoy* help validate an entire army of arrivistes." See Sarris, "Films in Focus," *Village Voice*, July 20, 1972, 47.

37. Fred M. Hechinger, "An Anti-Jewish Joke?" *New York Times*, Aug. 16, 1972, sec. 2, pp. 1, 9.

38. Bob Lardine, "Complaints About Portnoy," *Daily News*, Aug. 6, 1972; and Robert Alter, "Defaming the Jews," *Commentary* 55, no. 1 (June 1973): 77. Andrew Kopkind linked *Portnoy's Complaint* to several other current movies that concerned male sexual dysfunction: *Play It Again, Sam* (Paramount, 1972) and *Everything You Always Wanted to Know about Sex But Were Afraid to Ask* (United Artists, 1972), both written by and starring Woody Allen, and *The Last of the Red Hot Lovers* (Paramount, 1972), from the play by Neil Simon. All four had explicitly Jewish men

**1989**

East and West Germans tear down Berlin Wall, marking Cold War's end

Velvet Revolution in Czechoslovakia

Pro-democracy protests in Tiananmen Square in Beijing lead to Chinese government crackdown

Nicolae Ceausescu ousted from power in Romania

Ayatolla Khomeini declares a fatwa against Salman Rushdie, condemning writer to death for writing *Satanic Verses*

Comedian Jackie Mason forced to resign from Rudolph Giuliani's campaign after making a racist comment about then New York Mayor David Dinkins

Paul Mazursky directs *Enemies, a Love Story*, based on a novel by Isaac Bashevis Singer

*The Simpsons* premieres on Fox network

Spike Lee releases *Do the Right Thing*

Time Life acquires Warner Communications

**1990**

Germany is reunified under Helmut Kohl

Iraq invades Kuwait

Hollywood's X rating is replaced by NC-17

*Seinfeld* premieres on NBC

Dramatic series *Northern Exposure* debuts on CBS

**1991**

Operation Desert Storm defeats Iraq, liberating Kuwait

August coup in Soviet Union fails, leading to establishment of the Commonwealth of Independent States (CIS)

Slovenia and Croatia unilaterally declare independence from Yugoslavia

Rioting breaks out in mixed hasidic–African-American neighborhood of Crown Heights, Brooklyn

Oliver Stone releases *JFK*

as their protagonists. See Kopkind, "Play With It Again, Sam," *Boston Phoenix*, Aug. 12, 1972, 5.

39. Bruce Jay Friedman, "A Change of Plan," *Esquire* (Jan. 1966), 96–97. Dreamlike and elliptical, Friedman's story reads like a treatment for Simon's script. Although Friedman's protagonist is nominally Jewish, the movie vastly ups the ethnic ante—in good measure through Jeannie Berlin's characterization of the abandoned bride, who is barely a character in "A Change of Plan."

40. Colin L. Westerbeck, Jr., "The Screen," *Commonweal*, Feb. 23, 1973, 430.

41. Stephen Farber, "You See Yourself in 'Heartbreak,'" *New York Times*, Feb. 18, 1973, sec. 2, p. 1; and Stuart Byron, "The Heartbreak Kid," *Real Paper* (n.d.). Significantly, perhaps, Farber and Byron are able to connect the characters in *The Heartbreak Kid* with people they knew, growing up Jewish in America. A dissenting opinion in the *New York Times*, Sept. 9, 1973, characterized Lila as "a cruel compendium of every unpleasant trait that has ever been associated with Jewish girls—particularly from New York . . . noisy, vulgar, demanding, insanely possessive, impossibly overbearing and grimly committed to pre-marital virginity. In short, a Jewish princess of

unmistakably lower middle-class origins." Jeannie Berlin, who had played small roles in *Move* and *Portnoy's Complaint*, was nominated for an Oscar and named the year's Best Supporting Actress by the National Society of Film Critics.

42. Stragglers include *The Apprenticeship of Duddy Kravitz* (Paramount, 1974), a Canadian film, which confirmed Richard Dreyfuss as the last of the new-wave Jewish leading men; *The Gambler* (Paramount, 1974), a "bad boy" film written by bad boy James Tobak; the gangster movie *Lepke* (Warner Bros., 1975), with Tony Curtis playing a Jew for the first time since he appeared as Houdini; and the lone female version of a Jewish new-wave movie, *Sheila Levine is Dead and Living in New York* (Paramount, 1975), based on the novel by Gail Parent and starring Jeannie Berlin. Like her brethren, Sheila is over-involved with a demanding Jewish mother.

43. Mort Drucker and Larry Siegel, "The Heartburn Kid," *MAD*, no. 162, Oct. 1973, 4–10.

J. HOBERMAN
**"How the Jew Got into Show Business"**

1. Albert Goldman, "The Comedy of Lenny Bruce," *Commentary* 36 (Oct. 1963): 314.

JEFFREY SHANDLER
**At Home on the Small Screen: Television's New York Jews**

1. Todd Gitlin, *Inside Prime Time* (New York: Pantheon, 1983), 185.

2. For example, according to Leo Bogart, "by January 1948 there were 102,000 [television] sets in [the U.S.], two-thirds of them in New York." See Bogart, *The Age of Television: A Study of Viewing Habits and the Impact of Television on American Life* (New York: Ungar, 1956), 8–9.

3. Paddy Chayefsky, *Television Plays* (1955; reprint, New York: Touchstone, 1971), 132.

4. Gitlin, *Inside Prime Time*, 184.

5. Henry Popkin, "The Vanishing Jew of Our Popular Culture," *Commentary* 14, no. 1 (July 1952): 46.

6. Ibid.

7. The oblique, encoded presence of Jewishness as a performative element in *Your Show of Shows* is a telling case in point. See "*Our Show of Shows*" in this volume.

---

**1992**

Bill Clinton elected president

Republic of Bosnia-Herzegovina declares its independence from Yugoslavia

Exoneration of Los Angeles police in Rodney King case sparks three days of violence and vandalism

Art Spiegelman's *Maus* awarded Pulitzer Prize

Spike Lee releases *Malcolm X*

English-language edition of *The Forward* begins publication

**1993**

PLO leader Yasir Arafat and Israeli Prime Minister Yitzhak Rabin sign peace accord

United States Holocaust Memorial Museum opens in Washington, D.C.

Beit Hashoah: Museum of Tolerance opens in Los Angeles

Steven Spielberg releases *Schindler's List*

*The Nanny* debuts on CBS

**1994**

Muslim terrorists attack World Trade Center in New York

Lubavitcher Rebbe, Menachem Mendel Schneerson, dies

Adam Sandler performs "The Chanukah Song" on *Saturday Night Live*

Robert Redford directs *Quiz Show*

Steven Spielberg uses profits from *Schindler's List* to establish the Shoah Visual History Foundation

DreamWorks founded by Spielberg, Jeffrey Katzenberg, and David Geffen

8. Nathan Glazer and Daniel Patrick Moynihan, *Beyond the Melting Pot: The Negroes, Puerto Ricans, Jews, Italians, and Irish of New York City* (Cambridge, Mass.: MIT Press, 1963), 138.

9. George Lipsitz, "The Meaning of Memory: Family, Class, and Ethnicity in Early Network Television Programs," *Cultural Anthropology* 1, no. 4 (Nov. 1986).

10. Sig Altman, *The Comic Image of the Jew: Explorations of a Pop Culture Phenomenon* (Rutherford, N.J.: Fairleigh Dickinson University Press, 1971), 299.

11. See David Marc, *Comic Visions: Television Comedy and American Culture*, 2d ed. (Malden, Mass.: Blackwell, 1997), 70ff, 147. Carl Reiner played Petrie in the pilot of the series, which originally was titled *Head of the Family*. According to Vince Waldron, Reiner dismisses the notion that rejection of the pilot version was in any way a result of anti-Semitism: "'I never had Jewish rhythms in these shows,' [Reiner] insists. . . . 'Even in the very first pilot I did . . . , it was a very gentile show. I would never *not* admit that I was a Jew—but I wasn't going to do a show about Jewishness. I knew that the country was not looking for a Jewish ethnic show. Not yet.'" See Waldron, *The Official Dick Van Dyke Show Book* (New York: Hyperion, 1994), 34.

12. Caryn James, "A Great Place to Visit (At Least on Television)," *New York Times*, Oct. 23, 1997, E1.

13. Amy Meisler, "Mary Poppins She's Not," *New York Times*, Dec. 18, 1994, sec. 2, p. 45.

14. Jack Kugelmass, "From Cultural Pathology to Social Salubrity: Sitcoms and the Self-Representation of Jewish Difference," in Kugelmass, *Rites of the Tribe* (forthcoming).

15. Nora Lee Mandel, "Media Watch: What the World Sees in 'The Nanny,'" *Lilith* 21, no. 4 (winter 1996): 40.

16. Robin Cembalest, "Big Hair, Short Skirts—and High Culture: Taking Fran Drescher Seriously," *Forward*, Feb. 14, 1997, 9.

17. Marc, *Comic Visions*, 196.

18. Geoffrey O'Brien, "Sein of the Times," *New York Review of Books*, Apr. 14, 1997, 14.

19. See, for example, O'Brien, "Sein of the Times"; and Maureen Dowd, "Yada Yada Yuppies," *New York Times*, May 14, 1997.

20. Dowd, "Yada Yada Yuppies," *New York Times*.

21. Jedediah Purdy, *For Common Things: Irony, Trust, and Commitment in America Today* (New York: Alfred A. Knopf, 1999); and Richard Leiby, "But Seriously, Folks . . . : Pundits Say Irony Is Out. Don't Laugh," *Washington Post*, Sept. 27, 2001, C1.

22. For a discussion of how these two series present Jewishness, see Jon Stratton, "*Seinfeld* Is a Jewish Sitcom, Isn't It?" in *Coming Out Jewish: Constructing Ambivalent Identities* (New York: Routledge, 2000), 282–314.

23. Walter Goodman, "Critic's Notebook," *New York Times*, Feb. 2, 1999, E3.

24. Marc, *Comic Visions*, 201–2.

25. J. Hoberman, "Diasporama!" *Village Voice*, Apr. 18, 1995.

26. "What's So Funny About N.Y.C.?" *New York*, Feb. 20, 1995, 45.

27. See for example, Ron Rosenbaum, "*Seinfeld*: Requiem for a TV Heavyweight," *New York Observer*, Apr. 20, 1998, 33.

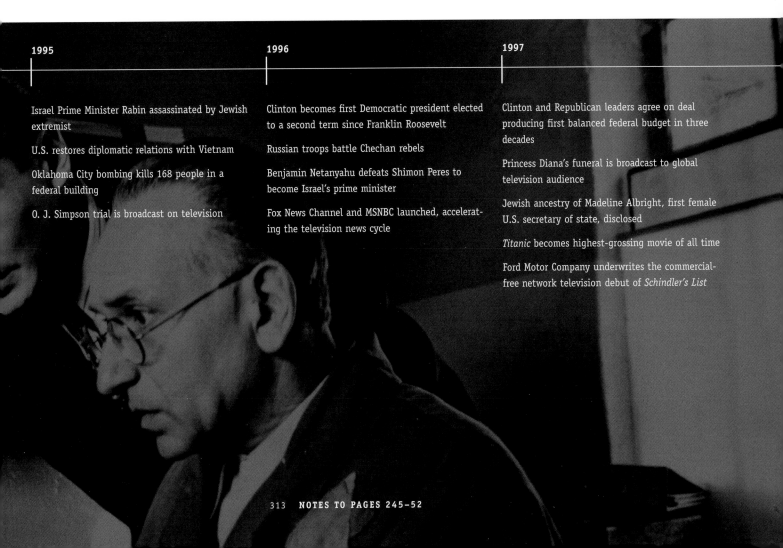

1995

Israel Prime Minister Rabin assassinated by Jewish extremist

U.S. restores diplomatic relations with Vietnam

Oklahoma City bombing kills 168 people in a federal building

O. J. Simpson trial is broadcast on television

1996

Clinton becomes first Democratic president elected to a second term since Franklin Roosevelt

Russian troops battle Chechan rebels

Benjamin Netanyahu defeats Shimon Peres to become Israel's prime minister

Fox News Channel and MSNBC launched, accelerating the television news cycle

1997

Clinton and Republican leaders agree on deal producing first balanced federal budget in three decades

Princess Diana's funeral is broadcast to global television audience

Jewish ancestry of Madeline Albright, first female U.S. secretary of state, disclosed

*Titanic* becomes highest-grossing movie of all time

Ford Motor Company underwrites the commercial-free network television debut of *Schindler's List*

28. James, "A Great Place to Visit," E8.

29. "For Seinfeld Fans: Kramer's Reality Tour," brochure, n.d.. See also www.kennykramer.com.

30. "The World According to *Seinfeld*," *TV Guide*, special edition spring 1998, 14–15; and Douglas Martin, "'Seinfeld' Party Is Sidetracked on Way to Bryant Park," *New York Times*, Apr. 30, 1998, B2.

31. Bruce Weber, "In Boise, Manhattan Kvetching Is Familiar as a Bagel," *New York Times*, Oct. 23, 1997, E1.

32. Jim Windolf, "To Neurotic New York, *Seinfeld* Is News at 11," *New York Observer*, Nov. 16, 1996, 1.

33. Lis Lipkin, "Long Live American Heroes," *Forward*, Nov. 22, 1996, 13.

34. Abraham H. Foxman, "The Holocaust Meets Popular Culture," *New York Times*, Oct. 31, 1998, A15; and O'Brien, "Sein of the Times," 12.

35. Amy Dockser Marcus, "Burden of Peace: American Jews Grapple with an Identity Crisis," *Wall Street Journal*, Sept. 14, 1994, A1, A6.

36. Craig Horowitz, "Are American Jews Disappearing?" *New York*, July 14, 1997, 31.

### Seinfeld (and Others) on *Seinfeld*

1. "What's So Funny About N.Y.C.?" *New York*, Feb. 20, 1995, 45.

2. Mike Flaherty and Mary Kaye Schilling, "The Seinfeld Chronicles," *Entertainment Weekly*, May 30, 1997, 24.

3. Ron Rosenbaum, "*Seinfeld*: Requiem for a TV Heavyweight," *New York Observer*, Apr. 20, 1998, 1, 33, 35.

4. Chaim Saiman, "Seidman, Seinfeld and Formalist Frustrations," *G-Cubed* 2 (1999): 17.

5. Karen Bender, "Why We Watch 'Seinfeld' and Cry: 'I Want to Be Elaine,'" *Forward*, Mar. 14, 1994. According to Tim Brooks and Earle Marsh, *The Complete Directory to Prime Time Network and Cable TV Shows 1946–Present*, 6th ed. (New York: Ballantine, 1995), Elaine's last name is spelled *Benes*.

JEFFREY SHANDLER
### American Media and the Holocaust

1. See the bibliography in this volume for major studies of the Holocaust in film and television.

2. *Paramount News* (Apr. 28, 1945), 4–69; National Archives and Records Administration, Washington, D.C., RG 200.

3. Annette Insdorf, *Indelible Shadows: Film and the Holocaust*, 2d ed. (Cambridge, U.K.: Cambridge University Press, 1989), 3.

4. Elie Wiesel, "Trivializing the Holocaust: Semi-Fact and Semi-Fiction," *New York Times*, Apr. 16, 1978, sec. 2, pp. 1, 29.

5. John Weisman, "If Only We'd Had TV during Hitler's Time," *TV Guide*, Dec. 31, 1988, 6–8.

6. "Elie Wiesel: A Search for Peace," *ABC News Nightline*, Dec. 2, 1992.

7. Abraham H. Foxman, "The Holocaust Meets Popular Culture," *New York Times*, Oct. 31, 1998, A15.

8. Dotson Rader, "We Can't Just Sit Back and Hope," *Parade*, Mar. 27, 1994, 7.

9. "America Remembers the Holocaust," *ABC News Nightline*, Dec. 28, 1993.

10. See, for example, essays by Lilianne Weissberg (Germany) and Haim Bresheeth (Israel) in *Spielberg's Holocaust: Critical Perspectives on "Schindler's List,"* ed. Yosefa

**1998**

Clinton impeached after scandalous affair with a White House intern, but the Senate votes not to remove him from office

India and Pakistan test nuclear weapons

Last episode of *Seinfeld* airs

*Sex and the City* debuts on HBO

DreamWorks releases *Prince of Egypt*, an animated film based on the story of Moses

**1999**

U.S. air-strikes against Serbia force Slobodan Milosovic to surrender in Kosovo

NATO expands to include Poland, Hungary, and the Czech Republic

Two heavily armed students at Columbine High School kill fifteen people, including themselves

Y2K bug inspires fears of international technological crisis

George Lucas revives the *Star Wars* cycle with *The Phantom Menace*

**2000**

Al Gore names Senator Joseph Lieberman his vice-presidential running mate

U.S. Supreme Court determines that George W. Bush is forty-third president

Israeli forces withdraw from southern Lebanon

Renewed Palestinian-Israeli violence in Al-Aqsa Intifada

AOL acquires Time Warner

Loshitzky (Bloomington: Indiana University Press, 1997); and Bernard Weinraub, "Islamic Nations Move to Keep Out 'Schindler's List,'" *New York Times*, Apr. 7, 1994, C15.

11. Amy E. Schwartz, "Laughter in the Movie House," *Washington Post*, Mar. 16, 1994, A19; see also Frank Rich, "*Journal*: 'Schindler's' Dissed," *New York Times*, Feb. 6, 1994, sec. 4, p. 17.

12. John E. Yang, "Rep. Coburn Apologizes for 'List' Tirade," *Washington Post*, Feb. 27, 1997; and Stuart Elliott, "Ford Will Travel High Road with Adless 'Schindler's List,'" *New York Times*, Feb. 21, 1997, D1.

13. Rader, "We Can't Just Sit Back and Hope," 7.

14. Terrence Rafferty, "Current Cinema: A Man of Transactions," *New Yorker*, Dec. 20, 1993, 132. In her introduction to *Spielberg's Holocaust*, Yosefa Loshitzky notes that "Spielberg's testimony in the summer of 1994 before a congressional committee examining the issue of 'hate crimes' itself testifies to the fact that the most successful commercial filmmaker in Hollywood's history has suddenly achieved 'expert' status on a controversial and complex social phenomenon—purely by virtue of having directed a film whose subject is the rescue of a handful of Jews."

JEFFREY SHANDLER
**The Virtual Rebbe**

1. According to Jerome Mintz, while "television is forbidden in many [hasidic] families, it nonetheless manages to surface in community life in one way or another." See Mintz, *Hasidic People: A Place in the New World* (Cambridge, Mass.: Harvard University Press, 1992), 182. Mintz offers several anecdotes of American Hasidim who stash television sets under the bed or in secret cabinets.

2. Menachem Mendel Schneerson, *Toward a Meaningful Life: The Wisdom of the Rebbe*, adapted by Simon Jacobson (New York: William Morrow, 1995), 189; spelling as per original.

3. Craig Horowitz, "Beyond Belief," *New York*, June 19, 1995, 42.

J. HOBERMAN
**Bill Clinton, Hollywood President: A Chronology**

1. John Baxter, *Steven Spielberg: The Unauthorized Biography* (London: Harper Collins, 1996), 373–74. According to Baxter, it was Warner Bros. executive Steve Ross who converted the apolitical filmmaker to a supporter of candidate Bill Clinton. After the election, Spielberg hosted the new president on several trips to Los Angeles, and the world premiere of Spielberg's *Jurassic Park* (1993) was held in Washington, D.C., as a benefit for Hillary Clinton's favorite charity, the Children's Defense Fund.

J. HOBERMAN AND JEFFREY SHANDLER
**Not the Last Word: A Conversation**

1. Norman L. Friedman, "Jewish Popular Culture in Contemporary America," *Judaism* 24 (summer 1975): 263–77.

2. Michael Rogin, *Blackface, White Noise: Jewish Immigrants in the Hollywood Melting Pot* (Berkeley and Los Angeles: University of California Press, 1996).

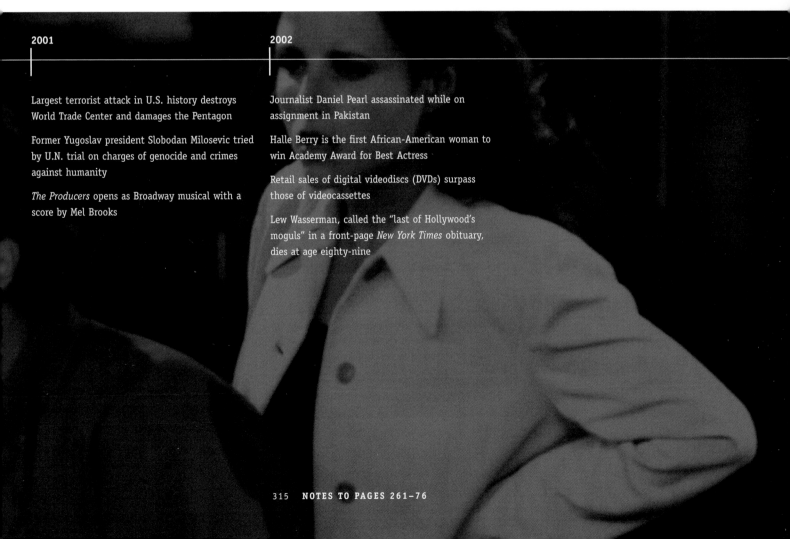

**2001**

Largest terrorist attack in U.S. history destroys World Trade Center and damages the Pentagon

Former Yugoslav president Slobodan Milosevic tried by U.N. trial on charges of genocide and crimes against humanity

*The Producers* opens as Broadway musical with a score by Mel Brooks

**2002**

Journalist Daniel Pearl assassinated while on assignment in Pakistan

Halle Berry is the first African-American woman to win Academy Award for Best Actress

Retail sales of digital videodiscs (DVDs) surpass those of videocassettes

Lew Wasserman, called the "last of Hollywood's moguls" in a front-page *New York Times* obituary, dies at age eighty-nine

# SELECTED BIBLIOGRAPHY

## FILM

### American Film History: General

Goodman, Ezra. *The Fifty-Year Decline and Fall of Hollywood*. New York: Simon and Schuster, 1961.

Izod, John. *Hollywood and the Box Office, 1895–1986*. New York: Columbia University Press, 1988.

Jacobs, Lewis. *The Rise of the American Film: A Critical History*. 1939. Reprint, New York: Teachers College Press, 1968.

Morden, Ethan, *The Hollywood Studios: House Style in the Golden Age of the Movies*. New York: Alfred A. Knopf, 1988.

Sklar, Robert. *Movie-Made America: How the Movies Changed American Life*. New York: Random House, 1975.

### Film History: Silent Era (1895–1928)

Abel, Richard. *The Red Rooster Scare: Making Cinema American, 1900–1910*. Berkeley and Los Angeles: University of California Press, 1999.

Bowser, Eileen. *The Transformation of Cinema, 1907–1915*. New York: Charles Scribner's Sons, 1990.

Eckhardt, Joseph P., and Linda Kowall. *Peddler of Dreams: Siegmund Lubin and the Creation of the Motion Picture Industry, 1896–1916*. Philadelphia: National Museum of American Jewish History, 1984.

Gunning, Tom. *D. W. Griffith and the Origins of American Narrative Film: The Early Years at Biograph*. Urbana: University of Illinois Press, 1991.

Hampton, Benjamin B. *History of the American Film Industry from Its Beginnings to 1931*. New York: Dover Publications, 1970.

Hansen, Miriam. *Babel and Babylon: Spectatorship in American Silent Film*. Cambridge, Mass.: Harvard University Press, 1991.

Koszarski, Richard. *An Evening's Entertainment: The Age of the Silent Feature Picture, 1915–1928*. New York: Charles Scribner's Sons, 1990.

May, Lary. 1980. *Screening Out the Past: The Birth of Mass Culture and the Motion Picture Industry*. New York: Oxford University Press, 1980.

Musser, Charles. *The Emergence of Cinema: The American Screen to 1907*. New York: Charles Scribner's Sons, 1990.

Ramsaye, Terry. *A Million and One Nights: A History of the Motion Picture through 1925*. New York: Simon and Schuster, 1926.

Ross, Steven J. *Working-Class Hollywood: Silent Film and the Shaping of Class in America*. Princeton: Princeton University Press, 1998.

Stokes, Melvyn, and Richard Maltby, eds. *American Movie Audiences: From the Turn of the Century to the Early Sound Era*. London: BFI Publishing, 1999.

### Film History: Studio Era (1928–1960)

Balio, Tino, *Grand Design: Hollywood as a Modern Enterprise, 1930–1939*. Berkeley and Los Angeles: University of California Press, 1995.

Buhle, Paul, and Dave Wagner, *Radical Hollywood*. New York: New Press, 2002.

Couvares, Francis G., ed. *Movie Censorship and American Culture*. Washington, D.C.: Smithsonian Institution Press, 1996.

Crafton, Donald. *The Talkies: American Cinema's Transition to Sound, 1926–31*. Berkeley and Los Angeles: University of California Press, 1997.

Doherty, Thomas. *Pre-Code Hollywood: Sex, Immorality, and Insurrection in American Cinema, 1930–1934*. New York: Columbia University Press, 1999.

———. *Projections of War: Hollywood, American Culture, and World War II*. New York: Columbia University Press, 1993.

Friedrich, Otto. *City of Nets: A Portrait of Hollywood in the 1940s*. New York: Harper and Row, 1986.

Giovacchini, Saverio. *Hollywood Modernism*. Philadelphia: Temple University Press, 2001.

Horne, Gerald. *Class Struggle in Hollywood, 1930–1950: Moguls, Mobsters, Stars, Reds, and Trade Unionists*. Austin: University of Texas Press, 2001.

Koppes, Clayton R., and Gregory D. Black. *Hollywood Goes to War: How Politics, Profits, and Propaganda Shaped World War II Movies*. New York: Free Press, 1987.

Leff, Leonard J., and Jerold L. Simmons. *The Dame in the Kimono: Hollywood, Censorship, and the Production Code from the 1920s to the 1960s.* New York: Grove Weidenfeld, 1990.

Mitchell, Greg. *The Campaign of the Century: Upton Sinclair's Race for Governor of California and the Birth of Media Politics.* New York: Random House, 1992.

Rosten, Leo C. *Hollywood: The Movie Colony, the Movie Makers.* New York: Harcourt, Brace and Company, 1941.

Schatz, Thomas. *Boom and Bust: American Cinema in the 1940s.* Berkeley and Los Angeles: University of California Press, 1999.

———. *The Genius of the System: Hollywood Filmmaking in the Studio Era.* New York: Pantheon, 1988.

Schwartz, Nancy Lynn. *The Hollywood Writers' Wars.* New York: Alfred A. Knopf, 1982.

Shindler, Colin. *Hollywood Goes to War.* Boston: Routledge and Kegan Paul, 1979.

Walsh, Frank. *Sin and Censorship: The Catholic Church and the Motion Picture Industry.* New Haven, Conn.: Yale University Press, 1996.

Wells, Walter. *Tycoons and Locusts: A Regional Look at Hollywood Fiction of the 1930s.* Carbondale: University of Southern Illinois Press, 1973.

### The Jazz Singer

Carringer, Robert L., ed. *The Jazz Singer.* Madison: University of Wisconsin Press, 1979.

McClelland, Doug. *Blackface to Blacklist: Al Jolson, Larry Parks, and "The Jolson Story."* Metuchen, N.J.: Scarecrow Press, 1987.

Rogin, Michael. *Blackface, White Noise: Jewish Immigrants in the Hollywood Melting Pot.* Berkeley and Los Angeles: University of California Press, 1996.

### The Movie "Moguls"

Berg, A. Scott. *Goldwyn: A Biography.* New York: Alfred A. Knopf, 1989.

Carey, Gary. *All the Stars in Heaven: Louis B. Mayer's MGM.* New York: E. P. Dutton, 1981.

Crowther, Bosley. *Hollywood Rajah: The Life and Times of Louis B. Mayer.* New York: Holt, Reinhart, and Winston, 1960.

French, Philip. *The Movie Moguls: An Informal History of the Hollywood Tycoons.* London: Weidenfeld and Nicolson, 1969.

Gabler, Neal. *An Empire of Their Own: How the Jews Invented Hollywood.* New York: Crown, 1988.

Marx, Samuel. *Mayer and Thalberg: The Make-Believe Saints.* New York: Random House, 1980.

Sinclair, Upton. *Upton Sinclair Presents William Fox.* Los Angeles: Upton Sinclair, 1933.

Thomas, Bob. *King Cohn: The Life and Times of Harry Cohn.* New York: G. P. Putnam's Sons, 1967.

———. *Thalberg: Life and Legend.* Garden City, N.Y.: Doubleday, 1969.

Warner, Jack L., with Dean Jennings. *My First Hundred Years in Hollywood.* New York: Random House, 1965.

Zierold, Norman J. *The Moguls.* New York: Coward-McCann, 1969.

### Images of Jews in American Film

Erens, Patricia. *The Jew in American Cinema.* Bloomington: Indiana University Press, 1984.

Friedman, Lester D. *Hollywood's Image of the Jew.* New York: Ungar, 1982.

———, ed. *Unspeakable Images: Ethnicity and the American Cinema.* Urbana: University of Illinois, 1991.

Miller, Randall, and Allen Woll. *Ethnic and Racial Images in American Film and Television.* New York: Garland Publishing, 1987.

### Jewish Filmographies

Fox, Stuart, comp. *Jewish Films in the United States: A Comprehensive Survey and Descriptive Filmography.* Boston: G. K. Hall, 1976.

Gellert, Charles Lawrence, comp. *The Holocaust, Israel, and the Jews: Motion Pictures in the National Archives.* Washington, D.C.: National Archives and Records Administration, 1989.

Rosenberg, Joel. "Jewish Experience on Film: An American Overview." In *American Jewish Year Book 1996,* ed. David Singer. New York: American Jewish Committee, 1996.

## BROADCASTING

### Broadcasting History: General

Barnouw, Erik. *A History of Broadcasting in the United States.* 3 vols. New York: Oxford University Press, 1966–70.

Sterling, Christopher H., and John M. Kittross. *Stay Tuned: A Concise History of American Broadcasting.* 2nd ed. Belmont, Calif.: Wadsworth, 1990.

### Radio: General

Douglas, Susan J. *Listening In: Radio and the American Imagination.* New York: Times Books, 1999.

Nachman, Gerald. *Raised on Radio.* New York: Pantheon, 1998.

### Television: General

Barnouw, Erik, *Tube of Plenty: The Evolution of American Television.* New York: Oxford University Press, 1975.

Boddy, William. *Fifties Television: The Industry and Its Critics.* Urbana: University of Illinois Press, 1990.

Gitlin, Todd. *Inside Prime Time.* New York: Pantheon, 1983.

MacDonald, J. Fred. *One Nation Under Television.* New York: Pantheon, 1990.

Marc, David. *Comic Visions: Television Comedy and American Culture.* 2nd ed. Malden, Mass.: Blackwell, 1997.

———. *Demographic Vistas: Television in American Culture.* Philadelphia: University of Pennsylvania, 1984.

Spigel, Lynn. *Make Room for TV: Television and the Family Ideal in Postwar America.* Chicago: University of Chicago Press, 1992.

### Images of Jews on Radio and Television

Pearl, Jonathan, and Judith Pearl. *The Chosen Image: Television's Portrayal of Jewish Themes and Characters.* Jefferson, N.C.: McFarland, 1999.

# AMERICAN JEWS AND THE MEDIA: SPECIAL TOPICS

## Yiddish Film and Broadcasting

Goldberg, Judith N. *Laughter Through Tears: The Yiddish Cinema.* Rutherford, N.J.: Fairleigh Dickinson University Press, 1983.

Goldman, Eric A. *Visions, Images, and Dreams: Yiddish Film Past and Present.* Teaneck, N.J.: Ergo Media. 1988.

Hoberman, J. *Bridge of Light: Yiddish Film between Two Worlds.* New York: Museum of Modern Art and Schocken Books, 1991.

Paskin, Sylvia, ed. *When Joseph Met Molly: A Reader on Yiddish Film.* Nottingham, U.K.: Five Leaves Publications, in association with the European Jewish Publication Society, 1999.

Sapoznik, Henry. *Klezmer! Jewish Music for Old World to Our World.* New York: Schirmer Books, 1999.

## Anti-Semitism and the Media

Baldwin, Neil. *Henry Ford and the Jews: The Mass Production of Hate.* New York: Public Affairs, 2001.

Birdwell, Michael E. *Celluloid Soldiers: Warner Bros.'s Campaign against Nazism.* New York: New York University Press, 2001.

Carr, Steven Alan. *Hollywood and Anti-Semitism: A Cultural History up to World War II.* Cambridge, U.K.: Cambridge University Press, 2001.

## Jews and Blacks and the Media

Diner, Hasia R. *In the Almost Promised Land: American Jews and Blacks, 1915–1935.* Westport, Conn.: Greenwood Press, 1977.

Gubar, Susan. *Racechanges: White Skin, Black Face in American Culture.* New York: Oxford University Press, 1997.

Melnick, Jeffrey. *A Right to Sing the Blues: African Americans, Jews, and American Popular Song.* Cambridge, Mass.: Harvard University Press, 1999.

Williams, Linda. *Playing the Race Card: Melodramas of Black and White from Uncle Tom to O. J. Simpson.* Princeton: Princeton University Press, 2001.

## The Holocaust and the Media

Avisar, Ilvan. *Screening the Holocaust: Cinema's Images of the Unimaginable.* Bloomington: Indiana University Press, 1988.

Bean, Henry, ed. *The Believer: Confronting Jewish Self-Hatred.* New York: Thunder's Mouth Press, 2002.

Doneson, Judith E. *The Holocaust in American Film.* Philadelphia: Jewish Publication Society, 1987.

Insdorf, Annette. *Indelible Shadows: Film and the Holocaust.* 2nd ed. Cambridge, U.K.: Cambridge University Press, 1989.

Loshitzky, Yosefa, ed. *Spielberg's Holocaust: Critical Perspectives on "Schindler's List."* Bloomington: Indiana University Press, 1997.

Mintz, Alan. *Popular Culture and the Shaping of Holocaust Memory in America.* Seattle: University of Washington Press, 2001.

Shandler, Jeffrey. *While America Watches: Televising the Holocaust.* New York: Oxford University Press, 1999.

Zelizer, Barbie, ed. *Visual Culture and the Holocaust.* New Brunswick, N.J.: Rutgers University Press, 2000.

## Blacklisting and the Media

Bentley, Eric. *Are You Now or Have You Ever Been: The Investigation of Show Business by the Un-American Activities Committee, 1947–1958.* New York: Harper and Row, 1972.

Bernstein, Walter. *Inside Out: A Memoir of the Blacklist.* New York: Alfred A. Knopf, 1996.

Bessie, Alvah. *Inquisition in Eden.* New York: Macmillan, 1965.

Buhle, Paul, and Dave Wagner. *A Very Dangerous Citizen: Abraham Lincoln Polonsky and the Hollywood Left.* Berkeley and Los Angeles: University of California Press, 2001.

Ceplair, Larry, and Steven Englund. *The Inquisition in Hollywood: Politics in the Film Community, 1930–1960.* Garden City, N.Y.: Doubleday, 1980.

Cogley, John, and Fund for the Republic. *Report on Blacklisting.* New York: Fund for the Republic, 1956.

Dick, Bernard F. *Radical Innocence: A Critical Study of the Hollywood Ten.* Lexington: University Press of Kentucky, 1989.

Foley, Karen Sue. *The Political Blacklist in the Broadcast Industry: The Decade of the 1950s.* New York: Arno, 1979.

Gordon, Bernard. *Hollywood Exile, or, How I Learned to Love the Blacklist: A Memoir.* Austin: University of Texas Press, 1999.

McGilligan, Patrick, and Paul Buhle. *Tender Comrades: A Backstory of the Hollywood Blacklist.* New York: St. Martin's Press, 1997.

Navasky, Victor. *Naming Names.* New York: Penguin Books, 1991.

Vaughn, Robert. *Only Victims: A Study of Show Business Blacklisting.* New York: G. P. Putnam's Sons, 1972.

## American Jews and Comedy

Altman, Sig. *The Comic Image of the Jew: Explorations of a Pop Culture Phenomenon.* Rutherford, N.J.: Fairleigh Dickinson University Press, 1971.

Cohen, Sarah Blacher, ed. *Jewish Wry: Essays on Jewish Humor.* Bloomington: Indiana University Press, 1987.

Goldman, Albert. *Freakshow: The Rocksoul-bluesjazzsickjewblackhumorsexpoppsych Gig and Other Scenes from the Counter-Culture.* New York: Atheneum, 1971.

Jenkins, Henry. *What Made Pistachio Nuts? Early Sound Comedy and the Vaudeville Aesthetic.* New York: Columbia University Press, 1992.

Romeyn, Esther, and Jack Kugelmass. *Let There Be Laughter! Jewish Humor in America.* Chicago: Spertus Press, 1997.

Winokur, Mark. *American Laughter: Immigrants, Ethnicity, and 1930s Hollywood Film Comedy.* New York: St. Martin's Press, 1996.

## American Jews and the Performing Arts

Cohen, Sarah Blacher, ed. *From Hester Street to Hollywood: The Jewish-American Stage and Screen.* Bloomington: Indiana University Press, 1983.

Kleeblatt, Norman L., ed. *Too Jewish? Challenging Traditional Indentities.* Exh. cat. New York: The Jewish Museum; New Brunswick, N.J.: Rutgers University Press, 1996.

Slobin, Mark. *Tenement Songs: The Popular Music of the Jewish Immigrants*. Urbana: University of Illinois Press, 1982.

Whitfield, Stephen J. *In Search of American Jewish Culture*. Waltham, Mass.: Brandeis University Press, 1999.

### Gender, Sexuality, and Images of Jews in the Media

Antler, Joyce, ed. *Talking Back: Images of Jewish Women in American Popular Culture*. Hanover, N.H.: University Press of New England, 1998.

Prell, Riv-Ellen. *Fighting to Become Americans: Assimilation and the Trouble Between Jewish Women and Jewish Men*. Boston: Beacon Press, 1999.

### American Jewish History

Alexander, Michael. *Jazz Age Jews*. Princeton: Princeton University Press, 2001.

Heinze, Andrew. *Adapting to Abundance: Jewish Immigrants, Mass Consumption, and the Search for American Identity*. New York: Columbia University Press, 1990.

Hertzberg, Arthur. *The Jews in America: Four Centuries of an Uneasy Encounter*. New York: Simon and Schuster, 1989.

Howe, Irving. *World of Our Fathers: The Journey of the East European Jews to America and the Life They Found and Made*. New York: Harcourt Brace Jovanovich, 1976.

Moore, Deborah Dash. *To the Golden Cities: Pursuing the American Jewish Dream in Miami and L.A.* New York: Free Press, 1994.

Shapiro, Edward S. *A Time for Healing: American Jewry Since World War II*. Baltimore: Johns Hopkins University Press, 1992.

## PERSONALITIES

### Biographies and Profiles of Performers, Directors, and Others

Baxter, John. *Steven Spielberg: The Unauthorized Biography*. London: Harper Collins, 1996.

Berg, Gertrude. *Molly and Me*. New York: McGraw Hill, 1961.

Brown, Jared. *Zero Mostel: A Biography*. New York: Atheneum, 1989.

Bruce, Lenny. *How to Talk Dirty and Influence People: An Autobiography*. Chicago: Playboy Press, 1965.

Davis, Sammy, Jr., Jane Boyar, and Burt Boyar, *Yes I Can: The Story of Sammy Davis, Jr.* New York: Farrar, Straus and Giroux, 1965.

Desser, David, and Lester D. Friedman. *American-Jewish Filmmakers: Traditions and Trends*. Urbana: University of Illinois Press, 1993.

Drescher, Fran. *Enter Whining*. New York: Regan Books/HarperCollins, 1996.

Freedland, Michael, *Jolson: The Story of Al Jolson*. London: Virgin, 1995.

Goldman, Herbert G. *Banjo Eyes: Eddie Cantor and the Birth of Modern Stardom*. New York: Oxford University Press, 1997.

———. *Fanny Brice: The Original Funny Girl*. New York: Oxford University Press, 1992.

———. *Jolson: The Legend Comes to Life*. New York: Oxford University Press, 1988.

Holtzman, Will. *Judy Holliday*. New York: Putnam, 1982.

Louvish, Simon. *Monkey Business: The Lives and Legends of the Marx Brothers*. London: Faber and Faber, 1999.

Marx, Groucho, and Richard J. Anobile. *The Marx Bros. Scrapbook*. New York: Darien House, 1973.

McBride, Joseph. *Steven Spielberg: A Biography*. New York: Simon and Schuster, 1997.

Milton, Joyce. *Tramp: The Life of Charlie Chaplin*. 1996. Reprint, New York: Da Capo Press, 1998.

Morris, George. *John Garfield*. New York: Jove Publications, 1977.

Robinson, David. *Chaplin: His Life and Art*. New York: McGraw-Hill, 1985.

Rosenblatt, Samuel. *Yossele Rosenblatt: The Story of His Life as Told by His Son*. New York: Farrar, Straus and Young, 1954.

Sklar, Robert. *City Boys: Cagney, Bogart, Garfield*. Princeton: Princeton University Press, 1992.

Spada, James. *Streisand: Her Life*. New York: Crown Publishers, 1995.

Yacowar, Maurice. *Loser Take All: The Comic Art of Woody Allen*. 2nd ed. New York: Continuum, 1991.

———. *Method in Madness: The Art of Mel Brooks*. New York: St. Martin's Press, 1981.

# CONTRIBUTORS

**J. Hoberman** is senior film critic for the *Village Voice*, where he has been a staff writer since 1983. He is an adjunct professor in the Department of Cinema Studies at New York University and in the Humanities Division at The Cooper Union. His publications include *The Magic Hour: Film at Fin de Siècle* (2003), *The Red Atlantis: Communist Culture in the Absence of Communism* (1998), *Bridge of Light: Yiddish Film between Two Worlds* (1991), and a cultural history of American movies in the 1960s, forthcoming.

**Jeffrey Shandler** is Assistant Professor in the Department of Jewish Studies at Rutgers University. His publications include *While America Watches: Televising the Holocaust* (1999), *Remembering the Lower East Side: American Jewish Reflections* (2000), and *Awakening Lives: Autobiographies of Jewish Youth in Poland before the Holocaust* (2002). Among the exhibitions he has curated are *Sholem Aleichem in America* (YIVO Institute for Jewish Research, 1990) and *Holy Land: American Encounters with the Land of Israel in the Century before Statehood* (National Museum of American Jewish History, 1998).

**Maurice Berger** is a Senior Fellow at the Vera List Center for Art and Politics of the New School for Social Research, New York, and Curator of the Center for Art and Visual Culture at the University of Maryland. He is the author of *White Lies: Race and the Myths of Whiteness* (1999), which will be adapted as a television documentary for PBS in 2004, as well as *The Crisis of Criticism* (1998), *Constructing Masculinity* (1995), *Modern Art and Society* (1994), *How Art Becomes History* (1992), and *Labyrinths: Robert Morris, Minimalism, and the 1960s* (1989).

**Michael Bronski** has published widely and is the author of *Pulp Friction: Uncovering the Golden Age of Gay Male Pulps* (2003) and *The Pleasure Principle: Sex, Backlash, and the Struggle for Gay Freedom* (1998). He is a Visiting Scholar at Dartmouth College in Jewish Studies.

**Mel Gordon** is the author of *Erik Jan Hanussen: Hitler's Jewish Clairvoyant* (2002), *Voluptuous Panic: The Erotic World of Weimar Berlin* (2001), *Lazzi: The Comic Routines of the Commedia Dell'arte* (1983), and, with Alma Law, *Meyerhold, Eisenstein, and Biomechanics: Actor Training in Revolutionary Russia* (1996). He has also edited a number of volumes, including *Grand Guignol: Theatre of Fear and Terror* (1988) and *Dada Performance* (1987).

**Amelia S. Holberg** is Assistant Professor of Media Studies and English at Catholic University in Washington, D.C. She is presently at work on a book entitled "Exhibiting Jewishness: Contemporary Jewish Identity, History, and Visual Narrative," and is the author of "Betty Boop: Yiddish Film Star," published in the December 1999 issue of *American Jewish History*.

**David Marc** is a writer whose work focuses on the history and criticism of American broadcasting. Among his books are *Bonfire of the Humanities: Television, Sub-literacy, and Long-Term Memory Loss* (1995), *Comic Visions: Television Comedy and American Culture* (1989), and *Demographic Vistas: Television in American*

*Culture* (1984). He recently completed an oral history project for the Newhouse School of Public Communications at Syracuse University, which includes more than two hundred taped and transcribed interviews with pioneering figures in the American television industry. He is an adjunct member of the Syracuse faculty.

**Deborah Dash Moore** is Professor of Religion at Vassar College. Her most recent book, written with Howard B. Rock, was *Cityscapes: A History of New York in Images* (2001). Among her publications is the two-volume *Jewish Women in America: An Historical Encyclopedia* (1997), which she edited with Paula Hyman. She is the author of *To the Golden Cities: Pursuing the American Jewish Dream in Miami and L.A.* (1994), *At Home in America: Second Generation New York Jews* (1981), and *B'nai B'rith and the Challenge of Ethnic Leadership* (1981).

**Samuel J. Rosenthal** received his M.A. at the Annenberg School of Communication at the University of Pennsylvania in 1993. His thesis was entitled, "Golden Boychik: Star-Audience Relations between John Garfield and the Contemporary American Jewish Community."

**Ben Singer** is Associate Professor in the Department of Communication Arts at the University of Wisconsin—Madison. He is the author of *Melodrama and Modernity: Early Sensational Cinema and Its Contexts* (2001). He is at work on a book about early film exhibition in New York.

**Mark Slobin** is Professor of Music at Wesleyan University and the author or editor of a dozen books in ethnomusicology, including *Fiddler on the Move: Exploring the Klezmer World* (2000) and *Tenement Songs: Popular Music of the Jewish Immigrants* (1982), both of which won the ASCAP-Deems Taylor Award, as well as *Subcultural Sounds: Micromusics of the West* (1993).

**Judith Thissen** is Assistant Professor of Film Studies at Utrecht University in the Netherlands. She is currently working on a book about moviegoing on New York's Lower East Side during the silent cinema era. She held a visiting Fulbright scholar position at the Department of Cinema Studies at New York University and was a post-doctoral fellow at the Center for Judaic Studies at the University of Pennsylvania. She has contributed essays to several anthologies, including *American Movie Audiences: From the Turn of the Century to the Early Sound Era* (1999) and *American Silent Film: Discovering Marginalized Voices* (2002).

**Donald Weber** is Professor of English and American Studies at Mount Holyoke College, and Chair of the English Department. He has published on a variety of subjects relating to Jewish-American culture, including literature, television, and film, and is the author of *Rhetoric and History in Revolutionary New England* (1988). He has just completed a book entitled, "Haunted in the New World: Mapping Modern Jewish-American Culture."

# INDEX

Howe, Irving, 163
humor, Jewish, 136, 154, 161–63, 201–2, 203, 220–21, 242–43, 246, 252, 276, 293n.3; and Charlie Chaplin, 37–39, 283n.12, 284n.19; and comedy writing, 144–45, 257; and Jewish jokes, 136, 232, 300n.1, 301n.2; and movie roles, 47; vaudeville traditions of, 120. *See also* comedians, Jewish
*Humoresque*: silent version, 140; sound version, 173–75
Hurst, Fannie, *Humoresque*, 174
Hymers, Rev. R. L., Jr., 72

*I'll See You in My Dreams*, 89, 294n.5
*I Love You, Alice B. Toklas!*, 230–31
*Immigrant, The*, 34
Ince, Ralph, "Balked," 18
Ince, Thomas, 49
*Isn't She Great*, 43

*Jack Benny Show, The*, 199–200, 250
Jacobowicz, Simcha, 74
Jaffe, Sam, *The Mad Dog of Europe*, 61
James, Caryn, 248
*Jazz Singer, The*: as movie, 12, 36, 46, 76–97, 139, 275–76, 277, 293n.2; as play, 77–78, 84–85, 87, 91; remakes of movie, 88–92, 125, 294n.5
Jeffries, Leonard, 74, 290n.53
Jenkins, Henry, 157
Jentes, Harry, "Since Sarah Saw Theda Bara," 277
Jessel, George, 77, 84–85, 157, 282n.3, 292n.2
Jewish Theological Seminary, 13, 103, 130–32
*Joley*, 91
Jolson, Al, 46, 55, 77–78, 84–92, 95, 154, 157, 190, 276, 292n.2; in blackface, 77–80, 84–85, 87–89, 92–93, 95–99, 190, 276; in *The Jazz Singer*, 77–81, 85–88, 93, 139; and *Joley*, 91; and *Jolson*, 91; and *Jolson: The Musical*, 92; and *The Jolson Story*, 88–90, 92, 294n.4; and *Jolson Sings Again*, 89
Jolson, Harry, 77
*Jolson*, 91
*Jolson Sings Again*, 89
*Jolson Story, The*, 88–90, 92, 294n.4
*Jolson: The Musical*, 92
*Judgment at Nuremburg*, 206, 259, 263; on TV, 259
*Juggler, The*, 209, 212

Kadar, Jan, 235
Kael, Pauline, 71, 228–29, 239, 289n.43, 311n.34
Kafka, Franz, 226, 228, 237, 252; *The Castle*, 302n.5
Kahn, Gus, 89
Kallen, Horace, 213
Kaminska, Ida, 87

Kandel, Abe, *City for Conquest*, 141
Kane, Bob, 303n.3
Kaplan, Rabbi Mordecai, 274
*Kasrilevka on the Mississippi*, 131
Katchor, Ben, 276
Katims, Milton, 131
Katz, Mickey, 203
Katz, Otto, 287n.18
Katzenberg, Jeffrey, 206, 269, 272–73
Kauffman, Stanley, 221, 228, 233, 239
Kaufman, George S., 66, 159
Kavner, Julie, 247
Kaye, Danny, 69, 178–81, 230, 298n.2
Kazan, Elia, 68, 297n.20
Kazantakis, Nikos, *The Last Temptation of Christ*, 72
Keaton, Buster, 147
Keeler, Ruby, 87, 92
Keller, Sheldon, 144
Kenneally, Thomas, *Schindler's List*, 259
Kennedy, John F., president, 190, 272
Kennedy, Joseph P., 64
Kent, Sidney, 67, 289n.35
Kert, Larry, 91
Kessel, Adam, 35
Keystone film company, 35
King, Alan, 181, 226–27
Kingsley, Ben, 260
Kinoy, Ernest, 244
Kirby, Jack, 303n.3
Klane, Robert, *Where's Poppa?*, 237
Klein, Joe, *Primary Colors*, 271
Knepper, Max, 60
Kober, Arthur, 141
Koch, Howard, 67
Kominsky, Sadie, 95
Kominsky-Crumb, Aline, 276
Kopkind, Andrew, 311n.38
Koplan, Ephraim, 32–33
Kramer, Kenny, 252, 256
Kramer, Stanley, 209
Krenek, Ernst, 63
Krents, Milton, 131
Krishtol, Moyshe, 169
Kristol, Irving, 136
Kugelmass, Jack, 163, 223, 250
Kunin, Rabbi Boruch Shlomo, 264

Laemmle, Carl, 18–19, 34, 47, 57, 65, 281n.12; Laemmle Film Service, 19
Lampert, Zohra, 227
Lancaster, Burt, 259
Landi, Elissa, 140
Lane, Nathan, 41, 43, 148, 279
Lardner, Ring, Jr., 69
Lasky, Jesse L., 47, 54, 57
*Last Days, The*, 263
*Last Temptation of Christ, The*, 72, 291–92n.3,

292n.6
*Laughter on the Twenty-Third Floor*, 43, 145, 148, 275
*Law and Order*, 251
Lawford, Peter, 189, 213
Lawson, John Howard, 62, 64, 70, 287n.20, 288n.27; *Success Story*, 141
Lear, Norman, 247, 290n.53; *All in the Family*, 191, 246–47, 250, 259
Le Baron, William, 67, 289n.35
Lederer, Francis, 63
Lederer, Otto, 78
Lee, Peggy, 90, 294n.6
Lee, Spike, 99; *Bamboozled*, 98–99
Lee, Stan, 303n.3
Lehman, Ernest, 240–42
Lehrer, Tom, 224
Leigh, Janet, 182
Lembeck, Harvey, 121
Lennart, Isabel, 154
*Lenny*, 198, 221
Levene, Sam, 68, 142–43
Levenson, Sam, 136, 139; *Meet the Folks*, 139
Levin, Meyer: "Anne Frank: Diary of a Young Girl," 193; *The Illegals*, 207, 209
Levine, Joseph E., 223, 228, 230
Levinshteyn-Strashunsky, Yoel-David, 84
Levinson, Barry, 253, 257
Levy, Eugene, 91
Levy's rye bread ad, 221, 226, 234
Lewinsky, Monica, 202, 271–72
Lewis, Jerry, 90–91, 157
Lewis, Richard, 251
Lewis, Sinclair, *It Can't Happen Here*, 287n.17
Lieber, Joel, *Move*, 236–37
Lieberman, Joseph, senator, 273
Lieberman, Rhoda, 276
Liebman, Max, 144
*Life Is Beautiful*, 261, 263
Lindbergh, Charles, 64, 288n.25
Linden, Hal, 251
Lipkin, Lisa, 255
Lipper, Ken, 263
Lipsitz, George, 122, 297n.10
*Little Girl with Big Ideas, A*, 107
Litvak, Anatole, 63
Livingston, Jerry, 127
Loeb, Phillip, 120–22, 124–25, 257, 297n.20, 298n.21
Loew, Marcus, 16, 18–19, 28–30, 47, 57
*Long Way Home, The*, 263
Lord, Daniel J., 62
Louis-Dreyfus, Julia, 253
Louvish, Simon, 163
*Love and War*, 251
*Love, Sidney*, 251
Lovitz, Jon, 251
Lubavitcher hasidim (Chabad), 206, 264–67;

# TEXT AND ILLUSTRATION CREDITS

## TEXT CREDITS

Page 29 ("The Grand Scandal"): Reprinted courtesy of BFI Publishing. From Melvyn Stokes and Richard Maltby, eds., *American Movie Audiences: From the Turn of the Century to the Early Sound Era* (London: BFI Publishing, 1999), 21.

Page 109: Reprinted courtesy of The Forward Association, Inc., New York.

Page 135: Excerpt from *I Married a Communist* by Philip Roth. Copyright © 1998 by Philip Roth. Reprinted by permission of Houghton Mifflin Company. All rights reserved.

Pages 136–43: Reprinted courtesy of Henry Popkin. Reprinted from *Commentary*, July 1952, by permission. All rights reserved.

Pages 169–70: Reprinted courtesy of The Forward Association, Inc., New York.

Page 195 ("Hollywood"): Words by Enid Futterman, music by Michael Cohen. Copyright © 1985 by Enid Futterman and Michael Cohen. Jem Associates and Williamson Music owners of publication and allied rights throughout the world. (Williamson Music administrator of all rights on behalf of itself and Jem Associates.) International copyright secured. All rights reserved. Used by permission.

Pages 196–97: Reprinted courtesy of Rhonda Lieberman. © *Artforum*, January 1993, "Glamorous Jewesses," by Rhonda Lieberman.

Page 222: *The Essential Lenny Bruce* Copyright © 1967, Douglas Music Corp. All rights reserved. Used by permission.

Page 249: "The Nanny Named Fran" reprinted courtesy of Ann Hampton Callaway.

## ILLUSTRATION CREDITS

The photographers and the sources of visual material other than those indicated in the captions are as follows (numerals in **boldface** refer to pages).

### ABBREVIATIONS

| | |
|---|---|
| CB | Cherney Berg |
| CSUN | Urban Archives Center, California State University, Northridge |
| FA | The Forward Association, Inc., New York |
| JH | J. Hoberman |
| JM | The Jewish Museum, New York |
| JS | Jeffrey Shandler |
| JTS | Joseph and Miriam Ratner Center for the Study of Conservative Judaism, Jewish Theological Seminary of America, New York |
| MoMA | The Museum of Modern Art/Film Stills Archive, New York |
| NCJF | Rutenberg and Everett Yiddish Film Library of the National Center for Jewish Film at Brandeis University, Waltham, Mass. |
| NJAB | National Jewish Archive of Broadcasting, The Jewish Museum, New York |
| NYM | The New Yorker Magazine, Inc. |
| NYPL | Billy Rose Theatre Collection, The New York Library for the Performing Arts, Astor, Lenox and Tilden Foundations |
| PF | Photofest, New York |
| YIVO | YIVO Institute for Jewish Research, New York |

Front cover: Frédéric Brenner
Spine: MoMA
Back cover: CB
Half title: CB
Frontispiece: MoMA
Contents spread: **6** Free Library of Philadelphia, Prints and Pictures Collection (top); MoMA (center, bottom) **7** MoMA

### Nickelodeon Nation

**14** MoMA **16** Q. David Bowers **17** MoMA (top left, top right); Maggie Valentine (bottom left); American Museum of the Moving Image, Astoria, N.Y. (bottom right) **19** MoMA **20–21** MoMA **22** NYM (top) **24** NCJF **26** Free Library of Philadelphia, Prints and Pictures Collection **26–27** Marc Wanamaker/Bison Archives **28** Stoney Shukat **29** Museum of the City of New York, Byron Collection **31** FA (left); Daniel Clowes and Landmark Theatres (right) **32–33** United States Department of the Interior, National Park Service, Edison National Historic Site, West Orange, N.J. **34** MoMA **35** MoMA **36** From Samuel Rosenblatt, *Yossele Rosenblatt: The Story of His Life as Told by His Son* (New York: Farrar, Straus and Young, 1954) **37** MoMA (top); From Wolfgang Gersch, *Chaplin in Berlin* (Berlin: Parthas Verlag GmbH, 1999) (bottom) **38** JS **39** MoMA **40** JH **41** MoMA **42** NYPL (top left); MoMA (right, bottom left) **43** PF (top); MoMA (bottom left)

## Moguldom

44 MoMA 47 MoMA 48 MoMA 49 NYM 51 YIVO 54–57 MoMA 58 CSUN 59 © Bettmann/Corbis 60 From Greg Mitchell, *The Campaign of the Century: Upton Sinclair's Race for Governor of California and the Birth of Media Politics* (New York: Random House, 1992) 61 CSUN 62 MoMA 63 Deutsches Historisches Museum, Berlin (top) 64 MoMA 66 JM 67 AP/Wide World Photos 68 MoMA 69 Southern California Library for Social Studies and Research, Los Angeles 70 Peter Schweitzer (top); © Bettmann/Corbis (bottom) 71 JM 72 AP/Wide World Photos 75 *Moment* Magazine (right) 76 Courtesy of the Academy of Motion Picture Arts and Sciences, Beverly Hills, Calif. 79 MoMA 80 MoMA 81–83 NYPL 85 © Museum of the City of New York, Gift of the Trio Press through the Hebrew Actors' Union (66.33.5) 86–87 MoMA 88 NCJF 89 MoMA 90 JM (left); MoMA (right) 91 Reprinted with permission from TV Guide Magazine Group, Inc., © 1959 TV Guide Magazine Group, Inc., *TV Guide* is a registered trademark of TV Guide Magazine Group, Inc. 92 MoMA (left); JM (right) 93 NYM (left); MoMA (right) 96 MoMA 98 New Line Productions, Inc., *Bamboozled* © 2000 New Line Productions, Inc., all rights reserved

## An American at Home, a Jew on the Air

100 CB 102 © Bettmann/Corbis 103 FA (top); MoMA (bottom) 104 American Jewish Historical Society, Waltham, Mass., and New York 105 American Museum of the Moving Image, Astoria, N.Y./Lawrence Williams Collection 106 JH 107 YIVO (top, bottom left); NCJF (bottom right) 108 Museum of the City of New York 110 JM (left); FA (top right, bottom right) 113 CB 114 Donald Weber 115 Syracuse University Library, Department of Special Collections, Syracuse, N.Y. 117–18 CB 120 Syracuse University Library, Department of Special Collections, Syracuse, N.Y. (top); CB (bottom) 121 CB 122 Stuart Schear 123 CB 124 *New York Post* (top); Peter Schweitzer (bottom) 125 George Karger/TimePix, New York 126 CB 127 CB (top); JM (bottom left, bottom right) 129 National Archives, Washington, D.C. 130 NJAB (left); JTS (right) 131 JTS 134 CBS Photo Archive, New York 137 JH 138 CB 139 MoMA 140 JH 142–43 MoMA 144 PF 145 *New York Times* (top); PF (bottom) 146 NYPL 147 MoMA (top, bottom left); PF (bottom right) 148 Rhino Entertainment, Los Angeles (top left); MoMA (top right, bottom left, bottom right) 149 Vice Waldron, *The Official Dick Van Dyke Show Book* (1994; reprint, New York: Applause Theatre Books, 2001), and Calvada Productions (top); MoMA (bottom left); PF (bottom right)

## Star Gallery

150 Frédéric Brenner 152 Columbia University Library, New York 153–56 MoMA 158–59 MoMA 160 National Portrait Gallery, Smithsonian Institution, Washington, D.C., © Al Hirschfeld, art reproduced by special arrangement with Hirschfeld's exclusive representative, the Margo Feiden Galleries, Ltd., New York 161 Frédéric Brenner (left); © 2002 Andy Warhol Foundation for the Visual Arts/ARS, New York, and © 2002 Ron Feldman Fine Arts, New York (right) 162 From Jerry Rubin, *Do It! Scenarios of the Revolution* (New York: Simon and Schuster, 1970) (top left); JM (top right); NYPL (bottom left); MoMA (bottom right) 164 MoMA 165 From Leslie Cabarga, *The Fleischer Story* (New York: Nostalgia Press, 1976) 166 Action Comics #1 © 1938 DC Comics, all rights reserved, used with permission 167 Tele Cinema, Inc., New York 168 © Bettmann/Corbis 169–73 MoMA 174 Zionist Archives, Jerusalem 175 YIVO (left); MoMA (top left, bottom right) 176 MoMA (left); PF (right) 177 PF 178–80 MoMA 183–85 Random House, Inc., New York 186–87 Christie's, New York 188 PF 191 MoMA (top, bottom right); PF (bottom left) 192 Loomis Dean/TimePix, New York 193 © AFF Basel CH/AFS Amsterdam NL 194 MoMA (top); NYPL (bottom) 195 JH (top); © Al Hirschfeld, art reproduced by special arrangement with Hirschfeld's exclusive representative, the Margo Feiden Galleries Ltd., New York (bottom) 196–97 *Artforum* and The New York Public Library and Photofest 198 MoMA (top); Milton Glaser (bottom) 199 PF 200 JS 201 PF 203 Robert de Michiell

## Stand-Up Jews

204 MoMA 208 Courtesy of the Academy of Motion Picture Arts and Sciences, Beverly Hills, Calif. 209–10 MoMA 212–18 MoMA 219 Gjon Mili/TimePix, New York 220 MoMA 221 Used by permission of Arnold Products, Inc. "Levy's" is a registered trademark of Arnold Products, Inc. (left); MoMA (right) 222 PF 223 MoMA 225 MoMA 227 MoMA 229–31 MoMA 232 © E.C. Publications, Inc., all rights reserved, used with permission 233–35 MoMA 236 MoMA (top); TimePix, New York (bottom left); JH (bottom right) 237–38 MoMA 239 MoMA (top); JH (bottom) 240–43 MoMA 244 JS 246 Vice Waldron, *The Official Dick Van Dyke Show Book*, and Carl Reiner (top left); Vice Waldron, *The Official Dick Van Dyke Show Book*, and Calvada Productions (bottom left); PF (right) 247 PF 248–49 NJAB 252 Thomas L. Fluharty 253 Castle Rock Entertainment, Beverly Hills, Calif. 254–55 Yan Nascimbene; reprinted with permission from TV Guide Magazine Group, Inc., © 1998 TV Guide Magazine Group, Inc., *TV Guide* is a registered trademark of TV Guide Magazine Group, Inc. 256 JS 257 MoMA 258 JH 259 PF (top); MoMA (bottom) 260 MoMA 261 JS 262 Shimon Attie 263 Art Spiegelman 264 JS 266 JS 268 © AFP/Corbis 269 © Bettmann/Corbis 270 MoMA 271 JH (top); MoMA (bottom) 272 MoMA

## Not the Last Word: A Conversation

276 Peter Schweitzer 277 National Museum of American History, Behring Center, Smithsonian Institution, Washington, D.C. 278 Mark Bennett 279 JH

## Timeline

280–81 MoMA 282–83 Q. David Bowers 284–85 MoMA 286–87 Marc Wanamaker/ Bison Archives 288–93 MoMA 294–95 American Museum of the Moving Image, Astoria, N.Y./Lawrence Williams Collection 296–97 MoMA 298–99 PF 300–305 MoMA 306–7 PF 308–13 MoMA 314–15 Castle Rock Entertainment, Beverly Hills, Calif.